ARTIFICIAL INTELLIGENCE IN ACCOUNTING AND AUDITING:

The Use of Expert Systems

MIKLOS A. VASARHELYI

AT&T Bell Laboratories
and Columbia University

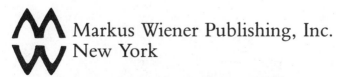 Markus Wiener Publishing, Inc.
New York

First published in 1989 by
Markus Wiener Publishing, Inc.
225 Lafayette Street
New York, N.Y. 10012

Library of Congress Cataloging-in-Publication Data

Artificial intelligence in accounting and auditing.

  Bibliography: p.
  1. Accounting—Data processing. 2. Auditing—
Data processing. 3. Expert systems (Computer science)
I. Vasarhelyi, Miklos A.
HF5679.A78 1988   657'.028'5633   87-40223
ISBN 0-910129-72-X

Printed in the United States of America

CONTENTS

ACKNOWLEDGMENTS

The editor and the publisher gratefully acknowledge the following authors and publishers:

Andrew D. Bailey, Jr., Karl Hackenbrack, Prabuddha De, Jesse Dillard, "Artificial Intelligence, Cognitive Science and Computational Modeling in Auditing Research: A Research Approach," JOURNAL OF INFORMATION SYSTEMS, pp. 20–40, Spring 1987. Reprinted with the permission of the authors.

William E. McCarthy, "On the Future of Knowledge-Based Accounting Systems," DR. SCOTT MEMORIAL LECTURES IN ACCOUNTANCY, Vol. 15, 1986. Reprinted with the permission of the author.

Thomas W. Lin, "Expert Systems and Management Accounting Research," MANAGEMENT ACCOUNTING, Vol. 4, No. 1, Spring 1986. Reprinted with the permission of the author.

Mohammad J. Abdolmohammadi, "Decision Support and Expert Systems in Auditing: A Review and Research Directions," ACCOUNTING & BUSINESS RESEARCH, Spring 1987, pp. 1–13. Reprinted with the permission of the author.

Jagdish S. Gangolly, "A Computational View of Financial Accounting Standards," unpublished working paper, State University of New York at Albany, 1987. Reprinted with the permission of the author.

William F. Messier, Jr., James V. Hansen, "Expert Systems in Auditing, The State of the Art," unpublished working paper, Fall 1987. Reprinted with the permission of the authors.

Graham Gal, Paul J. Steinbart, "The Use of Rule-Based Expert Systems to Investigate the Effects of Experience on Audit Judgments," unpublished working paper, Proceedings of the seventh International Conference on Information Systems, San Diego, Calif., December 15–17, 1986. Reprinted with the permission of the authors.

William F. Messier, Jr., "A Preliminary Investigation of EDP-XPERT," AUDITING: A JOURNAL OF PRACTICE AND THEORY, Fall 1986, pp. 109–123. Reprinted with permission of the authors.

J. E. Boritz, D. S. Broca, "Scheduling Internal Audit Activities," AUDITING: A JOURNAL OF PRACTICE AND THEORY, Vol. 6, No. 1, Fall 1986, pp. 1–19. Reprinted with the permission of the authors.

Rayman D. Meservy, Andrew D. Bailey, Jr., Paul E. Johnson, "Internal Control Evaluation: A Computational Model of the Review Process," AUDITING: A JOURNAL OF PRACTICE AND THEORY, Vol. 6, No. 1, Fall 1986, pp. 44–74. Reprinted with the permission of the authors.

Jesse F. Dillard, Janes F. Mutchler, "Knowledge-Based Expert Computer Systems in Auditing," unpublished working paper, The Ohio State University, 1986. Reprinted with the permission of the authors.

William F. Messier, Jr., "Scheduling the Monitoring of EDP Controls in Online Systems," INTERNATIONAL JOURNAL OF COMPUTER AND INFORMATION SCIENCES, Vol. 12, No. 1, February 1983, pp. 35–46. Reprinted with the permission of the authors.

Daniel E. O'Leary, Toshinori Munakata, "An Accounting Prototype Expert System," unpublished working paper, University of Southern California, 1987. Reprinted with the permission of the authors.

Daniel E. O'Leary, W. Thomas Lin, "An Expert System for Cash Flow Analysis," unpublished working paper, University of Southern California, 1987. Reprinted with the permission of the authors.

Paul J. Steinbart, Graham Gal, "The Role of Expert Systems in Accounting Research," unpublished working paper, University of Massachusetts, September 1986. Reprinted with the permission of the authors.

David Shpilberg, Lynford E. Graham, "Developing ExperTAX: An Expert System for Corporate Tax Accrual and Planning," AUDITING: A JOURNAL OF PRACTICE AND THEORY, copyright 1986 Coopers & Lybrand. Reprinted with the permission of the copyright owners.

Kirk P. Kelly, Gary S. Ribar, John J. Willingham, "Interim Report on the Development of an Expert System for the Auditor's Loan Loss Evaluation," PROCEEDINGS OF THE 1986 TOUCHE ROSS / UNIVERSITY OF KANSAS AUDITING SYMPOSIUM, May 1986. Unpublished working paper, reprinted with the permission of the authors.

Efraim Turban, Theodore J. Mock, "Expert Systems: What They Mean to the Executive," NEW MANAGEMENT, pp. 45–51. Reprinted with the permission of the authors.

Drake W. Smith, David J. Temple, "The Mortgage Loan Analyzer—An Expert System for Underwriting Residential Mortgage Loans", unpublished working paper, Arthur Andersen & Co., Seattle, 1987. Reprinted with the permission of the authors.

INTRODUCTION

The purpose of this book is to combine academic and practitioner literature that falls between accounting or auditing and computer science or knowledge engineering expert systems. It includes a collection of articles which were already published in scholarly journals as well as unpublished papers which were presented to small groups of scholars and practitioners.

This book is not an introductory text and is only suitable for readers with basic knowledge in artificial intelligence, expert systems, accounting, and auditing. The book is divided into five areas:

1. **Foundations:** covering some key concepts of ES, AI, and a view of the future.

2. **Methodology and Surveys:** involving an overview of published work in the field and methodological issues.

3. **Applications in Auditing:** covering a series of pre-paradigmatic works in auditing in subareas as auditor judgment, EDP audit, audit scheduling, internal control evaluation, etc.

4. **Applications in Accounting:** encompassing the first attempts of formalizing accounting issues in an ES framework.

5. **Applications in Practice:** describing some work performed in the professional world and its interpretation.

This introductory chapter examines some of the history of the field, its major domains, some basic concepts, their evolution, and key issues for the use of AI/ES in accounting and auditing.

Artificial Intelligence (AI) and Expert Systems (ES)

Artificial Intelligence (AI) is a field of science which attempts to get machines to exhibit behavior that we call intelligent behavior when we observe it in human beings. Since these machines are always computers, artificial intelligence (AI) in our day is a branch of computer science.

An expert system (ES) is a branch of artificial intelligence. An ES is a set of programs, computer routines and data which has a wide base of knowledge in a restricted domain and uses structured reasoning to perform tasks which a human expert could do.

1. **Game Playing:** involved computer usage for games such as chess playing machines, blackjack, and more menial games as tic-tac-toe.

2. **Problem solving:** efforts involved attempts to prove formulae, develop theorems and manipulate algebraic formulae.

3. **Language Translation:** problems involved many of the currently addressed problems of natural language manipulation, and related language constructs among languages for translation purposes.

4. **Pattern recognition:** focused in identifying particular patterns out of a string of events or cues.

It complained at the same time about the stagnation of the field of artificial intelligence. Its advance remained rather slow until the late seventies when developments in hardware and software as well as some major conceptual leaps allowed for substantial progress. AI research evolved from the search for generalizable solutions and algorithms to the concept of partial solution of problems based on expertise. This opened the domain of the field to the examination of problems with no clearcut solution, but where expert knowledge could improve the quality of outcomes.

Many branches of AI exist and work proceeds rapidly in these fields. Currently AI[2] main fields of research involve work in:

- **Natural languages:** where researchers work on problems related to natural language interface, machine translation, understanding the spoken language, etc.

- **Expert systems:** where no generalizable solutions are researched but expertise is used to deal with fuzzy problems and relationships.

- **Cognition and Learning:** dealing with models of thinking, learning, problem solving, etc.

- **Computer Vision:** developing principles and algorithms for machine vision and the interpretation of visual data.

- **Automatic Deduction:** this area deals with the resolution of problems, theorem proving, logic programming, etc.

Of particular interest to accountants and auditors was the development of expert systems (ES) in several fields of application.[3] These systems showed that complex problems with existing expertise could be modeled and systems built to supplement human decision processes.

"**Expert Systems** are a class of computer programs that can advise, analyze, categorize, communicate, consult, design, diagnose, explain, explore, forecast, form concepts, identify, interpret, justify, learn, manage, monitor, plan, present, retrieve, schedule, test, and tutor."[4] They deal with problems that usually require human beings in their solution and a substantial amount of expertise. They are typically developed with the help of human experts emulating these individuals working in their field of endeavor. Expertise consists of knowledge about a particular domain, understanding of domain problems, and skills relative to solving or partially resolving some of these problems.

Knowledge in most domains is either public or private. **Public knowledge** is articulated in the public domain, for example, the technical literature, and that which is propagated through formal means of instruction. **Private knowledge** includes knowledge that is available to the experts through both their conscious and subconscious levels of cognition. For example, an expert dealing with internal control system evaluation may have developed a set of rules that would find a single indicator that alone would require further investigation of a particular item. These rules may not be in the accounting firm's formal audit rules but are clear in the mind of the auditor and are applied by him or her in a conscious and articulatable manner. Auditors, when asked, could easily state these **heuristic rules.**

Auditors may, on the other hand, have internal control cues that indicate some trouble, but by themselves do not necessarily determine a need for further action. The combination of a few of these cues will determine the need for further audit examination. The auditor may, however, have difficulties in articulating these rules when asked by a third party. The subconscious rule combination process is a product of experience and may be used as the standard for determining how computer software should perform these functions. **Knowledge engineers** often resort to a series of methods to try to get experts to articulate their processes. Among these methods they use real-life examples as cases, think-aloud problem solving, panels of experts to evaluate outcomes, problems with a known outcome to evaluate expertise, etc.

Elements in an Expert System

Expert systems are software programs that emulate human knowledge and combine human-based rules to perform some application task. A series of different concepts evolved from the original work, not essential for ESs, but part of the way ESs are currently developed. An ES will typically have: 1) a series of **facts,** 2) a set of **rules,** 3) some type of rule **interpreter,** and 4) an **inference engine.**[5] Rules can be formulated in the IF-THEN format and may be used as a way to make factual statements about the problem area, "F"

An inference engine is a method of systematically choosing goals, evaluating rules, and interacting with the user in order to obtain a value for the final goal.

Expert systems will have a large set of rules organized in some fashion. In order to achieve some goals, rules must be interpreted (evaluated). The process of searching through the conclusions of rules to achieve goals is referred to as **backward chaining.**

Another equally valid method is **forward chaining.** This method searches the condition parts of the rules for any rule that may be true and performs its conclusion part. This adds new information to the context, and the process is repeated. The repetitive chaining process allows for the implementation of a common feature in ESs which are the WHY and HOW features that use the selected set of rules to explain the system actions.

Some Historical Examples of Expert Systems

The **DENDRAL**[6] program encoded the heuristic knowledge of expert chemists into rules that controlled the search for possible molecular structures, making it possible to obtain a satisfactory answer with a fraction of the effort. The idea of using rules to represent expert knowledge has permeated expert systems work.

CASNET[7] was developed for the diagnosis and therapy of glaucoma, and has been rated by professionals as having performance close to experts. It led to a methodology for modeling diseases in general and to the development of the software EXPERT, a general tool that also has been applied to rheumatology and endocrinology. The program introduced a causal network to model diseases.

The **MACSIMA**[8] program has achieved high competence in the symbolic computations associated with applied analysis.

CADUCEUS[9] **and MYCIN**[10] address different medical diagnosis problems. CADUCEUS (also known as INTERNIST-1) addresses a large semantic network of relationships between diseases and symptoms in internal medicine. MYCIN works on the diagnosis and treatment of infectious blood diseases. The first program encompassed approximately 100,000 associations in 1982. The second program comprises about 400 rules.

The efforts from researchers at Carnegie-Mellon University in conjunction with Digital Equipment Corporation led to the development of R1,[11] an expert system to configure DEC VAX computer systems.

Another interesting application of expert systems is speech-understanding systems. HEARSAY-II incorporates a 1000 word vocabulary and "its skill rivals that of a ten-year-old child."[12]

Figure 1 displays the evolution of a set of expert systems over the years. The figure is based on a chart presented by Hayes-Roth et al.[13] with some modifications.

Generic languages for the development of expert systems were often the by-product of early effects in expert systems. The MYCIN effort led to EMYCIN; Rand Corporation's efforts led to ROSIE;[15] the work at Carnegie-Mellon University led to the development of the OPS series of production system languages;[16] and the HEARSAY work led to AGE.

These early efforts shaped much of today's expert systems work. Many application efforts have since been attempted with more or less noteworthy effects. Noteworthy efforts include applications in: interpretation of oil drilling data (Schlumberger), equipment failure diagnosis, military threat assessment and targeting, VLSI design, crisis management, etc. Among the less noted areas of application are accounting and auditing applications.

Artificial Intelligence, Expert Systems, Accounting, and Auditing

Knowledge can be defined as **descriptions, relationships, and procedures in some domain of interest.** For example, an auditor has knowledge about a series of facts relative to accounting rules and data. Among these rules, for example, are how to compute depreciation and the methods to measure inventory. On the other hand auditors have a good feeling for certain data relationships such as the fact that a company in financial distress may have cash flow problems, a company preparing to enter Chapter 11 may hoard cash, and that these problems are reflected in the statement of sources and uses of funds. In addition, the auditor knows that the controller is responsible for accounting practices and the treasurer for cash flow management. These relationships, descriptions, and procedures (say as prescribed in GAAP and GAAS) are the **knowledge base** of auditors.

Expert systems have been used in: 1) design, 2) prediction, 3) diagnosis, 4) monitoring, 5) planning, 6) debugging, 7) repair, 8) instruction, 9) interpretation, and 10) control functions among many others. Potential applications to the audit area could be developed along each of these functions. For example:

1. **Design:** reconstructing the path of data flows in an integrated computer system based on client documentation, some program logic, and the structure of approvals and authorizations in the organization.

2. **Prediction:** an auditor examining relevant figures and issuing a "going concern" qualification.

3. **Diagnosis:** an auditor infers breakdown in controls from patterns in daily sales.

4. **Planning:** planning the steps in the audit process (audit planning).

5. **Monitoring:** keeping track of transactions in an online system to detect potential problems.

6. **Debugging:** evaluating the integrity of particular computer systems that may affect the accounting process and identification problems.

7. **Repair:** identifying problems with the software logic and their automatic correction.

8. **Instruction:** utilizing expert systems to resolve real problems and the ES's self-documentation and justification features for training new accountants (or auditors).

9. **Interpretation:** auditors examining variances in compliance with internal control standards and interpreting these as relevant or meaningless.

10. **Control:** interpreting, predicting, repairing, and monitoring system behavior.

In addition to the above generic areas, some accounting-related areas also deserve a different kind of consideration: tax advice, insurance coverage estimation, consolidation models, examination of the existing body of precedents (legal, audit), indexation of the standards in GAAP and GAAS, etc.

The tools emerging for usage by auditors endeavoring to use ES are many. Most traditionally, artificial intelligence-oriented systems were programmed in LISP,[17] a symbol manipulation-oriented language. A wide variety of LISP dialects exists and is used in the AI/ES field. These include a few micro-computer-oriented versions. Another programming language popular in this area is PROLOG.[18] These programming languages are complemented in the arsenal of AI/ES designers by a set of **knowledge engineering languages** such as ART, KEE, EMYCIN, and ROSIE. In addition, because of the intensive computing environment required in these problems, some special hardware is emerging for AI/ES work (e.g., Symbolics machines). In the late eighties, the generic corporate user of AI/ES work has tended to lean toward the use of generic mainframes instead of the acquisition of expensive specialized machines.

In 1984, 1986, and 1988 the School of Accountancy of the University of Southern California sponsored three Symposia on Decision Support Systems and Expert Systems in auditing. In these symposia several academics presented research into expert systems applications, particularly in the evaluation of internal controls and audit planning.

Many CPA firms are committed to programs of audit automation. Some of these efforts involve expert system technology. Coopers & Lybrand's ExperTAX aids in the process of tax accrual assessment. Arthur Andersen has been working in the areas of audit planning and risk assessment. Peat Marwick Main & Co. has developed an expert system for the evaluation of bank loan loss reserves. Touche Ross also has some efforts in this area.

Concluding, accounting, and auditing are complex judgment and rule-rich domains of knowledge. The complexity of modern economic means of production leads to a web of entangled and often conflicting professional standards, jurisprudence, and good professional judgment. Computer-based decision aids will consequently become very important tools for the profession. The areas of most immediate application potential are the constrained problems where a clear domain of judgment exists. Among these we find: 1) tax accrual assessment, 2) estimation of bad debt allowance, 3) audit risk assessment, 4) evaluation of internal controls in certain areas of computer systems, 5) statistical sampling, etc.

FIGURE 1
Evolution of Selected Expert Systems and
Expert System Building Languages[14]

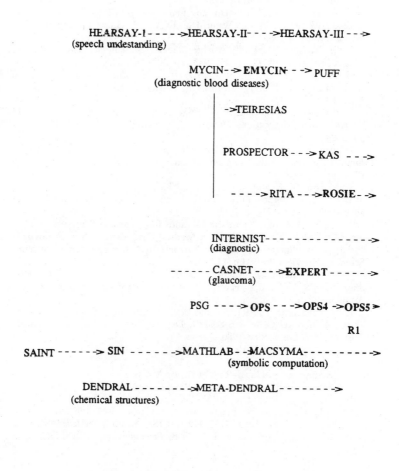

HEARSAY-I - - - - ->HEARSAY-II- - - ->HEARSAY-III - - ->
(speech understanding)

MYCIN- -> **EMYCIN** - -> PUFF
(diagnostic blood diseases)

->TEIRESIAS

PROSPECTOR - - -> KAS - - ->

- - - -> **RITA** - - -> **ROSIE** - ->

INTERNIST- - - - - - - - - - - - ->
(diagnostic)

- - - - - - CASNET - - - -> **EXPERT** - - - - - ->
(glaucoma)

PSG - - - -> **OPS** - - -> **OPS4** -> **OPS5** >

R1

SAINT - - - - -> **SIN** - - - - - ->MATHLAB - - **MACSYMA** - - - - - - - - - ->
(symbolic computation)

DENDRAL - - - - - - - ->META-DENDRAL - - - - - - ->
(chemical structures)

| 1965 | 1970 | 1975 | 1980 |

* Bold Face items are generic tools

Footnotes

1 Adapted from Hayes-Roth et al., op. cit p. 8.

2. See also the three-volume compendium entitled, "The Handbook of Artificial Intelligence" by Barr, Feigenbaum and Cohen published by HeurisTech Press in Stanford, California, 1981.

3. See Hayes-Roth Waterman, and Lenat (eds.), "Building Expert Systems," Addison-Wesley, 1983 and Waterman, D.A., "A Guide to Expert Systems," Addison-Wesley, 1986.

4. Michaelsen, R. H., D. Michie, and A. Boulanger, "The Technology of Expert Systems," *BYTE*, April 1985, pp. 303–312.

5. Waterman, D. A., *A Guide to Expert Systems*, Addison-Wesley, 1983 and B. A. Thompson and W. A. Thompson, "Inside an Expert System," *Byte*, Byte April 1985, pp. 315–330.

6. Buchanan, B. G. and E. A. Feigenbaum, "DENDRAL and Meta-DENDRAL: Their Applications Dimension," Artificial Intelligence, Vol. 11, 1978, pp. 5–24.

7. Weiss, S. M., C. A. Kulikowski, and A. Sfair, "A Model-based Consultation System for the Long-term Management of Glaucoma," IFCAI, Vol. 5, 1977, pp. 826–832.

8. Martin, W. A. and R. J. Fateman, "The MACSIMA System," Proceedings of the Second Symposium on Symbolic and Algebraic Manipulation, Los Angeles, 1971, pp. 59–71.

9. Pople, H. E. Jr., "Heuristic Methods for Imposing Structure on Ill-Structured Problems: The Structuring of Medical Diagnostics." In P. Szolovitz, (ed.), "Artificial Intelligence in Medicine," American Association for Advancement of Science, Westview Press, pp. 119–185.

10. "Computer–Based Medical Decision Making: From MYCIN to VM." In Shortliffe, W. J. II and E. Hance, "Readings in Medical Artificial Intelligence," Addison-Wesley, 1984.

11. McDermott, J., "R1: A Rule-Based Configurer of Computer Systems," Technical Report, CMU-CS-80-119, Department of Computer Science, Carnegie-Mellon University, 1980.

12. Hayes-Roth et al., op. cit., p. 11.

13. Op. cit. p. 8.

14. Adapted from Hayes-Roth et al., op. cit. p. 8.

15. A registered trademark of the Rand Corporation.

16. Forgy, C. L., "The OPS5 User's Manual, Technical Report CMU-CS-81-135, Computer Science Department, Carnegie-Mellon University.

17. Winsten, P. H. and B. K. P. Horn, *LISP,* Addison-Wesley, 1981.

18. Clocksin, W. F and C. S. Mellish, *Programming in PROLOG,* Springer-Verlag, 1981.

References

Aikins, J.S., "Prototypical Knowledge for Expert Systems," *Artificial Intelligence,* Vol. 20, 1983 North-Holland, pp. 163–210.

"Artificial Intelligence: The Second Computer Age Begins," *Business Week,* March 8, 1982.

Austin, Howard, "Market Trends in Artificial Intelligence," Knowledge Analysis, Inc., May 18, 1983.

Belew, R. and P. Ohmans, "The Mind of a New Machine," *TWA Ambassador,* February 1983.

Broad, W. J., "Building A Robot: The Crash Course," *The New York Times,* May 3, 1983.

Clancey, W. J., "The Epistemology of a Rule-Based Expert System," *Artificial Intelligence,* Vol. 20, 1983, North-Holland, pp. 215–251.

Clocksin, William F. and J. D. Young, "Introduction to PROLOG, A 'Fifth-Generation' Language."

Davis, Dwight, B., "English: The Newest Computer Langauge," *High Technology,* February 1984.

Dillard, J. F., K. Ramakrishna, and B. Chandrasekaran, "Expert System for Price Analysis: A Feasibility Study," Working Paper Series, College of Administrative Science, The Ohio State University, October 1983.

Ferguson, Ron, "PROLOG, A Step Toward the Ultimate Computer Language," *Byte,* November 1981.

Fikes, R. E., "Odyssey: A Knowledge-Based Assistant," *Artificial Intelligence,* Vol. 16, 1981, North-Holland, pp. 331–361.

Froiland, Paul, "The Case Against the Thinking Machine," *TWA Ambassador,* February 1983.

Gleick, James, "Exploring the Labyrinth of the Mind," *The New York Times Magazine,* August 21, 1983.

Grishman, R. and L. Hirschman, "Question Answering from Natural Language Medical Databases," *Artificial Intelligence,* Vol. 11, 1978, North-Holland, pp. 25–43.

Harris, L. R., "Fifth Generation Foundations," *Datamation,* July 1983.

Hayes-Roth, F., "Implications of Human Pattern Processing for the Design of Artificial Knowledge Systems," Academic Press, 1978.

Heuristic Programming Project, "Heuristic Programming Project 1980," Computer Science Department, Stanford University, Stanford, CA.

Kinnucan, P., "Machines That See," *High Technology,* April 1983, pp. 30–37.

Krolak, P. D. and J. H. Nelson, "A Man-Machine Approach for Creative Solutions to Urban Problems," *Krolak and Nelson,*

McCarty, L. T., "Reflections on TAXMAN: An Experiment in Artificial Intelligence and Legal Reasoning," *Harvard Law Review,* Vol. 90, No. 5, March 1977, pp. 837–893.

McClellan, David T., "LISPing with Your PC," *PC Magazine,* December 1983, pp. 519–528.

Michaelsen, R. H. "An Expert System for Federal Tax Planning," *Expert Systems: The International Journal of Knowledge Engineering,* October 1984, p. 149.

Ramakrishna, K., J. F. Dillard, T. G. Harrison, and B. Chandrasekaran, "An Intelligent Manual for Price Analysis," Working Paper Series, College of Administrative Science, The Ohio State University, October 1983.

Reitman, Walter, "Artificial Intelligence Application for Business: Getting Acquainted," *AI Symposium,* New York University, 1983, pp. 218–231.

Shank, R. G. and R. P. Abelson, *Scripts, Plans, Goals, and Understanding,* Lawrence Erlbaum Associates, 1977.

Shaw, A. N. and H. A. Simon, "Elements of a Theory of Human Problem Solving," *Psychology Review,* Vol. 65, No. 3, 1958, pp. 151–166.

Shimura, M. and F. H. George, "Rule-Oriented Methods in Problem Solving," *Artificial Intelligence,* Vol. 4, 1973, North-Holland, pp. 203–223.

Shwartz, S. P., "Natural Language Processing in the Commercial World," Cognitive Systems, Inc., New Haven, CN.

Simon, Herbert, "Information Processing Models of Cognition," *Annual Review Psychology,* Vol. '30, 1979, Annual Reviews Inc., pp. 363–396.

_____, "The Structure of Ill Structured Problems," *Artificial Intelligence,* Vol. 4, 1973, North-Holland, pp. 181–201.

Stefik, M., "Inferring DNA Structures from Segmentation Data," *Artificial Intelligence,* Vol. 11, 1978, North-Holland, pp. 85–114.

Stolfo, S. J. and G. T. Vesonder, "ACE: An Expert System Supporting Analysis and Management Decision Making," Department of Computer Science, Columbia University, October 1982.

Szolovitz, P. and S. G. Parker, "Categorical and Probabilistic Reasoning in Medical Diagnosis," *Artificial Intelligence,* Vol. 11, 1978, North-Holland, pp. 115–144.

Verity, J. W., "Endowing Computers With Expertise," *Venture,* November 1983.

Walker, Adrian, "Databases, Expert Systems, and PROLOG," Pre-final draft paper for NYU Symposium on AI Applications to Business, May 18–20, 1983.

Waltz, David, "Artificial Intelligence," *Scientific American,* Vol. pp. 118–133.

Waterman, D. A. and F. Hayes-Roth, "An Overview of Pattern-Directed Inference Systems," San Diego Academic Press, 1978.

Weiss, S. M., C. A. Kulikowski, S. Amarel and A. Safir, "A Model-Based Method for Computer-Aided Medical Decision Making," *Artificial Intelligence,* Vol. 11, 1978, North-Holland, pp. 145–172.

Weyhrauch, R. W., "Prolegomena to a Theory of Mechanized Formal Reasoning," *Artificial Intelligence,* Vol. 13, 1980, North-Holland, pp. 133–170.

White, C. E., A. D. Luzi, and D. L. Craig, "Knowledge-Based Expert Systems for Auditing Professionals," AMIS working paper No. 83–10, The Pennsylvania State University, August 1983.

Winograd, T., "Extended Inference Modes in Reasoning by Computer Systems," *Artificial Intelligence,* Vol. 13, 1980, North-Holland, pp. 5–26.

Woods, W. A., "Natural Language Communication with Machines: An Ongoing Goal," Draft, Beranek, Bolt and Newman Inc., May 1983.

Part I

FOUNDATIONS OF ARTIFICIAL INTELLIGENCE AND EXPERT SYSTEMS IN ACCOUNTING AND AUDITING

This part of the book relates AI and ES to the different problems in accounting and auditing. The Bailey, Hackenbrack, De, and Dillard article presents a framework to validate expert systems. The ". . . researcher can explicitly investigate human judgment processes and test whether the posited processes, represented in a computer program, explain observed behavior." The article lists in Table 1 accounting-based expert systems of which several are discussed elsewhere in the book. The article also attempts to distinguish academic journal research in ES from efforts that are developmental in nature, a major concern for researchers attempting to publish in this area and for journal editors deciding on the merits of an article.

Finally, the article has an appendix that classifies decision support systems (DSS) vis-a-vis their functions and level of expertise. This classification is of great interest in considering that progressive expertise will be impounded in corporate MISs and their level of ability must be gauged in some form.

The McCarthy paper is also classified as fundamental. It focuses on the implications of AI technology in general and expert systems (ES) in particular on accounting. The paper pinpoints the current stage of accounting information systems and extrapolates where they are going to be in the future. The representational formalisms of ESs (logic, rules, and semantic networks) are used to give the readers a feeling for DB (databases) and AI.

1

Artificial Intelligence, Cognitive Science, And Computational Modeling In Auditing Research: A Research Approach

ANDREW D. BAILEY, JR., KARL HACKENBRACK, PRABUDDHA DE, and JESSE DILLARD

The inability of traditional reseach methods to provide solution algorithms for large, ill-structured decision problems has created an interest in the study of expert decision processes and has resulted in numerous attempts to automate these processes. Advancements in Artificial Intelligence (AI) technologies have made possible an integrated approach to the study of expert decision-making behavior at a semantically rich level of analysis.

This paper has several interrelated objectives. First, a distinction is made between the application of AI technologies for product development purposes and for fundamental research. Not until the academic accounting profession comes to terms with this issue will it be able to develop criteria with which to evaluate academic efforts supported by AI applications. Second, a framework to study human information processing is de-

TABLE 1

Example Accounting-Based Expert Systems

SYSTEM	SHELL	REFERENCE	DOMAIN
Tax Advisor	EMYCIM	Michaelson [1982]	Estate Planning
Auditor	AL/X	Dungan [1983]	Allowance for Bad Debts for Commercial Clients
		Mock and Vertinsky [1984]	Choice of Audit Opinion
		Biggs [1984]	Going-Concern Judgments
	AL/X	Braun and Chandler [1983]	Allowance for Bad Debts in the Health Care Industry
CFILE	M1	Willingham and Wright [1985]	Collectability of Bank Loans
IL-ANALYZER		Gal [1985]	Interal Control in the Revenue Cycle
AUDITPLANNER		Steinbart [1984]	Materiality Judgments in Audit Planning
		Braun and Chandler [1983]	Analytic Review
		Dillard and Mutchler [1986]	Opinion Formulation

veloped. This process, which we call the Expert Systems Research Approach (ESRA), integrates traditional Human Information Processing (HIP) methodologies with AI research techniques currently considered controversial by many academic accountants. The fundamental goal of ESRA is not unlike that of more traditional behavioral research efforts in accounting, i.e., to understand, evaluate, and ultimately improve the quality of decision making. ESRA is simply an extension of HIP research. Third, the paper introduces some of the techniques necessary to implement the Expert Systems Approach (ESA). In the remainder of this section, the concept of an expert system is defined and the distinction between expert systems development and expert systems research is made.

Many researchers have argued that the best way to build "intelligent" machines is to emulate human information processing. When this perspective is chosen, the disciplines of psychology and computer science together define the concepts that constitute artificial intelligence. Expert systems use these concepts to solve problems in specific application domains. They are referred to as knowledge-based systems because it is generally held that "the problem-solving power exhibited in an intelligent agent's performance is primarily a consequence of the specialist's knowledge employed by the agent, and only very secondarily

4

related to the generality and power of the inference method employed. Our agents must be knowledge-rich even if they are methods-poor" (Feigenbaum, 1977, p. 1016). Identification and representation of the domain knowledge—both the knowledge states and related procedural knowledge—lie at the heart of human information processing and expert systems work. Appendix A develops the concept of an expert system as it relates to the more general area of decision-support systems.

Expert systems work in accounting continues to be criticized for its apparent lack of scientific rigor and/or its apparent product development orientation. In many cases one or both of these criticisms have, in our judgment, been well placed. However, we believe that much of the conflict has been fueled by a misunderstanding of the methods involved as well as by an apparent model-building or developmental focus in the research to date (see Table 1 for examples of accounting-based efforts).

One contribution of this paper is to make a distinction between those activities that should be preferred as academic research and those activities that should be considered developmental in nature. Basically, expert systems developmental activities are generally outcome-oriented while research activities also focus on expert decision-making processes. The explicit recognition of this distinction will help the academic community articulate the standards by which it evaluates the process that includes expert systems work. Only when these standards are apparent will the academic community be able to fully use its comparative advantage to do research in this area and thereby obtain the benefits that this approach has to offer. We hope that the discussion that follows will permit those who work in the area to better focus their efforts.

Developmental Activities Versus Research Activities

Developmental activities are those whose aim is to use existing technologies to program a computer to find solutions to problems that no computer program has previously been able to effectively solve. The primary focus of developmental projects is not the creation of new knowledge, but the creation of efficient and effective problem solvers using extant knowledge. These activities have substantive and potentially immense business

5

value, as they can have a significant impact on the practice of accounting, auditing, and taxation.

Many contend that it is not apparent that scientific knowledge is advanced by this type of work (McCarthy, 1984, p. 7). Others argue that developmental activities are a part of the continuous cycle of research to application and back. As this process represents advances in the totality of knowledge development, such development is clearly a part of the process of science (Danos et al., 1986). In our opinion, however, developmental activities are not the comparative advantage of the academic's efforts to extend knowledge. Generally, academics should concentrate on research while business pursues development. While we believe that academics may contribute in a consulting fashion to development projects, recent projects carried through to completion within the public accounting sector clearly demonstrate that the practitioner is often in a better position to pursue developmental projects than is the academic (Shpilberg and Graham, 1986). The boundaries between research and development may at times be unclear; nevertheless, this notion should be central to all academic efforts.

The primary focus of an expert systems research project is the creation of a theory of a single expert's decision-making processes (Newell et al., 1958, p. 151). Auditors are appropriate subjects for expert judgment research. They exhibit many of the characteristics normally associated with domain expertise, e.g., they can perform well in task environments where information is often incomplete and probabilistic in nature and where the task is semi- or ill-structured. This task-dependent behavior requires the auditor to use information processing strategies that rely on metaknowledge and heuristics. Metaknowledge is used by experts to organize and structure a task, while heuristics are rules of thumb that allow experts to work with incomplete information and make educated guesses. The ESRA provides a framework in which these processing strategies and domain knowledge can be identified and integrated into a theory of expert decision making where the expert system, in computer program form, embodies the theory. This research process may fill the void left by the inability of extant human information processing technologies to elucidate the heuristics used by expert auditors and may unlock what has traditionally been referred to as the "black box" of auditing expertise.

The distinction between the application of AI technologies for product development purposes and for fundamental research can be viewed from another perspective, i.e., the emphasis placed on each of the AI concepts embodied in the Expert Systems Approach (ESA), the generic form of the ESRA. In the next section we describe the ESA and present a brief discussion of several critical concepts within each of its stages. Only after the ESA has been discussed, without reference to either research or development, will we attempt to further distinguish between expert systems research and expert systems development.

The third and last section of the paper describes what we feel is a viable approach to human information processing research. This approach, ESRA, is an application of the ESA framework to the study of decision making at a process-oriented level in semantically rich task domains. This framework also provides a structure to test the researcher's understanding of the modeled behavior.

Expert Systems Approach (ESA)

The expert systems approach as defined in this paper includes four integrated stages: knowledge acquisition, knowledge representation, computational modeling, and validation. During the first three stages, problem-solving expertise is extracted from a knowledge source, structured, and converted to a machine-readable format. Validation, as the name implies, entails a process to ascertain the propriety of the results of the earlier stages. Each of these stages is discussed individually.

KNOWLEDGE ACQUISITION

To achieve a level of expert performance, an individual must bring to the problem-solving task more than static domain-specific facts and generic psychological processes. For example, an individual must know more than the rules of chess to understand the gamesmanship of a chess master and more than medical facts to appreciate the diagnostic skills of a physician (Johnson, 1983, p. 78). The critical dimension on which expert performance is distinguishable from novice performance is the use of heuristic knowledge—the art of good guessing or the knowledge of good judgment in an ill-structured domain (Dreyfus, 1984, p. 23). If knowledge-based systems are to perform at an expert level, the system must embody the knowledge that is

7

associated with successful human performance in sôlving ill-structured problems; i.e., large amounts of well-organized domain-specific facts and good problem-solving heuristics (Chi et al., 1981).

Unfortunately, experts can seldom accurately describe what they actually know and do in accomplishing their tasks (Johnson, 1983, p. 80). As individuals acquire the heuristics and facts that allow them to perform tasks at an expert level, they tend to lose the awareness of what they know. Experts understand, act, and learn without a conscious awareness of the process. What "obviously" must be done is done (Dreyfus, 1984, p. 32). Johnson calls this phenomenon the "paradox of expertise." This type of knowledge, which may include both heuristic knowledge and domain-specific facts, is commonly referred to as tacit knowledge.

Since experts cannot directly express tacit knowledge, those who work in this area must rely on a mix of indirect methods to elicit this knowledge. Three methods are discussed: descriptive, observational, and intuitive (Bailey et al., 1985, p. 30–4).

Descriptive methods elicit what Johnson (1983, p. 82) refers to as reconstructed methods of reasoning. The knowledge engineer and experts interact through interviews, lectures, and written materials (books, journals, audit working papers, etc.) to discover the domain facts and procedural knowledge that can be codified by experts. This type of knowledge takes the form of plausible rules for how a task might be done. It is fairly general, as it can typically be applied across a variety of forms of a given task.

Descriptive methods may adequately extract domain-specific facts. However, their ability to unlock the heuristics that give meaning to the concept of expertise is, by the definition of tacit knowledge, questionable. Methods that explicitly attempt to unlock tacit knowledge, sometimes referred to as authentic methods of reasoning (Johnson, 1983), are needed. Observational and intuitive acquisition methods attempt to accomplish this end.

Even though the status of process-tracing is controversial (Nisbett and Wilson, 1977), developers of knowledge-based systems have generally relied upon this observational technique to infer authentic methods of reasoning (Chignell and Smith, 1985, p. 5). The process-tracing technique that receives the most attention is the verbal protocol.

8

Closely related to the observational method is the intuitive method. Both rely on direct introspective access to higher-order cognitive processes. But, unlike the observational method, the intuitive method does not rely on interactions between the knowledge engineer and the expert. Here, the knowledge engineer becomes an expert and attempts to extract relevant problem-solving heuristics and domain facts from himself. Granted, the intuitive method is subjective and, like the process-tracing approach, suffers from the possibility that the process used to uncover the tacit knowledge may mask the very process that is being studied/elicited. However, even though the development of these techniques is in its infancy, enough work in this area has been done to conclude that representations of authentic reasoning are achievable (Johnson, 1983, p. 92).

Once the pertinent domain knowledge has been extracted, the architect of the system, the knowledge engineer, must add structure to it. This process, the knowledge representation stage, is discussed next.

KNOWLEDGE REPRESENTATION

This section surveys two representational schemes: (1) a rule-based system, and (2) a frame-based system. The rule-based system is used to discuss knowledge representation issues as they relate to the construction of the knowledge base and the inference engine. The interaction between these repositories of knowledge acquired during the acquisition stage defines the concept of a knowledge system. Aspects of processing control covered in the rule-based section are equally applicable to frame-based systems. As such, the distinction in this paper between the two representational schemes is based on how knowledge other than that needed to control system processing is represented, i.e., the frame-based representation is discussed only with respect to the knowledge base.

The general structure of a typical Rule-Based System (RBS) is illustrated in Figure 1. Roughly, the Components of an RBS can be classified as a member of either the knowledge base or the inference engine. The knowledge base contains data in the form of production rules and facts. Rules represent actions the system should initiate when specific conditions have been met, while facts specify true propositions about the problem-solving domain that hold across applications (Hayes-Roth, 1985, p. 924).

9

FIGURE 1

**General Structure of A
Rule-Based System**

Knowledge Base

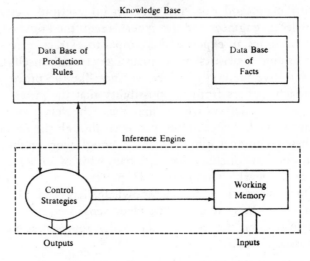

Inference Engine

Outputs   Inputs

The software that governs the selection of processing methods, directs the storage of intermediate calculations, and directs the processing methods themselves, is called the control strategies. Working memory is the repository of the results of intermediate processing. Together, the control strategies and working memory define the inference engine.

A rule-based system's problem-solving expertise is essentially captured in a few hundred to thousands of production rules. A rule might appear as follows:

R(n): IF   condition 1 LEP
                •
                •
                condition i
     THEN   action 1
                •
                •
                action j

The IF part is called the antecedent and the THEN part the consequent. A rule is triggered when all of its conditions are

10

matched with situation-specific facts or inferences generated by previously fired rules. A rule is fired when its actions are executed.

Control strategies (Sullivan and Fordyce, 1985), also called metaknowledge, direct the selection of rules and their execution. Rule selection is accomplished by a method of pattern matching between working memory or the database of facts and rule. The primary difference between existing systems is the method used to simplify pattern matching (Hayes-Roth, 1985, p. 925).

Two methods of controlling rule selection are forward chaining and backward chaining. Forward chaining involves a general movement from known facts to deduced facts by triggering rules as a result of pattern matching between a changing working memory and the antecedent of the production rules. A backward chaining system is goal driven. It selects or is given a hypothetical conclusion and then determines whether or not the supporting facts are present or can be inferred by successively examining production rules whose consequent matches structures in the working memory.

The working memory, sometimes referred to as the blackboard, is used to store both situation-specific information and inferences generated throughout a given session as a result of production rule firings. This situation-specific information is usually entered through a terminal at the beginning of a session or during the session in response to system queries of the user. Some systems also receive information directly from sensors (Sullivan and Fordyce, 1985).

Proponents of rule-based systems argue that whether or not this model correctly explains human problem-solving expertise, experts find it relatively easy to express problem-solving methods using production rules. They consider RBSs the method of choice for building knowledge-intensive systems (Hayes-Roth, 1985, p. 921).

Frame-based systems originated from a continuing stream of research on computer representations of human cognitive processes. The primary motivation of Minsky (1975, ch. 6) when he introduced the concept of frame systems was the modeling of scene analysis reasoning. Subsequent research has largely focused on structural representation issues.

The frame-based representation scheme resembles a hierarchical network whose nodes are individual frames. These sys-

11

FIGURE 2

Frame-Based System
Class Structure, Links, Inheritance

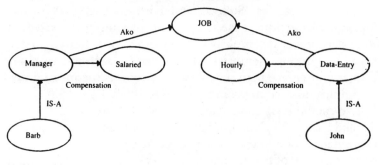

tems represent a prototypic description of an object or class of objects and exploit their hierarchical nature by enabling descriptive and procedural knowledge to be shared among multiple frames (Winsten, 1984, p. 255–260).

Within the network, there are three ways to connect (link) individual frames and characteristics within frames. IS-A links connect frames that describe specific objects to frames representing a relatively homogeneous group of objects, i.e., instance frames to class frames. AKO (a kind of) links connect homogeneous class frames to more heterogeneous class frames. Facets link characteristics called values or procedural knowledge to individual frames. In Figure 2, the BARB frame is identified as a member of the manager class by an IS-A link. The AKO link represents the fact that the MANAGER frame is a subset of the JOB frame. A value facet COMPENSATION is used to identify the type of compensation each job classification usually receives. This example illustrates the hierarchical organization common to all frame systems. It can also be used to illustrate the process that transfers information from class frames to instance frames. This process, called inheritance, mimics reasoning processes believed to exist in humans.

Inheritance is a search procedure that is initiated when information is not available at the instance frame being interpreted. Basically, the missing data are retrieved from related class frames (Sullivan and Fordyce, 1985, p. 12). In Figure 2, no COMPENSATION facet is directly attached to the BARB frame. But the value linked to the MANAGER frame is SALARIED. By virtue of the IS-A link, the value SALARIED would be inherited by the BARB frame. Likewise, unless evidence to the contrary is available, John is assumed to be an hourly employee simply because he is a data-entry person, and data-entry employees are usually paid an hourly wage.

Once the domain-specific knowledge has been represented, the knowledge engineer turns to the task of re-representing the domain-specific knowledge via the building of a computational model. This mapping of the results of the knowledge representation stage to a computer representation is discussed next.

COMPUTATIONAL MODELING

The knowledge engineer can choose from three categories of computational modeling tools—programming languages, shells, and representation languages (Hayes-Roth et al., 1983, p. 283–287). Those who wish to start the modeling process from "square one" tend to choose one of two general-purpose programming languages. To date, the most popular is the family of LISP languages. Their popularity stems from the language's symbolic manipulation capabilities and interactiveness. PROLOG, an acronym for PROgramming in LOGic, is gaining wider acceptance. The intent of this language is to apply one powerful rule of inference to a mechanical theorem-proving system, enabling "a programmer to make a computer stimulate the thinking process by making deductions from information given in logical formulas" (Colmerauer, 1985, p. 1296). This close link with logic proved to be burdensome and has resulted in the incorporation of practical constraints into the final package. Nonetheless, this model is considered an important milestone in the evolution of AI programming languages.

Rather than starting from scratch, it may be possible to use commercially available software packages, referred to as shells, sometimes with little or no modification. Shells, also referred to as skeletal systems, may greatly reduce modeling efforts and may provide the necessary support to enable those who lack the requisite programming skills to construct a computational model. In practice, however, this process is rarely simple. Some of the more popular shells are EMYCIN, GALEN, KAS, and EXPERT.

Representation languages are programming languages that have been specifically developed for AI applications. Since, unlike shells, they are not tied to a particular framework, they allow for a wider variety of control structures. This increased

13

flexibility is not costless, as the process of applying these models may be more difficult. Some commonly used systems include OPS5, HEARSEY-3, ROSIE, and RLL. Those interested in an overview of these and many of the other available AI tools should consult Bundy (1984) and Hayes-Roth et al. (1983, p. 301–326).

At this juncture in the ESA, the different paths followed by the cognitive science researcher and the problem-solver developer become more evident. Each must validate the results of the first three stages of the ESA; however, their orientations are not the same. The developer's criteria for model performance are based on outcome measures, not process measures. The problem-solver builder is more interested in modeling the "best" heuristics than in emulating any given expert. Therefore, in building the computational model, attempts to identify heuristics used by experts become secondary to identifying "good" problem-solving heuristics. In other words, a good solution is the desired result even if no particular expert follows the programmed process.

Researchers, on the other hand, are primarily concerned with understanding the expert's decision processes and thus require a more careful knowledge-acquisition effort attuned to identifying the expert's heuristics and modeling the expert's decision process. The researcher's formal validation process is therefore multifaceted, including both process and output measures.

When the researcher's model surpasses the required threshold of performance, he or she has validated his or her understanding of an individual's judgment process in the strictly defined domain from which it was built. This research approach is developed further in the next section of the paper. What follows is a description of the validation phase from the perspective of a problem-solver builder.

VALIDATION

Model 1 in Figure 3 represents the mapping of knowledge from the knowledge representation stage to a computational model format. Validation at this step entails comparing outcome measures between the model and the expert that were used during the knowledge acquisition and knowledge representation stages. If significant differences are found, the developer must tune the model. Tuning is a process that involves reverting to the

14

FIGURE 3

**Validation Framework
Development Perspective**

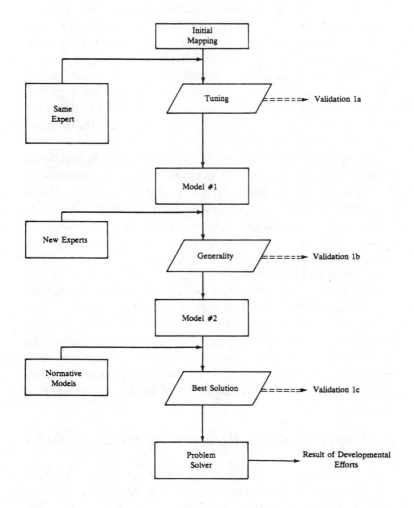

knowledge acquisition or knowledge representation stages to extract and represent additional facts or heuristics that will enable the computational model to pass this stage of the validation process.

During the second stage of the validation process, additional experts are used to address the following types of questions. Are the model's outcomes comparable with those found across experts? If not, what mechanisms could cause conclusions to differ across experts? Here, cue sets are given to a number of experts not used during earlier stages of the system's development. Outcomes are compared and significant variations, if any, are identified. Causation is hypothesized and reasonable alternatives, whether new facts or new heuristics, are included in the model. The developer seeks to include the best available heuristics in the model. No hard and fast rules are available to guide this process. The result of this validation effort is Model 2 in Figure 3.

Having constructed a model that works, the developer's focus shifts. He or she is now in a position to place a premium on efficiency and the ability to arrive at the best solution. Normative models may help streamline the knowledge base or inference engine by highlighting those cue sets that should be most relevant or the preferable outcomes from the previous step.

While we know of no theoretically tenable method to determine which problem-solving method is the best or what the best solution is in this context, this is the type of issue that the builder of a problem solver must consider. Validation at this step is not strictly outcome-oriented. It has a process orientation only to the extent that it relates to user friendliness, speed of processing, and the ability to provide *ex post* justification for actions and decisions. The consequence of this validation stage is a developed problem solver, the primary objective of the developmental process.

An Expert Systems Research Approach (ESRA)

In studying expert judgment, accounting researchers have focused on either judgment outcomes or the decision process leading to these outcomes. Johnson et al. (1982, pp. 201–202, 225) discuss the two traditional methodological approaches used in these investigations. The first is a statistical approach that analyzes judgment outcomes. The second is a process-tracing

16

approach that captures the outcome and the judgment process leading to the outcome.

In a typical judgment task using the statistical approach, subjects are given several stimulus cue sets, e.g., a case study, which must be analyzed in making either numerical judgments (How many hours should be assigned to an audit engagement?) or categorical classifications (Can the system of internal control be relied upon?) (Ashton, 1974; Joyce and Biddle, 1981a and 1981b). If the judgments associated with each cue combination are considered a dependent variable, one form or another of the general linear model can be used to identify the relative cue importance. If the various cue combinations are orthogonal, an analysis of variance technique is used to discover which cues or patterns of cues appear to be significant factors in making the decisions.

Although this class of methods generally explains significant levels of variation and yields interesting results, it is not wholly satisfactory in providing explanations for the observed results. First, the underlying theoretical constructs of these studies are often not well developed. In these cases, little can be said about the causal relationship of cues and decisions. Second, most of these studies deal in highly abstracted settings for which the mapping between the experimental objects and reality is often ill-defined. Third, such studies can tell us little about the judgment process followed by the subject in making the observed judgment.

Judgment requires more than domain knowledge. It requires metaknowledge, or strategies for using domain knowledge, to generate possible hypotheses, to recognize potential relationships among sets of cues, etc. The statistical modeling approach provides little insight into these processes or the processes used to determine which cues to attend to, in what order they are attended to, and what knowledge to associate with interpreting each cue. We do not wish to suggest that these efforts are not worthwhile, but neither are they flawless. New methods may contribute to our understanding of expertise.

Some human information processing researchers assert that the mental models used by individuals are intuitively constructed, i.e., constructed without rational thought or inference (Johnson, 1982, p. 225). Process tracing is a method for investigating intuitive judgment that concentrates on the judgment process, not merely the outcome judgment. In addition to

17

investigating the information highlighted by classical statistical methods, process tracing attempts to describe higher-order levels of expert cognition. One process-tracing method, the thinking-aloud protocol, may be used to identify both the domain knowledge and process used by the expert in interpreting cue sets. Although this method and others dealing in rich context environments may yield significant insights, the information gathered from studies employing these techniques is not invulnerable to criticism.

The models constructed from verbal protocol analyses may agree with a subject's intuitive notion of the problem-solving strategy, whereas the structure of input-output models may not. The "face validity" of the verbal protocol seems high (Ashton, 1982, p. 181). However, this conjecture may be misleading. One should be careful not to overstate the credibility of process-tracing results. The technique does not imply an isomorphism between actual judgment processes and the protocol results simply because it is process-oriented (Einhorn et al., 1979, p. 470).

There are several reasons why one should be conservative when analyzing or reviewing process-tracing results. First, the traditional appeal to statistical significance is not generally available in process-tracing studies because of the small sample sizes employed. Second, the act of requiring subjects deliberately to attend to possibly nondeliberate cognitive activities may distort the very processes that are the focus of the analysis. Some authors (e.g., Nisbett and Wilson, 1977, p. 233) suggest that any introspective access that individuals may have to their judgment processes is not sufficient to produce generally correct or reliable reports. "Subjective reports about higher mental processes are sometimes correct, but even the instances of correct report are not due to direct introspective awareness. Instead, they are due to the incidentally correct employment of *a priori* causal theories" (p. 233). Third, results obtained by Smith and Miller (1978) suggest that in tasks involving routine skills, cognitive processes may function automatically and be inaccessible via either introspection or active self-reporting. That is, an individual's ability to report accurately his cognitive processes may be inversely related to the degree of routineness associated with the task. This problem may be acute in expert judgment behavior verbal-protocol studies, as experimental tasks generally coincide with assignments that the expert considers routine.

18

Motivated by the recognition of these deficiencies, some cognitive researchers have adopted what we refer to as the expert systems research approach. The objective of this broad framework is not unlike that of other human information processing approaches. The intent is the study of decision making and human information processing at a process-oriented level in semantically rich task domains. But, unlike the traditional process-tracing approach, the ESRA provides a structure within which to test the researcher's understanding of human judgment behavior.

The ESRA entails the four integrated stages of the ESA, i.e., knowledge acquisition, knowledge representation, computational modeling, and (theory) validation. The first two stages involve identifying and organizing the many processes that together constitute domain expertise. The computational modeling stage takes this expertise and translates it into a computer-compatible representational framework. Once the researcher feels confident that the computational model adequately emulates the cognitive processes of the expert under study, the theory validation phase has begun. In one sense the computational model is a validation of the researcher's understanding, in that it already emulates the expert at some level. Additional efforts extend the degree of confidence the researcher can place in the model as a representation of the expert's judgment processes.

During the knowledge acquisition phase, the researcher attempts to elicit, usually from a single expert, the knowledge states and the related cognitive processes associated with the expert's judgment behavior. This information is then organized and formalized during the knowledge representation stage. The goal of these two stages is to develop a theory of behavior. Extant expert systems techniques and current knowledge as to expert decision processes require that this be a theory of judgment across the "narrowly" defined sphere of an individual expert (Newell et al., 1958, p. 151).

No attempt is made to replicate judgment processes at the most primitive levels of cognition (Newell et al., 1958, p. 153). Instead, the accounting researcher chooses some level of abstraction consonant with the available cognitive psychology and computer science technology and with the breadth of the domain that he or she has chosen to study. The breadth of the domain is a critical factor, since a necessary characteristic of the

19

results of this methodology is tractability. That is, there is usually an inverse relationship between the depth of understanding achievable and the breadth of the domain studied.

Process-tracing techniques are an integral part of the knowledge acquisition stage. The usefulness of a verbal protocol analysis is derived not only from its exploratory powers but also from the ability to produce a potentially rich representational model of judgment behavior (Payne et al., 1978, p. 29) based on the data collected. We are not aware of other methods that explicitly attempt to model more detailed levels of judgment processes.

As the process-tracing data are accumulated, but before enough information has been gathered to build a prototype of the computational model, the knowledge engineer needs a technique that allows him to gain a degree of confidence in the data. Fortunately, both process-tracing and input-output analysis capture the expert's decision processes, but at different levels of generality. ". . . [P]rocesses are neither more or less true or real as a function of a particular level of analysis. Rather, regression and process-tracing models both deal with underlying psychological process[es] . . ." (Einhorn et al., 1979, p. 470). We exploit this complementary relationship to justify the use of a multimethod, knowledge acquisition approach (Ashton, 1982, p. 185). Within the current scenario, input-output analyses can, in addition to providing unique data, serve as a benchmark from which to "confirm" the initial results of the knowledge acquisition stage, i.e., the verbal protocol results. If the results derived from the various methods are in agreement, the credibility of each is enhanced. However, a disagreement will not necessarily indicate which analysis is superior (Ashton, 1982, p. 183).

A researcher who applies a multimethod approach to human information processing research acquires and represents a pool of interrelated data and cross-validating results. Why should he or she build a computation model? The rewards are not directly associated with the model-building activity, but with the computational model's value as a research tool. This is the juncture at which individuals involved in the contemporary academic accounting debate over the propriety of expert systems research often fail to clearly articulate their positions. Most denigrate all attempts to use AI technologies largely because expert system "pioneers" in accounting research have tended to focus on the model-building activities, have tried to have their activities deemed research, and have, in the process, "muddied the waters." We believe that these early efforts were essential and important in their own right. However, we do not believe that they represent fundamental research efforts. Nor do we believe the assertion that all activities associated with a computational model are developmental in nature. An analogy can be drawn between the use of an expert system shell to build a computational model (e.g., GALEN) and a statistical package (e.g., SPSS) used to implement the lens model paradigm (Ashton, 1982, p. 124–151). In neither case is the construction of the computer representation a research activity. Instead, the activity represents the application of a tool by the researcher to a researchable issue.

We envision two distinct uses of these expert system research tools. The first and perhaps most fruitful application of the model, from the perspective of the individual researcher, may be its use to facilitate the transmission and reproduction of the researcher's expertise. The computational model is simply one possible representation of the researcher's theory. It can be thought of as a reasonably portable form of a theory, where the potential number of applications in subsequent research projects is limited only by the creativity of the individual researcher.

The computational model can also be used to validate theories developed using knowledge acquisition techniques such as the process-tracing method. A computational model, as an expert emulator, can help verify that the researcher has, at some level of abstraction, an understanding of the expert judgment process (Newell et al., 1958, p. 166). If the expert behavior identified by process-tracing and other knowledge acquisition techniques can be emulated by a computational model, the process provides evidence that the researcher's theory of an expert is valid. In other words, the ESRA is one process that can be used to study judgment behavior in which the expert system, an emulator, acts as a validation tool.

Validation in this context does not necessarily imply that the theory of judgment behavior is being directly "confirmed." Rather, validation implies that the discrete results from the theory development phase are reasonably consistent and mimic human performance on a process and outcome basis as measured by the technologies used to acquire the knowledge represented by the computational model. In addressing this issue, consider the views of Popper, an early member of the post-logical-positivism community within the philosophy of science. As

21

discussed by Christenson (1983, pp. 8–9), Popper accepts the process view of science. He agrees with the logical positivists who adopt the position that empirical science is a collection of propositions whose (truth or) falsity can be decided only by experience, and with Hume (1748) that experience can never conclusively establish the truth of any proposition since it is impossible to verify a theory by any number of confirming observations, i.e., falsificationism. In other words, absolute authenticity is an elusive concept. The appropriate question should therefore be: Does the expert systems research approach provide a framework within which to judge the verisimilar nature of a researcher's conjectures?

We suggest that it does if viewed within the context of Newton-Smith's (1981) "temperate" rationalist philosophy, which is discussed in Danos et al. (1986). In short, Newton-Smith sees both the process and results of scientific inquiry as dynamic. Therefore, as a result of scientific advancement, the process of science always becomes richer, and "better" theories are constantly formulated and accepted. Validation, then, should have a temporal connotation, where the acceptance of a researcher's theory is a function of the theory's ability to survive a series of attempts to refute it. The expert systems research approach is the contemporary answer to the increased sophistication needed to frame current investigations of human information processing. The richer levels of study dictated by the increasingly complex or "better" theories of judgment that the natural evolutionary process of science demands can be met by the ESRA. Within the expert systems research approach, the theory validation phase is a surrogate for the traditional activity of third-party replication of results, i.e., survival of refutation. The theory validation phase cannot, in principle, replace third-party replication because the degree of replication and robustness inherent in the theory validation phase admittedly falls short of the power of "confirmation" associated with replication by third parties. We believe, however, that this phase captures a significant portion of the replication process.

In sum, if the theory validation process, applied over a series of trials, suggests agreement between the computational model and the test subjects, then the researcher can be reasonably certain that he or she has captured the authentic methods of reasoning associated with a particular judgment task. The researcher has validated his or her claims at a level of abstraction consonant with the available judgment behavior technology. The researcher has demonstrated in a rigorous manner that he or she has a thorough understanding of the judgment task and that the propositions that follow from his or her work potentially belong to the body of empirical knowledge. Replication of the researcher's results by others extends the validation effort.

The theory validation framework we have presented in broad terms above begins at the point where the researcher or developer has enough comfort in the results of the knowledge representation stage to construct a computational model. For some, the model-building stage will begin long before the knowledge acquisition and knowledge representation stages are complete. Those who follow this strategy believe that the best way to build a computational model is through a process wherein an initial prototype evolves into "the model" as more domain information is revealed. Others wait until the formal knowledge representation stage is complete. We will assume, without loss of generality, that the latter course is chosen.

The initial validation (Validation 2a in Figure 4), after mapping from the knowledge representation stage to Computational Model 1, entails process and outcome comparisons between the model and the expert from whom the theory was derived, using cue sets similar to those used during the knowledge acquisition and knowledge representation stages. When the model surpasses the required threshold of performance, the researcher has validated his or her understanding of an individual's judgment process. The model can be considered a representation of the theory of an individual expert in the strictly defined domain from which it was built.

This is a necessary plateau within the ESRA. The researcher has one more hurdle. He or she must still explicitly define the boundaries of the domain with which a model (theory) can effectively deal. This test of robustness entails developing case materials which vary in subtle and methodic ways from the case materials used to extract, represent, and model the expertise. Validation testing at this stage still involves process comparisons and outcome comparisons between the tuned model and the original expert. The researcher may either use this as an opportunity to define in narrative terms the boundaries of the domain of discourse or to enhance the capacity of the tuned model at the periphery of the domain. In either case, the model should degrade gracefully. This version of the computational model

FIGURE 4

Validation Framework
Research Perspective

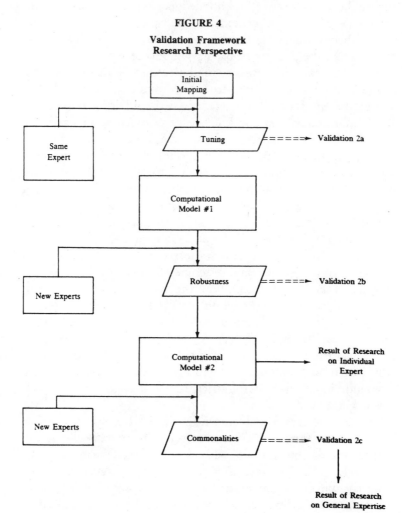

(Computational Model 2 in Figure 4) completes the expert systems research approach in defining a theory of the individual expert.

When the researcher compares the model of individual expert behavior to both the processes and outcomes of experts not previously involved, the intent is to discover the commonalities and differences between experts (Newell et al., 1958, p. 152). This special type of validation does not influence the acceptance of the researcher's theory of the original expert's judgment behavior. Any "discrepancies" between the model of the initial expert's behavior and any one of the experts used in this phase are assumed to be associated with the behavior that properly belongs to the model of the "new" subject's behavior. At this point, the researcher can only note what the commonalities and differences are. This information will probably not lead to a computational model of general expertise across the entire domain of discourse, as it is unlikely that a model composed solely of similarities found across all experts will be operational. After all, a specific application of expertise is, by definition, unique and not generalizable across groups of people or tasks.

There is no agreed-upon method of assessing which set of procedures that could potentially be applied in a specific validation situation is best. However, there does seem to be a consensus that the appropriate strategy to follow is to construct a web of convincing evidence (Johnson, 1983, p. 90). The key is to gather different types of evidence, each of which speaks to a different facet of the model's performance. The researcher must select the mix of techniques from the set of all available validation techniques that he or she feels addresses the unique characteristics of the task domain. Critical aspects of one model may differ significantly from those of another. As a result, the mix of validation tools can vary from one situation to the next.

The validation plan—a set of procedures to implement each phase within the general validation framework—that we feel adequately evaluates the model's performance combines two types of validation tests: tests of sufficiency (output results) and process comparison tests (Johnson, 1983, pp.85–89). The emphasis on each type of test is dictated by the goal of the project. Developmental projects would focus on tests of sufficiency, while research projects would place a greater emphasis on process-comparison testing. Statistical evaluation of process-comparison tests, while desirable, is generally not available because

25

of the small sample sizes dictated by the intricacies associated with the various techniques (Meservy et al., 1985). There are simply not enough researcher or expert hours, given extant technology and resources. As a result, researchers generally rely on tabular and graphical analyses of data (e.g., Johnson, 1983, pp. 88–89).

Sufficiency tests require the model to predict/postdict the behavior that they allegedly explain. Two standards of performance have been suggested (Buchanan and Shortliffe, 1984, p. 580): (1) the correct answer to the case and (2) the answer of a human expert(s) based on the same case materials. The former criterion is almost never applicable in the domains investigated by expert judgment researchers or modeled by builders of problem solvers. As a result, sufficiency testing usually involves giving the model and a number of subjects a reasonable range of cases that were not part of the model development phase and determining if they reach the same or similar conclusions.

While sufficiency testing is generally adequate in evaluating a problem solver, it does not adequately validate the researcher's understanding of the expert decision process, as any number of mechanisms can be organized into a system capable of producing a given outcome. Process comparisons are needed to ensure that, at some level of abstraction, the model employs the reasoning steps or lines of reasoning indicative of the expert's performance. The work of Meservy et al. (1985) illustrates process-comparison testing.

Meservy's model evaluation framework is based upon the comparison of model traces and verbal protocols of several expert auditors. The comparison is based upon the integration of results from two separate analyses: (1) a top-down, global analysis and (2) a bottom-up, knowledge state/cognitive-processes analysis. The top-down analysis identifies the specific goals, subgoals, and objectives that direct information processing, e.g., the representation or mental picture of the segregation of duties within a transaction cycle. Results of this analysis are rather general, but they provide the foundation from which more detailed analyses can be performed. The bottom-up analysis focuses on knowledge states, static sets of facts, concepts, and hypotheses, and the cognitive processes (e.g., reading, requesting information, and searching for information) that link them. This analysis allows the researcher to examine how the experts use old sets of facts, as well as to generate new knowledge states and the types of cognitive processes that link the knowledge states (Bailey et al., 1985, pp. 41–42).

A proviso is in order. The discussion so far may have created the impression that an individual researcher will necessarily work in all stages of the expert system research approach. Instead, what we have tried to lay out from the perspective of the individual researcher is a meta-process. We have developed a framework within which the contiguous parts of a possibly communal process can be integrated to form a more focused approach to either articulate current paradigms or move toward new paradigms. A researcher, over the course of his or her career, may wish to tackle, to some degree, all stages of the process. However, it is not reasonable to expect each of a researcher's projects, where a project is synonymous with a publication, to encompass all stages of the ESRA. Rarely would an individual possess the requisite skills in all areas. Still, significant incremental insights into judgment behavior might be gained if the researcher could evolve through the progression of the ESRA stages, since he or she would be in a position to capitalize, at any given point, on insights gained during earlier stages of the process.

In summary, the application of artificial intelligence concepts to build expert systems enables the researcher to describe and validate the strategies underlying decision-making processes. By identifying the interactions between static domain knowledge and cognitive processes, the expert systems research approach can provide a broad framework in which to investigate and understand human judgment behavior and to validate that understanding in such semantically rich task-domains as accounting and auditing.

Appendix A
The Continuum of Decision-Support Systems

Numerous researchers and practitioners use the term Decision-Support System (DSS) to describe/classify their work. What do they mean by a decision-support system? What distinguishes DSSs from Electronic Data Processing (EDP) or Management Information Systems (MIS)? A definitive answer to this question does not exist since different individuals have different notions as to the meaning of DSS (Bonczek et al., 1981).

An initial dichotomy suggested by Alter (1977, p. 39) classifies business computer applications as either an electronic data processing or a decision-support system. The dichotomy is based on whether the application promotes efficiency through improved processing or decision making. EDP systems are oriented toward the automation of transaction processing, recordkeeping, and reporting, i.e., mechanical efficiency. A DSS, on the other hand, has as its goal the improvement of the overall efficiency and effectiveness of individuals within the organization by supporting their decision-making processes in a fairly direct fashion. Where EDP systems perform largely clerical tasks, DSSs provide assistance ranging from simple information retrieval to suggesting solutions to sophisticated problems.

Alter (1977, p. 49) suggests a seven-cell classification scheme ranging from fairly simple "systems whose basic purpose was (is) to retrieve simply aggregations of raw data," through highly complex "systems whose basic purpose was (is) to suggest actions based on formulas or mathematical procedures." His taxonomy is based on a single dimension, the degree to which the system can directly aid the decision-making process. The Bailey et al. (1985, p. 13) framework discussed below is equally broad. It refers to a DSS as "any interactive computer application that helps a decision maker by providing access to large data banks or by implementing a decision model or both."

The following characteristics are indicative of those normally associated with decision-support systems (Bailey et al., 1985, p. 10). First, it is useful to narrow the definition to include only computer-based systems. Paper-based systems do exist; however, it is the computer's processing power that makes it possible to exploit the real potential of DSSs. Second, a DSS should provide an interactive user interface. During processing, the computer will query the user for additional information and/or supply intermediate results. Also, the user will query the computer and obtain additional feedback ranging from specific data to explanations of the system's "solution" to the problem under consideration. Third, DSSs should provide access to large data banks. The ability to selectively retrieve and manipulate large quantities of data and to produce useful information is what makes decision-support systems powerful and practical. Fourth and last, advanced DSSs will suggest solutions to problems by combining data and computer-based rules for processing the data.

28

DECISION AIDS

Based on the above, Bailey et al. (1985) classify decision-support systems as Decision Aids (DA), Non-Expert DSS (NEDSS) and Expert Systems (ES). Decision Aids are distinguished from the other decision-support systems by their lack of man/machine interaction. The auditor simply selects one from a list of available application packages and uses it in the prescribed manner. Examples of these applications include the use of Generalized Audit Software Programs (GASP) in the collection and manipulation of data from client systems and similar software used to develop and control working papers, e.g., trial balances. Many decision aids are able to support data analysis via normative models. Such aids do not guide the auditor through the decision process involved, but simply provide a solution, e.g., statistical sample size computations. The systems are user-dominated; i.e., the user, not the system, makes the decision at each crucial step. A list of currently operational decision aids would include ASK, AUDITAID, BASE, CARS, STAR, TRAP and PROBE (Weber, 1982).

NON-EXPERT DECISION-SUPPORT SYSTEMS

Non-Expert DSSs have evolved from decision aids by adding menu-driven, interactive components. Peat Marwick Main & Co.'s SEACAS system is a notable example. Deloitte, Haskins & Sells, Coopers & Lybrand, Arthur Young, and others use similar systems. More advanced systems are under development by most of the large public accounting firms. The newer systems are menu- and model-driven, but lack the emulation aspects of expert decision processes. It is mainly the lack of the expert judgment emulation processing characteristic that most differentiates non-expert from expert DSSs.

EXPERT SYSTEMS

Barr and Feigenbaum (1981) define artificial intelligence as "the part of computer science concerned with designing intelligent computer systems, that is, systems that exhibit the characteristics we associate with intelligence in human behavior—understanding language, learning, reasoning, solving problems, and so on." Expert systems apply AI concepts to

29

solve what we generally consider difficult problems requiring expertise in well-defined domains. As such, expert systems are a subspecialty or application of AI. Expert systems are most appropriate where an algorithmic solution to the problem addressed does not exist and where complete or certain data are not available (Sullivan and Fordyce, 1985, p. 4).

Expert systems are different from conventional computer programs (Sullivan and Fordyce, 1985) in that the former rely on symbolic representations and heuristic search processes while the latter depend on numeric representations and algorithmic solutions. Expert systems usually separate the control structure from the knowledge base, making modifications to each relatively easy. Conventional programs integrate information and control. Also, the expert system user tends to accept satisfactory answers while users of conventional programs often require optimal or near-optimal solutions.

In sum, expert systems represent, in machine-readable form, human knowledge and decision processes associated with a specific domain. This allows a computer to solve problems and provide information that previously would have required the presence of a human expert. The goal of AI/ES is not to replace human decision makers but to supplement human decision making, and thus to release human resources for more important questions. AI/ES is an important step in making the DDS a more viable participant in the decision-making process.

References

Alter, S., "A Taxonomy of Decision-Support Systems," *Sloan Management Review*, Fall 1977, pp. 39–56.
Anderson, J., "Cognitive Psychology," *Artificial Intelligence*, 1984, pp. 1–11.
Ashton, R. H., *Studies in Accounting Research #17: Human Information Processing in Accounting*, American Accounting Association, 1982.
Bailey, A. D., Jr., G. Duke, P. Johnson, R. Meservy, and W. Thompson, "Auditing, Artificial Intelligence, and Expert Systems," *NATO Advanced Study Institute: Decision-Support Systems: Theory and Application*, Maratea, Italy: 1986.
Barr, A. and E. Feigenbaum, *The Handbook of Artificial Intelligence*, Vol. 1, HeurisTech Press, 1981.
Bonczek, R., C. Holsapple, and A. Whinston, *Foundations of Decision Support Systems*, Academic Press, 1981.
Braun, H. and J. Chandler, "Development of an Expert System to

Assist Auditors in the Investigation of Analytic Review Fluctuations," Research Project for Peat Marwick Main & Co., 1983.

Buchanan, B. G. and E. H. Shortliffe, *Rule-Based Expert Systems,* Addison-Wesley, 1984.

Bundy, A., *Symbolic Computation, Catalogue of Artificial Intelligence Tools,* Springer-Verlag, 1984.

Chi, M. T., P. Feltovich, and R. Glaser, "Categorization and Representation of Physics Problems by Experts and Novices," *Cognitive Science,* 1981, pp. 121–152.

Chignell, M. S., and P. J. Smith, "An Introduction to Knowledge-Based Systems," working paper, University of Southern California, June 1985.

Christenson, C., "The Methodology of Positive Accounting," *The Accounting Review,* January 1983, pp. 1–22.

Colmerauer, A., "PROLOG in 10 Figures," *Communications of the ACM,* December 1985, pp. 1296–1310.

Danos, P., D. Holt, and A. D. Bailey, Jr., "The Interaction of Science and Attestation Standard Formation," working paper, University of Minnesota, 1986.

Dillard, J. and J. Mutchler, "A Knowledge-Based Expert System for the Auditor's Going Concern Decisions," working paper, The Ohio State University, 1986.

Dreyfus, H. L., "What Experts Systems Can't Do," *Raritan,* 1984, pp. 22–36.

Dungan, C., "A Model of an Audit Judgment in the Form of an Expert System," Ph.D. dissertation, University of Illinois, 1983.

Einhorn, H., D. Kleinmuntz, and B. Kleinmuntz, "Linear Regression and Process-Tracing Models of Judgment," *Psychological Review,* September 1979, pp. 465–485.

Feigenbaum, E., "The Art of Artificial Intelligence," *International Joint Conference on Artificial Intelligence,* 1977, pp. 1014–1029.

Gal, G., "Using Auditor Knowledge to Formulate Data Model Constraints: Expert Systems for Internal Control Evaluation," Ph.D. dissertation, Michigan State University, 1985.

Hayes-Roth, F., "Rule-Based Systems," *Communications of the ACM,* September 1985, pp. 921–932.

———, D. A. Waterman, and D. B. Lenat, (eds.) *Building Expert Systems,* Addison-Wesley, 1983.

Hume, D., *An Enquiry Concerning Human Understanding,* Open Court Publishing Co., 1927 [1748].

Johnson, P., "What Kind of Expert Should A System Be?" *The Journal of Medicine and Philosophy,* February 1983, pp. 77–97.

———, F. Hassebrock, A. Duran, and J. Moller, "Multimethod Study of Clinical Judgment," *Organizational Behavior and Human Performance,* 1982, pp. 201–230.

Joyce, E. J. and G. C. Biddle, "Anchoring and Adjustment in Probabilistic Inference in Auditing," *Journal of Accounting Research,* Spring 1981a, pp. 120–145.

——— and ———, "Are Auditors' Judgments Sufficiently Regressive?" *Journal of Accounting Research,* Fall 1981b, pp. 323–349.

31

McCarthy, J., "We Need Better Standards for AI Research," *The AI Magazine*, Fall 1984, pp. 7–8.

Meservy, R., A. D. Bailey, Jr., and P. Johnson, "Auditing Internal Controls: A Computational Model of the Review Process," *Auditing: A Journal of Practice & Theory*, Spring 1986.

Michaelsen, R. H., "An Expert System for Federal Tax Planning," working paper, University of Nebraska, 1982.

Minsky, M., "A Framework for Representing Knowledge," in P. Winsten (ed.), *The Psychology of Computer Vision*, McGraw-Hill, 1975, Chapter 6.

Mock, T. and I. Vertinsky, "DSS-RAA: Design Highlights," Summary paper presented at the Symposium on Decision Support Systems for Auditing, Sponsored by the University of Southern California and the Deloitte, Haskins & Sells Foundation, 1984.

Newell, A., J. Shaw, and H. Simmon, "Elements of a Theory of Human Problem Solving," *Psychology Review*, No. 3, 1958, pp. 151–166.

Newton-Smith, W. H., *The Rationality of Science*, Routledge & Kegan Paul, 1981.

Nisbett, E. and T. Wilson, "Telling More Than We Can Know: Verbal Reports on Mental Processes," *Psychological Review*, May 1977, pp. 231–259.

Payne, J., M. Braunstein, and J. Carroll, "Exploring Pre-decision Behavior: An Alternative Approach to Decision Research," *Organizational Behavior and Human Performance*, 1978, pp. 17–44.

Shpilberg, D. and L. E. Graham, "Developing ExperTAX: An Expert System for Corporate Tax Accrual and Planning," *Auditing: A Journal of Practice & Theory*, Fall 1986, pp. 75–94.

Smith, E. and F. Miller, "Limits on Perception of Cognitive Processes: A Reply to Nisbett and Wilson," *Psychological Review*, July 1978, pp. 355–362.

Steinbart, P., "The Construction of an Expert System to Make Materiality Judgments," Ph.D. dissertation, Michigan State University, 1984.

Sullivan G. and K. Fordyce, "Decision Stimulation (DSIM) One Outcome of Combining Expert Systems and Decision Support Systems," working paper, IBM, 1985.

Weber, R., *EDP Auditing: Conceptual Foundation and Practice*, McGraw-Hill, 1982.

Willingham, J. and W. Wright, "Development of a Knowledge-Based System for Auditing and Collectibility of a Commercial Loan," Research Proposal for Peat Marwick Main & Co., 1985.

Winsten, P., *Artificial Intelligence*, Addison-Wesley, 1984.

32

On the Future of Knowledge-Based Accounting Systems

WILLIAM E. MCCARTHY

In recent years, commercial advances in artificial intelligence (AI) in general and in expert systems (ES) in particular have received considerable attention in accounting. Accounting researchers have used ES methods to study a wide range of decision-making behavior in judgment areas such as going-concern opinions (Biggs and Selfridge, 1986), audit materiality assessments (Steinbart, 1984), internal control evaluations (Gal, 1985) (Meservy, 1985), and receivables writeoffs (Dungan and Chandler, 1985). In each of these cases, the researchers involved built a working expert system with the express goal of capturing computationally the accumulated wisdom of specific accounting experts, usually partners in public accounting firms. Additionally, these public accounting firms themselves have begun to devote a considerable amount of time, money, and manpower resources to assorted AI projects with the hope of benefiting from the tremendous upsurge which has been predicted repeatedly for commercial activity in this arena. For example, projections of fifteen-year increases in AI revenues to $113 billion and in AI employment to 650,000 have recently been made.

This paper will explore the implications of AI technology for accounting. However, it will do so in a manner unlike the ES projects above. That is, I intend not to discuss individual decision modeling by itself, but in the context of linking AI-type systems with traditional processing of accounting transaction cycles in a database (DB) environment. This linking of expert systems and database technology has received extensive research attention from computer scientists of late (Brodie, Mylopoulos, and Schmidt, 1984), and it has the potential I believe of extending the scope of accounting work within most companies considerably. Accounting transactions are the infrastructure on which all commercial data processing systems are built. Most knowledge-based systems will benefit from accounting systems specifically tailored for shared use and inference, and such a possibility is my primary thesis in this presentation.

The rest of this paper is organized as follows. My first major section will discuss the differences between knowledge representation methods in the separate computer science disciplines of database (DB) systems and artificial intelligence (AI) systems. These differences were once significant, but they are eroding rapidly, and I will also suggest here where knowledge-based accounting systems might fit as AI and DB come together. The second major section of the paper will be its longest—an overview of knowledge representation methods. My examples here will be quite simple, and they should equip a non-computer oriented reader with a basic understanding of the issues involved in these newer accounting systems. The paper will end by discussing the implications of the demonstrated new systems and by discussing possible future directions.

Accounting Information Systems in the Worlds of Databases and Artificial Intelligence

In trying to pinpoint where accounting information systems are now and where they might be in the future, I intend to use as reference points the world of database (DB) applications and the world of artificial intelligence (AI) applications (see Figure 1). The difference between these two worlds is admittedly arbitrary (Sowa, 1984), and its definition relies heavily on an equally arbitrary distinction between type and occurrence data. However, I think that readers will find both dichotomies useful even if the definitional edges becomes somewhat fuzzy at times.

Most database or data processing applications rely on just a few basic information groupings or record types, but their processing involves many, many instances of those structures. Figure 1 portrays the type/instance dichotomy for merchandise data in a

34

FIGURE 1

TYPES {

INSTANCES {

MERCHANDISE	STOCK #	DESCRIPTION	PRICE	QOH	COST
	8555	Cat tree	5.00	86	4.85
	5510	Poodle clipper	6.50	512	6.00
	1187	Budgerigar perch	11.00	729	4.85
	2751	Ordinary mousetrap	.75	902	.06
	2752	Improved mousetrap	10.50	804	3.29
	8400	Rat cage	50.00	165	11.04
	4563	Pet taxi	42.00	231	10.00
	8700	Hampster swing	26.00	231	25.00

Database (DB) World

1. Few types, many instances
2. Emphasizes performance, capacity, & security
3. Prime concern is "computational realism"
4. Examples:
   - Payroll
   - Order Entry
   - General Ledger

Artificial Intelligence (AI) World

1. Many types, few instances
2. Emphasizes functionality & flexibility
3. Prime concern is "epistemological adequacy
4. Examples:
   - Chess
   - New product decision
   - Audit judgement

CONTRASTING DB AND AI ORIENTATIONS

hypothetical pet store supply business. The "type" data (also known as the database *intention* would consist of a record name ("merchandise") and the various field names ("stock #," "QOH," etc.), and these intentional features will most often be defined in the data-definition sections of a programming language like COBOL or in the schema-definition language of a database management system or a data dictionary. The "instance" data (also known as the database *extension*) in the pet store supply example embraces the eight rows which individually describe the various kinds of merchandise (mousetraps, etc.) this company holds for sale. A name often used in AI research to denote an individual instance of a concept (for example, an individual row in the Figure 1 table) is a *token*.

Even with only this toy example as a reference, readers can see that the ratio of types to tokens in the DB world is heavily skewed toward large amounts of homogeneous occurrence data. This high degree of homogeneity allows for extremely efficient processing, hence the DB emphasis on computational realism in its choice of real-world problems to attack. Payroll, general ledger, and nearly all other kinds of normal accounting processing arising from transaction cycles also fall into this DB domain. This is why these accounting functions have been so heavily computerized for twenty years or more.

The world of AI applications, on the other hand, deals less with large sets of instance data and more with types. AI type/token ratios are much closer to unity. For example, audit judgment research will usually isolate many concepts to be considered in a final decision, but there will rarely be multiple instances of each concept to be reviewed in a single case. Emphasis in the AI arena of computer modeling swings decidedly toward an ability to represent definitional features of the environment faithfully (epistemological adequacy).

Recent work in expert database systems illustrates the point that many applications will require a mix of these two orientations. In business organizations today, there is certainly a heavy bias toward the DB world, but that bias is tempered by increasing needs for decision-making support in relatively unstructured areas of operational control, management control, and strategic planning. Such decisions were formerly the exclusive property of human managers, auditors, and investors (see Figure 2) who made their choices or plotted their strategies with information gleaned from internal reports and databases along their own

FIGURE 2

Knowledge-based accounting systems

Transaction processing with inside data

Unstructured decisions with inside/outside data
- Operational control
- Management control
- Strategic planning

COMPUTERIZED ACCOUNTING SYSTEM

DECISION-MAKER
- Manager
- Auditor
- Investor

SOURCE: Adapted from Patrick, p. 139.

understanding of the outside corporate environment. Expert system and decision-support research has indicated that at least some of this decision-making structure is amenable to computerized processing or support. However, such computerized support must also be able to access and "interpret" the pool of corporate data arising from cyclic transaction processing, hence the need for movement toward hybrid systems as shown in Figure 2.

For a system to combine the efficiency and capacity of database management with the flexibility and functionality of an AI system, it must be operating from a common definitional base. The basis for that commonality lies in the area of knowledge representation methods (the AI term) and semantic data modeling methods (the DB term). Both of these fields have borrowed heavily from each other (and from other disciplines such as psychology and linguistics), and their concepts will be reviewed without undue emphasis on either in the next section.

Knowledge Representation Methods

As illustrated in Figure 3, knowledge-based systems have three basic types of architecture. Readers should realize that the distinctions which I will be making among these three are not absolute in the sense that the types share many common features and in the sense that knowledge in one form is readily translatable to another. There also exists a number of other representation and modeling methods, and my categorizations are not ones with which all computer scientists would agree. Nonetheless, presentation of these three representational formalisms will pinpoint some basic philosophical differences which in turn will give readers an overall appreciation for the definitional nuances of both DB and AI. The three architectures are these:

1. *Logic*—This is the most theoretically appealing knowledge representation (KR) technique, and it forms the basis for the use of logic programming systems such as PROLOG. Based on the predicate calculus (Dahl, 1983), it has been used extensively in research work combining DB and ES realms (especially in Europe and Japan).

   In logical representation, each atomic fact (such as "Art is the father of Bob") is represented in a *proposition* such as

38

FIGURE 3

1. **LOGIC**
   - Art is the father of Bob

   > F (Art, Bob)

   - Art is Bob's parent if Art is the father of Bob

   > P (Art, Bob): - F (Art, Bob)

   - Art is Cap's grandparent if Art is Bob's parent and Bob is Cap's parent

   > G (Art, Cap): - P (Art, Bob), P (Bob, Cap)

SOURCE: Genesereth and Ginsberg, pp. 934-35.

2. **RULES**
   IF   Sex is male, and age
   is less than 40, and
   Marathon time is less than 3:00:00
   THEN Eligible to run in Boston

3. **SEMANTIC NETWORK**

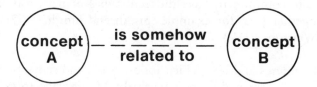

concept A — is somehow related to — concept B

REPRESENTATION FRAMEWORKS

"F(Art, Bob)") wherein the "F" is a *predicate* which relates the *arguments* "Art" and "Bob" via a father relationship. These propositions can be tied together by implication as seen in the second sentence of Figure 3 which states that a father relationship between two people generalizes to a parent relationship and in the third sentence of Figure 3 which states that a parent of a parent relationship implies a grandparent relationship.

2. **Rules**—Rule-based systems are the dominant form of ES architecture today. This is especially true for micro-computers whose software market is replete with expert system "shells" able to manage the creation and maintenance of rule knowledge bases quite efficiently.

   As seen in Figure 3, knowledge, representation in rules takes the form of one or more *antecedent* clauses (such as "IF sex is male") and a *consequent* clause (such as "THEN eligible to run in Boston") which logically follows.

3. **Semantic Networks**—This category can be subdivided into different types of networks, and these types collectively form the closest ties with traditional database research in the area of data modeling.

   Again as illustrated in Figure 3, semantic networks represent knowledge about some domain in the form of graphs which relate *nodes* (such as "concept A" and "concept B") together with labeled *edges*. Interpretation of the edges determines the type of network, although it is certainly quite common to have different types of networks used together (see, for example (Smith and Smith, 1977) and [Winston, 1984]).

In the figures and text which follow, rules and semantic networks will be covered more extensively. My decision to exlude logical systems from more detailed enumeration is not meant to imply that such systems have little promise for accounting. My coverage of rules and networks is keyed more toward easier intuitive understanding and toward easier integration with past modeling work in accounting domains.

40

FIGURE 4

Rule 1 ⌐IF: 1) the client is a public entity, and

PREMISE ⎨   2) there is no significant concern about the liquidity or solvency of the client

⎳THEN: it is assumed that the principal external users of the financial statements are primarily interested in information about the results of current operations.

CONCLUSION ⎨

Rule 2   IF: 1) the principal external users of the financial statements are primarily interested in the results of current operations, and

     2) net income is above the break-even point

THEN: the materiality judgment should be based on net income.

Rule 3   IF: 1) the basis for making the materiality judgment is known, and

     2) the percentage rate for making the materiality judgment is known

THEN: the materiality level equals the product of the percentage rate times the base used to make the materiality judgment.

}GOAL

RULE-BASED KNOWLEDGE AND INFERENCE

SOURCE: Steinbart, Chap. IV.

41

FIGURE 5

Semantic Networks

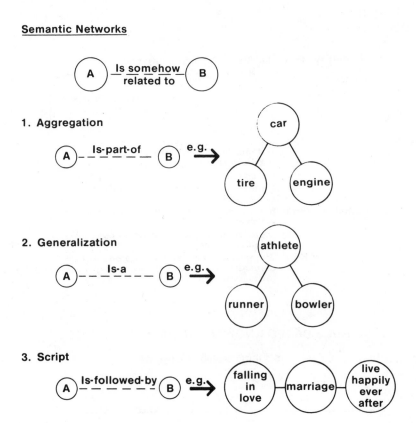

1. Aggregation

2. Generalization

3. Script

RULE-BASED KNOWLEDGE REPRESENTATION

Figure 4 illustrates a rule-based representation (also called a production system) of audit judgment. This subset of rules is taken from an expert system developed by Paul Steinbart [1984, 1987] to capture the expertise of an audit firm partner in the area of materiality judgments (that is, how auditors determine the threshold dollar amounts to investigate empirically during the conduct of an audit). Readers may see how "chunks" of knowledge are represented as a series of IF–THEN rules where the first part or the antecedent of the rule is called the *premise,* and the second part or the consequence is termed *the conclusion.* When a premise is judged to be true, the rule is "triggered," and its conclusion becomes a fact known to the rest of the production system. The particular production system shown in this figure uses *backward chaining* to mimic expert inference, because it first establishes a "goal" conclusion to work toward and then attempts to prove that goal by having all of its premises established as facts. Premises are established:

(1) by finding other rules which have those premises as conclusions and by then working to trigger those other rules.

(2) by appeal to the user of the expert system in the form of an interactive question (such as an inquiry concerning the control consciousness of a company's CEO which would be a very difficult fact to establish empirically [Gal, 1985]), or

(3) by reference to a database of facts.

The chaining in the Steinbart example is illustrated with the backwards arrows, and it proceeds simply by finding other rules which can help it to resolve its purpose of triggering the goal rule.

As mentioned previously, production systems are the dominant ES architecture today, especially in accounting research work on audit judgment (see also [Merservy, 1985] and [Dungan and Chandler, 1985]). In all of these implemented cases, the process of knowledge engineering consisted of having experienced audit decision makers work through a number of possible cases while the researcher attempted to elicit their expertise, capture it in the form of rules, and use it to build a system which could then perform in much the same manner as the expert auditors themselves would.

SEMANTIC NETWORK KNOWLEDGE REPRESENTATION

Figure 5 illustrates the basic idea of semantic nets: there are two concepts (which I have labeled as A and B) and there is some kind of relationship between them. Concepts are represented as nodes in the network, while relationships are portrayed as labeled edges or links drawn between the nodes. The three examples of Figure 5 illustrate some common interpretations of semantic nets:

(1) Aggregation .... A *is part of* B
     example: An engine is part of a car.

(2) Generalization .... A *is a* B
     example: A runner is an athlete.

(3) Script .... A *is followed by* B
     example: Falling in love is followed by marriage.

In each of these three cases, part of the impetus involved in the development of these interpreted networks was the desire of some computer scientists to use knowledge representation formalisms which bear strong resemblances to human cognition and belief structures in a particular domain of discourse. For instance, if I were to state, "I have my car parked outside this building," readers would logically assume with a high degree of certainty that "my engine" was there as well, because an engine is almost always a component part of a car. In the same vein, less certain statements such as "a bowler is an athlete" or "love and marriage go together" could be modeled with similar formalisms. However, the KR system in this case should allow for some degree of uncertainty or vagueness in the interpretation of the link. Some network representation methods do allow for such an interpretation, but such vagueness is rare in database management systems which adhere predominantly to the concept of "strict typing" (Tsichritzis and Lochovsky, 1982). Similar uncertainties, incidentally, can be accommodated in both rule-based and logic-based KR systems with methods such as uncertainty factors and fuzzy logic.

Each of the three types of semantic nets listed above is explained in sections and figures which follow. For each network

44

type, I will first use a commonsense example and follow it with some accounting interpretations.

AGGREGATION

Figure 6(b) portrays a semantic network in which aggregation is designated between the nodes as one goes up the page. In the first part of this figure, the component structures of two of the Figure 1 pet store merchandise items (the "improved mousetrap" and the "budgerigar perch") are shown pictorially, while the bottom half shows the detailed hierarchical representation of just the latter.

With the pictures, readers can see that a "frame," which itself is a component of two other items, has two parts: (1) a "base" and (2) an "arm." Much like the car and engine example, this semantic network structure illustrates how complex assemblages of ideas can be conceptualized at a higher level of abstraction as just one thing while simultaneous access to lower and more detailed levels is maintained for other purposes.

In Figure 6(b), interpretation of each link would be "is–part of" as one moves up the hierarchy. More commonly in business domains, this aggregation interpretation would refer less to the physical component structure of the merchandise (although such information would still be maintained in a bill of materials) and more to its data properties and to its relationships with other concepts. Thus we would find that the primary processing of merchandise information in a company would concern itself with characteristics like the price and cost of various inventory items. Figure 7 illustrates an aggregation hierarchy (Smith and Smith, 1977) for merchandise data items. Link interpretation would still be "is–part of," although "has property of" and "is-related-to" might be more intuitively descriptive. Higher data objects in the hierarchy, like "sale" and "customer," are abstractions which allow easier handling of the more detailed lower items. In most traditional data processing applications, which actually are driven by little or no "modeling" orientation, data aggregation like that illustrated in Figure 7 are accomplished with COBOL-type *records* and *fields*.

Figure 8 takes the same example as Figure 7 (along with additional data shown as dashed figures) and recasts it into another formalism for data aggregation: the widely–used and easily understood entity–relationship data model (Chen, 1976;

45

FIGURE 6

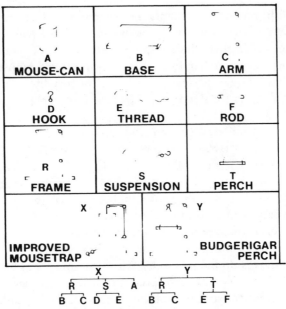

(a) Two component structures

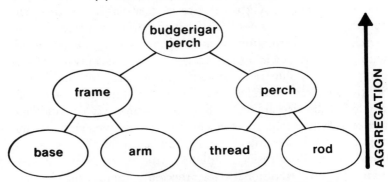

(b) Aggregation hierarchy for budgerigar perch

AGGREGATION HIERARCHY

SOURCE: Adapted from Howe, p. 138

FIGURE 7

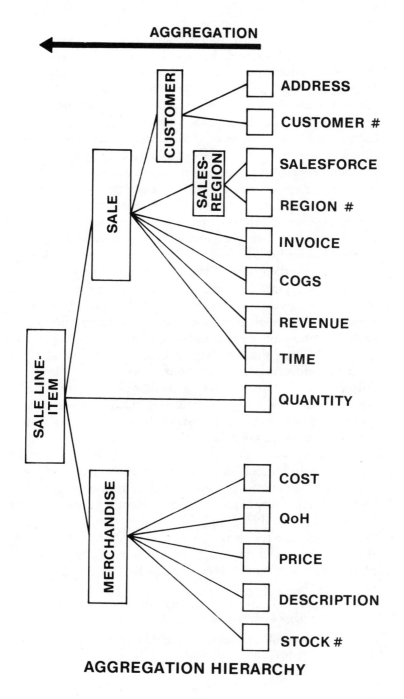

AGGREGATION

AGGREGATION HIERARCHY

McCarthy, 1979). This type of semantic network does not represent data aggregation as a hierarchy of objects being related as components of other objects, but as a collection of entities (boxes), relationships (diamonds), and attributes (circles). Each entity box in this example has also been labeled in accord with the REA prototype of a typical accounting transaction cycle (McCarthy, 1982). This REA approach to accounting data modeling has been successfully used in a number of implementations specifically tailored for the type of hybrid transaction-processing/decision-support-system environments shown in Figure 2 (Gal and McCarthy, 1986a; Denna and McCarthy, 1986).

Figure 9 depicts how aggregation is commonly handled in the AI world: as *frames* (Minsky, 1975). Frames are knowledge structures which represent prototypical constellations of elements or attributes. Figure 9 shows what a frame reconceptualization of the merchandise part of Figures 7 and 8 would look like. The central concept itself is the frame name, and its typical parts or properties are called "slots." The individual property tokens (like "8555" and "cat tree") are said to *fill* the slots, and as readers can see, there is generally no requirement that slot-fillers be declarative (for example, last-in-first-out periodic inventory costs could be virtual and materialized only when needed). As a matter of fact, it seems that nearly any kind of computable object, including procedures and assertions, can be placed there. Procedures, such as those shown for the last two slots of Figure 9, which are invoked when a certain behavior pattern (such as an insertion of new data or a data query) is recognized in a system, are called *triggers* or *demons.*

As readers may have noticed in this brief treatment of aggregation, different symbolic interpretations of the same real world phenomena are almost inevitable in any knowledge-based system. Such variability has been the concern of researchers (such as Smith and Smith ([978], and Sowa [1984] among others) who have studied the problem of *conceptual relativity.* Using terms already described in the paper, the problem of conceptual relativity can be restated as follows:

- One person's entity is another person's relationship is another person's attribute.

- One person's procedure is another person's declaration is another person's constraint.

FIGURE 8

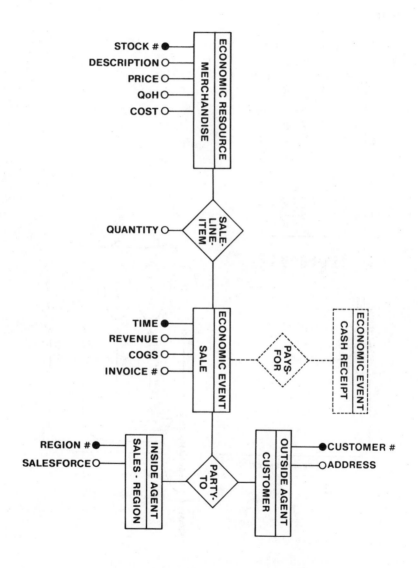

ENTITY-RELATIONSHIP REPRESENTATION

FIGURE 9

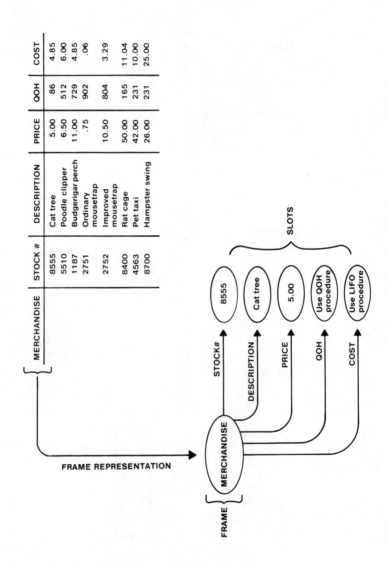

MERCHANDISE	STOCK #	DESCRIPTION	PRICE	QOH	COST
	8555	Cat tree	5.00	86	4.85
	5510	Poodle clipper	6.50	512	6.00
	1187	Budgerigar perch	11.00	729	4.85
	2751	Ordinary mousetrap	.75	902	.06
	2752	Improved mousetrap	10.50	804	3.29
	8400	Rat cage	50.00	165	11.04
	4563	Pet taxi	42.00	231	10.00
	8700	Hampster swing	26.00	231	25.00

FRAME REPRESENTATION

- One person's type is another person's token.
- etc., etc.

The paradox of fixed modeling primitives is that they facilitate individual thinking while simultaneously making the integration of different individuals' conceptualizations difficult. However, the facilitated thinking is worth the risk, and I believe that anybody who approaches this problem dogmatically can be rightly accused of pedanticism and overly-scholastic thinking (besides which, they will probably fail in their system-building efforts). It is perfectly justifiable to use entity–relationship modeling, for instance, even if one cannot give an absolute rule for deciding what *is* or *is not* an entity. Likewise, it makes little sense to agonize indefinitely over a representation choice such as modeling inventory quantity-on-hand as a fixed data value or as a procedure which materializes that value when needed. Such choices involve relative criteria, and they just cannot ever be characterized as absolutely right or wrong. My advice to accounting workers in this area (advice, incidentally, which applies to all types of representation choices) is to use the concepts rigorously first, but with a strong degree of flexibility when integration with the work of others is contemplated. In an excellent discussion on the issue of conceptual relativity, John Sowa summarizes this modeling viewpoint when he says that "Concepts are useful fictions that are not absolute" (1984, p. 350).

My discussion of the methods of Smith and Smith (1977), Chen (1976), and Minsky (1975) completes this paper's review of *aggregation* which is clearly the dominant type of semantic network used in database work. The next two types of networks I will address involve concepts whose intellectual roots deal more with the AI problem domains of property inheritance and natural-language processing: *generalizations* and *scripts*.

GENERALIZATION

Figure 10 portrays a network in which nodes going down the page represent increasing specialization of the concept at the top, while concepts at the bottom generalize upward. I have also cast each node in this hierarchy as a frame with an aggregation of properties, and there is a strong notion of property inheritance for the lower level nodes. Thus, readers can see that a shark "has

51

FIGURE 10

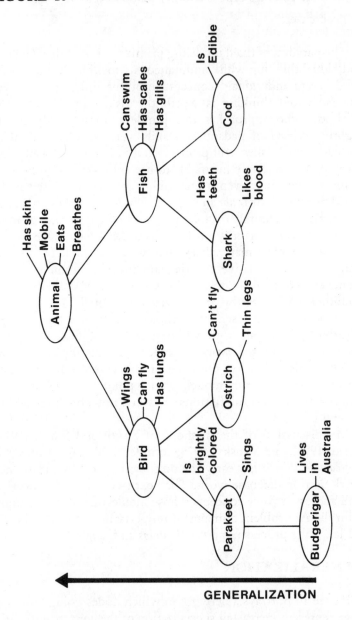

GENERALIZATION

GENERALIZATION (ISA) HIERARCHY

SOURCE: Adapted from Brachman, p.31.

52

teeth" and "likes blood," but they should also note that a shark "is-a" fish which in turn "is-a(n)" animal, so it also possesses characteristics like gills and skin.

The generalization and the "is-a" link interpretation of Figure 10 denote type-type relationships, but token-type generalizations could be specified as well. For example, I could have added a node with "Ollie" under the "Ostrich" branch of this tree and a "Sammy" under the "Shark" branch to denote two individual animals of those classes. Readers should be aware, however, that some AI and DB researchers would use different names and different link interpretations for those two different kinds of generalization abstraction. Token-type generalization is sometimes called "classification," and the links in type-type networks are sometimes labeled "AKO" (a-kind-of).

Figure 11 illustrates another frame-oriented generalization example (Winston, 1984), this one taken from natural language processing research work designed to interpret newspaper stories. If readers have followed the aggregation and generalization examples given earlier, they could see that an instantiation of a concept would involve filling slots for that individual frame and for all of its ancestor frames up the hierarchy. Thus, an "earthquake" story would need in addition to other attributes information on the quake's "magnitude" on the Richter scale, its "damage" estimates, and its approximate "time."

In the lower part of Figure 11, I have included some accounting frames which illustrate in a different manner the REA (McCarthy, 1982) template structure for the "sale" event first shown in Figures 7 and 8. Slots to be filled for this example would include "invoice #," "revenue," "cogs," and "time," the last of these coming from two hierarchical levels away. The "inside agent," the "outside agent," and the "resource" involved in the exchange event would also be needed, and in the case of the "sale" transaction, these would be filled by appropriate sales-region, customer, and merchandise tokens.

Figure 11 is adapted from a section of Winston's artificial intelligence book (1984, chapter 8) entitled "Digesting News Seems to Involve Frame Retrieving and Slot Filling" wherein he discusses the problems involved in representing symbolically the commonsense knowledge people use in performing the intelligent albeit simple task of understanding daily news events. In terms of the split between the machine domain of processing and the human domain of processing that we first saw in Figure 2,

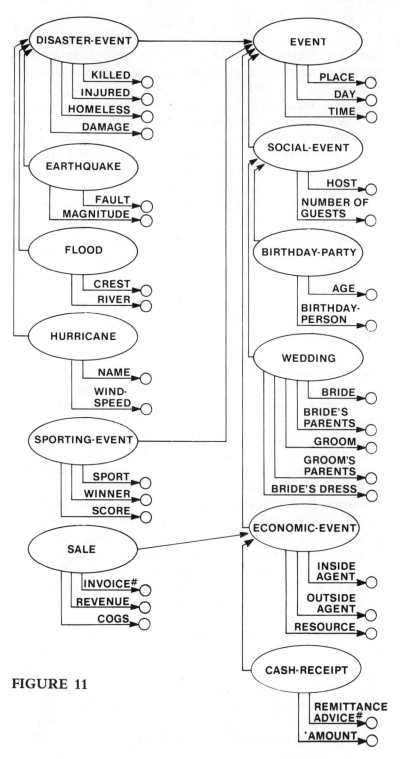

FIGURE 11

FRAME-ORIENTED AGGREGATION AND GENERALIZATION

SOURCE: Adapted from Winston, p. 267.

this act of "digesting news" would be very similar to the human information processing which would take place when a manager, auditor, or investor makes some kind of unstructured decision using accounting transaction data. Such human-computer linking illustrates the motivation for development of knowledge-based accounting systems. Systems which will mimic the expertise of accounting experts (like managers) will have to have access to the commonsense knowledge structures of transaction data (like its aggregation components or its generalization categories).

SCRIPTS

If people of various ages and backgrounds were to separately read sentence (1) at the top of Figure 12, there might certainly be some different interpretations of Graham's activities (did he go to a zoo or did he go to a ballgame?). To at least the sports-oriented reader of sentences (2) and (3) however, it would be fairly obvious what Paul and Howard did last night, because "Cubs" would seem to refer to the baseball team rather than to small animals and there are no "expos" at a zoo. Additionally, readers might be able to infer from experience other non-enunciated information about these activities such as the fact that Paul's night game didn't take place in Chicago (because the ballpark has no lights) or the fact that Howard's game might have included the singing of "O Canada" (because the Expos are a Montreal team).

Whatever ambiguity was present with regard to Graham's activities would probably dissipate for most readers when sentence (1) was followed with either sentence (1a) or sentence (1b), because this later information would certainly evoke the correct "script" from the reader's mind. This would be either the "zoo-script" following under sentence (1a) or the "ballgame-script" following under sentence (1b). (This particular ballgame-script incidentally is mine and thus it models my experience and understanding of what happens when one goes to a baseball game; the zoo-script is my daughter Molly's.)

Various Types of Scripts

Scripts are knowledge structures which represent stereotypical sequences of actions, and their primary AI use has been in the

55

FIGURE 12

(1) Graham went to see the tigers last night.
(2) Paul went to see the Cubs last night.
(3) Howard went to see the expos last night.

(1a) He saw Eric in the monkey house.   (1b) He saw Eric during the National Anthem.

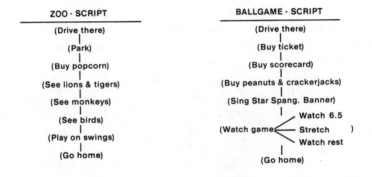

ZOO - SCRIPT

(Drive there)
|
(Park)
|
(Buy popcorn)
|
(See lions & tigers)
|
(See monkeys)
|
(See birds)
|
(Play on swings)
|
(Go home)

BALLGAME - SCRIPT

(Drive there)
|
(Buy ticket)
|
(Buy scorecard)
|
(Buy peanuts & crackerjacks)
|
(Sing Star Spang. Banner)
|
(Watch game   — Watch 6.5
                — Stretch   )
                — Watch rest
|
(Go home)

ACCOUNTING SCRIPT

(Subscribe to stock)→(Pay money)→(Get certificate)→(Receive dividends)

VARIOUS TYPES OF SCRIPTS

56

FIGURE 13

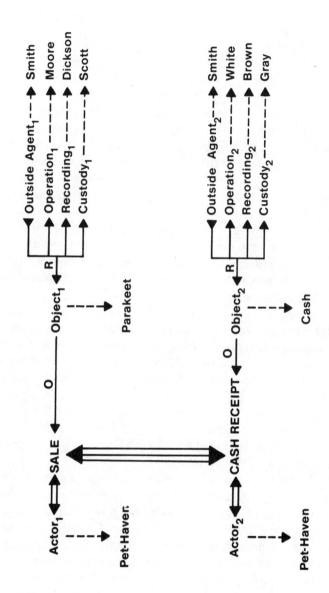

REVENUE - CYCLE SCRIPT

SOURCE: Adapted from Gal and McCarthy, 1986b.

57

research areas of natural-language processing and human memory understanding (Schank, 1984). Scripts can be conceptualized as semantic networks where the nodes represent the actions or *scenes* and the links interpret as "is-followed-by." Each scene can be a script in its own right (for example "watch game" which has three subscripts in Figure 12), and these sub-parts can be broken down all the way to their most elementary actions (such as the physical transfer of money involved in "buying popcorn") (Schank and Abelson, 1978). Additionally, each scene could itself be conceptualized as another type or node in a semantic net such as *a frame* (with slots for "home team" and "starting pitcher" for example in ballgames) or *a generalization hierarchy* (with an ancestor of "sporting-event" for ballgames). Conceptually, scripts can be specified at both higher and lower levels of abstraction to explore issues such as learning and analogous thinking (Lehnert, 1981). For example, a researcher might use this mechanism to explore why going to zoos might remind people of going to ballparks or to explore what happens to general cognitive structures when particular script instances don't comply (such as when a different national anthem is played or when the players use aluminum bats).

At the bottom of Figure 12, I have included an example of a script from the domain of accounting to show readers the types of actions which might need to be impounded in a machine representation of background knowledge for an accounting decision maker. Again, each of these four actions would probably be broken down into a number of more detailed subscripts. From the perspective of a corporation for instance, the "receive dividend" script for a stockholder might consist of "declare dividend" and "pay dividend," and each of these actions could be broken down further in turn.

In Figure 13, a much more elaborate script is presented which details not just stereotypical sequences of events, but also the allowable sets of actors and roles for those events. These particular representations and mechanisms for enforcing them in large complicated databases are currently being explored with regard to automating the images that auditors have of "good internal controls" for a company (Gal and McCarthy, 1985, 1986b). Audit knowledge to be represented in this domain would include, for instance, the concepts of "an approved transaction" and "sufficient separation of duties."

KNOWLEDGE REPRESENTATION METHODS SUMMARY

We have now completed our review of three different types of knowledge representation formalisms: (1) logic, (2) rules, and (3) semantic networks. The semantic networks were covered in particular depth because of their relationship to this paper's primary thesis which is the future integrated use of both DB and AI systems. Readers are reminded again, however, about the arbitrary nature of my review. Formalisms that I have deemphasized, such as logic, can be used extensively in combined DB-AI work, and representation examples that I have presented in one way are easily translated to other methods.

Future Directions

At the outset of this presentation, I speculated that AI-type or knowledge-based systems represent an arena into which accounting information system designers should naturally move as they become more interested in providing accounting data support for unstructured decision-making in areas of management control and strategic planning. In this last section of the paper, I intend to discuss what the architecture of these newer systems might look like and what changes in systems analysis methods might be required.

ARCHITECTURE OF ES-DBMS ENVIRONMENT

Figure 14 illustrates the tight coupling which will have to occur between the database software environment and the expert system software environment for the movement toward knowledge-based accounting systems to be successful.

At the top of Figure 14 is portrayed the database environment whose design iterates through the traditional systems analysis life cycle with the exception that much more attention is paid to semantically-oriented data model specifications (Armitage, 1985). The database which results from this process is controlled and used via DBMS software, and it consists of two kinds of information: (1) the database *extension* which is the accumulated store of various accounting transaction data and (2) the database *intention* which is the type information designated in the lan-

59

FIGURE 14

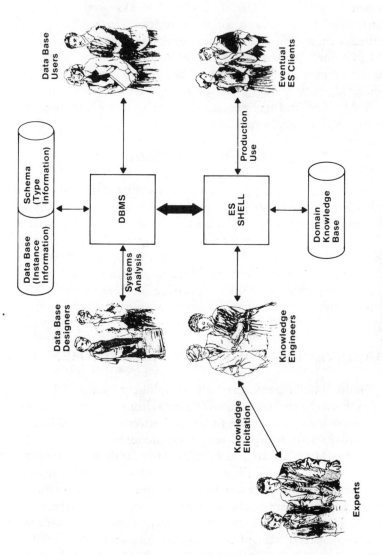

ES AND DBMS COUPLING

60

guage of one of the knowledge representation formalisms covered earlier.

The bottom of Figure 14 illustrates the expert system environment for some type of accounting-oriented expertise whose structure has been elicited and captured by knowledge engineers with an ES "shell." The shell is a commercially available piece of software which facilitates the construction of a system by automatically managing procedures such as chained inferencing and property inheritance. The shell takes care of the ES overhead, while the actual specifics of a certain expert process are stored in a separate "domain knowledge base."

For the coupled systems to work well together, the knowledge representation formalisms used in each will have to be compatible. Up to the present time, most accounting ES that have been built have not had to face this problem, because they have not depended on access to large accounting transaction databases. In other words, their "facts" came from outside the company or from the experts themselves. Quite obviously, there is a great opportunity for newer classes of computerized accounting systems whose processes on the one hand require heuristic or ES-type specification, but whose data needs on the other hand require access to elements of the large corporate database.

Technologically, the tight links shown in Figure 14 are not yet supported on a widespread basis, although there has been some encouraging work completed in research settings. In the meantime, there are some nontechnological changes which accounting information systems researchers and practitioners can explore, so that the structures of their accounting systems and the methods by which they build those systems can be ready when the new software technology is.

Changes in Analysis and Design Methods for Accounting Information Systems

More Semantic Infrastructures. First and foremost, there needs to be continued movement toward the goal of making accounting transaction databases more "epistemologically adequate." After our review of knowledge representation structures, I hope that readers would agree that our present methods of transaction processing and data representation in accounting are less ambitious than they need to be. Most computerized accounting systems remain philosophically closer to the insular mindset of

FIGURE 15

Bookkeeping structure

REA-based structure

Accountants

Enterprise of Interest

**SEMANTIC INFRASTRUCTURE FOR FUTURE GENERATIONS
OF KNOWLEDGE-BASED ACCOUNTING SYSTEMS**

the bookkeeper than to the more modern philosophy of shared usage and knowledge representation. As illustrated in Figure 15, this accounting restructuring requires a movement toward an *events* (Sorter, 1969; McCarthy, 1981) orientation which means that accountants move away from their "observe-interpret-record" methods of value-accounting and toward simpler "observe-record" systems. Events models are driven by the same knowledge representation philosophies that database systems are driven by in the sense that both primarily endeavor to build information systems whose users can act as if they had actually observed the actual phenomena of interest (that is, the company's transaction activity). Too often, modern accounting systems contain account classifications and valuations which are interpretations indigenous only to bookkeeping. Such interpretations are not epistemologically correct, and they should be relegated to user views. As I have argued elsewhere, (McCarthy, 1984) I believe that REA-type structures form a solid basis on which to build conceptual structures of accounting activities.

More Use of Enterprise Modeling and Prototyping. Second, many of the more fundamental activities used in analysis and design of accounting systems will have to be supplemented with newer methods specifically designed for the less-structured environment. For example, Davis's contingency theory for the specification of information system requirements (see Figure 16) predicts that environments characterized by high uncertainty because of the absence of a stable set of requirements and because of user and analyst inexperience will not be served well by traditional accounting system life cycle methods (like asking users or using existing systems as models). This is exactly the type of environment in which knowledge-based systems will operate. In other words, the "way we have always done it" will *not* be the model of the future. Designers will find it necessary to become familiar with more heuristic methods associated with the high uncertainty end of the spectrum shown in Figure 16. These will include methods that emphasize firm-wide analysis (such as enterprise data modeling) and methods that emphasize the use of experimental AI prototypes as a method for explicating the genuine needs of users.

Summary

I have titled this paper, "On the Future of Knowledge-Based Accounting Systems." We have looked together at some initial

63

FIGURE 16

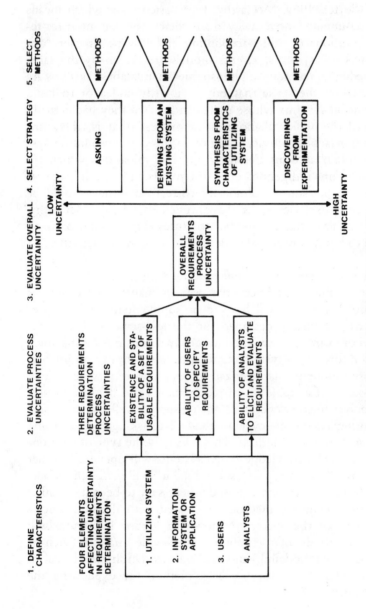

DAVIS CONTINGENCY APPROACH TO
INFORMATION REQUIREMENTS DETERMINATION

SOURCE: Davis and Olson, p. 489.

definitions of knowledge-based systems and taken a fairly extensive review of the conceptual structures used within them. I finished with an enumeration of my own ideas of the changes that these techniques would bring upon accounting information system users and designers. As I mentioned in the paper, technology in the areas of both database systems and artificial intelligence is still changing rapidly, and the study of computerized systems which combine these two technologies is still in its infancy. Commercial interest and activity seems to indicate, however, that the effect of all of these areas upon corporations will be pervasive. Since most of this new technology will ultimately depend upon data sourced from accounting transaction systems, I believe that the changes upon accounting will be quite dramatic as well.

References

Armitage, H. M., *Linking Management Accounting with Computer Technology*, Society of Management Accountants of Canada Research Monograph Series, 1985.

Biggs, S. F and M. Selfridge, "GC-X: A Prototype Expert System for the Auditor's Going Concern Judgment," working paper, University of Connecticut, January 1986.

Brachman, R. J., "What IS-A Is and Isn't: An Analysis of Taxonomic Links in Semantic Networks," *Computer*, October 1983, pp. 30–36.

Brodie, M. L., J. Mylopoulos, and J. W. Schmidt, (eds.), *On Conceptual Modeling*, Springer-Verlag, 1984.

Chen, P. P., "The Entity-Relationship Model—Toward a Unified View of Data," *ACM Transactions on Database Systems*, March 1976, pp. 9–36.

Dahl, V., "Logic Programming as a Representation of Knowledge," *Computer*, October 1983, pp. 106–111.

Davis, G. B. and M. H. Olson, *Management Information Systems: Conceptual Foundations, Structure, and Development*, McGraw-Hill, 1985.

Denna, E. and W. E. McCarthy, "An Events-Accounting Foundation for DSS Use," *Proceedings of the NATO Advanced Study Institute*, Maratea, Italy, 1986.

Dungan, C. W. and J. S. Chandler, "Auditor: A Microcomputer-Based Expert System to Support Auditors in the Field," *Expert Systems*, October 1985, pp. 210–221.

Gal, G., "Using Auditor Knowledge to Formulate Data Model Constraints: Expert Systems for Internal Control Evaluation," Ph.D. dissertation, Michigan State University, 1985.

———, and W. E. McCarthy, "Specification of Internal Accounting Controls in a Database Environment," *Computers and Security*, March 1985, pp. 23–32.

―――― (1986a), "Operation of a Relational Accounting System," *Advances in Accounting*, 1986.

―――― (1986b), "Semantic Specification and Automated Enforcement of Internal Control Procedures Within Accounting Systems," working paper, Michigan State University, 1986.

Genesereth, M. R. and M. L. Ginsberg, "Logic Programming," *Communications of the ACM*, September 1985, pp. 933–941.

Howe, D. R., *Data Analysis for Database Design*, Edward Arnold, 1983.

Lehnert, W., "Plot Units and Narrative Summation," *Cognitive Science*, Vol. 5, 1981.

McCarthy, W. E., "An Entity-Relationship View of Accounting Models," *The Accounting Review*, October 1979, pp. 667–686.

―――――, "Multidimensional and Disaggregate Accounting Systems: A Review of the 'Events' Accounting Literature," *MAS Communication*, July 1981, pp. 7–13.

―――――, "The REA Accounting Model: A Generalized Framework for Accounting Systems in a Shared Data Environment," *The Accounting Review*, July 1982, pp. 554–578.

―――――, "Materialization of Account Balances in the REA Accounting Model," Invited Presentation to the British Accounting Association, Norwich, England, April 1984.

Meservy, R. D., "Auditing Internal Controls: A Computational Model of the Review Process," Ph.D. dissertation, The University of Minnesota, 1985.

Minsky, N., "A Framework for Representing Knowledge," in P. H. Winsten (ed.), *Psychology of Computer Vision*, McGraw-Hill, 1975, pp. 211–277.

Patrick, R. L., "Auditing and DP: Redressing the Relationship," *Datamation*, November 15, 1978, pp. 139–144.

Schank, R. and R. Abelson, *Scripts, Plans, Goals, and Understanding*, Lawrence Erlbaum Associates, 1977.

―――――, *The Cognitive Computer*, Addison-Wesley, 1984.

Smith, J. M. and D. C. Smith, "Database Abstractions: Aggregation and Generalization," *ACM Transactions on Database Systems*, June 1977b, pp. 105–133.

―――――, Principles of Database Conceptual Design," *NYU Symposium on Database Design*, New York University, 1978, pp. 35–49.

Sorter, G. H., "An 'Events' Approach to Basic Accounting Theory," *The Accounting Review*, January 1969, pp. 12–19.

Sowa, J. F, *Conceptual Structures: Information Processing in Mind and Machine*, Addison-Wesley, 1984.

Steinbart, P. J., "The Construction of an Expert System to Make Materiality Judgments," Ph.D. dissertation, Michigan State University, 1984.

―――――, "Materiality: A Case Study Using Expert Systems," *The Accounting Review*, January 1987.

Tsichritzis, D. C. and F. H. Lochovsky, *Data Models*, Prentice-Hall, 1982.

Winsten, P. H., *Artificial Intelligence*, Addison-Wesley, 1984.

Part II

METHODOLOGY AND SURVEYS

Part II presents four papers of generic nature, dealing respectively with ES and management accounting research, research directions for ES in auditing and a computational view of financial accounting standards. The Lin article introduces expert systems to an audience of managerial accountants, describes ES as composed of five major components (knowledge base, inference engine, knowledge acquisition module, explanation module, and language interface) and then discusses the implications, opportunities, and difficulties for ES research in managerial accounting.

Abdolmohammadi, examining the decision process of the auditor, uses the Simon framework to place it into phases and discusses the relationships of these phases with task structure. Knowledge-based expert systems (KES) are defined and compared with decision support systems. This analysis should be contrasted with the appendix of the Bailey et al. paper presented in Part I. Finally, the author presents a critical evaluation and research directions by asking some important questions which include:

1. How does one identify an audit expert?

2. What methodology should be used to elicit an expert's decision rules?

3. How long and how costly is it to develop DSSs and KESs?

4. What would be the effect of KES on the legal liability of auditors?

5. What would be the organizational impact of KES on auditing firms?

Gangolly focuses on knowledge organization for financial accounting standards. A declarative representation of knowledge is proposed in regards to accounting standards. Then the development of a knowledge base for SFAS No. 48 is discussed to illustrate the point of the paper. This work is of great importance as a building block in the development of knowledge bases to support the instruction of accounting and in the support of the disclosure evaluation function of the auditor. Several professional accounting firms already are working in the structuring of SFAS statements in a knowledge base format.

Messier and Hansen survey the state-of-the art in expert systems in auditing. They overview expert systems, review existing expert systems, review the difficulties in successful development of expert systems, and discuss the impact of expert systems on practice.

Expert Systems and Management Accounting Research

Thomas W. Lin

A current topic of interest in accounting is the subject of expert systems. Expert systems are one area of research related to the subject of artificial intelligence. Artificial intelligence and expert systems have been identified by the AICPA (1985) Future Issues Committee as one of the major issues significant to the accounting profession with rapidly emerging implications for the future. Recently, several articles have shown the use of expert systems in accounting and auditing, e.g., Dugan and Chandler (1985), Elliott and Kielich (1985), Hansen and Messier (1982), and Messier and Hansen (1984). The USC Symposium on Expert Systems and Audit Judgment, held in February 1986, had more than 200 accounting researchers and practitioners attend. These events are indicative of the growing degree of interest in expert systems research in accounting.

This article first presents an overview of expert systems in terms of definitions and components of expert systems. It then describes the implications for management accounting research by providing potential management accounting application areas, research issues/opportunities, and difficulties encountered in expert systems research.

Expert Systems: What Are They?

ARTIFICIAL INTELLIGENCE AND EXPERT SYSTEMS

Artificial Intelligence (AI) is a subfield of computer science which is concerned with developing intelligent computer sys-

69

tems to simulate human reasoning. AI has focused on research areas of robotics, natural language understanding, voice recognition, image processing, and expert systems.

Expert systems (ES) are problem-solving computer programs that use expert knowledge and inference procedures to perform functions similar to those normally performed by a human expert in some specialized problem areas.

The major benefits of ES are saving money, sharing knowledge, obtaining better quality decisions, and providing training tools. The major limitations of ES are difficulties in extracting expertise from humans, and long development times to build ES and in developing ES that are creative, adaptive, and have common sense.

COMPONENTS OF EXPERT SYSTEMS

There are five major components of an ES: (1) the knowledge base, (2) the inference engine, (3) the knowledge acquisition module, (4) the explanation module, and (5) the language interface.

A knowledge base contains facts, decision-making rules, and hypotheses. Barr and Feigenbaum (1982) described several techniques of knowledge representation. The most common techniques are production rules, frames, and semantic nets. Under production rules, knowledge is represented by a set of rules; it is a formal way of specifying a recommendation or strategy expressed in the IF CONDITION (premise), THEN ACTION (conclusion) statements. In the frames method, knowledge is represented by a cluster of statements that associate features with nodes representing concepts or objects. Semantic nets consist of a network of nodes standing for concepts, events or objects connected by areas describing the relation between nodes.

The brain of the ES is the inference engine with reasoning capabilities. It controls the search through the knowledge base. Goodall (1985) described various ways of reasoning about rules. The most common reasoning procedures are forward chaining and backward chaining. Forward chaining involves reasoning from data to hypotheses; that is, rules are matched against facts to establish new facts. Backward chaining starts with a goal or hypothesis, and then attempts to find data or evidence that support the goal or hypothesis. There are three common ways of representing uncertain information in an ES: Bayesian inference,

70

certainty factor, and fuzzy logic approaches. (See Goodall [1985] for details.)

The knowledge acquisition module requires a knowledge engineer to accumulate, transfer, and transform expertise from some knowledge source, e.g., an expert, to a computer program for constructing or modifying the knowledge. The common knowledge acquisition techniques are interviewing, protocol analysis, and simulation methods.

The explanation module can explain why the system reached a particular decision or why it is requesting a particular piece of information.

The language interface provides English-like query language or graphics for the user to interact with the ES.

Implications for Management Accounting Research

POTENTIAL MANAGEMENT ACCOUNTING APPLICATIONS

Expert systems have been used for diagnosis, design, planning, control, prediction, monitoring and training purposes. Management accountants can use ES to solve the complex problems of capital budgeting, transfer pricing, variance analysis and investigation, performance evaluation, incentives and compensation systems, corporate planning and budgeting, product pricing, and information systems selection. An ES can also be used to train management accountants.

RESEARCH ISSUES/OPPORTUNITIES

Expert systems provide new research opportunities for management accounting professors. The following is a list of potential research issues/opportunities:

1. Research on psychological characteristics of expert decision makers. For example, see Shanteau (1986).

2. Research on how experts formulate and solve complicated, semi-structured management accounting problems.

3. Evaluate different knowledge representation techniques such as rules vs. frames in representing various management accounting problems.

71

4. Evaluate different reasoning procedures such as forward chaining vs. backward chaining for various management accounting tasks.

5. Evaluate different ways of representing uncertain information such as Bayesian inference vs. the certainty factor approach for various management accounting problems.

6. Evaluate the effectiveness of different knowledge acquisition techniques such as protocol analysis vs. simulation methods on various management accounting problems.

7. Evaluate the effectiveness of a management accounting ES vs. other decision aids or models.

8. Develop a normative framework on how knowledge should be elicited and represented in the knowledge base.

9. Research on memory organization and structure as well as the strategy for memory retrieval.

10. Research on how to effectively validate an ES and compare the effectiveness of different validation techniques. See O'Leary (1986) and Hayes-Roth et al. (1983) on various validation techniques.

POTENTIAL DIFFICULTIES IN ES RESEARCH

Prospects for expert systems research in management accounting can be summarized as typical good news/bad news. The good news is that there is a demand for research in ES as shown in the above management accounting application areas. The bad news is that this type of research is time-consuming, costly, and difficult. The development of most expert systems usually take four to fifteen man-years.

Several companies have developed expert systems programs called "shells." A shell has a specific set of inference engine approaches, an explanation module, and an empty knowledge base. Shells shorten the ES development time and cost. But these packages have drawbacks of providing only one reasoning mechanism and one knowledge representation technique as well as poor documentation and maintenance. The researcher has to justify the selection of a particular shell before conducting ES research or an application. Another shortcoming of most shells is that they lack traditional computer capabilities, such as database management: and sophisticated computations that many management accounting applications require. Most of the existing ES research focuses on "system development" instead of "scientific research." Management accounting researchers should undertake a systematic research approach to making contributions to accounting knowledge, and let management accountants take an engineering approach to developing management accounting expert systems.

References

AICPA, "The Future Issues Committee—First Annual Report to the Board of Directors," June 1985.

Barr, A. and E. Feigenbaum, *The Handbook of Artificial Intelligence*, Vol. 2, Kaufmann Publications, 1982.

Dungan, C. W. and J. S. Chandler, "Auditor: A Microcomputer-Based Expert System to Support Auditors in the Field," *Expert Systems*, October 1985, pp. 210–221.

Elliott, R. K. and J. A. Kielich, "Expert Systems for Accountants," *Journal of Accountancy*, September 1985, pp. 125–134.

Goodall, A., *The Guide to Expert Systems, Learned Information*, Medford, NJ, 1985.

Hansen, J. V. and W. F. Messier, Jr., "Expert Systems for Decision Support in EDP Auditing," *International Journal of Computer and Information Sciences*, 1982, pp. 357–379.

Hayes-Roth, F, D.A. Waterman, and D. B. Lenat (eds.), *Building Expert Systems*, Addison-Wesley, 1983.

Messier, W. F, Jr. and J. V. Hansen, "Expert Systems in Accounting and Auditing: A Framework and Review," in E. Joyce and S. Moriarity (eds.), *Decision Making and Accounting: Current Research*, University of Oklahoma, 1984.

O'Leary, D. E., "Validation of Business Expert Systems," paper presented at the University of Southern California Symposium on Expert Systems and Audit Judgment, February 17–18, 1986.

Shanteau, J., "Psychological Characteristics of Expert Decision Makers," paper presented at the University of Southern California Symposium on Expert Systems and Audit Judgment, February 17–18, 1986.

Decision Support and Expert Systems in Auditing: A Review and Research Directions

MOHAMMAD J.
ABDOLMOHAMMADI

Introduction

Auditors are using computers with increasing frequency in their engagements, and computer-based decision aids such as decision support systems (DSS) and knowledge-based expert systems (KES) are receiving substantial support for use in auditing (Messier and Hansen, 1984). What makes DSS and KES particularly desirable is their ability to enhance the effectiveness (and possibly efficiency) of audit decision making (Luzi, 1981, p. 16). They also provide better expertise to each auditor by bringing the experience of an accounting firm to individual auditors (Elliott and Kielich, 1985). For these reasons, Vasarhelyi and Bao (1984, p. 12) call these decision aids "ideal." Consideration of these effective audit tools is especially desirable now, because the profession is coming increasingly under market and legislative pressure to enhance the quality of audit services at more competitive prices.[1]

The purpose of this paper is to (1) provide a model of task complexity to identify areas of application of DSS and KES in auditing, (2) provide specific audit examples of DSS and KES from the literature, (3) review critically the literature relating to the potential uses of KES and DSS in auditing, and (4) suggest research directions in KES and DSS. The paper is organized as

75

follows: the next part provides the proposed model, and definitions and illustrations of KES and DSS in auditing. A critique of KES and DSS in auditing, followed by a section on future research, comprise the rest of the paper.

A model of the decision process and task structure

To identify the areas of application of DSS and KES in auditing, a model of the auditor's decision process is needed. According to a well-cited theory, any decision process encompasses three iterative phases: intelligence, design, and choice (Simon, 1960). Carlson (1983) summarizes these phases as presented in Figure 1. The intelligence phase relates to the definition of the problem under consideration and collection of data relating to the problem. At the design phase, the decision maker would generate alternative courses of action and collect further data if necessary to support each alternative. Analysis of the alternatives and the selection and explanation of the best alternative is done in the choice phase.

For example, suppose that an auditor is involved with the task

Figure 1
Decision making phases

Intelligence
    Gather data
    Identify objectives
    Diagnose problem
    Validate data
    Structure problem

Design
    Gather data
    Manipulate data
    Quantify objectives
    Generate alternatives
    Assign risks or values to alternatives

Choice
    Generate statistics on alternatives
    Simulate results of alternatives
    Explain alternatives
    Choose among alternatives
    Explain choice

Adapted from Carlson (1983, p. 137)

of evaluating the adequacy of a client's allowance for doubtful debts. He or she might take the following approach: (1) prepare (or have the client prepare) a list of credit customers with their corresponding account balances (intelligence phase), (2) classify customers into different risk groups by preparing an aging schedule (design phase) and send confirmation letters accordingly, and (3) choose a given percentage of the balances of each risk group (choice phase).

In some tasks, the problem can be well-defined at the intelligence phase, and alternative solutions are very limited at the design phase leaving very little judgment at the choice phase. These tasks are considered to be "programmable" (Simon, 1960) or "structured" (Keen and Scott-Morton, 1978). There are other tasks where the problem is ill-defined at the intelligence phase or the alternative solutions may be numerous at the design phase, requiring the decision maker to use considerable judgment and insight to choose an alternative at the choice phase. These tasks are called "nonprogrammable" or "unstructured."

Somewhere between the "programmable-unprogrammable" or "structured-unstructured" continuum lay other tasks. These tasks may be called "semi-programmable" or "semi-structured." The problem in these tasks could be reasonably defined at the intelligence phase, alternative solutions may be limited and specified at the design phase, leaving some judgment to the decision maker in choosing among the alternatives at the choice phase of the decision process. The top panel of Figure 2 summarizes the phases of the decision process along the structured-unstructured continuum.

There are several implications of the above model in the context of auditing. First, although a given level of audit expertise is

Figure 2
Relationships between the task structure and decision making phases

Decision Phase	Factor	Task Structure	
		Semi-Structured	Unstructured
Intelligence: Problem is	Well-defined	Reasonably defined	Ill-defined
Design: Alternatives are	Well-specified	Limited, specified	Numerous
Choice: Requires	Little judgment	Some judgment	Judgment and insight
Expertise level	Low	Medium	High (speciality)
Decision support	Automation	Decision support system	Knowledge-based system

necessary to handle any audit task,[2] it is in the semi-structured to unstructured task category where expertise plays a major role (Messier and Hansen, 1984, p. 183). The tasks considered to be structured require very little judgment and could be accomplished by the lowest level of expertise. For example, the task of recomputing depreciation expense could be accomplished easily by a junior accountant. As the task under consideration gets less structured, higher level expertise, judgment, and insight become more and more crucial to get the job done. In fact, Abdolmohammadi and Wright (1986) found significant correlation between task structure and staff level recommended by eighty-eight audit managers and partners in a survey questionnaire: the less structured the task, the higher the level of staff required to get the task done.

A second implication of the above model in auditing is that the less structured the task, the more the need for decision support. At the structured task level, automation of the process is feasible. A major portion of these types of tasks is in fact already automated in major accounting firms (see Grease, 1984 for Peat Marwick Main & Co.'s experience).

Semi-structured tasks, on the other hand, require more than automation. The decision maker can use data and models to assist him or her in choosing between alternatives. DSSs have been proposed to provide this assistance (see below). For example, internal control evaluations are considered by auditors to be a semi-structured task (Abdolmohammadi and Wright, 1986). This is because, while the problem of internal control evaluation is reasonably defined at the intelligence phase, and alternative decisions are limited (e.g., strong, mediocre, or weak) at the design phase, the auditor needs to use some judgment to choose between alternatives at the choice phase. Bailey et al. (1985) have developed a decision support system called TICOM to assist auditors in designing, evaluating, and analyzing internal control systems.

In the unstructured task category, consider the task of evaluating the controls in an advanced electronic data processing system. This task may be unique for each audit with many possible alternatives, leaving the choice phase of the decision process in need of much judgment and insight on the part of the advanced EDP-auditor. Thus, the decision aids necessary in this task would require the consideration of the decision rules used by a specialist auditor (e.g., computer audit specialists). KESs have been proposed for these task domains (see below). The EDP-XPERT system developed and tested by Hansen and Messier (1986) is an example of such a system.

The lower panel of Figure 2 summarizes the implications discussed above. Of course, there are other implications of the model as well, but discussion of them is beyond the scope of this paper. In the following section, DSSs and KESs are defined, illustrated, and compared.

Decision support and expert systems in auditing

As proposed in the previous section, while DSSs have promise in the semi-structured task domain, KESs are more appropriate in unstructured tasks. This distinction, however, is not widely recognized in the auditing literature. In fact, DSS and KES terms have been used almost interchangeably in some studies (see, for example, Bedard, Gray, and Mock, 1984). While a KES is a system of decision support, it has several features that distinguish it from a DSS. However, these features make KES different from DSS more by degree than type. In this section, DSS and KES are defined and illustrated first, followed by a discussion on their similarities and differences.

DECISION SUPPORT SYSTEMS

A DSS is an interactive computer-based software which assists decision makers in using *data* and *models* to make their decisions in *semi-structured* task domains (Keen and Scott-Morton, 1978, p. 11, emphasis added). Johnson (1983) calls these models "mechanical optimization methods" and argues that these methods are optimal models developed specifically to find the "best" solution to a given problem. Examples of these methods include regression equations, linear programming algorithms, and Bayesian inference models (Johnson, 1983, p. 82).

DSSs are intended to improve the effectiveness of decision makers by providing support without automating the whole decision process. At the intelligence phase of the decision process, a DSS would acquire relevant data from the user or the existing database. The DSS would then use a pre-specified normative model (e.g., a statistical model) to assist the decision maker in the design phase to develop viable alternatives and acquire data for the analysis of each of these alternatives. The DSS would then use the model to assist the decision maker in the final choice of an alternative.

For example, consider the tasks of tests of transactions and account balances. The auditor collects, evaluates, and integrates various types of non-sampling and sampling evidence. To quantify and integrate non-sampling evidence with the sampling evidence, the auditor normally uses professional judgment. A DSS to support him or her in this task could use a formal model such as the Bayesian statistical model. This model has been advocated in the past as a systematic method of integrating sampling and non-sampling evidence (Bailey and Jensen, 1977; Blocher and Robertson, 1976), which would provide much efficiency over the classical approach currently being used in auditing (Crosby, 1980; Abdolmohammadi, 1986).[3] The sampling task in general (and a Bayesian sampling task in particular) is considered to be a semi-structured task in auditing[4] and has been reported as a popular area for DSS in auditing.[5]

As an illustration of a DSS in auditing, a Bayesian assisted sampling system (BASS) is presented. The discussion that follows is based on a feasibility study of BASS using a microcomputer with spreadsheet graphics capability. Although much detail work remains, the prototype developed so far could be used to illustrate a sampling system DSS.

BASS takes a cycle approach to auditing. For each cycle (e.g., sales and collection cycle, inventory acquisition, and warehousing cycle), the auditor concurrently collects non-sampling and sampling evidence and makes an audit decision. A Bayesian model approach for this purpose is presented in Figure 3. Boxes A and B in Figure 3 are the focus of BASS.

In each of the tasks represented in Boxes A and B in Figure 3, BASS would assist the auditor in all phases of the decision process as explained below:

Intelligence Phase—In this phase the auditor enters:

(1) The data relating to the prior probability distribution (PPD) of the parameter of interest (expected compliance error rate in Box A and expected account balance in Box B). This PPD is quantified using the questioning modes of the probability distribution function technique for compliance errors (Box

80

FIGURE 3
A Baysian audit model

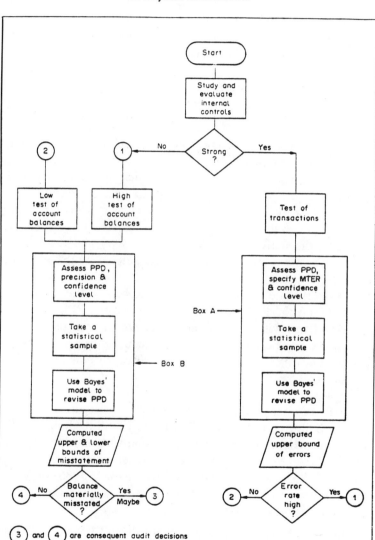

A) and the most likely, maximum and minimum technique for account balances (Box B).[6]

(2) The maximum tolerable error rate (MTER) (Box A) and precision or materiality (Box B). In accounting firms where MTER and materiality judgments are subject to specific formulae, the DSS would automatically calculate these inputs. For example, the accounting firm of Peat Marwick Main & Co. uses a materiality formula called "gauge" (Elliott, 1983) which is defined as $G = 1.6X^{2/3}$ where X is the greater of assets or revenues. By a programming gauge, BASS would automatically compute G using the assets or revenues already in the database or entered by the auditor.

(3) Finally, the auditor would enter the level of confidence (e.g., 90% or 95%) he or she is seeking from the statistical results. *Design Phase*—The alternatives implicit in BASS are that the error rate (Box A) is either high or low. Similarly, the account balances (Box B) are either misstated or not. So the system would proceed to collect data to evaluate each of these alternatives (see below).

Choice Phase—Based upon the data entered by the auditor in (1)–(3) above, BASS would suggest a sample size and instruct the auditor to enter the sample results after sampling is undertaken. BASS would then update the PPD using the Bayesian revision model and calculate the computed upper and lower bound of errors or account misstatements and present this information to the auditor for consequent decisions, as presented in Figure 3.

There are many other examples of DSS in auditing. As cited earlier, Bailey et al.'s (1985) TICOM is a DSS to design, evaluate, and analyze internal control systems. Bedard, Gray, and Mock (1984, p. 260) propose an impressive list of application areas in DSS (and KES). Hansen and Messier (1986) provide a survey of practicing auditors indicating several areas of application of decision aids.

KNOWLEDGE-BASED EXPERT SYSTEMS

Knowledge-based expert systems (KES) came out of much work in the area of artificial intelligence. Artificial intelligence refers to the use of computers to simulate human intelligence. Thus, "the goal of (artificial intelligence) is to construct computer software that performs tasks which normally require human intelligence" (Hansen and Messier, 1982, p. 363). Early research in artificial intelligence was " . . . concerned with making computers perceive, reason, and understand" (Duda and Gasching, 1981, p. 238). This research not only attempted to develop software that would perform a task as well as a human decision maker, but it would also attempt to capture the decision makers' cognitive processes (perception, reasoning, etc.). This research, however, generated disappointing results, as many cognitive scientists provided evidence casting much doubt that computers will ever approach the power of human thinking or give much of an insight into how people think (*Economist,* 1985, p. 87). Consequently, the general goal of artificial intelligence evolved around the concept of figuring out how to represent knowledge in some formal symbols such as "IF-THEN" or "production" rules. These rule-based systems may not think like human beings, but they are capable of accomplishing useful work. By Ten Dyke's (1985) analogy, "in the past people wanted to fly, like a bird; today they fly, though not like a bird" (p. 30).

A popular application of artificial intelligence has been KES, also called expert consultant system (Nilsson, 1980).[7] KES can be defined as a computational system which embodies organized knowledge concerning some specific area of human expertise by using an explicit representation of knowledge (Bramer, 1984; Chingell and Smith., 1985). Furthermore, although KES can be, and has been, successfully applied to certain semi-structured tasks in the past, the most challenging area of its use is in the unstructured task domain, because in these problem situations "one does not know at the beginning what to model" (Humphreys, 1985, p. 1). Therefore, mechanical optimization models used in DSS are of limited use in the unstructured tasks. Rather, the KES model is developed, using KES techniques, by bootstrapping the expert. Furthermore, because it is more costly to develop a KES than a DSS (see next sections), building DSSs for semi-structured tasks may be more economical than KESs.

KES seeks to capture the decision rules (knowledge base) used by "an expert."[8] The decision rules are elicited and modeled by a KES specialist, called a knowledge engineer. This model is then programmed in an expert "shell" such as AL/X (Advice Language X) (Paterson, 1981), using a programming language such as LISP or PROLOG, in terms of a series of IF-THEN or production rules. A user of the system would respond to certain

Figure 4
KES development and use

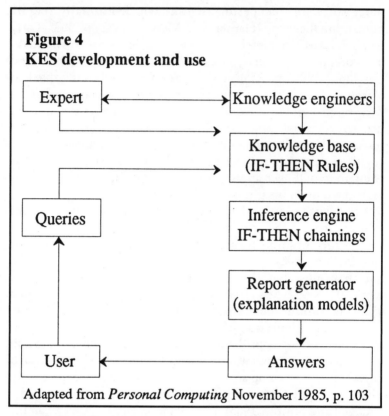

Adapted from *Personal Computing* November 1985, p. 103

queries from the KES. The KES then uses a combination of IF-THEN rules called chaining (inference engine) to recommend a course of action. Figure 4 depicts the relationships described above.

For example, suppose that an auditor is assessing the collectibility of a bank loan in a bank audit. The objective is to assess the adequacy of bank loan loss reserve for commercial loans. An expert system developed by Peat Marwick Main & Co. (Elliott and Kielich, 1985, p. 128) has an IF-THEN rule number 121, as follows:

If current-ratio	= yes [sic] and
current-ratio-industry	= moderate and
quick-ratio-industry	moderate and
unused line of credit	= x^2
loan-officer-liquidity evaluation	= x^3 and
sell-noncurrent-assets	= x^4 and
other-short-term liabilities	= x^5
Then short-term liquidity	= moderate

Because of the vast amount of time required to turn an expert's knowledge into a knowledge base using standard knowledge engineering methods, whereby the expert declares relevant rules in answering to the knowledge engineer's questions, development of KES has been very slow (Humphreys, 1985, p. 8). The KES development successes in medicine, geology, and computer manufacturing, among other fields,[9] are significant enough, however, to generate much interest in developing KES in other fields. For example, MYCIN is an infectious disease diagnoser with some 500 decision rules (Shortliffe, 1976). PROSPECTOR, another example of a KES, is a mineral exploring diagnoser with 1600 decision rules (Duda et al., 1980). Similarly, R1 (McDermott, 1980) and its commercial counterparts XCON and XSell (Kraft, 1984) is a VAX computer configurator with over 2000 decision rules. In all these KESs, the user is charged with providing the relevant data requested by the KES as input. The KES then processes the data using the inference engine and recommends a course of action. The user can, of course, compare the recommendation with a decision that he or she would otherwise have made and then resolve the difference.

The success of the KESs mentioned above has encouraged interest in the use of KES in auditing, among other fields. For example, Hansen and Messier (1986) have been working on the development and testing of the EDP-XPERT system since 1981. This system seeks to simulate an EDP audit specialist in evaluating the controls of an advanced EDP system. The following is an example of a decision process that EDP-XPERT would support.[10] Suppose that the objective of the auditor is to assess the adequacy of the control system of the EDP of his client. The auditor has collected certain evidence relating to the EDP system and uses EDP-XPERT in a session as following:

Intelligence Phase—The auditor makes an a priori decision as to whether controls are adequate. Suppose the auditor chooses 50/50 as the decision (controls being equally likely to be adequate or inadequate). Relating to this goal of evaluating the adequacy of the EDP controls, the EDP-XPERT asks for certain input from the auditor. For example, one question would be: "How certain are you that all incoming messages are logged?" The auditor would respond by giving a number between   -5 (extreme lack of evidence) and 5 (presence of evidence) where 0 indicates no information. Suppose that the auditor answered 0.5.

Design Phase—The alternatives possible at this phase are either there is a more than 50% chance that the controls are adequate or there is a less than 50% chance that they are adequate.

Choice Phase—EDP-XPERT uses a Bayesian updating procedure to revise the auditor's prior expectation using a chain of IF-THEN rules programmed in the system. In the example given in the intelligence phase above, Messier and Hansen (1984) report that in an actual session the probability of the adequacy of the controls was assessed by the EDP-XPERT to be 61%. Of course, the auditor needs to use judgment as to whether or not he or she agrees with EDP-XPERT and, if so, whether he or she would consider the controls to be adequate for audit purposes.

There are other examples of KES in the auditing literature. Dungan and Chandler have developed AUDITOR (a bad debt expense estimator) (Dungan, 1983). Braun and Chandler (1983) are extending the work of Dungan and Chandler to hospital audits. These projects and the EDP-XPERT use the AL/X software borrowed from oil platform diagnosis in geology. The accounting firm of Peat, Marwick Main & is using a microcomputer-based expert system software shell called M1 to develop a KES for assessing the collectibility of bank loans (Elliott and Kielich, 1985: Willingham, Ribar, and Kelly, 1985; Willingham and Wright, 1985). Finally, Steinbart (1984) developed a KES for materiality decisions in auditing using EMYCIN. Other areas of application have been suggested in Elliott and Kielich (1985) and Hansen and Messier (1986), among others.

SIMILARITIES AND DIFFERENCES BETWEEN DDS AND KES

Both DSS and KES were developed to provide decision aids to auditors. According to Sprague (1983), such decision aids should (a) provide support in all phases of the decision process (i.e., intelligence, design, and choice), (b) be easy to use by non-computer people in an interactive mode, and (c) be flexible so that they could be adapted to accommodate changes in the

86

environment. Furthermore, the decision aid developed should (d) provide an explanation of the decision process used. Gorry (1973) asserts that decision makers are more willing to accept a system if they understand its decision process. Given the above common requirements, there are several similarities and differences between DSSs and KESs as discussed below.

Similarities. The top panel of Figure 5 summarizes the similarities between DSS and KES: (1) Both DSS and KES provide a mechanism for training staff in accounting firms. Elliott and Kielich (1985) assert that "expert systems can be used to simulate real situations, thereby teaching inexperienced professionals what information is combined in reaching a decision" (p. 132). Simulation can also be used with DSS for the same purpose. (2) The models programmed in DSS or KES can be shared with all decision makers within an organization, expecially when human expertise is either scarce or not available (Elliott and Kielich, 1985; Sullivan and Fordyce, 1985). Thus, both DSS and KES provide a vehicle to pass the availability of optimal models in a DSS and expertise of a top expert in a KES down to the lowest level of staff in an accounting firm. (3) Computers process data and models faster than human beings. Thus, while DSS provides efficiency in processing data and models, KES would provide efficiency by focusing the attention of the auditor on factors considered to be relevant to the task domain (Elliott and Kielich, 1985; Sullivan and Fordyce, 1985). (4) The decision support of the DSS will be the provision of an "optimal solution" resulting from the normative model used. The KES, on the other hand, would suggest a solution which is based on the decision rules of

---

Figure 5
Similarities and differences between DSS and KES

Factor	Decision Support Systems	Knowledge-Based Systems
Similarities:		
Staff training	Provide online training	Provide online training
Knowledge sharing	The model in DSS is shared by all decision makers	The expertise of an expert is shared with all decision makers
Efficiency	Process data and model faster	Focus only on factors (decision rules) relevant to the decision
Final decision support	Provides optimal solution	Provides second opinion
Differences:		
Task domain	Semi-structured	Unstructured
Model	Normative optimal model	An expert's decision rules
Search	Numeric/algorithmic	Symbolic/heuristic
Output	Optimal solution	Satisfactory answer
Flexibility	Modification difficult	Modification generally easy
Cost	Inexpensive	Very expensive

the expert programmed in the KES. Thus, the decision support would essentially appear as a "second opinion" (Elliott and Kielich, 1985). The important point is that, in either DSS or KES, the decision maker is ultimately responsible for making decisions, although he or she would use the output of a DSS or KES as an input into his or her terminal decision.

Differences. The bottom panel of Figure 5 summarizes the differences between DSSs and KESs: (1) While the task domain of DSS is primarily semi-structured, the task domain of KES is primarily unstructured as presented earlier. (2) It was also argued earlier that DSS uses certain normative models such as statistical sampling models to process data and suggest solutions to the decision maker. The model in KES is a set of decision rules elicited from an expert. These decision rules are chained together in the inference engine to produce the final recommendation. (3) As a result of the above two characteristics, the search process in DSS is numeric and follows certain algorithmic relationships relating to the model programmed in the DSS. The search process in KES, on the other hand, is primarily symbolic (i.e., IF-THEN rules) and follows the heuristics and insights of an expert whose decision rules are programmed in the KES. Thus, while the normative models programmed in DSS are primarily borrowed from other fields such as statistics, mathematics, and operations research, there is a need for at least one human expert acknowledged to perform the task well to develop a KES. As Duda and Gasching (1981, p. 262) argue, such an expert should possess exceptional performance skills resulting from special knowledge, judgment, and experience. (4) A DSS generates an "optimal" solution based on the normative model used. For example, the Bayesian revision model is presented in statistics as an optimal revision model. Thus, the output from a DSS using a Bayesian approach can be considered an optimal solution. The output from a KES, on the other hand, relates to the decision rules of the expert programmer. Given the uncertainty inherent in unstructured tasks, the solution may be "satisfactory" rather than being "optimal." (5) DSSs are developed using structured languages such as COBOL, PASCAL, and spreadsheet programs, among others. These languages have severe limitations which would make modification to DSSs time-consuming and difficult. While KES languages such as LISP or PROLOG also suffer from certain limitations, they provide more flexibility than structured languages. Furthermore, the goal of expert systems software developers is to develop languages or expert "shells" that would do to KES what spreadsheet programs have done to worksheet programming and manipulations. These languages would a provide high-level modeling approach to AI-related computations that could relieve users of the need to deal with programming details (Khoshnevis and Chingell, 1985).

Finally, the cost of developing DSS is less than that of KES. While both KES and DSS require the purchase and maintenance of certain hardware and software programs, KES development requires acquisition of knowledge from an expert, in addition to the programming time and cost required for both DSS and KES. The knowledge acquisition is extremely costly and time-consuming, pushing the cost of developing a KES easily to $1 million, depending on the complexity of the system (Elliott and Kielich, 1985, p. 133). Similarly, Keith (1985) argues that the cost estimates range anywhere up to the low millions.

There are also, of course, detailed technical and programming differences between DSS and KES, the discussion of which is beyond the scope of this paper. The conclusion from this section is that, while both DSS and KES have the objective of providing decision support, DSS is primarily concerned with semi-structured tasks, leaving the more unstructured tasks to KES where expertise plays a significant role in solving such problems. Furthermore, while DSSs are low cost decision aids, KESs are more expensive to develop for use in auditing. The differences discussed in this section provide significant direction for rigorous research, as discussed in the next section.

A critical evaluation and research direction

From the above discussion and examples, it is clear that both KES and DSS have potential in auditing. Once developed, both DSS and KES would uniformly provide decision aid to all levels of audit decision makers, although the auditor will make the final decision. There is no evidence, however, indicating whether an auditor would deviate from the decision suggested by a DSS or a KES, given that the auditor knows the decision is presumably supported by an "optimal" or an "expert" model in the firm.

To evaluate DSS and KES, a traditional cost-benefit analysis could be undertaken. A KES would provide the benefit of putting the expertise of a firm's most experienced auditor at the fingertips of auditors at all levels, thus reducing the need for extensive training and experience in making audit decisions. It would, however, entail high costs in terms of numerous technical details requiring tremendous effort over a long period. A DSS would require a relatively inexpensive developmental cost over a short period, but its benefits would be limited to the amount of "support" it could provide the auditor in semi-structured audit tasks.

To do a cost-benefit analysis of DSS and KES in auditing, the problems associated with development of these decision aids should be identified and investigated through rigorous research. In this section, some issues are identified from the literature to set the stage for research directions. These issues include:

- classification of audit tasks by complexity
- search for a "normative model" or an "expert"
- methods of eliciting knowledge
- flexibility
- developmental time and cost

CLASSIFICATION OF AUDIT TASKS BY COMPLEXITY

To identify the areas of application of DSS and KES in auditing, there is a need for an inventory of audit tasks classified by the level of task structure. Such a classification would identify the structured tasks for simple automation, the semi-structured tasks for DSS development, and the unstructured tasks for KES development. Although accounting firms are increasingly incorporating structured audit approaches (standardized tools and techniques) and a top-down approach to the design and execution of an audit engagement (Cushing and Loebbecke, 1984), no general classification of audit tasks is reported in the literature. Some authors (e.g., Bedard et al., 1984; Elliott and Kielich, 1985; Hansen and Messier, 1986, Keith, 1985) have proposed certain audit tasks for DSS and KES development. A general audit task classification study would be desirable to evaluate these tasks for the purpose of DSS and KES development.

In a preliminary study, Abdolmohammadi and Wright (1986)

engaged eighty-eight audit managers and partners to rank ten audit tasks according to their perceived task complexity. Although much variation between auditors (mostly firm effects) was observed, the authors were able to classify these ten audit tasks into three clear levels of task structure (structured, semi-structured, and unstructured) using the analysis of variance paradigm. For example, while the task of looking up tables for sample size decisions, was considered to be a structured task, the task of determining expected population deviation rates (as an input to sample size decisions in compliance testing) was considered to be semi-structured. A comprehensive listing of audit tasks and their classification according to task complexity seems desirable for the development of DSS and KES in auditing. So far, the development of DSS and KES has been based on a "one-task-at-a-time" method.

SEARCH FOR A "NORMATIVE MODE" OR AN "EXPERT"

Once tasks are identified for DSS and KES development, appropriate "normative models" for DSS and "experts" for KES need to be identified. Since normative models are borrowed from other fields (e.g., statistics), the choice for a model for DSS requires some library research to match appropriate models against specific semi-structured tasks. For example, for statistical sampling tasks, the choice is between classical, Bayesian, and other models, and within each of these models, of course, there are different methods that need to be analyzed.

The choice of an expert to develop a KES for an unstructured task is less clear and requires more research. The factors that constitute an expert are not known and previous research shows that there is significant inconsistency among auditors confronting the same task (Joyce and Libby, 1982, p. 108), both within each accounting firm and across different accounting firms. Keith (1985, p. 5) states that " . . . it might be tough, maybe impossible, to get all 692 of us (partners in Price Waterhouse) to agree on the same proposed individuals (as experts)."

Thus the question arises as to how one should identify an audit expert? What are the educational and experience determinants of such an expert? While these questions can be easily answered in some professions, such as medicine, research has not as yet investigated these issues in auditing. For example, the medical

91

profession has well-specified training, residency programs, specialty education, and continuing education to qualify a physician as a specialist (expert). Of course, each accounting firm has its own guidelines for required education and training to qualify an individual as a specialist. For example, Elliott (1983) reports that Peat Marwick Main & Co. has specific guidelines to qualify auditors as computer audit specialists or statistical audit specialists. However, the fact remains that no generally recognized guidelines have been established by the profession as a whole for identifying experts.

Keith (1985) argues that to identify experts, attributes such as common sense, wisdom, intuition, insightfulness, imagination, creativity, and resourcefulness should be considered. Keith admits that definition and measurement of these attributes is difficult, but he proposes that proper representation of these in a KES is desirable. Research in the identification and measurement of these attributes and other determinants of expertise is needed in order to make KES generalizable to a broad group of users. Furthermore, recent literature suggests that expertise should be closely identified with specific and narrowly defined audit tasks (Abdolmohammadi and Wright, 1987), and that experience with the defined tasks makes a significant difference in judgment of auditors (Fredrick and Libby, 1986; Abdolmohammadi and Wright, 1987). This literature suggests that even when experts are identified, their judgments may change over time as their level of experience with the contextual task improves. Thus, KES development should provide enough flexibility in design such that KES is easily revised for the effect of new experience.

METHODS OF ELICITING KNOWLEDGE

Once an expert is identified, his or her knowledge needs to be elicited by a knowledge engineer. To do this, a method of eliciting knowledge must be developed, such as the methodology of process tracing (thinking aloud when doing a job) (Ericsson and Simon, 1980; Biggs and Mock, 1983; Anderson, 1984). The problem is that experts in fields other than auditing are reported to have seldom been able to describe what they know. Even if the experts try to specify it, their "knowledge is incomplete and ill-specified" (Davis, 1982, p. 8). Thus, it is important to first investigate whether auditors suffer from the same limitation in describing their expertise as do other professionals, and whether the methodology of process tracing is sufficient to overcome this problem.

Biggs, Messier, and Hansen (1985) report encouraging results for the use of a protocol analysis of the processes that three computer audit specialists used to do EDP audits. This analysis, however, generated certain IF-THEN rules that indicate auditing around the computer rather than auditing through the computer. The authors were seeking to find the latter IF-THEN rules for use in Hansen and Messier's (1986) EDP-XPERT system. This indicates that there is a need for further refinement and empirical testing of the process tracing paradigm as a means of eliciting KES knowledge.

Of course, other methods of knowledge representation have been offered. For example, Johnson (1983) offers the "reconstructed method of reasoning," where what an expert "should" be doing is inferred from the writings of a practitioner group (p. 82). Thus, this method would involve "using currently available information (e.g., textbooks, firm materials) to construct the inference network of rules" (Hansen and Messier, 1986, p. 2). Johnson, however, states that, in his observation of a physician, he noticed that the physician "did not teach what he seemed to do," and when the phsyician was asked why, he replied, " . . . you see I don't know how I do diagnosis, and yet I need things to teach students" (p. 81). Thus, the method of reconstructed reasoning is used to develop the initial knowledge base (Hansen and Messier, 1986) to be later refined by experts. There is still a need to elicit explicitly what decision rules the experts use when they make decisions to complete the knowledge base.

FLEXIBIITY

Auditors use professional judgment extensively in every audit phase, and judgments are different across clients and for the same client over time. Consequently, they appear to develop numerous patterns or heuristics for judgments. As asserted by Duda and Gasching (1981), "real world problems use semi-logical methods such as recognizing one of a thousand familiar patterns" (p. 238). The success of a KES depends on whether it is flexible enough to accommodate these patterns and heuristics of human judgment. This is not an easy task, as it would be difficult to try to recognize all of the patterns and heuristics present and program them in terms of IF-THEN rules. Even for MYCIN and

93

PROSPECTOR, which attack well-understood tasks, the knowledge bases are incomplete (Duda and Shortliffe, 1983, p. 265).

Compared with other professionals, auditors' experience is limited but expanding over a long period. For example, consider the effect of the following differences between auditors and physicians: (1) While physicians have repetitive experience with hundreds of patients, auditors have a very limited number of clients. In fact, a physician has experience with more patients in a day, typically twenty-five patients (Owens, 1983, p. 106), than the auditor has in a whole year, typically ten to fifteen clients. The repetitive task nature of the physician makes him or her more experienced in medical tasks over a short period than an auditor in auditing tasks. This, of course, indicates the importance of studying experts in auditing for the purpose of passing experience on to others in the profession.

(2) Physicians receive frequent feedback on the results of their decisions; the patient's health either improves, deteriorates, or remains stable. Auditors, on the other hand, may never find out exactly what is "right" or "wrong" about their clients. Only in the case of audit failures (about 0.2% of all audits, according to Philip B. Chenok, AICPA President)[11] would the auditors know what happened.

(3) Most patients go to a physician voluntarily to improve their health. They will generally not try to outsmart the physician. On the other hand, most clients are required by regulatory agencies (i.e., SEC) or interested third parties (e.g., banks) to engage auditors for an audit opinion. The client may have a number of reasons (e.g., financing from a bank) to try to influence the auditor or outsmart him or her in certain regards.

Furthermore, the auditing/accounting body of knowledge is in a constant state of change. New accounting and auditing pronouncements and statements are constantly being issued, which affect the way auditors audit. Moreover, different auditors interpret and use these pronouncements in different ways, as is evidenced in their lack of agreement, discussed earlier. The implication of the above factors is that decision aids developed for auditing should be particularly flexible to accommodate the necessary changes over time. The technology of artificial intelligence has the great promise of enhancing the flexibility of an already flexible rule-based software. Structured languages used

94

in DSS development at this point may be less flexible in programming than KES.

DEVELOPMENT TIME AND COST

Based on experience with KESs developed in other fields, David (1984, p. 26) estimated that, for the best understood problems, an expert system would require at least five work-years to develop (and up to forty work-years for a complex system). Given the complexity of auditing, this forty work-years time estimate may not be unrealistic. For example, Messier and Hansen (1984) report that their EDP-XPERT is still in its "embryonic stage" after four years of development (p. 199). A DSS, on the other hand, can be developed in a short period, since it does not require the knowledge engineering step that is required for developing a KES.

The research question that arises is how to measure objectively the costs and benefits associated with KES and KDS. The experience with the DSS and KES that have been developed or are under development will provide much needed data to investigate this question.

Summary of Research Directions

Many questions were raised in the previous section relating to the use of KES and DSS in auditing. These questions can be viewed as avenues for future research. For example, KES requires modeling of an expert in auditing. (1) How does one identify an audit expert? What are the educational and experience requirements of such an expert? (2) What methodology should be used to elicit an expert's decision rules? Is the process-tracing paradigm a sufficient method for this purpose? (3) Given that auditors have rather poor agreement on their audit judgments, how feasible is it to build a DSS and a KES that would represent a consensus-building paradigm, rather than a single audit expert? Would structured aids such as KES lead to higher agreement among auditors?

Other questions arise for other arguments in the paper. For example, (4) Do auditors have difficulty in describing their knowledge, as has been shown for other professionals? (5) There are now KES modeling languages available on micro-computers. Are these sufficient for developing KES or are they too limited in terms of the number of IF-THEN rules they allow? How do these languages perform in audit settings? Is there any need for other languages specifically developed for auditing? Because of the proliferation of micro-computers in audit applications, this issue is important. (6) How long does it take and how costly is it to develop operational DSS and KES in auditing? (7) How does one validate the usefulness of DSS and KES in auditing?

Finally, suppose that operational DSS and KES are developed; (8) Would such systems be generalizable to all auditors? Would auditors accept or resist these systems? What are the behavioral implications? Do auditors feel threatened? (9) Would DSS and KES improve upon the quality of audit services? (10) How would clients of auditors react to the use of DSS and KES, since auditors are presumably sensitive to the biases and preferences of their clients? Would they react positively to some (e.g., data security evaluation systems) or negatively (e.g., internal control weakness identification systems)? (11) How would the legal liability of accountants be affected by the use of these systems? (12) Would DSS and KES development impact on the organizational structure of accounting firms by shifting the need from certain areas (e.g., detailed accounting knowledge) to other areas (e.g., working knowledge of computers and systems)? What implications would these have for educational institutions providing entry-level education to the accounting profession? Research is needed to study these issues but, as Keith (1985) argues, a good way of finding out is to build fully-fledged working prototype systems and use such systems to study the research questions identified above, among others.

Footnotes

1. For example, see *Wall Street Journal,* January 26, 1985 for a report on aggressive bidding by auditors, and February 19, 1985 for a report on Representative John Dingell's Committee relating to investigation and oversight of auditing in the United States.

2. An expert is a trained and experienced individual who calls forth his or her expertise "in appropriate situations according to the demands of specific tasks" (Johnson, 1983, p. 80). Thus, the "expert" would employ certain heuristics and insights from experience to generate good decisions in a short period (Hayes-Roth et al., 1983).

3. A discussion of the characteristics and limitations of the Bayesian approach in auditing is beyond the scope of this paper. The interested reader is referred to Abdolmohammadi (1985).

4. Determination of the components of the sample task were rated semi-

structured by the manager-partner subjects in the Abdolmohammadi and Wright (1986) study.

5. Hansen and Messier (1985) report that thirteen of their seventeen practicing auditors chose statistical sampling as an appropriate task for application of computer-based decision aids.

6. Having reviewed the PPD assessment techniques, Abdolmohammadi (1985) identified the probability distribution function technique as particularly congruent with the task of compliance error estimation. In this technique the auditor is given a number of exclusive and exhaustive error intervals (e.g., 0%–1%, 1.01%–2%. . . , 8% or greater) and is asked to attach a probability of occurrence to each of these intervals for the client under study (probabilities assigned should sum to one). BASS would use the auditor's responses to draw graphically a probability distribution using a beta function. Similarly, for the account balance estimations, the method of most likely, minimum and maximum values is used. The most likely value and the minimum (maximum) value is assessed such that the auditor believes there will be only an X% chance that the account balance would be less (greater) than this value. BASS would use the auditor's responses to draw graphically a probability distribution using a normal function. For a detailed discussion of the strengths and weaknesses of these PPD assessment methods and others, see Abdolmohammadi (1985).

7. Other applications of artificial intelligence include natural language processing, intelligent retrieval from databases, robotics, and automatic programming. For a detailed discussion, see Nilsson (1980).

8. Messier and Hansen (1984) and Wright (1984) assert that current practice does not allow for integration of the knowledge of multiple experts. Willingham, Ribar, and Kelly (1985), however, report that CFILE is based on "consensus" of several experts. This expert system is a bank loan loss reserve estimation system.

9. See Bramer (1984) for a listing and discussion of existing KES in different fields.

10. The discussion of EDP-Xpert is a non-technical summary of much detailed and technical discussion in Messier and Hansen (1984).

11. See *Wall Street Journal,* February 19, 1985, p. 4.

References

Abdolmohammadi, M. J., "Bayesian Inference Research in Auditing: Some Methodological Suggestions," *Contemporary Accounting Research,* Vol. 2, Fall 1985, pp. 76–94.

———, "Efficiency of the Bayesian Approach in Compliance Testing: Some Empirical Evidence," *Auditing: A Journal of Practice and Theory,* Vol. 5, Spring 1986, pp. 1–16.

——— and A. Wright, "A Classification of Audit Task Complexity for Developing Decision Aids," *Proceedings of the Eighteenth Annual Meeting of the Decision Sciences Institute,* November 1986.

——— and ———, "An Examination of the Effects of Experience and Task Complexity on Audit Judgments," *Accounting Review,* January 1987, pp. 1–13.

Anderson, M. J., "The Process Tracing Paradigm: A General View," in S. Moriarity and E. Joyce (eds.), *Decision Making and Accounting: Current Research,* University of Oklahoma, Center for Economic and Management Research, 1984, pp. 158–172.

Bailey, A. D. and D. L. Jensen, "A Note on the Interface Between

Compliance and Substantive Tests," *Journal of Accounting Research,* Autumn, 1977, pp. 293–299.

———, G. L. Duke, J. Gerlach, C. Ko, R. D. Meservy, and A. B. Whinston, "TICOM and the Analysis of Internal Controls," *Accounting Review,* April 1985, pp. 186–201.

Bedard J., G. L. Gray, and T. J. Mock, "Decision-Support Systems and Auditing," *Advances in Accounting,* Vol. 1, 1984, pp. 239–266.

Biggs, S. F., W. F. Messier, Jr., and J. V. Hansen, "A Study of the Predecisional Behavior of Computer Audit Specialists in Advanced EDP Environments," paper presented at the American Accounting Association National Meeting, 1985.

——— and T. J. Mock, "An Investigation of Auditor Decision Processes in the Evaluation of Internal Controls and Audit Scope Decisions," *Journal of Accounting Research,* 1983, pp. 234–255.

Blocher, E. and J. C. Robertson, "Bayesian Sampling Procedures for Auditors: Computer-Assisted Instruction," *Accounting Review,* April 1976, pp. 359–363.

Bramer, M. A., "A Survey and Critical Review of Expert Systems Research," in D. Michie (ed.), *Introductory Readings in Expert Systems* Gordon and Breach Science Publishers, 1984, pp. 3–29.

Braun, H. M. and J. S. Chandler, "Development of an Expert System to Assist Auditors in the Investigation of Analytical Review Fluctuations," Peat Marwick Main & Co. Research Opportunities in Auditing Program, 1983.

Carlson, E. D., "An Approach for Designing Decision-Support Systems," in W. C. House (ed.), *Decision-Support Systems,* Petrocelli Books, 1983, pp. 125–155.

Chignell, M. H. and P. J. Smith, "An Introduction to Knowledge-Based Systems," working paper, University of Southern California, 1985.

Crosby, M. A., "Implications of Prior Probability Elicitation on Auditor Sample Size Decisions," *Journal of Accounting Research,* Autumn 1980, pp. 585–593.

Cushing, B. E. and J. K. Loebbecke, "The Implications of Structured Audit Methodologies," *Auditor's Report,* Vol. 8, Summer 1984, pp. 1, 10, 13.

Davis, R., "Expert Systems: Where Are We? And Where Do We Go From Here?" working paper, Massachusetts Institute of Technology, 1982.

———, "Amplifying Expertise with Expert Systems," in P. H. Winsten and K. A. Prendergast (eds.), *The AI Business,* MIT Press, 1984, pp. 17–40.

——— and J. G. Gasching, "Knowledge-Based Expert Systems Come of Age," *Byte,* September 1981, pp. 238–281.

———, ——— and P. E. Hart, "Model Design in·the PROSPECTOR Consultant System for Mineral Exploration," in D. Michie (ed.), *Expert Systems in the Microelectronic Age,* Edinburgh University Press, 1980.

Duda R. O. and E. H. Shortliffe, "Expert Systems Research," *Science,* April 1983, pp. 261–268.

Dungan, C., "A Model of an Audit Judgment in the Form of an Expert

System," unpublished Ph.D. dissertation, University of Illinois, Urbana-Champaign, 1983.

Economist, "Seeking the Mind in Pathways of the Machine," June 29, 1985, pp. 87–90.

Elliott, R. K., "Unique Audit Methods: Peat Marwick Main & Co., *Auditing: A Journal of Practice and Theory,* Vol. 2, 1983, pp. 1–12.

—— and J. A. Kielich, "Expert Systems for Accountants," *Journal of Accountancy,* September 1985, pp. 126–134.

Ericsson, K. A. and H. A. Simon, "Verbal Report as Data," *Psychological Review,* Vol. 87, 1980, pp. 215–251.

Fredrick, D. and R. Libby, "Expertise and Auditors' Judgments of Conjunctive Events," *Journal of Accounting Research,* Autumn 1986, pp. 270–290.

Gorry, G. A., "Computer-Assisted Clinical Decision Making," *Methods of Information in Medicine,* 1973, pp. 45–51.

Grease, C. E., "Accounting for Change," *World,* Vol. 18, 1984, pp. 16–17.

Hansen, J. V. and W. F. Messier, Jr., "Expert Systems for Decision Support in EDP Auditing," *International Journal of Computer and Information Sciences,* AU: Please Provide Vol. If Available 82, pp. 357–379.

—— and ——, "A Preliminary Test of EDP-XPERT," *Auditing Journal of Practice and Theory,* Vol. 6, Fall 1986, pp. 109–112.

Hayes-Roth, F., D. A. Waterman and D. B. Lenat (eds.). *Building Expert Systems,* Addison-Wesley, 1983.

Humphreys, P., "Intelligence in Decision Support," paper presented at the Tenth Research Conference on Subjective Probability, Utility, and Decision Making, 1985.

Johnson, P. E., "What Kind of Expert Should a System Be?" *Journal of Medicine and Philosophy,* ? Vol. 1983, pp. 77–97.

Joyce, E. J. and R. Libby, "Behavioral Studies of Audit Decision Making," *Journal of Accounting Literature,* Vol. 1, 1982, pp. 103–123.

Keen, P. G. W. and M. S. Scott-Morton, *Decision Support Systems: An Organizational Perspective,* Addison-Wesley, 1978.

Keith, J. R. "Expert Systems in Auditing: A Practitioner's Perspective," paper presented at the 1985 Price Waterhouse Auditing Symposium, 1985.

Khoshnevis, B. and M. H. Chignell, "A Framework for Artificial Intelligence Applications Software Development," working paper, University of Southern California, 1985.

Kraft, A., "XCON: An Expert Configuration System at Digital Equipment Corporation," in P. H. Winsten and K. A. Prendergast (eds.), *The AI Business,* MIT Press, 1984. pp. 41–49.

Luzi, A. D., "Computers in the Audit Process: Current Issues," working paper, Pennsylvania State University, 1981.

McDermott J., "RI: The Formative Years," *AI Magazine,* Vol. 2, 1980, pp. 21–29.

Messier, W. F., Jr. and J. V. Hansen, "Expert Systems in Accounting and Auditing: A Framework and Review," in S. Moriarity and E. Joyce (eds.). *Decision Making and Accounting: Current Research,* University of Oklahoma, 1984, pp. 182–202.

Nilsson, N. J., *Principles of Artificial Intelligence,* Palo Alto, CA: Tioga Publishing, 1980.

Owens, A., "Where the Primary-Care Squeeze is Hurting GPs and FPs," *Medical Economics,* June 13, 1983, pp. 104–135.

Paterson, A., *AL/X User Manual* (Oxford: Intelligent Terminals, 1981).

Shortliffe, E. H., *Computer-Based Medical Consultations: MYCIN,* American Elsevier Publishing Co. Inc., 1976.

Simon, H., *The New Science of Management,* Harper and Row, 1960.

Sprague, R. H., Jr., "A Framework for the Development of Decision Support Systems," in W. C. House (ed.). *Decision Support Systems,* Petrocelli Books, 1983, pp. 85–123.

Steinbart, P., "The Construction of an Expert System to Make Materiality Judgments," Ph.D. dissertation. Michigan State University, 1984.

Sullivan G. and K. Fordyce, "Decision Simulation (DSIM): One Outcome of Combining Expert Systems and Decision Support Systems," working paper, IBM, 1985.

Ten Dyke, R. P., "Outlook on Artificial Intelligence," *Journal of Accounting and EDP,* Summer 1985, pp. 30–37.

Vasarhelyi, M. A. and D. H. Bao. "Control Simulation as a Decision Aid," paper presented at Symposium on Decision Support Systems in Auditing, University of Southern California, 1984.

Willingham, J. J., G. R. Ribar, and K. P. Kelly, "Interim Report on the Development of an Expert System for the Auditor's Loan Loss Evaluation," working paper, Peat Marwick Main & Co., 1985.

—— and W. F. Wright, "Development of a Knowledge-Based System for Auditing the Collectibility of a Commercial Loan," research proposal, 1985.

Wright, W. F., Discussant's Comments on "Expert Systems in Accounting and Auditing: A Framework and Review," in S. Moriarity and E. Joyce (eds.), *Decision Making and Accounting: Current Research,* University of Oklahoma, 1984, pp. 207–213.

A Computational View of Financial Accounting Standards

JAGDISH S. GANGOLLY

Introduction

The German mathematician and philosopher Gottfried Leibnitz once observed "If controversies were to arise, there would be no more need of disputation between two philosophers than between two accountants. For it would suffice [for them] . . . to say to each . . . Let us calculate" (quoted in Frank 1949, pp. 206–208). The present day civilization is more charitable toward accountants in recognizing the value of their services; we accountants would now perhaps like to believe that disputation on points of theory is possible and necessary in accounting and that accountants' accomplishments today are not limited to mechanical manipulations of numbers whereby "answers come tumbling out when the right levers are pushed." On the other hand, the epistemological status of accounting theory is perhaps not as hopeless as the alleged status of legal theorizing which drove Rodell (1959) to assert without hesitation, "Legal words and concepts and principles float in a purgatory of their own, halfway between the heaven of abstract ideals and the hell of plain facts and completely out of touch with both of them. And that is why, in the last analysis, the language of the law is inherently meaningless" (Rodell 1959, p. 136). Only diehard sceptics in accounting would state something to that effect about the status of accounting theory.

Any undertaking that aims to view epistemic aspects of accounting in a computational framework is sure to draw intense fire. I shall nevertheless argue in this paper that such a view can help us in: (1) reducing (or at least bringing into the open view) semantic as well as syntactic ambiguities in accounting standards, (2) deriving principles governing drafting of accounting standards that minimize dysfunctional (usually syntactic) ambiguities, (3) studying the logical consequences of introduction, deletion, and alteration of accounting standards, and (4) gaining insights into the operation of accounting standards and the way we accountants reason about such standards, in the very process of representing our knowledge regarding accounting standards in a computational framework.

In section 2 I draw parallels between philosophy of law and accounting theory to highlight the similarities between law and accounting in an epistemological sense, and their implications for the development of a computational framework for financial accounting standards. In section 3 I introduce basic concepts of declarative representation of domain knowledge in "PROLOG," and in section 4 present various issues involved in the representation of knowledge regarding accounting standards, using paragraph 6 of FASB 48 on "Revenue Recognition Where the Right of Return Exists" as an example. In section 5 I provide concluding observations.

1. The Philosophy of Law and Accounting Theory

The idea of organizing extant knowledge systematically in definitions, postulates (or necessary assumptions), axioms (or common notions) and theorems proved by application of inference rules is an old one. Euclid's Elements, the Principia Mathematica of Whitehead and Russell (1962), and the celebrated "entscheidungsproblem" of Hilbert for determining the completeness, consistency, and decidability of mathematical systems are examples of attempts to axiomatize mathematical knowledge (Hodges, 1984). Mechanical jurisprudence (Pound, 1908) and legal positivism (Austin, 1885; Hart, 1961) in jurisprudence and the efforts of Moonitz (1961), Sprouse and Moonitz (1962), and the FASB conceptual framework project in accounting are also examples of attempts to axiomatize domain knowledge.

In the philosophy of law literature, one can discern at least three schools of judicial reasoning: legal realism, legal

102

positivism, and sociological jurisprudence (see for example Smith and Deedman, 1987 or Gardner, 1987). Legal realism denies "the applicability of logical deduction for legal reasoning" and considers that "legal rules are not the major determining factor in reaching a judicial decision, but are [a] mere rationalization of a decision reached for other (generally unarticulated) reasons." (Smith and Deedman, 1987, p. 86.) The well-known quote that summarizes the legal realist position is that of Oliver Wendell Holmes (1881, p. 5): "The life of the law has not been logic: it has been experience." As Gardner has observed, the legal realists view law as behavior or predictions of behavior (of judges in handing down cases). The legal realist position is also the jurisprudential version of pragmatic philosophy, the dominant American version of empiricism. Legal realist position on the law, according to Dworkin (1967) essentially is an attack on "mechanical jurisprudence" and their analysis differs only in emphasis from that of classical philosophers and legal positivists.

The key tenets of legal positivism, as summarized by Dworkin (1967) are (1) Law is a set of special rules used for the purpose of determining which behavior will be punished or coerced by the public power, and these rules can be identified and distinguished by specific criteria, by tests having to do not with their content but with their pedigree or the manner in which they were developed or adopted, (2) The set of these valid rules is exhaustive of "the law"—a case can not be decided by "applying the law" if such case is not covered by a rule; such a case must be decided by "judicial discretion," and (3) To say that someone has a "legal obligation" is to say that his or her case falls under a valid rule that requires him to do or to forbear from doing something. Legal positivism has been criticized for treating rules and principles as equivalents. Further, as Dworkin (1967) has observed, "positivism . . . stops short of just those puzzling, hard cases[1] that send us to look for theories of law. When we reach these cases, the positivist remits us to a doctrine of discretion that leads nowhere and tells nothing."

In sociological jurisprudence, it is deemed a duty of a judge "to weigh and balance the conflicting interests which are at stake in any particular dispute, and to decide the case accordingly" (Smith and Deedman, 1987, p. 87). In a version of this theory due to Dworkin (1967), judicial standards include principles and policies in addition to rules. Whereas rules apply in an all-or-nothing fashion, he defines policies in terms of goals to be

103

reached (economic, political, or social) and principles in terms of standards to be observed "not because it will advance or secure an economic, political, or social situation deemed desirable, but because it is a requirement of justice or fairness or some other dimension of morality." Moreover, "only rules dictate results, come what may. When a contrary result has been reached, the rule has been abandoned or changed. Principles [on the other hand] . . . incline a decision one way, though not conclusively, and they survive intact when they do not prevail. It hardly makes sense to speak of principles . . . as being 'overruled' or 're-pealed.' When they decline they are eroded, not torpedoed" (Dworkin 1967). The principles thus form the background in which rules are interpreted. The principles and policies may be conflicting, and it is the duty of the judge deciding a hard case to consider the principles and policies having a bearing on the case, weigh them and arrive at a decision.

In accounting, there has been a tradition of designating an organized inventory of existing practices as theory; examples often cited for this view include Paton and Littleton (1940) and Grady (1965). (Also see Sterling, 1967). In this empiricist tradition (in its American pragmatist version), knowledge is derived from observations in the "real world" (sensory experience), abstraction, and generalization obtained by the study of such observations. This view of the world is akin to the legal realist perspective in that any rules cited in the argument for or against an existing practice are rationalizations.

Some significant departures from this tradition are Moonitz, 1961; (Sprouse and Moonitz, 1962), AAA monograph titled "A Statement of Basic Accounting Theory" (ASOBAT), and the FASB conceptual framework project. Rejecting the idea of building a theory of accounting purely from a priori knowledge on the ground of its inapplicability in dealing with issues such as measurement and disclosures, Moonitz suggested a strategy in which we "first recognize and define the problems to be solved, then move to their solution by careful attention to what 'ought' to be the case, not what 'is' the case." Interestingly, this is the approach of what has been called the "rationalist tradition" by Winograd and Flores (1986). On the one hand both Moonitz (and Sprouse and Moonitz) and ASOBAT were attempts to axiomatize accounting and were therefore in the legal positivist tradition of cataloging accounting standards (although neither claimed their catalogue to be exhaustive) and on the other hand

104

some of their postulates (such as continuity, objectivity, consistency, and disclosure in the Sprouse and Moonitz study; relevance, verifiability, freedom from bias, and quantifiability in ASOBAT) could be interpreted as "principles" in the Dworkin sense and hence these studies could be looked upon, in retrospect, as attempts in the sociological jurisprudential tradition. Similarly, the primary and secondary qualitative characteristics of accounting information in FASB Concepts Statement No. 2 (predictive value, feedback value, timeliness, comparability, consistency, verifiability, neutrality, and representational faithfulness) could be interpreted as "principles" in the Dworkin sense if "shall" is added to their use.

The above discussion[2] has some very important implications on the way we view accounting "standards" and consequently on the development of a computational framework for them. The first obvious implication is for us to sort out "standards" into principles and rules. In accounting, we have traditionally used the terms principles and standards rather ambiguously, and a study of their use in the philosophy of law can help us sharpen our analysis of standards into principles and rules.

The second implication is the need for us to develop descriptive theories of reasoning in accounting which help us to interpret the rules in the context of principles and policies at any point in time and to resolve conflicting rules by evoking principles and policies. Yuji Ijiri's (1975) "Theory of Accounting Measurement" is probably the only effort in this area of research. It is important to recognize that, as in law, principles need to originate "in a sense of appropriateness developed in the profession and the public over time. Their continued power depends upon this sense of appropriateness being sustained" (Dworkin 1967). Accounting rules (and FASB statements, in some sense, can be construed as rules), on the other hand, are adopted in the context of the status of principles and policies at a particular point in time.

The third implication is that efforts at axiomatization of accounting are futile and doomed to failure, because principles are conflicting of necessity (traditional apparatus of logic demands consistency) and in general rules also can be inconsistent (such inconsistencies are noticed when new types of transactions or securities evolve). The fourth implication is that since accounting rules (and ultimately even accounting principles) are adopted in a sociological setting, criticism of failure of specific accounting

rules to conform to specific basic accounting principles is tanta-
mount to arrogance in claiming pre-emptive status for accounting principles over public policy objectives. Just as legal rules (in
statutes) are enacted in the context of certain public policy objectives and are interpreted with legal principles in the background,
we would need to consider accounting rules as formulated in the
context of certain public policy objectives and interpreted with
the accounting principles in the background. Viewed in this
light, subordination of an accounting principle by public policy
in any particular rule does not torpedo such a principle, but only
erodes it in that specific context. Subordination of the "representational faithfulness" or "substance over form" principle by the
public policy objective (higher productive investment in the
economy) in the context of accounting for investment tax credit,
for example, did not bury the "substance over form" principle,
but only eroded it in the context of accounting for certain types
of assets.

The consequences of the above discussion on the development
of a computational framework for accounting standards (and
hence for the development of "intelligent" decision support systems for accounting standards) are indeed profound. The first
consequence is that we can not look upon accounting as a closed
and consistent system. Until we develop principles, rules, and
theories for resolving conflicting rules, and models for evocation
of principles to determine the accounting treatment of "hard"
transactions (which are our analogs of hard cases in law), it is
unrealistic to attempt development of what may be termed a
"GAAP machine." It is difficult to make a convincing case for
the mere possibility of such a machine considering the "open
texture" of accounting concepts (we do not even have semantically unambiguous understanding of such basic concepts as
"assets") and absence of theories of reasoning in accounting. (See
Gardner [1987] or Hart [1961] for a discussion of "open texture"
in law.)

What has been said above may convey an impression that the
future for computational work in the area of accounting standards is not very bright. Far from it. The computational view
forces us to ask questions (to clarify definitions, reduce ambiguities, to discover the way we reason about problems) we accountants may not have asked before—it strikes at the very
foundations of what we believe accounting to be. To twist a
saying of Alfred North Whitehead (1925) in the context of

science, if accounting is not to degenerate into a medley of ad hoc hypotheses (and definitions and rules), it must become philosophical and must enter upon a thorough criticism of its own foundations.

The second consequence is that decision support systems for accounting which incorporate knowledge regarding accounting standards belong to a category that Smith and Deedman call "hairy systems"; such systems need to incorporate knowledge regarding accounting standards as well as accounting theory.

The third consequence is that development of an intelligent decision support system, at the present state of development of accounting theory and standards, is possible only in narrow domains for determining GAAP conformity accounting treatment of relatively easy (or perhaps well understood) transactions, since semantic as well as syntactic ambiguities here can be controlled (1) at the systems development stage by suitable disambiguation of the rules and enforced consistency of rules in the narrow domain, and (2) at run-time by providing for effective user-interaction. I will return to these issues after some rudimentary discussion of representation of knowledge in a declarative framework in the next section.

3. On A Declarative Representation of Knowledge Regarding Accounting Standards

The accounting standards, like written law, contain ambiguities, complex logical structures, considerable rhetoric, confusing mixture of object language, and meta-language statements, primitives that are open to differing interpretations, predicates that are "open textured"[3] and counterfactual conditionals. The process of disambiguation of accounting standards and their representation in a logical schema therefore is not a trivial task, but such an undertaking has many advantages. It can aid in generating accounting alternatives that are logical consequences of a set of current standards or in locating inconsistencies in the set of such standards. It can aid in the study of logical consequences of introduction, deletion or alteration of an existing standard. At a fundamental level, the very process of representation of knowledge regarding accounting standards in a logical fashion can provide insights into the operation of such standards. The study of knowledge representation schemes can

107

also considerably enhance our understanding of the generally accepted accounting principles.

The generally accepted accounting principles are an element of the environment in which accounting information systems function, and therefore representation of knowledge regarding accounting standards can contribute toward the building of "intelligent" information and decision support systems for accounting as well as auditing. In particular, alternative GAAP conforming accounting treatments of a given transaction for recording and financial reporting purposes can be obtained in such an intelligent decision support system by utilizing forward chaining (or bottom-up or data-driven) inference, starting from the details of a given transaction. Auditing a transaction for GAAP conformity, on the other hand, is equivalent to deducing the actual treatment of the transaction as a theorem of the GAAP knowledge base, using backward chaining (or top-down or goal-driven) inferences. In all of the discussions for the remainder of the paper, I treat accounting standards as rules as defined in the previous section, and assume that we are talking about a sufficiently narrow domain. The fact that deduction is not necessarily the only reasoning mechanism used for thinking about accounting standards also should be borne in mind in reading this section. I shall, however consider only deduction in this paper.

In the remainder of this section, I shall discuss the differences between imperative and declarative styles of knowledge representation, and provide a brief discussion of the logic programming language "PROLOG."

Most current representations of our knowledge regarding specific aspects of GAAP are imperative in the sense that our preoccupation is with the flow of control in deduction within the framework of GAAP rather than with the description of our knowledge regarding GAAP. For example, we draw flowcharts to apply specific accounting principles (e.g., APB 29 on nonmonetary exchanges or FASB 15 on accounting for troubled debt restructuring). Our preoccupation is with determining the flow of control (i.e., how we traverse through the flowchart). While flowcharts are extremely useful tools to understand GAAP and to answer routine questions, they are essentially one-dimensional in that they can answer only a pre-determined set of questions. Such charts are also "dumb" in the sense that there is only one way of traversing through them; there is no way of using the cumulative facts gathered in the course of traversing through the flowchart except the way in which the flowchart has already incorporated them. Moreover, if the questions we want answered are different, so must the flowcharts be. If there are changes in the accounting standard, revisions to the flowcharts must be extensive. If such changes are extensive, then the existing flowcharts may be rendered entirely irrelevant.

In a declarative representation of knowledge regarding accounting standards, we describe the knowledge regarding such standards in a knowledge base and let the "inference" mechanism do the job of controlling the flow of reasoning. The advantage here is that our preoccupation is with describing our knowledge regarding accounting standards (as it ought to be) rather than with telling the computer how to go about answering the questions—with logic rather than with control. (See Kowalski, 1979). In some sense, in this approach the epistemological and heuristic aspects of the design of "intelligent" systems is handled separately (but not necessarily independently). (See McCarthy and Hayes, 1969). This of course does not mean that in the design of a knowledge base we can safely ignore the control aspects; one can do so only at the cost of efficiency.

One popular language which encourages declarative programming is "PROLOG." It has been referred to in the literature variously as object-oriented[4] (Robinson, 1986), relational (Walker et al., 1987), non-von Neumann (Sterling and Shapiro, 1986), and a goal-oriented language (Bratko, 1986). PROLOG has gained considerable attention in the artificial intelligence community because of its declarative style (Clark and McCabe, 1984), programmability (Levesque, 1986), ease of object-oriented programming style (Hogger, 1985), its foundations in first-order predicate logic (Kowalski, 1974), and its close relationship with the relational database structure (Frost, 1986). For the rest of this paper we will use the micro-PROLOG[5] version of the language (McCabe et al., 1985) and an augmented PROLOG development system APES. (Hammond and Sergot, 1985).

In PROLOG,[6] a program consists of a set of clauses (or axioms). The clauses may be facts such as

table is__asset__surrendered	(1)
chair is__asset__received	(2)
cash is__monetary__asset	(3)
receivable is__monetary__asset	(4)

109

or rules[7] such as

transaction is＿monetary
    if ＿X is＿asset＿surrendered and
    ＿X is monetary＿asset   (5)

transaction is monetary
    if ＿X is＿asset＿received and
    ＿X is＿monetary＿asset   (6)

In the above, (1) and (2) say that in the transaction under consideration, table and chair are respectively asset given up and asset received. The next two facts indicate that cash and receivable are both monetary assets. Rule (5) (rule (6)) states that a transaction is monetary if the asset surrendered (asset received) is monetary; ＿X being a variable. In the above, table, chair, cash, receivable, and transaction are all objects; is＿asset＿surrendered, is＿asset＿received, is＿monetary＿asset are all propositions about the objects. This object orientation, as can be seen from the above, is natural in PROLOG.

In the PROLOG language, clauses in the program are assumed to be universally quantified in the variables and therefore rule (5) for example can be read as "for all ＿X, if ＿X is asset surrendered and ＿X is a monetary asset, then the transaction is monetary," which is the declarative reading of the rule. This rule can also be given an imperative interpretation as follows: "To prove that the transaction is monetary, we need to prove that the asset surrendered is monetary." Such an imperative reading of clauses is used in PROLOG to break down goals into sub-goals (for details see Clocksin and Mellish, 1984).

It should be observed that the right-hand side (called condition, antecedent, or protasis) of rules (5) and (6) consist of a conjunction of conditions whereas the left-hand side (called conclusion, consequent, or apodasis) is a single conclusion. Clauses which consist of a single conclusion but conjunction of conditions is called a Horn clause. All PROLOG clauses must be Horn clauses (also referred to in the literature as Kowalski clausal form). It can be shown that any problem that can be expressed in logic can be re-expressed in Horn clauses, and therefore Horn clause representation is adequate for most purposes (Kowalski 1979).

Now given a goal such as

    is (transaction is＿monetary)   (7)

computation in PROLOG consists of deriving a constructive proof of (7) from the axiom system (1)-(6). The axiom system and the goal together constitute a PROLOG program.

In general, if goals contain variables, they are assumed to be existentially quantified. If we give goal (7), the PROLOG compiler (or interpreter) searches the data/knowledge base (consisting of (1)-(6)) for a clause with a conclusion that matches the goal "transaction is___monetary." Since it finds such a conclusion in rule (5), the imperative interpretation of this rule is invoked and therefore the two sub-goals "___X is___asset___surrendered" and "___X is___monetary___asset" are substituted for goal (7). To satisfy the sub-goal "___X is___asset___surrendered," the interpreter will search the knowledge base for an instance of the relation "is___asset___surrendered"; when it is found in rule (1), the variable ___X will be bound to the object "table." The first sub-goal having been achieved, the next sub-goal "table is___monetary___asset" is considered; since there are no clauses in the knowledge base satisfying this sub-goal, it fails. At this stage, the interpreter will backtrack to the earlier sub-goal to see if there are any other facts about the relation is___asset___surrendered. Not finding any other instances of this relation, the interpreter will search the knowledge base to see if there are any other rules whose conclusion matches the goal. Since the conclusion in rule (6) matches the goal "transaction is___monetary," the process delineated above is repeated for this rule. It is easy to see that the final answer that the program will come up with is "no."

What we have described above is in fact an algorithm for answering the question: Is the transaction monetary? We described our knowledge regarding transactions and posed a question in a program; the resultant behavior of the PROLOG interpreter in executing the program was an algorithm. An interesting observation here is that such an algorithm can also provide the chain of reasoning used to arrive at the conclusion, i.e., it can answer the question: Why is the transaction not monetary?

Now, let us suppose we wanted to know if note is a monetary asset. If we pose this query as below

$$\text{is (note is\_\_monetary\_\_asset)} \tag{8}$$

we get the rather disturbing answer "no." We know that this can not be so because note is a monetary asset as defined in Paragraph No. 3 of APB Opinion No. 29. The reason for the negative answer is what is called "closed-world assumption," under which a relation not known to hold is assumed not to hold (Reiter, 1978). In PROLOG,[8] the closed-world assumption is implemented by the meta-rule called "negation as failure": We infer not X if every proof of X fails. In our example above, since note is not known to be monetary it is not assumed to be monetary.

It is important to note in the above that the PROLOG interpreter will search the knowledge base in the order in which the clauses are arranged, from top to bottom and from left to right. This is a necessity because most computers used presently are sequential (or von Neumann). In the execution of the above program, rule (6) was verified before rule (7) simply because the former appeared earlier in the program. Similarly, the sub-goal "__X0 is__asset__surrendered" was examined before the sub-goal "__X is__monetary" simply because the former appeared to the left of the latter in rule (6). In general, the sub-goals can be pursued in parallel if the program is run on a parallel machine. Our earlier comment that in the design of a knowledge base, control aspects can be ignored only at the cost of efficiency is relevant here. The arrangement of the clauses in the knowledge base and the arrangement of the conditions in the clauses determine the program execution time.

In answering the query in (7), the interpreter matched it with the conclusion and then invoked the imperative reading of the relevant rule to substitute the sub-goals. The sub-goals were taken up from left to right; a sub-goal considered for execution by the program only when all the sub-goals to the left have been achieved. In other words, PROLOG uses a top-down (backward chaining)[9] depth-first strategy in searching for solutions.

It should be apparent from the above discussion that the emphasis has been on describing our knowledge in terms of objects and relations between objects or propositions about objects. As observed earlier, this object orientation is natural to PROLOG programming. This object orientation is crucial from the point of view of developing intelligent decision support systems for accounting as well as auditing, since such orientation is the foundation for the conceptual framework of GAAP. The entity assumption is central to accounting; so are the concepts of elements of financial statements such as assets, liabilities, equities, and so forth. These elements also can be looked upon as objects. The focus of accounting theory, in such a scenario, is on such objects, relations between them, and propositions about them.

Nothing that has been said so far should create an impression that PROLOG is the only language in which declarative programs can be written. Such an interpretation would be confusing the representation framework we have adopted (declarative) with its implementation (PROLOG). One could in fact implement the framework in any language that permits recursion, such as LISP, SMALLTALK, or even perhaps PASCAL. Our choice of PROLOG is motivated by ease of programming, its affinity to first order logic and the relational database model (which is perhaps the dominant paradigm for accounting databases at the present time), and the ease of writing parsers (for creating natural language front-ends to build "user-friendly" systems).

4. Development of a Knowledge Base for FASB 48

The accounting standards are written in a natural language (English) and therefore exhibit ambiguity, semantic richness, and extremely complicated rules for inference that make automated inference virtually impossible. To accomplish automation of inference, we must look for a formal language that sacrifices semantic richness in return for reduced ambiguity and simpler rules of inference. The development of a knowledge base for accounting standards involves selection of such formalism. Once the formalism is chosen, the next step involves the translation of the standards from the natural language English into the formalism chosen. This step in turn involves gaining an understanding of what the standards actually mean (semantic analysis) and the choice of level of detail desired in the representation. This section deals with all these issues and provides an illustration of development of a toy knowledge base for FASB Statement No. 48 on "Revenue Recognition Where Right of Return Exists."

The three popular formalisms suggested in the literature for representing domain knowledge that are relevant to our discussions here are propositional logic (Sommers, 1985), predicate logic in various forms (Levesque and Brachman, 1985), and semantic networks (Quillian, 1969; Woods, 1975; and

Brachman, 1979). It is well known that propositional logic is not expressive enough. Semantic network representations, while being alternatives to predicate logic, are cumbersome in representing predicates with more than two arguments and lack standard representation (for details see Grishman, 1986). The semantics of predicate calculus, on the other hand, is quite standard and well understood. In this study, we represent accounting standards in an extended Horn clause subset of first order predicate logic implemented in PROLOG. This representation has been found adequate in studies in knowledge representation in law (Sergot et al., 1985), geology, medicine, biochemistry, engineering, and statistics (for details see Hammond and Sergot, 1985; Chapter 7) and taxation (Schlobohm, 1985).

The accounting standards contain ambiguities which may be intentional or unintentional in nature. The standard setters may, on purpose, introduce ambiguities to cover situations not foreseen at the time the standards are adopted, to preclude substitution of mechanical rules for professional judgment or simply to reflect the incompleteness or fuzziness of our understanding of certain accounting concepts. Such ambiguities are usually semantic in nature, make the accounting standards "open textured," and generally serve useful purposes. On the other hand, there are ambiguities in the standards simply because they are poorly drafted. These are usually syntactic in nature and are a source of much confusion because of their susceptibility to alternate and conflicting interpretations (see Allen, 1957, 1963, 1980; Allen and Engholm, 1978; Allen and Saxon, 1987). The most common ambiguities of the latter kind are a result of using confusing logical connectives such as "unless" and "only if." Allen suggests "normalization" of the text to reduce such ambiguities. Normalized text replaces all "maskers of meaning" by the "lowest common denominators of structural discourse": conjunction (and), disjunction (or), conditional (if . . . then . . .), and equivalence (if and only if). The accounting standards, as they are written, are syntactically perhaps far less ambiguous than some statutes (the Internal Revenue Code, for instance). In this paper, syntactic ambiguities are resolved by examining the intent of the standard as provided in the background information.

The choice regarding the level of detail in representation is crucial from the point of view of integrity, readability, and maintainability of programs. The level of detail involves the choice of predicates. The literature in computational linguistics suggests two possibilities. The first possibility is to observe a close correspondence between words in the natural language text and predicates (Grishman, 1986). The other possibility is to decompose predicates in such a way that any two synonymous sentences will have identical semantic representation, as suggested in the "conceptual dependency theory" of Schank (1977). We follow the first possibility because of the criteria given above and the ease of programming.

In the remainder of this section, I shall illustrate the development of a toy knowledge base to represent paragraph 6 of FASB Statement 48 on "Revenue Recognition Where the Right of Return Exists." My objective here is to study the problems that one encounters in the process and not to develop a finished product.[10] I shall use the principles of top-down design where concepts are successfully refined till we reach a stage where they are primitives. This strategy in software design has the advantage in our context that as accounting theory develops, concepts which are currently primitives can be refined by new definitions at a still lower level. When APES is used, for example, this strategy is ideal since concepts which are to be treated as primitives can be set interactive so that if facts do not exist in the knowledge base the program will request the user for information.

The FASB Statement 48 "specifies criteria for recognizing revenue when the buyer has the right of return" (para 3), so that given a transaction one can determine if the revenue from the sale can be recognized at sale date: if the criteria are satisfied by the transaction, revenue is recognized at sale date, otherwise not. The main rule is given in paragraph 6 which states: "If an enterprise sells its product but gives the buyer the right to return the product, [then] (revenue from the sales transaction shall be recognized at time of sale only if all of the following conditions are met)" and proceeds to list six conditions. Here we have inserted the word "then" in brackets and stated the rest of the conditional in braces to clearly identify the antecedents and the consequents. Since the outer conditional specifies the conditions in which the rule within braces applies, we have the first rule

FASB__48__para__6 applies
    if transaction is__a__sale and
        buyer has__right__of__return   (9)

The conditional in braces is ambiguous and we can interpret it in at least two different ways as follows:

Interpretation I: (Logical "only if" in object language). "If revenue from the sales transaction shall be recognized at time of sale, [then] the six conditions [will] have been met."

Interpretation II: (Logical "only if" in meta-language). "If the six conditions are met [then] revenue from the sales transaction shall be recognized at the time of sale" expresses the only condition in which the statement "Revenue from the sales transaction shall be recognized at time of sale" holds.

While these two interpretations are different, they entail the same conclusions which are justified in different, but structurally same ways. (Kowalski, 1979, Ch. 11). It should be noted that neither of the above interpretations imply in the object language that if the six conditions are satisfied, then revenue can be recognized at sale date, which obviously is the FASB intent. It is therefore reasonable to conclude that what FASB intended was the following interpretation:

Interpretation III: (Logical "if and only if").

    A. "If the six conditions are met, then revenue from the sales transaction shall be recognized at the time of sale" (the "if" part).

and B. "If the six conditions are not met, then revenue from the sales transaction shall not be recognized at the time of sale" (the "only if" part).

It is extremely difficult to represent "if and only if" statements in Horn clause logic because of infinite looping (in the imperative reading of programs). It may be observed in the interpretation III that we need part B, in general, for answering queries involving negation (e.g., is it not the case that revenue is recognized at time of sale?). In natural language, it is common to leave unstated the "only if" part of "if and only if" definitions. In PROLOG, "only if" halves of definitions are assumed to be intended by the closed world assumption implemented in the meta-rule "negation as failure" and therefore they can be left unstated. With this discussion in view, we have the rule:

116

sale date is revenue recognition date
    if FASB—48—para—6 applies and
    FASB—48—para—6a—f are—met   (10)

where FASB—48—para—6a—f are the six conditions, and the following rule to define deferral of revenue recognition.

sale date is—not—revenue—recognition—date
    if not (sale—date is—revenue—recognition—date)   (11)

To make explicit what we mean by the six conditions being met, we have the following:

FASB—48—para—6a—f are—met
  if FASB—48—para—6a   is—met and
      FASB—48—para—6b   is—met and
      FASB—48—para—6c   is—met and
      FASB—48—para—6d   is—met and
      FASB—48—para—6e   is—met and
      FASB—48—para—6f   is—met   (12)

FASB—48—para—6a—f are—not—met
    if not (FASB—48—para—6a—f are—met)   (13)

The above rules illustrate the awkwardness of representing number restrictions in first order logic. As Levesque and Brachman (1985) observe, one would require a sentence with 10^{11} conjuncts to say that there are a hundred billion stars in the Milky Way galaxy.

The first condition of paragraph 6 is satisfied if "the seller's price to the buyer is substantially fixed or determinable at the date of sale." The semantic ambiguity arises here because of the use of "substantially" and "determinable," the accountant being required to exercise professional judgment. In designing decision support systems, one can write rules defining "substantial" and "determinable" to account for all conceivable situations or leave the ambiguity in the predicate and allow the user to provide the information. The syntactic ambiguity arises because of the use of "or"—whether the condition is to be interpreted as "(substantially fixed) or (substantially determinable)" or as "(substantially fixed) or (determinable.)" In the legal context, such issues would be clarified by case law or by an examination of the objective of the statute. In financial accounting, interpretations and technical bulletins are issued when FASB is called upon to clarify such issues. If such pronouncements do not exist, in the final analysis, courts can be called upon to rule on them if they are issues under dispute or are arguments for a specific position in the dispute. For our purposes here, if the latter interpretations are adopted, we have the rules:

> FASB__48__para__6a is__met
> if price__to__buyer is__substantially__fixed__at
> sale__date   (14)

> FASB__48__para__6a is __met
> if price__to__buyer is__determinable__at
> sale__date   (15)

The second condition is straight forward and we have the rules:

> FASB__48__para__6b is__met
> if buyer has__paid seller   (16)

> FASB__48__para__6b is__met
> if buyer is__obligated__to__pay seller and
> obligation__to__pay is__not__contingent__on
> product__resale   (17)

A COUNTERFACTUAL:

The sentence fragments that we have come across until now were in the indicative mood, and were (or could be interpreted as) basically declarative in nature. The antecedents as well as the consequents in such statements are usually grammatical sentences and are propositions which are "not put forward as matters of fact, but simply as propositions to be entertained and indicated as related in terms of cause, conclusion, consequence" (see Appiah, 1986 and Palmer, 1986). The condition in 6.c on the other hand, is in the subjunctive mood and states that the "buyer's obligation to the seller **would not be** changed in the event of theft or physical destruction or damage of the product." Since the use of "if," or "in case of" in place of "in the event of" does not alter the meaning, the condition can be restated as "if there were theft or . . . the buyer's obligation would not be changed." (Curme, 1931). Subjunctive conditionals with antecedents known or expected to be false are called counterfactuals (Anderson, 1951).

The material conditionals that we have been using until now in this paper are truth-functional in the sense that the truth value of such conditionals are determined exclusively by the truth values of the corresponding antecedents and consequents; the truth value of counterfactual conditionals, on the other hand, depend on more than the truth values of their components. Counterfactual conditionals are vague and context dependent (Ginsberg, 1986). For example, substituting "pigs would fly" for "obligation to pay the seller would not be changed" in the above conditional, when it is interpreted as a material conditional, would make it true;[11] interpreted as a counterfactual, on the other hand, the condition in 6.c is likely to be true but not the conditional with "pigs would fly" substitution. The counterfactual conditionals tell us something other than what merely the truth values of their components would suggest. Many well-known rules of inference such as contraposition are not valid for counterfactuals (see Lewis, 1973 and Kvart, 1986).

The analysis of counterfactuals has attracted the attention of many logicians and philosophers. While there is considerable dissension among them with regard to the appropriate analysis of such conditionals, we follow Rescher's (1964) analysis of counterfactuals. In such analysis, the conditional in 6.c is to be viewed as a counterfactual specification of the covering generalization "theft, damage, or physical destruction does not alter the buyer's obligation" in the same way as the Rescher's counterfactual statement, "If Julius Caesar had been a lion, he would have had a tail" is the counterfactual specification of the covering law "all lions have tails." The Uniform Commercial Code section 2-509 and 327 specify that, **in the absence of agreement to the contrary,** the risk (for theft, damage, or loss) for the goods of sale is transferred to the buyer on receipt (if seller is a merchant), tender (if seller is not a merchant), receipt of title (when goods are held by bailee to be delivered without being moved) or acceptance (if sale on approval). We can therefore interpret the condition in 6.c as requiring the absence of an agreement whereby the seller bears the risk. We now have:

FASB__48__para__6c is__met
  if not (risk__transfer__clause is__in__
    sales__agreement)   (18)

The next three conditions provide us the following rules:

FASB__48__para__6d is__met
if buyer acquires__product__for resale and
buyer has__economic__substance and
not (buyer economic__substance__provided__only__by
seller)   (19)

FASB__48__para__6e is__met
if seller has__no__significant__obligation__for
future__performance   (20)

FASB__48__para__6f is__met
if future__returns can__be__reasonably
__estimated   (21)

It should be obvious from the above that paragraph 6 is replete with concepts that require exercise of professional judgment: "substantially fixed," "economic substance," "significant obligations," and "reasonably estimated." In building intelligent decision support systems, we need to specify what such terms mean. It also contains syntactic ambiguities. My purpose in this section has been to show that representation of accounting standards in extended Horn clauses is feasible, and in some sense desirable since it forces us to examine the "open textured" nature of accounting standards. In this section, I have directed my attention to the syntactic ambiguities except in the discussion of the counterfactual in 6.c. An in-depth semantic analysis of the accounting standards requires us to go beyond the realms of accounting and consider the use of language particularly in law.

5. Concluding Remarks:

In this paper I have drawn parallels between the philosophy of law and accounting theory and examined the feasibility of representation of accounting standards in the computational framework of extended Horn clause logic. In accounting, we generally emphasize syntactic knowledge at the expense of a fuller understanding of semantics of accounting standards. The framework provided here forces us to clarify the use (or abuse) of language in the formulation of accounting rules. It also provides a basis for examining the epistemological prerequisites for developing intelligent accounting information and decision support systems for accounting standards.

Footnotes

1. "A hard case is one which does not fall under an existing rule of law, or which appears to fall under two rules, the application of which could lead to differing or opposing solutions one from the other, or a case which falls clearly under a rule of law, the application of which would produce an irrational result." See Smith and Deedman (1987, p. 85).

2. The preceding discussion should not be construed as a summarized history of accounting thought. I have, for example, not considered the jurimetrics movement in law and its counterpart market-based empirical research in accounting. Both of these are, in some sense, in the tradition of behaviorism rather than cognitivism; the emphasis being on not on how attorneys (and judges) or accountants (and users of accounting information) do or should reason but on "what statistical measures will most conveniently summarize the(ir) behavior." See Gardner (1987).

3. The term "open texture" is due to Hart (1961) and refers to "inherent indeterminacy of meaning in the words by which fact situations are classified into instances and non-instances of legal concepts." See Gardner (1987), and also Putnam (1975).

4. In object-oriented programming, procedures (called methods) are local to and determine the behavior of objects. Methods are also "messages" which, if sent to objects, are recognized by them. In PROLOG, on the other hand, predicates double as procedures, and their invocation is pattern-directed. PROLOG is, therefore, strictly speaking, not object-oriented. It has nevertheless been referred to as being such, because of the prominence of objects in thinking about programs. Two of the important characteristics of object-oriented programming (inheritance and message sending) are natural to PROLOG. Because of this and its declarative nature, building an object-oriented programming environment in PROLOG is relatively straightforward (Stabler 1986). An object-oriented PROLOG implementation is available on top of the language "SMALLTALK" in the dialect "SMALLTALK v" (see DIGITALK 1986). Nevertheless, object-oriented programming in PROLOG is currently in experimental stages.

5. The fragments of PROLOG code presented in this paper are written in the syntax of the "simple" natural language front-end of the micro-PROLOG interpreter, or something like it. This syntax is very English-like and therefore easy to "sentence" since that is what it looks like.

6. What follows is by no means a rigorous introduction to PROLOG programming. Interested readers may refer to Clocksin and Mellish (1982), Clark and McCabe (1984), Sterling and Shapiro (1986), Bratko (1986), Marcus (1986), or Giannesini et al. (1986).

7. By rules, we mean that which logicians call "material conditionals." For details, see Quine (1982). For an interesting discussion in an accounting context, see Christenson (1984).

8. The closed world assumption makes the knowledge base complete, but in general, it also makes it inconsistent. Negation as failure is not the same as logical negation. Because of these, care needs to be exercised in designing systems using PROLOG. The language, however, is versatile enough to be useful for many types of problems. For details on these issues, please see Flanagan (1986) and Reiter (1978).

9. While most PROLOG implementations use this strategy, it by no means precludes one from using forward chaining strategy. For an example of forward chaining in PROLOG see Walker et al. (1987) or Merritt (1986).

10. To keep the discussion short, I shall not discuss the representation for transactions, which is very important in development of commercial applications.

11. This is so since, as Quine (1982) points out, a conditional is commonly felt

more as a conditional affirmation of the consequent rather than the affirmation of the conditional. A statement "If X then Y" is therefore false only when X is true and Y is false.

References

AAA, *A Statement of Basic Accounting Theory,* AAA, 1966.

Allen, Lyman, "Symbolic Logic: A Razor-Edged Tool for Drafting and Interpreting Legal Documents," *Yale Law Journal* 66, 1957, pp. 833–879.

———, "Beyond Document Retrieval, Toward Information Retrieval," 47 *Minnesota Law Review* 713, 1963.

———, "Language, Law and Logic: Plain Drafting for the Electronic Age," in Bryan Niblett, (ed.), *Computer Science and Law,* Cambridge University Press, 1980, pp. 75–100.

——— and C. Rudy Engholm, "Normalized Legal Drafting and the Query Method," *Journal of Legal Education,* Vol. 29, 1978, pp. 380–412.

——— and Charles S. Saxon, "Some Problems in Designing Expert Systems to Aid Legal Reasoning," in *Proceedings of the First International Conference on Artificial Intelligence and Law,* ACM Press, 1987, pp. 94–103.

Anderson, A. Ross, "A Note on Subjunctive and Counterfactual Conditionals," in *Analysis,* Vol. 12, 1951, pp. 35–38.

Appiah, Anthony, *Assertion and Conditionals,* Cambridge University Press, 1986.

Austin, John, *Lectures on Jurisprudence.* 2 vols. 5th ed. Revised and edited by Robert Campbell, John Murray (pub.), 1885.

Brachman, Ronald J., "On the Epistemological Status of Semantic Networks," in *Associative Networks: Representation and Use of Knowledge by Computers,* Nicholas V. Findler (ed.), Academic Press, 1979, pp. 3–50.

Bratko, Ivan, *PROLOG Programming for Artificial Intelligence,.* Addison-Wesley, 1986.

Christenson, Charles, "The Methodology of Positive Accounting," *Accounting Review,* January 1983, pp. 1–22.

Clark, K. L. and F. G. McCabe, *Micro-PROLOG: Programming in Logic,* Prentice-Hall, 1984.

Clocksin, W. F. and C. S. Mellish, *Programming in PROLOG,* Springer-Verlag, 1984.

Curme, George O., *Syntax,* D. C. Heath, 1931.

Digitalk, Inc., *Smalltalk/v Tutorial and Programming Handbook,* Digitalk, 1986.

Durant, Will, *The Story of Civilization: The Life of Greece,* Simon and Schuster, 1966.

Dworkin, Ronald M., "The Model of Rules," 35 *University of Chicago Law Review* 14, 1967. Reprinted in *Philosophy of Law,* 2nd ed. Joel Feinberg and Hyman Gross (eds.), Wadsworth, 1980.

———, *Taking Rights Seriously,* Harvard University Press, 1977.

Flanagan, Tim, "The Consistency of Negation as Failure," *The Journal of Logic Programming,* July 1986, pp. 93–114.

Frank, Jerome, *Courts on Trial,* Princeton University Press, 1949.

Frost, Richard, *Introduction to Knowledge-Based Systems,* Macmillan, 1986.

Gardner, Anne von der Lieth, *An Artificial Intelligence Approach to Legal Reasoning,* MIT Press, 1987.

Gardner, Howard, *The Mind's New Science,* Basic Books, 1985.

Giannesini, Francis, Henry Kanoui, Robert Pasero, and Michel van Caneghem, *PROLOG,* Addison-Wesley, 1986.

Ginsberg, Matthew L., "Counterfactuals," *Artificial Intelligence,* Vol. 30, No. 1. 1986, pp. 35–80.

Grady, Paul H., *Inventory of Generally Accepted Accounting Principles,* Accounting Research Study No. 7, AICPA, 1967.

Grishman, Ralph, *Computational Linguistics: An Introduction,* Cambridge University Press, 1986.

Hammond, Peter and Marek Sergot, *APES Programmer's Reference Manual,* Logic Based Systems, 1985.

Hart, H. L. A., *The Concept of Law,* Oxford, 1961.

Hodges, Andrew, *Alan Turing: The Enigma,* Simon and Schuster, 1983.

Hogger, Christopher J., *Introduction to Logic Programming,* Academic Press, 1984.

Holmes, Oliver Wendell, *The Common Law,* edited by Mark DeWolfe Howe, Little, Brown, 1963.

Ijiri, Yuji, *Theory of Accounting Measurement,* Studies in Accounting Research, No. 10, AAA, 1975.

Kowalski, Robert A., "Predicate Logic as a Programming Language," in *Proceedings of IFIP-74,* North-Holland, 1974, pp. 569–574.

———, *Logic for Problem Solving,* American Elsevier Publishing Co. Inc., North-Holland, 1979.

Kvart, Igal, *A Theory of Counterfactuals,* Hackett, 1986.

Levesque, Hector J. and Ronald J. Brachman, "A Fundamental Tradeoff in Knowledge Representation and Reasoning," in *Readings in Knowledge Representation,* R. J. Brachman and H. J. Levesque (eds.), Morgan Kaufmann, 1985.

———, "Knowledge Representation and Reasoning," in *Annual Review of Computer Science,* Vol. 1, 1986, pp. 255–288.

Lewis, David, *Counterfactuals,* Harvard University Press, 1973.

Marcus, Claudia, *PROLOG Programming: Applications for Database Systems, Expert Systems, and Natural Language Systems,* Addison-Wesley, 1986.

McCabe, F. G., K. L. Clark, B. D. Steel, and P. A. Parker, *Micro-PROLOG Professional Programmer's Reference Manual,* Logic Programming Associates, 1985.

McCarthy, John and Patrick Hayes, "Some Philosophical Problems from the Standpoint of Artificial Intelligence," in *Machine Intelligence 4,* B. Meltzer and Donald Michie (eds)., Edinburgh University Press, 1969, pp. 463–502.

Moonitz, Maurice, *The Basic Postulates of Accounting,* Accounting Research Study No. 1, AICPA, 1961.

Palmer, F. R., *Mood and Modality,* Cambridge University Press, 1986.

Paton, W. A., *Accounting Theory,* Ronald Press, 1922.

—— and A. C. Littleton, *Introduction to Corporate Accounting Standards,* AAA, 1940.

Pound, Roscoe, "Mechanical Jurisprudence," 8 *Columbia Law Review* 605, 1908.

Putnam, Hilary, "The Meaning of 'Meaning' " in H. Putnam, *Philosophical Papers, Vol. 2., Mind, Language, and Reality,* Cambridge University Press, 1975. pp. 215–271.

Quillian, M. R., "Semantic Memory," in *Semantic Information Processing,* M. Minsky (ed.), MIT Press, 1968, pp. 227–270.

Quine, W. V., *Methods of Logic,* Harvard University Press, 1982.

Reiter, Raymond, "On Closed World Databases," in *Logic and Databases,* H. Gallaire and J. Minker (eds.), Plenum Press, 1978.

Rescher, Nicholas, *Hypothetical Reasoning,* North-Holland, 1964.

Robinson, Philip R., *Using Turbo PROLOG,* McGraw-Hill, 1986.

Rodell, Fred, *WOE UNTO YOU, LAWYERS!,* Pagent-Poseidon, 1959.

Schank, Roger C., "Identification of Conceptualizations Underlying Natural Language," in *Computer Models of Thought and Language,* R. Schank and K. Colby (eds.), W. H. Freeman, 1973.

Schlobohm, D. A., "A PROLOG Program which Analyzes Income Tax Issues under Section 381(a) of the Internal Revenue Code" in *Computing Power and Legal Reasoning,* C. Walter (ed.), West Publishing, 1985, pp. 765–815.

Sergot, M. J., F. Sadri, R. A. Kowalski, F. Kriwaczek, P. Hammond, and H. T. Cory, "The British Nationality Act as a Logic Program," *Communications of the Association for Computing Machinery,* May 1986, pp. 370–386.

Smith, J. C. and Cal Deedman, "The Application of Expert Systems Technology to Case-based Law," in *Proceedings of the First International Conference on Artificial Intelligence and Law,* ACM Press, 1987, pp. 84–93.

Sommers, Fred, *The Logic of Natural Language,* Oxford University Press, 1982.

Sprouse, Robert T. and Maurice Moonitz, *A Tentative Set of Broad Accounting Principles for Business Enterprises,* Accounting Research Study No. 3, AICPA, 1962.

Stabler, Edward, "Object-Oriented Programming in PROLOG," *AI Expert,* October, 1986. pp. 46–57.

Sterling, Leon and Ehud Shapiro, *The Art of PROLOG: Advanced Programming Techniques,* MIT Press, 1986.

Sterling, Robert R., "A Statement of Basic Accounting Theory: A Review Article," *Journal of Accounting Research,* Spring 1967, pp. 95–112.

Walker, Adrian (ed.), Michael McCord, John F. Sowa and Walter G. Wilson, *Knowledge Systems and PROLOG: A Logical Approach to Expert Systems and Natural Language Processing,* Addison-Wesley, 1987.

Whitehead, A. N., *Science and the Modern World,* Macmillan, 1925.

———— and Bertrand Russell, *Principia Mathematica,* Cambridge University Press, 1927.

Winograd, Terry and Fernando Flores, *Understanding Computers and Cognition,* Ablex, 1986.

Woods, W. A., "What's in a Link? Foundations for Semantic Networks," in *Representation and Understanding,* D. G. Bobrow and A. M. Collins (eds.), Academic Press, 1975. pp. 35–82.

Expert Systems in Auditing: The State of the Art

WILLIAM F. MESSIER, JR., and
JAMES V. HANSEN

1. Introduction

Over the last five years there has been a growing interest in the development of expert systems for various audit problems. This interest has included both academic researchers and public accounting practitioners. There are several reasons for this interest in expert systems.

First, the audit environment is becoming more complex. The amount and type of knowledge that auditors must possess has increased tremendously over the last fifteen years. This has led to increased specialization within the profession. Industry specialists (e.g., banking, insurance), statistical sampling specialists, and computer audit specialists are examples of this trend. Once this special knowledge has been developed by individuals within a firm, the demands on their time can be enormous. By capturing this special knowledge in an expert system, it is possible to make this domain-specific knowledge available to less experienced members of the firm. This also protects the firm if the expert leaves the firm unexpectedly.

Second, the changes in the Code of Professional Ethics related to competitive bidding, solicitation, and advertising have led to increased competition between firms, resulting in lower audit fees. To combat these changes, public accounting firms are searching for ways to be more efficient while maintaining the same level of effectiveness. One way of improving efficiency is to support auditors with decision aids that allow them to do their work more quickly.

The third force behind expert systems is a desire on the part of practitioners to improve the consensus or agreement of their staffs' judgments across the firm. Early behavioral auditing research (Joyce, 1976; Mock and Turner, 1982) showed that there was low agreement among auditors when making certain audit judgments. From a quality control perspective, public accounting firms would like to minimize such lack of agreement. Structured decision aids are one alternative available to firms for increasing the consensus of their staffs' judgments.

Finally, the successful development of expert systems in medicine, geology, and other related areas has provided the impetus for the possibility of developing such systems to assist auditor judgments.

The remainder of this paper will cover four major topics. First, we present an overview of expert systems. This is followed by a review of eight existing expert systems in auditing. Third, challenges to the successful development of expert systems in auditing are discussed. Fourth, the potential impact of expert systems on audit practice is analyzed. Finally, some concluding comments are made.

2. An Overview of Expert Systems

Expert systems are computer programs that solve complex problems that require some type of expertise. In this part of the paper we discuss, in general terms, the types of problems that are amenable for expert systems, selecting the problem domain for developing expert systems, and the current state of the art in expert systems.

2.1 AMENABLE PROBLEM DOMAINS AND EXPERTISE

Expert systems in auditing are intended to support, not replace, the auditor. As such, we classify them as a type of decision aid. Decision aids vary in their format. At a very basic level, items like internal questionnaires or sample size worksheets (Elliott, 1983) can be viewed as decision aids. More complex decision aids would include computerization of a firm's audit approach and expert systems for specific audit decisions.

128

One way of determining the appropriate type of decision aid is to examine the amount of structure that exists within the problem domain. Problem domains may be classified along a continuum with *highly structured* and *highly unstructured* as the end points and *semi-structured* as a mid-point (Messier and Hansen, 1984). Tasks or decisions that are well specified and which have a unique solution are considered to have highly structured problem domains. As we move away from the structured end of the continuum to the semi- or highly unstructured end, we encounter problem domains where the tasks are not well defined and where more than one solution may be feasible. At the structured end of the continuum, relatively simple-(e.g., questionnaires) or deterministic-(e.g., management science) type decision aids are appropriate. In semi-structured or highly unstructured problem domains, decision aids such as decision support systems (e.g., database management systems) or expert systems are more applicable. The reason why expert systems are more appropriate in unstructured problem domains relates to the fact that the quality of the decision, in many instances, is a function of the expertise of the decision maker.

2.2 SELECTING THE PROBLEM DOMAIN

As suggested above, not all problem domains may be suitable for expert system development. Duda and Gaschnig (1981, p. 262) indicate that the following conditions are necessary for the successful development of an expert system:

1. There must be one human expert acknowledged to perform the task well.
2. The primary source of the expert's exceptional performance must be special knowledge, judgment, and/or experience.
3. The expert must be able to explain the special knowledge and experience and the methods used to apply them to particular problems.
4. The task must have a well-bounded domain of application.

These factors are indeed necessary, but they may not be sufficient. Experience has suggested other criteria which should be added:

First, the completed system should be expected to provide a significant benefit (preferably measurable) to the organization.

That is, the problem being addressed should occur frequently enough to justify the investment. Second, if the problem primarily involves numerical computation, other methods may be more effective. However, if the task involves rules of thumb, symbolic reasoning, handling a very large number of possibilities, or decisions based on incomplete or uncertain information, then an expert system may be the appropriate choice. Third, as the operation's researchers know, the most meticulously constructed model may be of no value if potential users are not enthusiastic about the completed product. Similarly, an expert system may fail if the developers do not consider how to make the system acceptable to the users. Fourth, there must be an appropriate measure for assessing the quality of the expert system's judgments. If the results produced cannot be agreed to by the expert(s), they will certainly be open to challenge. Fifth, the skills required by the task should be teachable to novices. That is, there is experience in teaching the domain knowledge to neophytes. Sixth, the need for the expert system should be likely to continue for several years. This condition is necessary in order to allow the requisite development time and opportunity for payoff.

2.3 STATE OF THE ART

Given the previous discussions, let's examine the current state of the art in expert systems. Buchanan (1982) and Davis (1982) point out that expert systems can handle narrow domains of expertise, have limited languages for knowledge representation, have limited or stylized input/output interfaces, have stylized explanation of their lines of reasoning, and have difficulty handling knowledge from more than one expert.

Expert systems have to deal with relatively narrow domains of expertise mainly because current technology places some limits on the size of the knowledge base. Current knowledge representation languages are also limited to simple frameworks such as frames and IF-THEN rules. Many times, experts have difficulty expressing their knowledge within such frameworks. There is, however, a substantial amount of current research examining alternation knowledge representation schemes.

Since we are unable to communicate with the computer in natural language, expert systems are straddled with very stylized and inflexible input/output communication interfaces. These are usually keyword parsing of input terms and template-generated production of text for output (Davis, 1982). Again, there are major research efforts underway to improve communication capabilities (e.g., more input and output). Similarly, explanation of the expert system's reasoning process is also limited. For example, the answer to a user's question, "How did you arrive at that conclusion?" usually results in a display of the rules used in arriving at the goal.

Current technology is also limited in the use of multiple experts because there is no way of reconciling differing and conflicting views. So while it is helpful to have several experts contributing to the knowledge base, one expert must be responsible for monitoring changes.

3. A Review of Existing Expert Systems

We will briefly review the eight expert systems in auditing that we are aware of that have reached the prototype stage of development. We will also mention a number of other systems that are currently under development.

3.1 AUDITOR

AUDITOR (Dungan and Chandler, 1985) is an expert system that assists an auditor in assessing the adequacy of a client's allowance for bad debts. The system was constructed using the AL/X expert system shell (Paterson, 1984) and was built in three stages: (1) initial modeling of the system goal, rules, and rule weights, (2) refinement of the system using expert auditors operating the system interactively, and (3) a validation test of the system (Dungan and Chandler, 1985, p. 212). After completion of the refinement stage, AUDITOR contained approximately twenty-five primary rules in its knowledge base.

AUDITOR was validated using two procedures. First, an auditor (not involved in the development of AUDITOR) served as a judge by comparing AUDITOR's judgment of the allowance for bad debts with the actual judgments made by the auditors in the field. The expert system's conclusions were judged acceptable in nine out of ten cases. The second procedure was a "blind" validation. In this instance, the auditor judged the acceptability of the judgments without knowing their source. AUDITOR's judgments were rated acceptable in ten of eleven cases. Dungan and Chandler (1985) point out that these results were achieved in clear cut cases (i.e., reserve all or nothing) and that the system will require further refinement to work with accounts that require a partial reserve.

3.2 EDP-XPERT

EDP-XPERT (Hansen and Messier, 1986a, b) is an expert system which is intended to assist Computer Audit Specialists (CASs) in making judgments of the reliability of controls in advanced computer environments. The system also uses the AL/X shell for implementation. The rule base in EDP-XPERT was initially developed based on textbook knowledge and public accounting firm materials. EDP-XPERT, at that point, contained a partial set of rules for controls in a distributed processing system. This initial knowledge base was refined with the help of a Senior CAS. After refinement with the Senior CAS, the system contained 133 rules structured into four goals (the reliability of supervisory, input, processing, and output controls).

A preliminary investigation (Hansen and Messier, 1986b) of the quality of the system's judgments was undertaken using seventeen participants in an initial CAS training program. All subjects evaluated the same case three times: prior to using EDP-XPERT, with EDP-XPERT, and after using EDP-XPERT. The results indicated that, with the exception of the output controls, the subjects' revisions of their control judgments were in the direction of the expert system's conclusions. The subjects' evaluations of EDP-XPERT across nine criteria were reasonable given the state of development of the system.

Since the preliminary investigation, EDP-XPERT's rule base has been expanded to include controls for online, real-time systems and database management systems. The prior rules and the basic goal structure were revised to accommodate the new additions. The rule base was again refined with the assistance of a Senior CAS. The system now has three major goals: supervisory, database management, and application controls. This latest prototype is currently being tested by senior CASs on two major cases and on selected clients.

3.3 CFILE

CFILE is being developed by Peat Marwick Main & Co. (Kelly, Ribar, and Willingham, 1986) to assist auditors in assessing bank loan loss reserves. The current version of CFILE is limited to loans that are due on demand or within one year, and are either unsecured or secured by bank deposits or marketable securities. The system requires two years of audited information or three years of unaudited financial information. It is also limited in its ability to perform and integrate cash flow analysis. Many of these limitations will be overcome with subsequent system development.

The system is implemented in a micro-computer environment using INSIGHT 2 (Level Five Research, 1985) which is a rule-based expert system shell. CFILE has a modular structure with individual modules for sub-goals such as current financial condition of borrower, strength of borrower's collateral, and guarantees. The system has reasonable explanation capabilities, allows for limited sensitivity analysis, and produces adequate documentation for the decision.

Some preliminary field testing has been conducted using CFILE. The testing was carried out using sixteen loans selected from four client bank files. Three subjects (two partners and a senior) participated in the testing. One of the partners was the expert who assisted in CFILE's development. The other partner was experienced in bank auditing while the senior had no bank audit experience.

Each subject made an assessment of each loan without using CFILE and then with the use of CFILE. CFILE classifies a loan into one of nine percentage reserve categories. The results showed that CFILE's judgments were consistent with the expert partner's judgments in nine out of ten loans (90%) using a reserve or no reserve classification. CFILE agreed with the second partner's reserve/no reserve judgments in eleven out of sixteen loans (69%). The results for the inexperienced senior were, as expected, slightly lower (62%). The developers of the system attribute the differences in performance to the expert partner's intimate understanding of the questions and the impact of the responses on CFILE's judgment.

At this point, CFILE performs quite well on loans that require no reserve. Its performance falls off as the loan analysis becomes more difficult, i.e., require a percentage of the loan to be reserved. It appears that additional work will be required to expand the depth of CFILE's knowledge base.

3.4 EXPERTAX

Coopers and Lybrand have developed an expert system called ExperTAX (Shpilberg and Graham, 1986; Shpilberg, Graham and Schatz, 1986) which supports the corporate tax accrual and planning process. More specifically, the system "provides guidance and advice, through issue identification, to auditors and tax specialists in preparing the tax accrual for financial statement purposes. It also identifies relevant issues for tax planning, tax compliance and tax service purposes" (Shpilberg et al., 1986, p. 136).

ExperTAX is unique in that it was not developed using an existing software shell. It was programmed using Common LISP to meet the special needs of the problem domain. The system is frame-based and contains an inference engine which uses forward chaining; a knowledge base which contains the frames, rules, and facts; a user interface for communication with the user; and a knowledge base maintenance system. The system is designed to contain several hundred frames and over 1000 rules.

ExperTAX was developed through the extensive involvement of 20 experts who devoted more than 1000 hours to the project. The initial structure for the knowledge base was obtained in a rather unique manner. Data from a recently completed corporate tax accrual was assembled in a conference room. Two experts (one audit and one tax) were separated by a curtain in the middle of the conference room from the data and an inexperienced staff auditor. The staff auditor was instructed to complete the tax accrual. The experts served as a resource to the staff auditor. Only verbal communication was allowed. Variations of this process were conducted for a total of twelve hours. Two video cameras taped the entire simulation experiment. The data from this experiment and the firm's tax accrual questionnaire served as the basis for the first prototype.

The system was further refined through interactive sessions with partners and managers who regularly conduct tax accrual and planning, tax specialists, and staff auditors. (Shpilberg and Graham, 1986). ExperTAX was validated in an informal manner by having a group of practice partners and managers test the system on a representative set of clients. Shpilberg et. al. (1986, p. 145) conclude that "ExperTAX and its knowledge base performed the task of collecting information better than the former paper method." Subsequent revisions to ExperTAX should make the knowledge base perform even better.

3.5 AUDITPLANNER

Steinbart (forthcoming) developed an expert system as a way of studying auditors' planning stage materiality judgments. He used the EMYCIN (van Melle, 1981) software to implement AUDITPLANNER. The initial rules for the system were taken from the procedures noted in a firm's audit manual and an initial interview with an audit partner who would serve as the expert. The prototype was then refined through a series of five half-day sessions in which the expert ran AUDITPLANNER on a number of actual clients. After each session AUDITPLANNER's knowledge base was edited to reflect specific situations uncovered during the interactive session.

A preliminary evaluation of AUDITPLANNER was conducted using three audit managers and three audit seniors. Five subjects evaluated two client companies and one subject evaluated three companies. The client companies included a wide range of industries. Each evaluator used the information contained in the workpapers to run AUDITPLANNER. The system's judgments were compared to the actual materiality level used on the audit. AUDITPLANNER's recommendations were evaluated as acceptable on eight of the thirteen companies. The results indicate that AUDITPLANNER was more conservative than the firm's auditors; i.e., it recommended lower materiality levels in twelve of the thirteen companies. The subjects felt that with additional refinement the system would be useful as a decision aid or training device.

3.6 GC/X

GC-X (Biggs and Selfridge, 1986) is an initial, prototype expert system that makes going concern judgments. The purposes of the research have been to develop a model of an expert auditor making going concern judgments, and to develop a plausible framework for future detailed work. Based on the literature and interviews with two experts, the GC-X system

135

incorporates six types of knowledge: (1) measures financial performance, (2) measures of financial performance for making going concern judgments and how to explain those judgments, (3) the target firm's business and its environment, (4) usage and explanation of business and environmental knowledge in making going concern judgments, (5) linkages of business and environmental factors of financial performance, and (6) business and environmental, and financial knowledge to evaluate management plans.

The system has been programmed in LISP and operates on a VAX 11/780 computer. GC-X has three system modules (a rule-based system that operates on financial knowledge; an event-chain network system that operates on business and environmental knowledge; and a plan evaluator that operates on both financial knowledge and business and environmental knowledge) and three databases (financial statement facts and facts concluded by the system; financial and judgment rules; and business and environmental events). GC-X is goal oriented in that it works on goals and subgoals in a goal-stack that is initialized with the goal to assess whether a company is a going concern. GC-X will make judgments directly from data in its databases, or it can operate interactively with a user. GC-X has a simple natural language interface that allows it to interact with the user, and the ability to explain its reasoning to the user.

3.7 AOD

AUDIT OPINION DECISION (AOD) (Dillard and Mutchler, 1986) is an expert system designed to assist an auditor in making judgments relating to going concern opinion decisions. The task was specified through an analysis of authoritative pronouncements and verbal protocols collected from audit experts. A knowledge-based system was constructed within the menu-based framework of the XINFO system and contains 445 frames. The user is guided through the decision process by the frame sequence presented. AOD has no logic capability. Its "intelligence" is structuring the intermediate decisions and presenting them to the user in the form and sequence evidenced in expert behavior. This type of system is seen as a requisite phase of expert system development having practical value as an online decision aid. AOD is currently being adapted for PC implementation and AOD-II is being developed which incorporates logic capabilities into the AOD system.

3.8 INTERNAL-CONTROL-ANALYZER

INTERNAL-CONTROL-ANALYZER (Gal, 1985) is a prototype expert system which evaluates internal controls in the revenue cycle. Like AUDITPLANNER, it relies on the EMYCIN software. Its development followed the now familiar pattern of starting with "book knowledge" and following that by refinement with an expert on a series of actual audit situations.

3.9 OTHER DEVELOPMENTAL SYSTEMS

In addition to the expert systems that were just reviewed, there are a number of other systems in various developmental stages. These include systems for: (1) investigating analytical review fluctuations (Braun and Chandler, 1983), (2) audit planning (Lewis and Dhar, 1985; Boritz, Wensley, and Dittner, 1986), and (3) internal control evaluation (Meservy, Bailey, and Johnson, 1986).

4. Challenges to Successful Development of Expert Systems

In this section, we address what we believe are two major issues facing expert systems developers in auditing. These are knowledge acquisition and assessing the quality of the expert system's judgments.

4.1 KNOWLEDGE ACQUISITION

There is general agreement that knowledge acquisition is a major bottleneck in an expert system's development (Wellbank, 1983). Notwithstanding the considerable intelligence and experience accumulated in such fields as psychology and systems analysis, there is no proven methodology for this complex and essential process. Problem domains can be quite disparate in terms of their types of knowledge and reasoning. The appropriate knowledge elicitation approach is largely dependent on the domain being studied.

A number of methods, sometimes in combination, have been utilized in an attempt to elicit the expert's knowledge: (1) questionnaires, interviews, and protocol analyses (e.g., Biggs, et al. 1986; Dillard and Mutchler, 1986); (2) an expert system shell (e.g., Dungan and Chandler, 1985; Steinbart, forthcoming); and (3) inductive methods (Quinlan, 1979). One difficulty with all of these methods is that many times experts have difficulty communicating their knowledge and reasoning processes. It may also be difficult to convert the elicited knowledge into a knowledge representation scheme such as a logic tree. It is also possible that the way in which the expert is led to describe his or her reasoning may not be the method normally used (Bell, 1985). We will briefly discuss each of the knowledge elicitation methods just mentioned.

4.1.1 Questionnaires, Interviews, and Protocol Analyses

The use of questionnaires, interviews, and protocol analyses have been the most common approaches to knowledge elicitation in audit settings. Each of these techniques requires sessions that can be rather lengthy and must often be tape recorded in order to capture all the necessary detail. Typically, the process of analyzing the data is very cumbersome and time consuming. The results often need to be broken down into sub-areas: identifying facts, assumptions, rules, heuristics, and goals. Additionally, some terms used by experts such as "good," "low," and "often" may be fuzzy and ill-defined.

A major challenge with these techniques is the fact that the expert may never have analyzed how he or she goes about making decisions. Thus, the expert may have difficulty describing the process. The interviewer can partially deal with this situation by allowing the expert to represent his or her approach to decision making in a form that is most natural. This may be a decision table, a diagram, a set of rules; or may be a documented set of cases.

4.1.2 Using an Expert System Shell

An alternative approach to knowledge acquisition is to involve the expert directly in the construction of the system. Use of an expert system shell does not require that the expert learn any programming skills. An initial prototype may be constructed using "published" knowledge about the problem. This initial prototype can be refined through interaction between the system and the expert on a series of increasingly difficult problems. The system is refined as the expert identifies where the system failed on individual cases. Steinbart's (forthcoming) work on AUDITPLANNER is a good example of this approach. A major

138

drawback is that this approach requires a substantial time commitment from the expert.

4.1.3 Inductive Methods

Inductive inference is a process of going from the particular to the general. An inductive inference system discovers regularities (rules) by analyzing a series of examples from the problem domain. These examples can be provided by the expert (or firm) based on actual or hypothetical situations. Software (e.g., EXPERT-EASE) currently exists which can be used for inducing rules from such examples. The resulting rules can then be implemented in an expert system.

Once an expert system has been so derived, the resulting rules can be tested by the expert and modifications made where necessary. While there has been no inductive work in auditing that we are aware of, there have been experiments in restrictive domains (e.g., chess) where rules derived from inductive methods have been shown to be very accurate (Quinlan, 1979). This approach is currently being used in taxation by Garrison and Michaelsen (1986) to identify rules from court cases and by Messier and Hansen (1986) to predict bankruptcy.

4.1.4 Comments

Whatever the elicitation method, it is important to have the expert work with the system as it is coded. In this way, the expert can identify results which are unusual, or with which he or she disagrees, so that appropriate modifications can be made to the system. Examining the reasoning process of the expert system as it arrives at a conclusion assists the expert in analyzing his or her own reasoning process.

Developers of expert systems also should be aware that for some problem domains the sheer complexity of analysis means that the human "experts" may be mediocre at best. Simply encoding such an "experts"'s knowledge in an expert system may not provide much gain. It may be that the rules extracted from the expert demonstrate empirical associations that lack a firm theoretical foundation. In such instances, deeper analysis of the system may be useful in improving performance. Certainly, the explanatory capability of an expert system is enhanced when the "deeper" reasons for conclusions or hypotheses generated by the expert system can be demonstrated.

4.2 THE QUALITY OF AN EXPERT SYSTEM'S JUDGMENTS

Builders of expert systems may have two different motivations for constructing an expert system. One reason may be to develop a cognitive simulation (i.e., a computational model) of the expert. The work by Steinbart (forthcoming) and Merservy et al. (1986) is representative of this approach. The second reason may be to develop a program that performs the task as well as the expert with little concern about whether the program performs the task similar to the expert. AUDITOR (Dungan and Chandler, 1985) and EDP-XPERT (Hansen and Messier, 1986a, b) are examples of this approach. It is important to keep this distinction in mind because they can lead to different design considerations. More important, they may lead to different evaluation considerations.

Buchanan and Shortliffe (1984) have proposed two standards for evaluating expert systems: (1) the "correct" answer to the problem or (2) what the expert states is the correct answer. In many problem domains including auditing, we seldom know the "correct" answer. As a result, the second approach is usually followed. Thus, the quality of the expert system's judgments is usually evaluated by comparing its output with the expert's answer. One difficulty with this approach is that different experts may not agree on the solution.

In addition to measuring the correctness of a decision, researchers who build expert systems as cognitive simulations face an additional problem. They must compare the *process* followed by the expert system with that of the expert. There are few, if any, rigorous ways of making such comparisons. Also, different experts may not solve the problem in a similar manner.

Our research on EDP-XPERT (Hansen and Messier, 1986a, b) confirms suggestions in the expert systems literature (Buchanan and Shortliffe, 1984) that the validation process should be undertaken throughout the life of the system. With early prototypes, the evaluation can be very informal. However, as the system's development progresses, the evaluation process must include complex cases and more objective measures of the system's performance. The reader is referred to Hansen and Messier (1986b) for some additional criteria for measuring performance.

5. IMPACT OF DECISION AIDS ON PRACTICE

We would like to discuss the potential impact that decision aids, and more specifically expert systems, may have on audit practice. Our comments on the effect of decision aids on audit practice will extend beyond expert systems and include the effect of automation on the audit process.

Most of the major public accounting firms are automating their audit approaches. We suspect that this automation will eventually take place in smaller firms as the software becomes available. These decision aids (or audit support tools) offer a number of benefits and costs to public accounting firms. First, audit support tools should remove lower level staff from a number of mundane audit tasks. This will free lower-level staff for more challenging work. The related costs will be that public accounting firms will have to hire better trained students and/or revise their current entry-level training programs.

Second, audit support tools should provide more consistency in how the audit is conducted and documented. A potential cost here is that the decision aids may be too rigid to accommodate the differences which exist between clients.

Turning more specifically to expert systems, we note three potential benefits. These are: (1) knowledge sharing, (2) augmented professional judgment, and (3) shorter decision times (Elliott and Kielich, 1985, p. 132). The development of an expert system results in capturing the expert's specialized knowledge in the system. This allows specialized expertise to be available to more staff members. The complexity of many audit judgments requires that auditors consult with other members of the firm before making certain decisions. A successful expert system could perform this function within the firm for selected decisions. Finally, an expert system could lead to shorter decision times by helping the user focus on the important issues and, therefore, not waste time on irrelevant factors.

The development and implementation of expert systems also involves a number of costs: (1) hardware and software, (2) knowledge acquisition, and (3) maintenance (Elliott and Kielich, 1985, p. 133). The cost of hardware and software will vary with the application. With small applications, micro-computers and available expert system shells (e.g., AL/X) may be adequate. For very large or sophisticated applications, specialized artificial intelligence computers and special programming languages may be necessary. Thus, costs for hardware and software could run from $75–$100,000. As we mentioned previously, the most difficult and costly part of an expert system construction is capturing the expert's knowledge and programming it into the system. Elliott and Kielich (1985, p. 133) estimate that this could run up to $1 million depending on the complexity of the system. Finally, after implementation, there will be ongoing maintenance for the system to accommodate changes in the problem domain.

Concluding Comments

In this article, we have discussed the reasons for the growing interest in expert systems, presented an overview of expert systems, reviewed a number of existing expert systems, and discussed the impact of expert systems on audit practice. The structural changes that decision aids and expert systems will have on our profession may be enormous. These changes make this an exciting time to be an audit researcher and practitioner.

FIGURE 1

Relationship of Types of Decision Aids With Type of Problem Domain

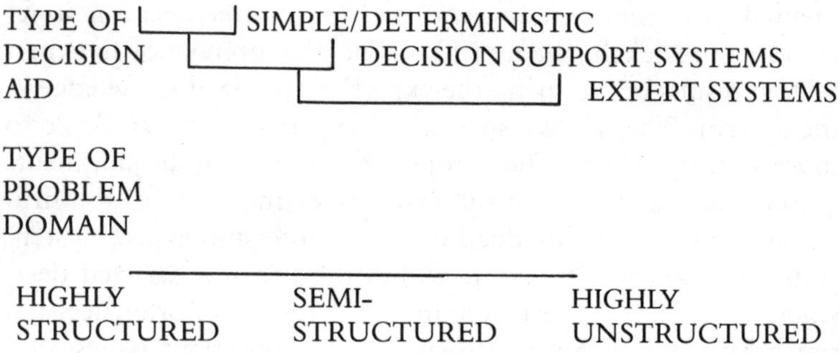

TYPE OF |_____| SIMPLE/DETERMINISTIC
DECISION |_____| DECISION SUPPORT SYSTEMS
AID |_____| EXPERT SYSTEMS

TYPE OF
PROBLEM
DOMAIN

HIGHLY   SEMI-   HIGHLY
STRUCTURED   STRUCTURED   UNSTRUCTURED

FIGURE 2
Overview of Existing Expert Systems

PANEL A: EXISTING PROTOTYPE SYSTEMS.

System	Problem Domain	Software Shell
AUDITOR	Adequacy of allowance for bad debts	AL/X
EDP-XPERT	Reliability of controls in advanced EDP environments	AL/X
CFILE	Adequacy of loan loss reserve	insight2
ExperTAX	Guidance for corporate tax accrual and planning process	Specific program in LISP
AUDITPLANNER	Setting preliminary stage materiality	EMYCIN
GC/X	Evaluates companies' ability to be going concerns	Specific program in LISP
AOD	Audit opinion decisions	XINFO
INTERNAL-CONTROL-ANALYZER	Evaluate internal controls	EMYCIN

PANEL B: DEVELOPMENTAL SYSTEMS.

System Developers	Problem Domain
Boritz, Wensley, and Dittner	Audit planning
Braun and Chandler	Investigation of analytical review fluctuation
Lewis and Dhar	Audit planning
Meservy, Bailey, and Johnson	Internal control evaluation

References

Bell, M. Z., "Why Expert Systems Fail," *Journal of the Operational Research Society,* Vol. 36, 1985, pp. 613–619.

Biggs, S. F and M. Selfridge, "GC-X: A Prototype Expert System for the Auditor's Going Concern Judgment," working paper, University of Connecticut, January 1986.

———, W. F Messier, Jr., and J. V. Hansen, "A Descriptive Analysis of Computer Audit Specialists' Decision Making Behavior in Advanced Computer Environments," working paper, September 1986.

Boritz, Wensley, and Dittner, "An Expert System for Assertion-Driven Audit Planning," working paper, 1986.

Braun, H. M. and J. S. Chandler, "Development of an Expert System to Assist Auditors in the Investigation of Analytical Review Fluctuations," research proposal, The Peat Marwick Foundation, 1983.

Buchanan, B. G., "New Research on Expert Systems," in J. E. Hayes, D. Michie, and Y-H Pao (eds.), *Machine Intelligence,* Vol. 10, Halsted Press, 1982.

———— and E. H. Shortliffe, *Rule-Based Expert Systems: The MYCIN Experiments of the Stanford Heuristic Programming Project,* Addison-Wesley, 1984.

Davis, R., "Expert Systems: Where Are We? and Where Do We Go From Here?" *AI Magazine,* Spring 1982, pp. 3–22.

Dillard, J. F. and J. F. Mutchler, "Knowledge-Based Expert Systems for Audit Opinion Decisions," technical report submitted to The Peat Marwick Foundation, 1986.

Duda, R. O. and J. G. Gaschnig, "Knowledge-Based Expert Systems Come of Age," *Byte,* September 1981, pp. 238–281.

Dungan, C. W. and J. S. Chandler, "AUDITOR: A Microcomputer-Based Expert System to Support Auditors in the Field," *Expert Systems,* October 1985, pp. 210–221.

Elliott, R. K., "Unique Audit Methods: Peat Marwick International," *Auditing: A Journal of Practice and Theory,* Spring 1983, p. 8, 1–12.

———— and J. A. Keilich, "Expert Systems for Accountants," *Journal of Accountancy,* September 1985, pp. 126–134.

Gal, G., "Using Auditor Knowledge to Formulate Data Model Constraints: An Expert System for Internal Control Evaluation," unpublished Ph.D. dissertation, Michigan State University, December 1985.

Garrison, L. R. and R. H. Michaelsen, "Computer Induction: A New Approach to Determining Scholarship or Fellowship Grant Status for Tax Purposes," working paper, University of Nebraska-Lincoln, April 1986.

Hansen, J. V. and W. F. Messier, Jr., "A Knowledge-Based Expert System for Auditing Advanced Computer Systems," *European Journal of Operational Research,* September 1986a, pp. 371–379.

————, "A Preliminary Investigation of EDP-XPERT," *Auditing: A Journal of Practice & Theory,* Autumn 1986b.

Joyce, E. J., "Expert Judgment in Audit Program Planning," *Studies of Human Information Processing in Accounting,* Supplement to *Journal of Accounting Research,* 1976, pp. 29–60.

Kelly, K. P., G. S. Ribar, and J. J. Willingham, "Interim Report on the Development of an Expert System for the Auditor's Loan Loss Evaluation," in *Auditing Symposium VIII,* University of Kansas, 1986.

Level Five Research, *User's Manual for INSIGHT 2,* Melbourne, FL: Level Five Research, Inc., 1985.

Lewis, B. L. and V. Dhar, "Development of a Knowledge-Based Expert System for Auditing," research proposal, The Peat Marwick Foundation, 1985.

Merservy, R. D., A. D. Bailey, Jr., and P. E. Johnson, "Internal Control

Evaluation: A Computational Model of the Review Process," *Auditing: A Journal of Practice & Theory,* Autumn 1986.

Messier, W. F, Jr. and J. V. Hansen, "Expert Systems in Accounting and Auditing: A Framework and Review," In E. Joyce and S. Moriarity, (eds.), *Decision Making and Accounting: Current Research,* University of Oklahoma, 1984.

———, "Inducing Rules for Expert Systems: An Example Using Bankruptcy Data," working paper, University of Florida, September 1986.

Mock, T. J. and J. L. Turner, *International Accounting Control Evaluation and Auditor Judgment,* New York: AICPA, 1981.

Paterson, A. *AL/X User Manual,* Oxford, England: Intelligent Terminals Ltd., 1984.

Quinlan, J. R., "Discovering Rules by Induction from Large Collections of Examples," in *Expert Systems in the Microelectronic Age,* D. Michie, (ed.), Edinburgh University Press, 1979.

Shpilberg, D. and L. E. Graham, "Developing ExperTAX: An Expert System for Corporate Tax Accrual and Planning," presented at the Symposium on Expert Systems and Audit Judgment, University of Southern California, February 1986.

——— and H. Schatz, "ExperTAX: An Expert System for Corporate Tax Planning," *Expert Systems,* July 1986, pp. 136–51.

Steinbart, P., "Materiality: A Case Study Using Expert Systems," *The Accounting Review,* (forthcoming).

van Melle, W. J., *System Aids in Constructing Consultation Programs,* UMI Research Press, 1981.

Wellbank, M., "A Review of Knowledge Acquisition Techniques for Expert Systems," Martlesham Consultancy Services, British Telecommunications, United Kingdom, 1983.

Part III:

APPLICATIONS IN AUDITING

Part III presents academic articles in the applications of ES to auditing. Gal and Steinbart analyze two rule-based expert systems (RBES) one of which is called INTERNAL-CON-TROL-ANALYZER and the second AUDITPLANNER. These systems are first described and then compared in terms of functions and structure.

Hansen and Messier (1986) present the results of a preliminary investigation of EDP-XPERT, an expert system for assisting computer audit specialists' judgments on the reliability of controls in advanced computer environments. The paper discusses the evaluation of expert systems and uses nineteen subjects to test EDP-XPERT.

The Boritz and Broca article is not a traditional expert systems paper but discusses models for scheduling internal audit activities. It demonstrates the relative application potential of management science techniques to scheduling. These approaches can be used as building blocks in the construction of expert systems that contain human knowledge associated to operations research based models.

Meservy, Bailey, and Johnson focus on the process of internal control evaluation. They investigate the strategies by which experienced auditors evaluate systems of internal accounting controls. The article includes: observations, using protocols of practicing auditors, interviews with one auditor, formalization as a computational model, and the validation of the model. The model is implemented as an expert system and tuned. It is tested with new cases and cross-validated against the performance of additional auditors.

Dillard and Mutchler provide guidance for expert systems

147

research and development in auditing. This illustrative example explores the formulation of a going concern audit opinion decision. This is divided into the following stages: 1) problem selection, 2) task domain, 3) prototype stage one system, and 4) stage two prototype development. The methodological and conceptual nature of this paper allows substantial insight for the reader, particularly in the development of frames and their relationship with a step in the auditor decision process.

Messier and Hansen introduce in their 1983 article the concepts around scheduling the monitoring of EDP controls in online systems. With the increased capability of embedding audit modules in the processing system, the question of frequency of monitoring becomes a concern in the system design itself. The authors present a general analytical model for monitoring, discuss embedded audit modules, define software monitors, and conclude with general advice for system designers and auditors.

The Use of Rule-Based Expert Systems to Investigate the Effects of Experience on Audit Judgments

GRAHAM GAL and PAUL J. STEINBART

Introduction

Rule-based expert systems (RBES) are currently the focus of a great deal of research interest. Most of that work has concentrated on the development of such systems; that is, the construction of the RBES is the *goal* of the research. The construction of an RBES, however, can also serve as the *means* for conducting descriptive empirical research on decision making behavior. The potential benefits of building an RBES for conducting descriptive research have been recognized by some researchers in the field of artificial intelligence:

> The aim here (in building an RBES) is thus not simply to build a program that exhibits a certain specified behavior, but to use the program construction process itself as a way of explicating knowledge in the field, and to use the program text as a medium of expression of the many forms of knowledge about the task and its solution (Davis and Lenat, 1982, p. 471).

There are two reasons why the construction of an RBES is useful for conducting descriptive research. First, the RBES is

149

developed by being used in the natural setting in which the judgments under study are normally made. Research on decision making and judgment behavior indicates that seemingly minor changes in either the content or the setting of the judgment task can significantly affect the behavior being studied (Adelman, 1981; Cox and Griggs, 1982; Ebbesen and Konecni, 1980; Einhorn and Hogarth, 1982; Hayes and Simon, 1977; Hoch and Tschirgi, 1983; Kahneman and Tversky, 1979). Second, the rules used by the RBES specify not only which factors influence a given judgment, but also specify the situation in which the rules apply. Thus, the set of rules, taken together, provides a model of the judgment process that explicitly includes the effect of the task environment.

Work on expert systems suggests that expert performance requires a large amount of domain-specific knowledge, the most important of which consists of heuristic rules-of-thumb for dealing with specific situations (Brachman, et al., 1983; Feigenbaum, 1979; Hayes-Roth, et al., 1983; Stefik, et al., 1983). This heuristic knowledge is acquired through experience (Abelson, 1981; Einhorn and Hogarth, 1982; Hogarth, 1981; Kahneman and Tversky, 1982; Tversky and Kahneman, 1981). Previous auditing research has focused on the effects of experience on general metrics of decision making behavior such as consensus, stability, and self-insight (Ashton, 1974a, 1974b; Ashton and Brown, 1980; Ashton and Kramer, 1980; Hamilton and Wright, 1982; Messier, 1983). In contrast, this study examines how experience affects the audit judgment process by changing the store of domain-specific knowledge used to make a particular judgment.

The remainder of this paper consists of three sections. The first section provides some background information about the two audit judgment tasks that were studied and describes the research method used in building the RBESs. The second section two examines the knowledge bases of the refined versions of each RBES and discusses how they differ from their initial prototype versions. The final section summarizes our findings and explores implications for future research.

Research Method

AUDIT JUDGMENT TASKS

This study examines the effect of experience on two audit judgment tasks: (1) the evaluation of the quality of a client's

150

internal controls and (2) the determination of materiality in the planning stage of the audit process. Each of these tasks is described in more detail below.

Evaluation of internal controls

A company's business activity consists of a number of economic transactions that affect its resources. Business organizations create and implement a set of procedures called internal controls to ensure that transactions are executed in accordance with management's intentions and are accurately recorded in the firm's information system. The specific internal controls implemented by a company result from management's assessment of the types of risks likely to affect normal transactions. For example, one of the risks related to credit sales transactions includes the possibility that the revenue will not be collected. Formal policies for granting credit represent one of the internal controls that can be used to minimize that risk.

As part of an audit engagement, the auditor assesses the quality of a client's set of internal controls. This assessment has two aspects. First, the auditor evaluates the efficacy of the client's internal controls for controlling the risks likely to be faced by the client. Second, the auditor evaluates how well those controls are actually functioning by performing tests of employee compliance with the stated controls.

INTERNAL-CONTROL ANALYZER (Gal, 1985) is designed to perform the former analysis for sales and cash receipts transactions. That is, it evaluates the overall efficacy of the controls designed by management, but does not test actual compliance with them. Figure 1 illustrates the evaluation process used by INTERNAL-CONTROL-ANALYZER. The figure indicates that the overall evaluation of the controls for the sales and cash receipts transaction cycle is the result of combining evaluations about three types of controls applied to those transactions: (1) population controls, (2) separation of duties, and (3) accuracy controls.

Population controls relate to the validity of the transactions, and can be broken down into controls designed to ensure that all valid transactions are recorded (completeness controls) and controls designed to ensure that all recorded transactions are indeed valid (authorization controls).

Separation of duties is based on the notion that no one person should be responsible for all phases of an economic transaction:

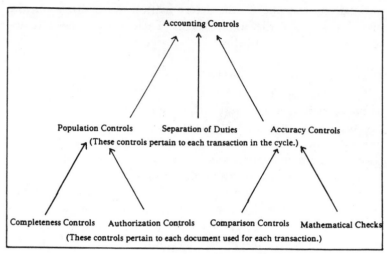

Figure 1: Types of Controls Examined in the Overall Evaluation.

having custody of a resource, possessing the ability to authorize transactions involving that resource, and being responsible for recording information about that resource.

Accuracy controls are designed, as their name implies, to ensure that transactions are recorded correctly. There are two types of accuracy controls: (1) checks on the consistency of information throughout the execution of the transaction (comparison controls) and (2) checks on the mathematical accuracy with which the transaction was recorded (mathematical controls). In summary, INTERNAL-CONTROL-ANALYZER combines judgments about all of these controls to evaluate the overall quality of the entire set.

Planning stage materiality judgment

Planning stage materiality is basically a judgment about the "importance" of any misstatements that might be present in a company's financial statements. Importance is defined in terms of potential impact on the users of the financial statements. Auditors do not examine every single transaction that occurred during a year; rather, they apply detailed audit procedures to a selected subset of those transactions. Materiality judgments made during the planning stage help determine the size of that subset. The auditor designs the audit program to be reasonably certain that any errors or misstatements that would be likely, either singly or in aggregate, to significantly affect the judgments of financial statements will be detected by the audit procedures that are used. AUDITPLANNER (Steinbart, 1985) is designed to determine the materiality level that should be used in planning the nature, timing, and extent of audit procedures.

Figure 2 shows the judgment model followed by AUDITPLANNER. The determination of planning stage materiality involves two sub-decisions: (1) the choice of a base for calculating materiality, and (2) the choice of a percentage rate to multiply by that base. The choice of a materiality base involves an assessment of what aspects of the client's financial statements users are most interested in. That decision is based on information about the client's (1) plans for future financing, (2) ownership structure (public or privately-owned), (3) the industry classification, and (4) financial characteristics. The choice of a percentage rate involves the auditor's assessment of any situations that would represent a greater than normal level of risk associated with the audit. That assessment is based on information about the intended uses of the financial statements and the auditor's prior experiences with the client.

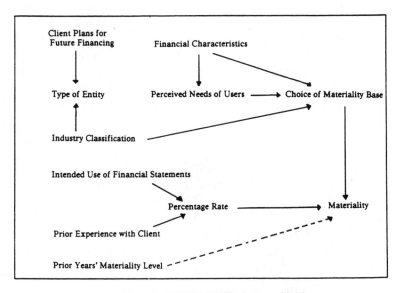

Figure 2: AUDITPLANNER's Judgment Model

CONSTRUCTION OF THE RBESs

The objective of this study is to examine the effect of experience on the audit judgment process. The method chosen to accomplish that objective involved a comparison of the knowledge base of an RBES that represents the judgment model used by a novice auditor with the knowledge base of an RBES that represents the judgment model used by an experienced auditor. The construction of each knowledge base is described below.

DEVELOPMENT OF NOVICE RBES

Novice audtitors can be characterized as possessing a fair amount of "book knowledge," but very little practical experience. They usually begin their careers in public accounting by attending a series of courses designed to teach them that firm's audit methodology. Thus, the training manuals used in those courses contain most of the novice auditor's knowledge about how to make different audit judgments.

The initial knowledge bases of both INTERNAL-CONTROL-ANALYZER and AUDITPLANNER consisted only of rules gleaned from the training manuals of two public accounting firms. The rules were first developed by reading the training materials. Then the proposed rules were discussed with an experienced auditor in each firm to ensure that the researchers had correctly interpreted the materials. The accuracy of the rules was then further verified by testing both RBESs on sample problems contained in the training materials. Both AUDITPLANNER and INTERNAL-CONTROL-ANALYZER reached the conclusions suggested in the training materials.

Development of experienced RBES

The initial prototype RBESs were refined by having an experienced auditor use them to make audit judgments for actual clients. Each RBES was built using the shell EMYCIN. EMYCIN's question and answering capabilities were used to facilitate the refinement process. Whenever the auditor disagreed with the RBES, EMYCIN's question and answering program was used to identify the rules that were the cause of the disagreement. The auditor was then asked to explain what was wrong

154

with the rules and to recommend how the system could be improved. Those suggestions were written down and implemented before the next interactive session. At that time, the revised RBES was tested to determine whether or not the correction had solved the problem. The revised RBES was also rerun on clients for which it had previously made correct decisions, to ensure that there were no unintended side effects from the revisions. Iterations of this interactive refinement process continued until the experienced auditors indicated that the systems were performing acceptably. Each RBES was then tested on a set of additional clients that had not been used to develop the system, and was found to make those judgments reasonably and acceptably. The contents of the knowledge bases of each RBES was then examined to investigate the effects of experience. The next section presents the results of that investigation.

Analysis

The knowledge bases of the refined versions of both AUDITPLANNER and INTERNAL-CONTROL-ANALYZER differ from those of the initial prototype versions of each system. Those changes resulted from the use of each system by an experienced auditor, and were necessary to enable the RBES to reach the same conclusions as had the experienced auditor. Consequently, the changes in the knowledge base of each RBES can be taken to represent the effects of experience on making particular audit judgments.

One obvious difference between the initial and refined knowledge bases is the number of rules contained in each. The refined versions contained several times the number of rules in the initial prototypes. This merely tells us, however, that experienced auditors have larger knowledge bases than novice auditors. Of more interest is the nature of new rules and the types of changes made to rules in the intial prototype knowledge bases. The remainder of this section provides examples of rules in the knowledge bases of both AUDITPLANNER and INTERNAL-CONTROL-ANALYZER to illustrate how experience affects the audit judgment process.

NEW RULES

Most of the rules included in the intial knowledge bases of both INTERNAL-CONTROL-ANALYZER and AU-

155

DITPLANNER were very general, and applied to a wide variety of "average" clients. Many of the new rules added during the refinement of each system were designed to deal with situations representing exceptions to those general conditions. For example, AUDITPLANNER initially contained several rules that could be used to classify the type of entity that a client is:

IF—the client has publicly-traded debt or equity securities, or

—the client has restrictive debt covenants that are measured by or depend on periodic financial statement amounts or ratios that involve the results of operations

THEN the client is a public entity.

Should neither premise clause be true, AUDITPLANNER concludes that the client is likely to be a private entity. The following rule is then applied to make this determination with certainty:

IF—the client is likely to be a private entity *and*

—the client is filing with a regulatory agency in preparation for the sale of its securities in a public market or

—the client intends to go public within the next two or three years

THEN the client is a public entity.

If this rule was not satisfied, AUDITPLANNER concluded that the client was a private entity. During the refinement process the experienced auditor indicated that the following rule needed to be added to the knowledge base:

IF the client is an insurance company

THEN the client is a public company.

In other words, even if the client met all of the conditions for being considered a private entity, if it could be classified as an insurance company, then it should be treated as a public entity. The rationale for this rule is that the regulators of insurance companies generally have the same needs and interests as do investors and creditors of public entities.

The refinement process added many rules of this type to the knowledge bases of both AUDITPLANNER and INTERNAL-

CONTROL-ANALYZER. The common aspect of all such rules was that they described specific situations which were not explicitly mentioned in the accounting firms' training manuals (probably because it would not be practical to list every specific situation). They serve to highlight exceptions to more general situations, and also prescribe a method for dealing with those exceptions.

MODIFICATION OF EXISTING RULES

The second type of change made to the knowledge bases of both INTERNAL-CONTROL-ANALYZER and AU-DITPLANNER involved a modification of some of the clauses of rules in the initial version of the knowledge base. Changes of this type generally reflect the experienced auditor's belief that the rules in the initial knowledge base were too general, and that their scope of application needed to be limited. An example of this type of change is found in the way that INTERNAL-CONTROL-ANALYZER determines whether there are problems with a lack of separation of duties. The initial knowledge base contained the following rule:

IF the various functions responsible for the execution of sales transactions are not performed by different people

THEN there is a problem with incompatible functions.

Information about incompatible functions was then used as follows:

IF there is a problem with incompatible functions

THEN there is a problem with separation of duties.

The experienced auditor indicated that this rule was too general. In particular, he stated that there were several other conditions which could mitigate the problem of incompatible functions so that there would not be any problem with separation of duties. The refined knowledge base of INTERNAL-CONTROL-ANALYZER, therefore, contains the following modified version of the previous rule:

IF—there is a problem with incompatible functions *and*

—the number of employees performing these functions is small, *and*

—there is adequate supervision of those employees

THEN there is no problem with separation of duties.

There were numerous changes of this type for both AU-DITPLANNER and INTERNAL-CONTROL-ANALYZER. In general, they serve to moderate some of the general rules in the audit manuals by taking into account mitigating circumstances which represent situations in which those rules should not be applied.

Conclusions and Implications

The initial knowledge bases of both INTERNAL-CON-TROL-ANALYZER and AUDITPLANNER contained only those rules that represented the book knowledge possessed by a novice auditor. Experienced auditors were used to refine each system, and suggested changes and additions to the knowledge base that would enable each RBES to more closely match the auditor's actual judgments. The refined knowledge bases of each RBES were then compared with the initial knowledge bases to examine the effects of experience.

The changes made to the knowledge bases were analyzed and classified into two categories: (1) the addition of new rules to deal with special situations, and (2) the modification of existing rules to alter the scope of their application. Examples of each type of change were presented. Both types of change represent methods for dealing with exceptions to general rules. Thus it appears that a major effect of experience is the development of the ability to make and recognize exceptions to more general courses of action.

There are several areas for future research. This study used qualitative methods for comparing novice and experienced knowledge bases, drawing on examples to illustrate differences. Research is needed on the development of quantitative measures for making such comparisons. This is not an easy task. Obvious measures, such as the size of the knowledge base, are of dubious worth because the number of rules can be easily changed by decisions on whether or not to include multiple clauses in the premises and conclusions of rules.

Another avenue for future research concerns the comparison

of knowledge bases developed by working with different auditors, both from the same and from different public accounting firms. Holstrum (1981) reviewed empirical research on a wide range of audit judgments and concluded that:

> In general, the most crucial aspect of the auditor judgment research to date is the lack of consensus among auditors in typical judgments made in the audit process (pp. 31–32).

The comparison of knowledge bases that reflect the judgment strategies of different auditors may provide some insight into the true causes of the observed lack of consensus.

Finally, this study illustrates that the construction of an RBES can help answer research questions about human decision making and judgment behavior, and need not be viewed simply as a means to automate those processes. Additional studies which use RBESs as a *means* for conducting research on aspects of human decision making and judgment behavior are needed.

References

Abelson, R. P., "Psychological Status of the Script Concept," *American Psychologist*, Vol. 36, No. 7, July 1981, pp. 715–729.

Adelman, L., "The Influence of Formal, Substantive, and Contextual Task Properties on the Relative Effectiveness of Different Forms of Feedback in Multiple-Cue Probability Learning Tasks," *Organizational Behavior and Human Performance*, Vol. 27, No. 3, June 1981, pp. 423–442.

Ashton, R. H., "An Experimental Study of Internal Control Judgments," *Journal of Accounting Research*, Vol. 12, No. 1, Spring 1974a, pp. 143–157.

———, "Cue Utilization and Expert Judgment: A Comparison of Independent Auditors with Other Judges," *Journal of Applied Psychology*, Vol. 59, No. 4, August 1974b, pp. 437–444.

——— and P. R. Brown, "Descriptive Modeling of Auditors' Internal Control Judgments: Replication and Extension," *Journal of Accounting Research*, Vol. 18, No. 1, Spring 1980, pp. 269–277.

——— and S. L. Kramer, "Students as Surrogates in Behavioral Research: Some Evidence," *Journal of Accounting Research*, Vol. 18, No. 1, Spring 1980, pp. 1–15.

Brachman, R. H., S. Amarel, C. Engelman, P. S. Engelmore, E. A. Feigenbaum, and D. E. Wilkins, "What Are Expert Systems?" in *Building Expert Systems,* F. Hayes-Roth, D. A. Waterman, and D. B. Lenat (eds.), Addison-Wesley, 1983, pp. 31–57.

Cox, J. R. and R. A. Griggs, "The Effects of Experience on Performance in Wason's Selection Task," *Memory & Cognition,* Vol. 10, No. 5, September 1982, pp. 496–502.

Davis, R. and D. Lenat, *Knowledge-Based Systems in Artificial Intelligence,* McGraw-Hill, 1982.

Ebbesen, E. B. and V. J. Konecni, "On the External Validity of Decision-Making Research: What Do We Know About Decisions in the Real World? in *Cognitive Processes in Choice and Decision Behavior,* T. S. Wallsten (ed.), Lawrence Erlbaum Associates, 1980, pp. 21–45.

Einhorn, H. J. and R. M. Hogarth, *A Theory of Diagnostic Inference: I. Imagination and the Psychophysics of Evidence,* working paper, University of Chicago, 1982.

Feigenbaum, E. A., "Themes and Case Studies of Knowledge Engineering," in *Expert Systems in the Microelectronic Age,* D. Michie (ed.), Edinburgh University Press, 1979, pp. 3–25.

Gal, G., "Using Auditor Knowledge to Formulate Data Model Constraints: An Expert System for Internal Control Evaluation," unpublished Ph.D. dissertation, Michigan State University, 1985.

Hamilton, R. E. and W. F. Wright, "Internal Control Judgments and Effects of Experience: Replications and Extensions," *Journal of Accounting Research,* Vol. 20, No. 2, Autumn 1982 (Part 2), pp. 756–765.

Hayes, J. R. and H. A. Simon, "Psychological Differences Among Problem Isomorphs," in *Cognitive Theory: Volume 2,* N. J. Castellan, Jr., D. B. Pisoni, and G. R. Potts (eds.), Lawrence Erlbaum Associates, 1977, pp. 21–41.

Hayes-Roth, F., D. A. Waterman, and D. B. Lenat, "An Overview of Expert Systems," in *Building Expert Systems,* F. Hayes-Roth, D. A. Waterman, and D. B. Lenat (eds.), Addison-Wesley, 1983, pp. 3–29.

Hoch, S. J. and J. E. Tschirgi, "Cue Redundancy and Extralogical Inferences in a Deductive Reasoning Task," *Memory & Cognition,* Vol. 11, No. 2, March 1983, pp. 200–209.

Hogarth, R. M., "Beyond Discrete Biases: Function and Dysfunctional Aspects of Judgmental Heuristics," *Psychological Bulletin,* Vol. 90, No. 2, September 1981, pp. 197–217.

Holstrum, G. L., *Improving Auditor Judgment Through Decision Modeling and Computer Assistance: Part I "Consensus in Audit Judgments,"* working paper, Deloitte, Haskins & Sells, 1981.

Kahneman, D. and A. Tversky, "Prospect Theory: An Analysis of Decision Under Risk," *Econometrica,* Vol. 47, No. 2, March 1979, pp. 263–291.

——, "The Psychology of Preferences," *Scientific American,* Vol. 246, No. 1, January 1982, pp. 160–173.

Messier, W. F., Jr., "The Effect of Experience and Firm Type on Materiality/Disclosure Judgments," *Journal of Accounting Research,* Vol. 21, No. 2, Autumn 1983, pp. 611–618.

Stefik, M., J. Aikins, R. Balzer, J. Benoit, L. Birnbaum, F. Hayes-Roth, and E. Sacerdoti, "Basic Concepts for Building Expert Systems," in *Building Expert Systems,* F. Hayes-Roth, D. A. Waterman, and D. B. Lenat (eds.), Addison-Wesley, 1983, pp. 59–86.

Steinbart, P. J., "The Construction of an Expert System to Make Materiality Judgments," unpublished Ph.D. dissertation, Michigan State University, 1985.

————, "The Construction of a Rule-Based Expert System As A Method for Studying Materiality Judgments," *The Accounting Review,* forthcoming.

Tversky, A. and Kahneman, D., "The Framing of Decisions and the Psychology of Choice," *Science,* Vol. 211, No. 4481, January 30, 1981, pp. 453–458.

A Preliminary Investigation of EDP-XPERT

JAMES V. HANSEN and WILLIAM F. MESSIER, JR.

With the introduction of low-cost computer technology, more organizations have been automating their accounting systems and the automation has been more extensive than in the past. These changes present some serious challenges to auditors in that typical internal controls and traditional audit trails will no longer be present. These challenges will require auditors to make evidential judgment decisions in more complex environments and will therefore require the development of better audit technology (Hansen and Messier, 1982). In this paper, we present the results of a preliminary investigation of EDP-XPERT, an expert system which is intended to assist computer audit specialists (CASs) in making judgments as to the reliability of controls in advanced computer environments.

Because of known human cognitive limitations, tools which help to improve the control reliability judgment process are needed. For example, Einhorn (1972) and Hogarth (1980) point out that psychological research suggests that the best role for individuals in judgment is in *evaluating* the data. The *combination* of the evaluated data, however, is best performed by *mechanical* means. These mechanical means can vary from simple additive models with few variables to expert systems such as the one described in this paper. The basic idea of all mechanical models is to support, and we hope, to improve the judgment process.[1]

In addition to presenting the results of the preliminary investigation of EDP-XPERT, we discuss the issue of evaluating expert systems. Our purpose is to point out the difficulty in evaluating expert systems and to suggest a number of criteria that can be used in the evaluation process. The remainder of the paper is as follows: the first section discusses the evaluation of expert systems; the second and third sections contain the method and results of the preliminary investigation; and the final section contains suggestions for future research and concluding comments.

Evaluation of Expert Systems

There may be two different (although not necessarily independent) reasons or motives in constructing computer programs that perform some task (Glass and Holyoak, 1986). In one instance, the motive is to "simulate" one expert. Here the program developers would not only be concerned with the program's ability to reach the same conclusion as the expert, but they would also be concerned with mimicking the expert's reasoning process. This approach takes a cognitive psychology perspective. The second reason is narrower in focus in that it attempts to produce a program that only performs the task as well as the expert with minimum concern for modeling human cognition. This is consistent with the development process for expert systems. The discussions in this paper relate specifically to evaluation of the expert system's conclusions and are not concerned with comparing the program's reasoning process with the cognitive processes of the expert.

THE EVALUATION PROCESS

There is no single best approach to the evaluation and validation of expert systems. It is apparent from the recent literature (Gaschnig et al., 1983; Buchanan and Shortliffe, 1984, Chapter 30) that the validation process must be undertaken *throughout* the life of the system and that the evaluations should become more formal as the expert system matures. In the early stages of development, the evaluation can be very informal with a demonstration that the initial prototype can be used on simple cases. Next, as the knowledge base is expanded, the evaluation process can begin to include more complex cases and feedback from experts and potential users. This is the stage at which EDP-XPERT is being evaluated in this paper. In later stages, the system can be formally evaluated, perhaps in "blinded" studies (Yu et al., 1979) or actual field studies (McDermott, 1984). (See Chandrasekran (1983) for a detailed proposed evaluation schedule.)

Evaluations typically require a standard by which performance can be measured. Two approaches have been suggested as standards for evaluating expert systems: (1) the "correct" answer to the particular case, or (2) what a human expert states is the correct answer based on the available information (Buchanan and Shortliffe, 1984, p. 580). In many of the problem domains where expert systems are built, the "correct" answer is not available. This is particularly true in a number of auditing situations. (Ashton, 1983)[2] As a result, the evaluations of most expert systems have been along the lines of the second approach (Dungan and Chandler, 1985). Since a "correct" answer is not immediately known when the reliability of EDP controls is evaluated, the second approach to examining EDP-XPERT's advice was followed.

SUGGESTED EVALUATION CRITERIA

Comparison of the expert's conclusion with that of the expert system is one major criterion for evaluating an expert system. A number of other criteria are also important based upon previous research (Gorry, 1973; Shortliffe, 1976). For example, it is important to assess items such as the wording of the questions posed by the expert system. Poor or unclear wording may cause user uncertainty about what is being asked. Second, the explanation capabilities of the system should include an ability to provide (1) additional explanation for a particular question, and (2) an explanation for why a particular question is being asked. Third, the mechanisms for providing input data (e.g., the response scale for a question) to the system are also extremely important. Finally, the program's reasoning capabilities are another important criterion. Explanation of the reasoning process (i.e., ability to show the user how a conclusion was reached) and reliability of the program's advice are important issues that should be examined as part of the evaluation process. All of these issues were examined during the preliminary investigation of EDP-XPERT.

Our purpose in this section was to elucidate how expert systems might be evaluated and the potential difficulties in such a process. Perhaps Gaschnig et al. (1983, p. 277) summarize this process best: "At this stage of expert systems' evolution, the evaluation process is more of an art, however primitive, than a science."

Method

DEVELOPMENT OF EDP-XPERT

Our initial work involved determining the feasibility of applying artificial intelligence (AI) techniques to the EDP audit environment. We reviewed the existing literature on the subject including the EDP audit materials of several Big Eight firms. We also conducted interviews with Computer Audit Specialists (CASs) from five Big Eight firms. While some of the firms we examined had structured approaches to dealing with the problem, in many instances the CAS still relied heavily on his or her expertise in advanced computer environments.[3] The initial efforts also involved establishing an appropriate AI structure for representation of the CASs' knowledge. A production system architecture (If-Then rules) was adopted mainly because our interview work indicated the problem domain was not static and that knowledge would have to be continuously updated. Rule-based systems provide easy modification of the knowledge base. Details of this research are contained in Hansen and Messier (1981, 1982). We do not, however, assert that auditors think in a rule-based manner. We do believe that a rule-based approach can capture the thought process in a fashion that will result in an expert system following "lines of reasoning" similar to those followed by the expert. But, as noted earlier, our work does not address the cognitive issues directly.[4]

The second phase of our research was taken in three major steps. First, we conducted a verbal protocol experiment with three senior CASs. Our intent was to examine the decision making behavior of CASs in some detail and to identify any decision rules (If-Then) that might be appropriate for the knowledge base of the expert system. Second, we identified a software package that would be appropriate for our problem domain. Third, we developed an initial prototype system.

The protocol study (Biggs, Messier, and Hansen, 1986) provided some insight into the decision making behavior of CASs but it did not provide many If-Then rules appropriate for an expert system in support of auditing advanced computer systems. Two possible reasons exist for this outcome. First, where we did identify a decision rule, it was usually very tentative or not in an obvious If-Then form. Second, the case used in the protocol study had strong user controls. As a result, the CASs used decision rules more appropriate for auditing *around* the computer. (See Biggs et al. (1986) for more detail.) The CASs' *overall* approach to computer auditing did provide general input to our modeling effort and did affect the goal structure used in EDP-XPERT (discussed below).

After examining the software available at the time, we chose AL/X (Advice Language/X) (Patterson, 1984) as our expert system software "shell." AL/X is based on the PROSPECTOR system (Duda et al., 1980) and was originally developed to diagnose the underlying causes of oil platform shutdowns. AL/X was chosen because at the time we started development it was the only software commercially available at a reasonable price. More important, however, the system seemed appropriate for the diagnostic-type problem we were investigating. The software does have certain limitations which we discuss in the last section.

The initial EDP-XPERT prototype (Hansen and Messier, 1986) contained approximately sixty rules. Since the protocol study failed to produce usable If-Then rules, we resorted to *reconstructed methods* (Johnson, 1981) to develop this initial knowledge base. Such an approach involves using currently available information (e.g., textbooks, firm materials) to construct the inference network of rules. This initial knowledge base contained a partial set of rules for controls in a distributed processing system[5] and had *one* overall goal (the reliability of the control system). We initially tested this knowledge base using a series of small problem situations. This initial testing, our protocol results (Biggs et al., 1986), and further discussion with our expert pointed out that CASs address the general or supervisory controls *before* looking at the application (input, processing, output) controls. Further, our expert indicated that unless supervisory controls were adequate, there would be no reliance on controls for specific accounting applications. Based on these findings, EDP-XPERT's knowledge base was restructured to include *four* separate goals, the reliability of supervisory, input, processing, and output controls. Additional If-Then rules were added after this restructuring.

We next met with our expert (a senior CAS) for two days to go through the rules in detail to determine if we had appropriate controls, structure, and terminology. The senior CAS also provided the degrees of belief ("weights") for the rules. All of his proposed changes were made to EDP-XPERT's knowledge base. This is the version of EDP-XPERT that was used in the preliminary investigation reported in this paper. The resulting system contained 133 rules. The breakdown of the rules by goals was 66 rules for the supervisor goal, 25 for input, 24 for processing, and 8 for the output goal.

EDP-XPERT'S SOFTWARE

AL/X (Paterson, 1984) contains two major components: a knowledge base and an inference engine. The knowledge base contains the inference network of If-Then rules which form the evidence-hypothesis relationships of the problem domain. The inference engine contains the analytical framework for generating and explaining advice to the user. The underlying model in AL/X's inference engine is based on a subjective "Bayesian-like" updating method for rule-based systems suggested by Duda et al. (1976).

We provide a brief overview of AL/X in order to help the reader understand some of the testing. The rules in EDP-XPERT contain degrees of belief (priors) provided by the expert which indicate the strength of the rules. The user chooses which model (goal) to use and AL/X then chooses a question to ask the user. The question chosen is the one that would have the maximum effect on the goal, i.e., the one which causes the greatest shift in the degree of belief of the current goal (Paterson, 1984). AL/X will ask all of the relevant questions related to the goal under consideration. The user normally responds to a question by providing a certainty factor: a number in the range of -5 to 5. This response scale is equivalent in AL/X's inference engine to probabilities ranging from zero to 100. After the user has responded to all questions relevant to a particular goal, the system provides a report on the likelihood of the truth of the hypothesis (goal). The following is an example of such a report:

After considering all significant questions, the degree that supervisory controls are complete and functioning well (supercontrols) initially was 0.0. It is now 9.5.

There are no more significant questions for the current goal. Investigated goals with degree of belief > = 0.0 are:

The supervisory controls are complete and functioning well. Prior degree was 0.0. Current degree is 9.5.

The current degree of belief can be converted to a probability since

$$p = \frac{odds\ (H)}{odds\ (H) + 1}$$

In this example,

$$degree\ (H) = 10log_{10}\ (odds\ (H)) = 9.5$$

and $p = .90$. During the preliminary investigation, the subjects were provided with a table that contained conversion values for the degrees of belief. Significant research exists with respect to the use of "probability-like" rules in expert systems. We do not address these issues in this paper; our interest, as noted earlier, is in developing a problem solver, not an expert emulator. The interested reader is referred to Buchanan and Shortliffe (1984, Chapters 10–13).

SUBJECTS

The seventeen subjects who participated in the preliminary investigation of EDP-XPERT were students in an initial CAS training course for a Big Eight public accounting firm. The subjects had an average of 3.3 years of audit experience, ranging from one to eight years. There were two managers, six supervisors, and nine seniors. All but one were CPAs and two subjects had Master's degrees. On average, the subjects had completed 2.5 computer courses in college, ranging from one to ten courses.

PROCEDURE

The test was administered during the second week of the two-week training course. The subjects were required to complete two large case studies during their training. In conjunction with the Senior CAS who was assisting us in developing the system, we determined that one of these cases would be appropriate for testing purposes. The case contained the following information on a hypothetical company (approximately sixty pages):

1. Audit planning and background information.

2. A description of the EDP control environment.

3. Documentation of the client's accounts receivable–sales system.

4. Information on access controls.

5. Various client data file layouts and system reports.

As part of the training course, the subjects were required to: (1) complete an EDP control environment worksheet; (2) document the accounting system and identify controls; (3) review and evaluate access controls, systems development, program changes, and manual follow-up procedures; and (4) apply computer audit software to test controls in the client's revenue cycle.

The investigation of EDP-XPERT was carried out in five parts. First, the subjects were given a 15-minute presentation on expert systems and an overview of the testing. They were then presented with some audit test results for the case. These results were provided by the senior CAS who was assisting us. Second, they completed the first part of a questionnaire which asked a series of questions about applications of computers in auditing, and in particular, questions about expert systems. This part of the instrument was based on a questionnaire used by Teach and Shortliffe (1981) for assessing physicians' comments on computer-based decision supports. The questions were adapted for an audit setting.[6] Third, the participants assessed the reliability of controls (supervisory, input, processing, and output) for the case company. Fourth, the subjects used EDP-XPERT to assist their assessment of the reliability of the company's controls. Fifth, they completed the final part of the questionnaire which included another assessment of the company's controls, completion of the same questions about expert systems, an evaluation of EDP-XPERT, and some demographic data. The subjects were allowed to use any material that they felt was relevant during the test.

Results

In examining the system at this stage, we realized that the knowledge base was incomplete (i.e., it did not contain all of the rules for an advanced computer system) and that the explanation capabilities of the system were not fully developed. However, we felt it was important to receive some feedback on the system's performance to assist us in further development efforts. We will discuss the results of the preliminary investigation under two categories: (1) the subjects' evaluations of expert systems and EDP-XPERT, and (2) the subjects' EDP control judgments.

TABLE 1
Number of Subjects Noting Applications of Computers to Auditing

Which of the following do you think are appropriate uses of computers in auditing? Mark *all* that apply.

	Number of Subjects (n = 17)
1. Preparing audit workpapers (e.g., replacing conventional paper copies).	17
2. Selecting transactions from client files.	17
3. Testing transactions from client files.	15
4. Monitoring client's internal control systems (e.g., embedded audit modules).	15
5. Computer-based decision aids ("expert systems") for *assisting* auditor judgment.	16
6. *Substituting* a computer-based decision aid for auditor judgment.	1

If you checked item 5. above, please indicate which of the following areas would seem appropriate for the application of computer-based decision aids ("expert systems").

Inherent risk evaluation	10
Auditing accounts receivable	7
Statistical sampling	13
Analytical review	10
Financial modeling	9
Internal control - manual or semi-automated environment	6
Internal control - advanced computer environment	10
Going concern evaluation	6
Audit opinion judgments	5

TABLE 2
Mean Ratings for Expectation Statements

	Before	After
Will be hard for auditors to learn.	− 1.41	− 1.12
Will force auditors to think like computers.	− 1.29	− 1.24
Will result in reliance on cookbook auditing and in time diminish auditor judgment.	− .12	− .12
Will dehumanize audit practice.	− .94	− .94
Will result in serious legal and ethical problems (e.g., increase malpractice suits).	− .29	− .47
Will diminish clients' image of auditor.	− .59	− .71
Will threaten an auditor's self-image.	− .59	− .77
Will depend on knowledge that cannot be kept up-to-date easily.	− .35	− .24
Will reduce the cost of auditing.	− .06	.06
Will result in less efficient use of auditor time.	− .59	− .47
Will alienate auditors because of electronic gadgetry.	− 1.12	− 1.12
Will reduce the need for specialists.	− .94	− 1.12
Will be unreliable because of computer malfunctions.	− .94	− .59
Will be blamed by clients for audit errors.	− .24	− .29
Will threaten personal and professional privacy.	− .82	− .89

TABLE 3
Mean Ratings for Demand Statements

	Before	After
Should respond to voice command and not require typing.	.41	.41
Should simulate auditor thought processes.	1.18	.65
Should never make an incorrect judgment.	− .29	− .06
Should become the standard for acceptable audit practice.	− .47	− .65
Should improve the cost efficiency of audit tests.	.65	.59
Should demand little effort from an auditor to learn or use.	.76	.59
Should significantly reduce the amount of technical knowledge an auditor must learn and remember.	− 1.35	− .77
Should display common sense.	.71	.77
Should be able to explain decisions to auditors.	1.59	1.41
Should automatically learn new information when interacting with audit experts.	.82	.65
Should display an understanding of their own audit knowledge base.	.94	.71
Should *not* reduce the need for specialists.	.71	.41
Should be portable and flexible so that the auditor can access them at any time and place.	1.71	1.41

TABLE 4
Subjects' Evaluation of EDP-XPERT

Please evaluate the expert system (AL/X) used in this experiment in terms of the attributes listed below:

	Mean Subject Response
1. Wording of questions	2.88
2. Explanation of questions (E command)	3.31
3. Explanation of why a question was asked (W command)	3.08
4. Explanation of program's reasoning (C command)	3.00
5. User response scale (+5 to −5)	3.24
6. Program's usefulness	2.77
7. Reliability of program's advice	2.63
8. Program performance	2.81
9. Educational capability	3.18
OVERALL	2.98

Response Scale:
1 = Very Poor 3 = Good   5 = Excellent
2 = Poor   4 = Very Good

SUBJECTS' EVALUATIONS OF EXPERT SYSTEMS AND EDP-XPERT

We gathered attitudinal data related to expert systems from the subjects. These data included subjects' responses on: (1) applications of computers to auditing, (2) the subjects' expectations and demands from expert systems, and (3) the subjects' evaluation of EDP-XPERT. Since these data are based on a small sample of auditors from one firm, no statistical tests were performed on these attitudinal questions. The results are shown in Tables 1–4.

Table 1 contains the number of subjects' responses to six areas where computers could be used in auditing. Items 1–4 on this table are current applications in practice. Virtually all of the subjects indicated that these items would be appropriate uses of computers in auditing. Items 5 and 6 were included to elicit the subjects' beliefs concerning expert systems. In particular, sixteen of 17 subjects indicated that expert systems would be an appropriate use of computers for *assisting* auditor judgment. On the other hand, only one subject thought that computer-based decision aids should be *substituted* for audit judgment. The subjects who thought that expert systems were appropriate for assisting auditor judgment were also asked to indicate which of nine audit areas might be appropriate for expert systems application. These areas were selected based on areas where expert systems in auditing are currently under development and areas where their use might be applicable.

Tables 2 and 3 present the mean ratings for a series of expectation and demand statements concerning expert systems. Each of the statements was preceded by the following: "Computer-based decision aids (expert systems) when FULLY developed . . ." The response scales and their corresponding values were: strongly disagree (-2), somewhat disagree (-1), not sure (0), somewhat agree (1), and strongly agree (2). The questionnaire was administered both *prior to* and *after* the use of EDP-XPERT. The second administration was conducted in order to see if the actual use of an expert system would change the subjects' beliefs.

In Table 2 we note that all of the mean values are negative. Thus, the participants disagree to some extent with all the expectation statements and, therefore, do not see a negative impact on themselves as individual auditors or on the profession from the use of expert systems. There is very little difference between the two administrations of the questionnaire. It is interesting to note that the responses by the physicians in the Teach and Shortliffe study (1981, p. 549) were positive for thirteen of these questions.

Table 3 provides the CASs' mean ratings on a series of questions related to what a user should expect from an expert system. The CASs have some definite views on a number of these statements. For example, there is high agreement that the system should: (1) simulate the auditor's decision processes, (2) be able to explain decisions to auditors, and (3) be portable and flexible. There is also strong agreement that the system will *not* reduce the amount of technical knowledge an auditor must learn and remember. The strength of these evaluations decreased after the use of the expert system.

Table 4 presents the subjects' evaluation of EDP-XPERT. Nine attributes, based on the previously mentioned criteria, were evaluated on a five-point scale (1 = very poor, 2 = poor, 3 = good, 4 = very good, 5 = excellent). The overall evaluation of the system (mean responses averaged across all nine attributes) was good (2.98). However, four items (1, 6, 7, and 8) which deal directly with the performance of EDP-XPERT received average

Applications in Auditing

ratings less than 3.0. These results show areas in which the EDP-XPERT system needs improvement. Given the current state of development of EDP-XPERT, we view these overall results as encouraging.

SUBJECTS' EDP CONTROL JUDGMENTS

In Table 5, we present the CASs' overall evaluations of the company's EDP controls. There were two evaluations of the EDP controls made by the subjects: (1) prior to the use of EDP-XPERT (PRE), and (2) after the use of EDP-XPERT (POST). EDP-XPERT's evaluation (SYS) of the reliability of the controls is also shown. Note that EDP-XPERT's evaluation is based on

TABLE 5
Subjects' Evaluations of EDP Controls

Controls

SUBJECT NUMBER	SUPERVISORY			PROCESSING			INPUT			OUTPUT		
	PRE	SYS	POST	PRE	SYS	POST	PRE	SYS	POST	PRE	SYS	POST
1	80	15	15	50	95	95	80	0	50	80	65	65
2	65	15	40	60	95	50	60	40	50	60	65	50
3	75	75	75	75	90	75	95	50	95	80	50	80
4	25	10	8	75	95	95	50	90	90	85	60	60
5	40	20	50	40	80	80	40	50	50	40	50	50
6	80	25	60	80	95	80	95	50	90	95	50	90
7	95	5	5	95	90	90	95	30	30	95	55	55
8	75	45	60	85	95	90	85	50	65	85	65	70
9	40	50	40	40	80	50	30	30	30	30	60	30
10	65	20	65	65	70	65	40	50	70	85	65	85
11	75	70	70	80	70	70	90	50	80	85	65	70
12	60	15	40	75	95	60	65	50	50	80	70	50
13	50	10	50	60	95	60	70	20	70	70	50	70
14	75	30	70	75	95	70	80	30	75	80	60	70
15	80	25	80	40	55	40	80	20	80	80	50	80
16	20	10	15	60	90	70	80	20	60	70	65	60
17	40	5	10	70	90	70	70	50	60	65	50	60

175

TABLE 6
Correlations of Subjects' Overall EDP Judgments and EDP-XPERT's Advice by Type of EDP Control

$\star = p < .05 \quad \star\star = < .10$

Supervisory Controls:

	PRE	SYS	POST
PRE	1.0		
SYS	.280	1.0	
POST	.416★★	.646★	1.0

Input Controls:

	PRE	SYS	POST
PRE	1.0		
SYS	−.235	1.0	
POST	.353	.407★★	1.0

Processing Controls:

	PRE	SYS	POST
PRE	1.0		
SYS	.430★★	1.0	
POST	.494★	.494★	1.0

Output Controls:

	PRE	SYS	POST
PRE	1.0		
SYS	.103	1.0	
POST	.711★	−.266	1.0

In this paper we presented the results of the preliminary investigation of EDP-XPERT. We also provided some insights into how expert systems can be evaluated. It is our hope that this paper will provide useful information to those researchers interested in expert system development.

the individual subjects' responses to the questions posed during the interactive session.

Table 6 presents the Pearson correlations of the subjects' judgments (both prior to and after the use of EDP-XPERT) and EDP-XPERT's conclusion.[7] The correlations are calculated by type of EDP control (system goal). An examination of the correlations for the supervisory controls indicates that the subjects' judgments prior to the use of EDP-XPERT (PRE) are not highly correlated with EDP-XPERT's evaluations (SYS), but they are correlated (p < .10) with the subjects' POST judgments.

176

Note, however, that the subjects' POST judgments are more highly correlated (p < .05) with EDP-XPERT's conclusion. The results of the correlations for the application controls are mixed. With the input controls, the results follow the general pattern found with the supervisory controls. The correlations of the judgments for the processing controls show similar correlations between PRE, POST, and EDP-XPERT. The output controls show that there was a high correlation between the subjects' PRE and POST judgments and that EDP-XPERT's conclusion was not highly correlated with either the subjects' PRE or POST judgments. This result for the output controls is not surprising since that part of the knowledge base contained only eight rules at the time of the test.

We infer from these results that the subjects' judgments after the use of EDP-XPERT were affected by their use of the expert system and its conclusion, and that the subjects' revisions of their control judgments (except for output controls) were in the direction of the expert system's conclusions.

Limitations, Future Research, and Concluding Comments

There are a number of limitations associated with this research which limit the generalizability of the results. First, this work is only a preliminary investigation of EDP-XPERT. As a result, the testing used in this study was not as rigorous as that required for formal testing (e.g., a blinded study). This work is consistent, however, with the suggestions made by Buchanan and Shortliffe (1984) that expert systems be subjected to various types of testing during their development. However, conducting formal tests of EDP-XPERT (and we suspect other expert systems in auditing) will be relatively difficult and costly. For example, the amount of information a subject needs to run *one* case for an interactive session is enormous; basically, all information on the client's EDP system. Additionally, there are only a limited number of CASs and access to them is very costly.

Second, we used a small number of subjects from one firm. Third, these subjects were not as experienced as the intended users (senior CASs) of the system.[8] Our results might have been different if we had used senior CASs. Finally, the expert system software has some built-in capabilities which may have affected the results. For example, the way the system selects the next question to be asked (the question which causes the greatest shift in the degree of belief) may not always appear to be logical. The reader is referred to Kidd and Cooper (1985) for a more detailed discussion of some of the potential difficulties with the AL/X software.

Our future work on EDP-XPERT will involve expansion of the knowledge base to include rules for controls in online and database systems. We are continuing to use reconstructed methods for gathering this knowledge followed by refinement with an expert. After this work is completed, EDP-XPERT will be subjected to two forms of testing. First, we will evaluate EDP-XPERT across a series of case studies using senior CASs. Second, if this previous testing proceeds well, EDP-XPERT will be field tested on a number of actual audit engagements.

Footnotes

1. Research in expert systems is still in its infancy. Very few systems are being used on an ongoing basis in the field. It may be optimistic at this point to think that expert systems will achieve a performance level greater than an expert.

2. We initially thought that expert systems researchers in the medical area always had outcome feedback, and therefore, tests of such systems were somehow more objective. However, Shortliffe (1984) points out: "The evaluation of expert systems that deal with medical therapy advice is actually very similar to the situation you describe for computer audit specialists. In the area of treatment, only one decision can be made and applied and it is not possible to back up and try again without having changed the situation. Since there are no gold standards for what is 'correct,' and even experts disagree about the preferred mode of treatment, this situation has presented real challenges in evaluating therapy advice systems."

3. Our definition of advanced computer systems follows Davis and Weber (1983) and includes three categories: distributed processing systems, database management systems, and online, real-time systems.

4. No existing expert system that we are aware of claims to make decisions *exactly* the way an expert does, although there is recognition that a better understanding of *how* experts solve problems may be necessary before expert systems achieve expert-level performance (Buchanan and Shortliffe, 1984).

5. We felt it was important to our work to develop an initial prototype. We chose to concentrate our initial efforts on controls in a distributed processing system. See Hansen (1984) for a discussion of audit considerations in a distributed processing system.

6. The authors would like to thank Professor Edward Shortliffe for allowing us to use and adapt this questionnaire for our study.

7. After making their POST judgments of the controls, the CASs were asked if they revised their judgments of the company's controls as a result of using EDP-XPERT. Fourteen subjects indicated that they revised their probabilities

based on the use of EDP-XPERT. Deletion of the three subjects that did not rely on EDP-XPERT does not significantly change the results reported in Table 6.

8. The firm that was assisting us with the project has three levels of CASs and there are only a small number of senior CASs (approximately thirty-five) distributed throughout their offices in the United States (Elliott, 1983). Given the preliminary nature of this investigation, we determined that these less experienced subjects would be adequate.

References

Ashton, R. H., *Research in Audit Decision Making: Rationale, Evidence and Implications,* Research Monograph No. 6, (Vancouver, Canada: Canadian Certified General Accountants' Research Foundation, 1983.

Biggs, S. F., W. F. Messier, Jr., and J. V. Hansen, "A Descriptive Analysis of Computer Audit Specialists' Decision-Making Behavior in Advanced EDP Environments," working paper, April 1986.

Buchanan, B. G. and E. H. Shortliffe, *Rule-Based Expert Systems: The MYCIN Experiments of the Stanford Heuristic Programming Project* Addison-Wesley, 1984.

Chandrasekran, B., "On Evaluating AI Systems for Medical Diagnosis," *The AI Magazine,* Summer 1983, pp. 34–38.

Davis, G. B. and R. Weber, *Auditing Advanced EDP Systems: A Survey of Practice and Development of a Theory,* Minneapolis, MN: The Management Information Systems Research Center, 1983.

Duda, R. O., J. G. Gaschnig, and P. E. Hart, "Model Design in the PROSPECTOR Consultation System for Mineral Exploration," in *Expert Systems in the Microelectronic Age,* D. Michie, (ed.), Edinburgh University Press, 1980.

————, P. E. Hart, and N. J. Nilsson, "Subjective Bayesian Methods for Rule-Based Inference Systems," *AFIPS Conference Proceedings of the 1976 National Computer Conference,* 1976, pp. 1075–1082.

Dungan, C. W. and J. S. Chandler, "AUDITOR: A Microcomputer-Based Expert System to Support Auditors in the Field," *Expert Systems,* October 1985, pp. 210–221.

Einhorn, H. J., "Expert Measurement and Mechanical Combination," *Organizational Behavior and Human Performance,* 1972, pp. 86–106.

Elliott, R. K., "Unique Audit Methods: Peat, Marwick International," *Auditing: A Journal of Practice & Theory,* Spring 1983, pp. 1–12.

Gaschnig, J., P. Klahr, H. Pople, E. Shortliffe, and A. Terry, "Evaluation of Expert Systems," In F. Hayes-Roth, D. A. Waterman, and D. B. Lenat (eds.), *Building Expert Systems,* Addison-Wesley, 1983.

Glass, A. L. and K. J. Holyoak, *Cognition,* Random House, 1986.

Gorry, G. A., "Computer-Assisted Clinical Decision-Making," *Methods of Information in Medicine,* 1973, pp. 45–51.

Hansen, J. V., "Audit Considerations in Distributed Processing Systems," *Communications of the ACM,* August 1983, pp. 562–569.

———— and W. F. Messier, Jr., "The Feasibility of Using Artificial Intelligence Techniques for EDP Auditing," Research Report on Project 80-145, The Peat Marwick Foundation, December 1981.

———— and ————, "Expert Systems for Decision Support in EDP Auditing," *International Journal of Computer and Information Sciences* 1982, pp. 357–379.

———— and ————, "A Knowledge-Based Expert System for Auditing Advanced Computer Systems," *European Journal of Operations Research,* 1986, in press.

Hogarth, R., *Judgment and Choice: The Psychology of Prediction,* New York: John Wiley & Sons, 1980.

Johnson, P.E., "What Kind of Expert Should a System Be?" *Journal of Medicine and Philosophy,* Vol. 8, 1983, pp. 77–97.

Kidd, A. L. and M. B. Cooper, "Man-Machine Interface Issues in the Construction and Use of an Expert System," *International Journal of Man-Machine Studies,* 1985, pp. 91–102.

McDermott, J., "R1 Revisited: Four Years in the Trenches," *The AI Magazine,* Fall 1984, pp. 21–35.

Paterson, A., *AL/X User Manual,* Oxford, England: Intelligent Terminals Ltd., 1984.

Shortliffe, E. H., Personal communications, December 27, 1984.

————, *Computer-Based Medical Consultations: MYCIN,* American Elsevier Publishing Co., Inc., 1976.

Teach, R. L. and E. H. Shortliffe, "An Analysis of Physicians' Attitudes Regarding Computer-Based Clinical Consultation Systems," *Computers and Biomedical Research,* Vol. 14, 1981, pp. 542–558.

Treisman, A. and G. Gelade, "A Feature-Integration Theory of Attention," *Cognitive Psychology,* 1980, pp. 97–136.

Yu, V. L., L. M. Fagan, S. M. Wraith, W. J. Clancey, A. C. Scott, J. F. Hannigan, R. L. Blum, B. G. Buchanan, and S. N. Cohen, "Antimicrobial Selection by Computer: A Blinded Evaluation by Infectious Disease Experts," *Journal of the American Medical Association,* 1979, pp. 1279–1282.

Scheduling Internal
Audit Activities

J. EFRAIM BORITZ and D. S. BROCA

Internal auditing, a key function in many organizations, is an integral part of the overall system of internal control, designed to ensure that other controls in an organization function as they should. Planning plays a crucial role in ensuring the effectiveness and proper focus of the activities of an internal audit department. However, recent surveys have found that the use of planning by the internal audit function has not been given adequate consideration (Boritz, 1983, p. 49). Often missing is a formal method for developing a comprehensive set of integrated departmental plans. A planning framework suggested by Boritz (1983) is subdivided into a network of six main sets of related activities:

1. defining the role, responsibility, and audit orientation of the internal audit department;

2. establishing facilities and procedures to be used;

3. identifying and managing the "portfolio" of auditable units and activities;

4. planning personnel-skill availability and utilization commensurate with the "portfolio" of audit task;

5. planning work activities and resource requirements of the department and its staff over appropriate time horizons and coordinating them with outside parties; and

181

6. scheduling, monitoring, and evaluating departmental work activities.

In this paper we consider the important audit planning problem of determining the audit schedule for each of the auditable units in a "portfolio" of such units over a specified planning horizon.[1]

Auditable Units

In today's corporate environment, a company may have several lines of business with operations across the globe, and may exhibit a myriad of authority-responsibility and reporting structures. In order that the auditor not get lost in the complexity of corporate structures, an "inventory" of all significant auditable units is usually compiled. The definition of auditable units would depend on specific organizational characteristics; e.g., whether the enterprise was functionally organized or product-centered. Analysis of business objectives, management processes, organizational relationships, information systems, and interviews with top management could all help in establishing an appropriate definition.[2]

The Audit As a Loss-Control Mechanism

One way of viewing internal audit activities is as a loss-control mechanism (Wilson and Ranson, 1971). This approach identifies two kinds of costs:

1. costs of fraud, error, waste, etc. which occur in the absence of auditing; and

2. the cost of the internal auditor and his or her work.

Compliance with controls within auditable units is assumed to deteriorate naturally over time (see Figure 1) unless appropriate action is taken at some point to restore compliance to its proper level (Barefield, 1975). Associated with this deterioration are economic consequences representing the costs of accumulated frauds, errors, or inefficiencies. The rate and extent of this deterioration would depend on a variety of factors, including the characteristics of the auditable unit and the auditors' skill in

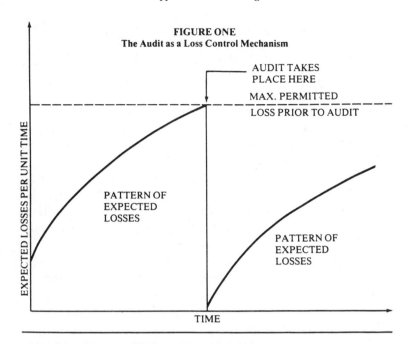

FIGURE ONE
The Audit as a Loss Control Mechanism

AUDIT TAKES PLACE HERE

MAX. PERMITTED LOSS PRIOR TO AUDIT

EXPECTED LOSSES PER UNIT TIME

PATTERN OF EXPECTED LOSSES

PATTERN OF EXPECTED LOSSES

TIME

discovering problems and recommending solutions. Audits are viewed as being instrumental in helping to restore compliance to its proper level (Hughes, 1977).[3]

There are costs associated with auditing, including costs of evaluating the controls and costs of correcting flaws and failures. Some of the costs of running the internal audit department are fixed and/or "sunk," and would be incurred irrespective of how much actual auditing was going on. Thus, they are considered to be irrelevant in our analysis. The cost of an audit, therefore, is the direct audit time plus direct audit-related expenses such as travel.

The auditor's goal is to audit as little and as infrequently as possible, but often enough to minimize deleterious economic effects upon the corporation due to significant deterioration of controls.[4] The optimal audit frequency should balance the expected losses if an audit does not take place against the cost of performing the audit.

AUDIT FREQUENCY

In conventional approaches to audit planning, it is assumed that all units will be audited at least "so often" during some period. This planning horizon typically covers three to seven years. The issue is, "How often within this planning horizon should each auditable unit be audited?"[5] There are three main policy alternatives for such decisions.

1. Fixed Frequency Policy

A fixed frequency policy is based on the implicit assumption that there are natural frequencies associated with audit units. The problem then becomes to find the "right" fixed frequency for each unit. This approach is followed by many internal audit departments, although frequencies may be adjusted periodically. It may be argued, however, that if auditees learn the fixed frequency, they may be motivated to perform at peak levels only at or near the audit dates. In addition, to the extent that the frequencies are imperfect, some auditable units would be consistently overaudited while others would be consistently underaudited.

2. Random Audit Frequency

Under this policy the frequency and timing of audits is unpredictable. Since auditees cannot guess when and to what extent they will be audited, it is argued that they would be motivated to maintain their controls and procedures at reasonable levels. However, such a policy is based on a relatively narrow view of auditee motivation, does not highlight the management assistance role of auditors, and may be difficult to justify to management; e.g., surprise audits, an example of this policy, are not performed in many organizations (IIA, 1979).

3. Conditional Audit Approach

Under a conditional audit approach, all auditable units might be monitored continuously or at specified intervals for signs of abnormal activity. Audits would be scheduled when units exhibited evidence of impaired controls. The reasoning behind this is that when compliance deteriorates, this affects the optimal functioning of economic activity. Thus, abnormal economic activity may be an indicator of control failures and by monitoring various relevant indicators, the internal auditor might be alerted to control problems. A variety of indicators is often used individually or in combination with other factors, as discussed below.[6]

Two approaches to conducting such monitoring activities are

analytical review and risk analysis. The latter is the basis of the discussion herein.

Riskiness Factors

In determining how often a particular audit unit is to be audited, several factors are implicitly or explicitly taken into account. In Section 520.04, the Standards for the Professional Practice of Internal Auditing suggest that criteria used for setting audit priorities should include:

* the date and results of the last audit;
* financial exposure;
* potential loss and risk;
* requests by management;
* major changes in operatiõns, programs, systems, and controls;
* opportunities to achieve operating benefits; and
* changes to and capabilities of audit staff.

However, a larger set of criteria might be drawn from the list provided by Patton et al. (1982); e.g., quality of the internal control system, competence of management, time since last audit, liquidity of assets, complexity of transactions, distance from the main office, changes in accounting systems, unit size, and level of employee morale.

Usually, subjective judgment about the relative importance of these factors cannot be avoided, especially when the benefits from auditing are intangible or difficult to predict.

Risk/Exposure/Concern Evaluation

After relevant criteria for establishing relative loss riskiness of auditable units have been identified, the next step is to use them in an organized fashion to arrive at an Audit Unit Priority Score (AUPS) for each auditable unit. Several approaches for doing this have been described by Boritz (1983).

1. Direct Assessment Method (Objective)
It is possible to set priority scores objectively by reference only to size attributes of auditable units (e.g., dollars of throughput,

value of assets, number of personnel, volume of transactions). Then, translating the appropriate largest unit attributes(s) to represent the highest number on a rating scale (e.g., ten on a one to ten rating scale), all other units can be ranked relative to this unit.

2. Direct Assessment Method (Subjective)

This evaluation is made using a rating scale. For each auditable unit, a subjective assessment is made using an importance scale (e.g., a scale ranging from one to ten) representing degrees of concern with respect to each risk factor for that auditable unit. These raw scores may simply be totaled, or differentially weighted and then totaled, arriving at the unit's priority score. For example, Wilson and Ranson (1971) suggest that each unit's "throughput dollars" be analyzed and classified into various categories of dollars processed. To each of these categories, an estimated (subjective) basic loss factor is assigned, representing a standard percentage of throughput dollars in that category typically considered at risk due to possible mismanagement. This "percentage at risk" is multiplied by the throughput dollars in that category and the results for all categories are summed, arriving at the risk of loss estimated for the auditable unit. When this is systematically carried out for all auditable units, the resultant risk of loss rating represents a relative priority score for ranking the units according to their riskiness. Other examples may be found in Boritz (1983).

3. Pairwise Comparison

This approach was suggested by Patton et al., (1982). For each risk factor, all pairs of auditable units are compared, one pair at a time, and a number from one to nine is assigned to the one with greater risk. When this has been done for all possible pairs of auditable units for one factor, the same process is repeated for the next factor, and so on, until all factors have been covered. The judgments so obtained are manipulated through matrix operations to yield a set of normalized eigenvectors whose elements represent the corresponding units' risk measures for that factor. These weights can in turn be weighted to reflect the relative importance of the risk factors, or equal weighting can be used.

4. Base Rate Assessment Method

This method is similar to the Pairwise Comparison Method except that some factor is chosen to represent a base for comparison and all other factors are evaluated in comparison with this base.

The pairwise comparison method yields a useful scale for setting priorities, but its applicability to very large organizations may be limited because of the need for an excessive number of comparisons. In contrast, the objective direct assessment method makes a more modest demand on planning time, but a poorer scale might result.[7] Depending on organizational size and characteristics, a combination of methods can be applied. Regardless of the method used, it is important to predefine clear guidelines for evaluating each factor properly.[8]

Previous Research

Wilson and Ranson (1971) pioneered the use of systematic methods to schedule audits. They considered four basic variables—size, risk, management quality, and cost of auditing—and suggested a framework for quantifying them. Their approach was based on the assumption that losses in the absence of auditing keep rising exponentially from zero to an asymptotic level of E dollars per year. Audit costs, on the other hand, are assumed to be incurred at a uniform rate. Once the audit is completed and the recommendations go into effect, after a certain delay the losses drop to zero and the pattern begins to repeat itself. Under these assumptions they derived an equation for an audit frequency that minimized the discounted present value of all costs, including operating losses susceptible to auditing and the direct costs of the audit itself. Although their model led to an equation which could not be solved explicitly, they developed an iterative solution procedure and also suggested an approximate formula.

Hughes (1977) constructed a general decision model appropriate for determining the optimal timing of internal audits. He viewed the problem as one of maintaining an internal control system. Hughes considered audits to be sets of actions which may lead to a restoration of a system to a desired level of effectiveness. The audits must be chosen at the beginning of each of an infinite number of periods conditional upon all information available concerning the state of the system. The objective is to select a policy for choosing actions to optimize relative to the cumulative economic consequences of the decisions made, i.e., minimize total expected discounted costs. In this vein Hughes models the problem as an infinite state, time-varying Markov decision process for which solutions can be obtained using dynamic programming methods.

Despite their existence in the literature, these papers have found limited application in internal audit departments. One reason may be the level of mathematical complexity, especially in Hughes' approach. The models also require data which may not be easily available even through the use of a heavy dose of subjective judgment. Moreover, reported computational experience on the behavior of the models in real-world settings is lacking.

Consequently, our objective in this paper is to examine a few robust and fairly general models that yield reasonable schedules, with inputs that are readily available or are capable of being estimated without too much difficulty. Beginning with a conceptual standpoint, several replacement-type models are examined whose solution techniques range from classical optimization to heuristics for achieving the cost tradeoffs. The emphasis here is on *understanding, applying,* and in some cases *extending* models that are fairly standard in the management science literature (see, for example, Jardine [1973] and Wagner [1975]).

A Conceptual View

We assume the following problem: the determination of an audit interval which minimizes the sum of audit costs and expected losses over the planning horizon. The tradeoffs in these costs and the resultant total cost function is depicted in Figure 2.[9]

Generally, audit units require some maximum period between successive audits, but within this constraint, their audit schedule typically depends on their relative importance or riskiness as measured by some index of loss riskiness. We call the index an Audit Unit Priority Score (AUPS). Figure 3 shows a typical pattern of audit cycles over a horizon of length T.

In situations where a large number of audit units are involved and in which an "ideal" long-range plan is to be determined, it is unwise to ignore the time value of money. Consequently, all future cash flows consisting of audit costs and expected losses should be discounted back to their present value as at the beginning of the planning horizon.

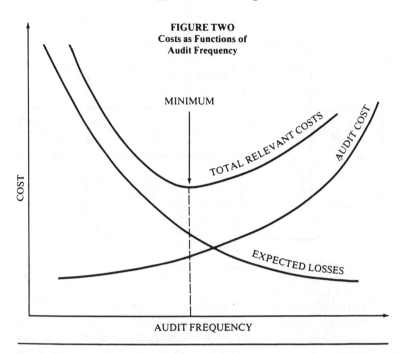

FIGURE TWO
Costs as Functions of
Audit Frequency

MINIMUM

TOTAL RELEVANT COSTS

AUDIT COST

EXPECTED LOSSES

COST

AUDIT FREQUENCY

THE ASSUMPTIONS

The model developed in this section assumes that for each identified auditable unit a conditional frequency policy is being adopted, in which the problem is to relate the frequency of auditing to a set of factors indicating an economic need for an audit. However, recognition is given to the usual constraint that all units must be audited at least once over a pre-specified planning horizon.

1. It is assumed that expected losses *(L)* accrue if a unit remains unaudited. It is further assumed that losses *(L)* rise exponentially over time *(t)* from zero and asymptotically approach a limiting level of M dollars per year.[10] Above this critical level the losses would be so high as to immediately alert management, who would call for an audit. The rate β at which the losses grow with time can be modeled by the function:[11]

$$L(t) = M(1 - e^{-\beta t})$$

189

FIGURE 3
Audit Cycles over the Planning Horizon

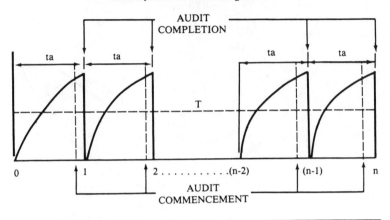

This type of curve is popular in modeling new product launches where the market is limited to some maximum value. The sales rate drops with the passage of time as market penetration increases and approaches the limit. In the above function, β is the growth rate coefficient which can be represented by the AUPS. This interpretation is reasonable since a higher AUPS represents a potentially risky unit in which losses grow at a much faster rate toward the limiting level than in one exhibiting a relatively low AUPS. Figure 4 depicts the behavior of the function for increasing values of β.

2. For determining M, the unit's assets or throughput may be taken as the starting point. This figure is typically in millions of dollars. Audit costs of the respective units, on the other hand, are in thousands of dollars. In order to balance the two, the throughput/asset figure may be scaled down proportionately so as to lie in the same range as the audit costs. This is accomplished by adding to the minimum audit cost a proportion of the audit cost range. The proportion added is determined by the ratio of the unit's throughput/assets to the maximum throughput or asset size in respect of all units.

$$M = Min.\ Audit\ Costs + \left[\frac{Unit\ Throughput}{Max\ Throughput}\right]$$
$$x\ Range\ of\ Audit\ Costs$$

190

In the absence of other methods and in view of the difficulty in directly estimating *M,* this scaled value is a proxy for the maximum expected loss if the unit is unaudited. When used in the loss function, it reflects the impact of asset or throughput size on loss accumulations and ensures meaningful tradeoffs between these losses and audit costs. *M* should not be given too literal an interpretation. Conceptually, this parameter should be regarded as a "trigger" value; accumulation of waste, inefficiencies, etc. beyond this benchmark would force management to call for an audit immediately, irrespective of the unit's established schedule.

3. The magnitude and range of the AUPS, which serves as the growth rate coefficient β in the loss function, is of utmost importance. As described earlier, several methods can be used to estimate the AUPS; but the basic objective is always to assign to each unit a number that expresses its relative riskiness. We assume that the internal audit department has a method based on judgment and/or mathematical techniques that yields a number representing the AUPS, the higher numbers representing more risky units.[12] It is not the purpose of the present paper to demonstrate all possible variations in method that could be employed for obtaining risk scores. The

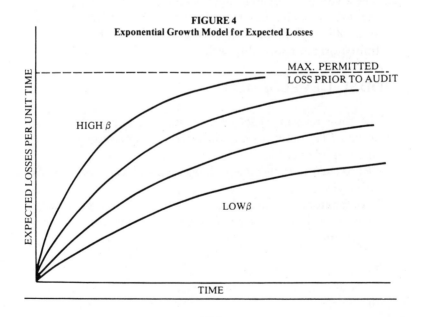

FIGURE 4
Exponential Growth Model for Expected Losses

MAX. PERMITTED LOSS PRIOR TO AUDIT

HIGH β

LOW β

EXPECTED LOSSES PER UNIT TIME

TIME

important point to note here is that the raw AUPS, computed by whatever method, when scaled by an appropriate factor and inserted in place of β in the exponential function, determines the relative speed at which losses accumulate over time (refer to Figure 4).

4. Each time the decision to audit is made, an audit cost, C, is incurred. It is assumed that a reliable estimate can be obtained by multiplying the standard hours required for auditing by the standard cost per hour incurred. These figures are usually available from the time summaries maintained by internal audit departments. Significant overheads (e.g., travel costs) should also be considered. As shown in Figure 3, audit costs are incurred over a small time period towards the end of each cycle. Since this interval is usally small in relation to total cycle length, it is assumed that they are incurred at the end of each cycle. The expected losses, on the other hand, are assumed to accrue continuously over the entire cycle length.

5. The relevant interest rate to be applied has in itself been a lively topic of research. For purposes of this article, it is assumed that the appropriate interest rate (r) is known or can be estimated.

6. The assumption of an infinite planning horizon also underlies the analysis. This is for mathematical convenience. The results obtained should, on average, approximate those for a finite horizon reasonably well.

MODEL DEVELOPMENT

The total relevant costs (TRC) over a planning horizon of duration (T) are a function of the interval (t_o) between successive audit completions.

$TRC = $ *audit costs over the planning horizon + expected losses during this period.*

To obtain total discounted costs, the problem is approached on a cycle-by-cycle basis. Two steps are necessary for each audit cycle (Jardine, 1973]:

1. Using appropriate formulae, the expected losses and audit costs are discounted to their present value as at the start of that cycle.

192

$$Discounted\ audit\ cost = C\,e^{-r't_o} \qquad (1)$$

and
Discounted expected losses =

$$\int_0^{t_o} L(t)e^{-rt}dt \qquad (2)$$

where L *(t)* is approximated by

$$M\,(1 - e^{-Bt})$$

2. The "intermediate" discounted cash flow so obtained is again discounted back to its present value as at the start of the first cycle (or the planning process). The results are then summed for all cycles forming an infinite series.

Thus, total discounted costs $TDC\ (t_o)$ over a long period of time, with an audit interval of size t_o, are given by equation (3).[13]

The objective is to seek a cost minimization solution, so we differentiate with respect to t_o and equate to zero as in equation (4).

The value of t_o which satisfies the above equation is the desired interval.

Since equation (4) does not yield an explicit solution for t_o in terms of the other known parameters, standard numerical techniques would be required; for example, we demonstrate a graphical plot method (Jardine, 1973):

1. Evaluate the left-hand of the equation and mark off this value on the vertical axis.

2. For various values of t_o sufficiently close, evaluate the right-hand side and plot these values forming a smooth curve.

3. Draw a horizontal line from the left-hand side to the smooth curve, then drop a perpendicular from this point to the x-axis. The intersection between the horizontal axis and the perpendicular yields the optimal value of t_o.

The graphical procedure is illustrated in Figure 5. Admittedly, if the number of audit units is large, some programmed numerical method, such as the Bisection method, [14] would have to be used.

$$TDC(t_o) = \frac{\dfrac{M}{\beta+r}e^{-(\beta+r)t_o} - \dfrac{M}{r}e^{-rt_o} + \dfrac{M}{r} - \dfrac{M}{\beta+r} + Ce^{-rt_o}}{1-e^{-rt_o}} \qquad (3)$$

$$\frac{d[TDC(t_o)]}{dt_o} = \frac{-Me^{-(\beta+r)t_o} - Cre^{-rt_o} + Me^{-(\beta+2r)t_o} - \dfrac{Mr}{\beta+r}e^{-(\beta+2r)t_o} + \dfrac{Mr}{\beta+r}e^{-rt_o}}{(1-e^{-rt_o})^2}$$

or, $\quad 0 = \quad -Me^{-(\beta+r)t_o} - Cre^{-rt_o} + Me^{-(\beta+2r)t_o} - \dfrac{Mr}{\beta+r}e^{-(\beta+2r)t_o} + \dfrac{Mr}{\beta+r}e^{-rt_o}$

or, $\quad r\left[\dfrac{1}{\beta+r} - \dfrac{C}{M}\right] = e^{-rt_o}\left[1 - \dfrac{\beta}{\beta+r}e^{-rt_o}\right]$ $\qquad (4)$

MODEL SENSITIVITY

By examining the kurtosis of the total cost curve around the optimal t_o value, it is possible to study the sensitivity of total cost to changes in the audit interval (see Figure 6). A fairly flat behavior around this region would, for example, show that violation of the schedule is not likely to have a significant impact on the total costs. But on the other hand, if the total cost function rises steeply on both sides of the optimal value, then every effort should be made to adhere to the schedule.

If there is uncertainty about the values of the input parameters, the total cost function can be plotted for each value in the uncertain range. A scrutiny of the differing slopes of this function in response to these changes would reveal the sensitivity of the parameter in question. For an audit situation, the estimate of input parameter C is fairly reliable, based on historical time summary data. But it would be interesting and useful for audit planners to verify the effect of varying β by applying a scaling factor (in, say, multiples of ten) to the raw AUPS. A drastic change in the shape of the total cost function in response to

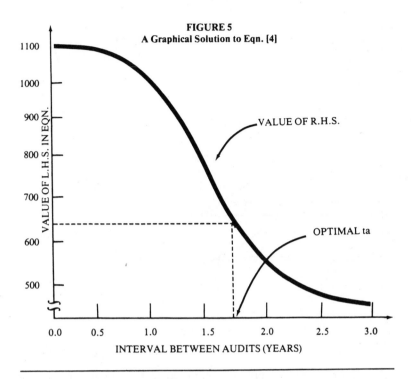

FIGURE 5
A Graphical Solution to Eqn. [4]

VALUE OF R.H.S.

OPTIMAL ta

VALUE OF L.H.S. IN EQN.

INTERVAL BETWEEN AUDITS (YEARS)

parameter changes might necessitate reexamining the estimation procedures for that input.

A Practical Approach

In this section we demonstrate a way that the above approach might be used in practice without overwhelming the internal auditor with mathematical complexity. The approach has been motivated by a heuristic developed by Silver and Meal (1973) which has wide applicability in production planning problems. The heuristic determines a minimum-cost replenishment policy for the case of time-varying demand given demand forecasts for a number of discrete time periods. The essence of its working is as follows. Starting at period one it tries to find a replenishment (order) quantity that will cover forecasted demand for as many future periods as possible, but is constrained in doing so by the fact that a trade-off between replenishment costs and carrying costs is involved. An order quantity covering five future demand

195

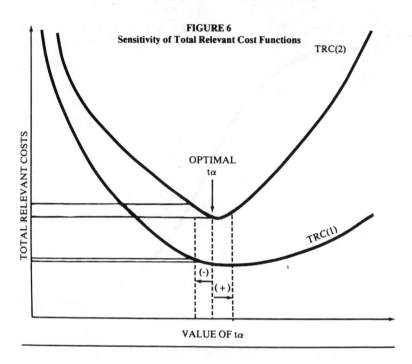

FIGURE 6
Sensitivity of Total Relevant Cost Functions

periods may reduce replenishment costs but greatly increases carrying charges. Therefore, the "optimizing" criterion used by the heuristic is to select the order quantity that minimizes the total relevant costs (replenishment plus carrying costs) per unit time for the duration of the replenishment. Having determined the duration of the first replenishment, the time period immediately following this duration is the next reference point to repeat the tradeoff procedure. The heuristic continues in this fashion until all future demand periods have been covered.

Suppose, in extending these ideas to the audit scheduling problem, that the internal audit department is charged with a planning horizon of *T* months. This might result from management's requirement that all units have an audit at least once during a period of six years. The objective is to systematically examine all possible audit cycles using a pre-specified step size until a cycle is obtained for which the sum of the total audit cost and expected losses is minimized. To see how this happens, consider a planning horizon of one year and a cycle period (i.e., the time between successive audits) of two months. Six cycles are generated and the end of each cycle represents the point in time when recommendations go into effect and losses drop to zero. The cost per cycle is the sum of expected losses and standard auditing cost of that unit. The expected losses are obtained by computing the integral of the loss function between the limits of zero and two. The total relevant costs *(TRC)* for the cycle are therefore:

$$TRC = \int_0^2 M(1-e^{-Bt})dt + C$$

Suppose the cycle period is increased to three months. The number of cycles reduces to four and the audit cost is also reduced because only four audits take place. But at the same time, the expected losses are greater per cycle because of the increased width of each cycle—the upper limit of integration is now three instead of two. The issue is whether the decrease in audit costs is large enough to more than offset the increase in expected losses during the planning horizon such that total relevant costs actually decrease. If the answer is affirmative, it is worthwhile to consider the three-month cycle.

Generalizing these concepts, we designed an algorithm that systematically searches through all possible cycles using a specified step increment; it then permits identification of that cycle which minimizes the sum of audit costs and expected losses over the planning horizon. The algorithm seeks to find a cycle which results in a unit being audited as infrequently as possible.

The cycle length, t_o, is increased in small equal steps until that cycle is obtained for which the *average discounted cost (ADC)* is minimized. In order to develop a precise mathematical expression an assumption is made, without loss of generality, that losses accrue at the end of each cycle. Thus the total cost per cycle for an audit interval t_o is:

$$TC(t_o) = \int_0^{t_o} L(t)dt + C$$

In the perfectly general case, an interval t_o generates n integer cycles and a fractional cycle t_f over the planning horizon whose cost is given by:

$$TC(t_f) = \int_0^{t_f} L(t)dt$$

197

Therefore, the total discounted costs for the time period under consideration may be calculated as follows:

$$TDC(t_a) = TC(t_a)e^{-r t_a} +$$

$$TC(t_a)e^{-2r t_a} + TC(t_a)e^{-3r t_a} + \ldots$$

$$+ TC(t_a)e^{-nr t_a} + \ldots + TC(t_f)e^{-rT}$$

Using the summation formula for a finite geometric series:

$$TDC(t_a) =$$

$$\left\{ TC(t_a)e^{-r t_a} \times \frac{(1-e^{-nr t_a})}{(1-e^{-r t_a})} + TC(t_f)e^{-rT} \right\}$$

The average discounted costs can now be obtained by dividing total costs by T:

$$ADC(T) = \frac{TDC(t_a)}{T}$$

The interval t_o which minimizes $ADC(T)$ determines the auditor's schedule.

ALGORITHM

A streamlined procedure for making the computations comprises the following steps:

1. Read the inputs—length of planning horizon, and the β, C, and M associated with the audit unit, together with the step-size to be used by the program.
2. Set the value of the current cycle length = 0.
3. Do the following while the current cycle length is less than or equal to T.

    a. Set the current cycle length = previous value + step size.

b. Compute the integer number of cycles in the planning horizon by dividing T by the current cycle length; thereafter, determine the length of the resulting fractional cycle, if any, at the end of the planning horizon.

c. Compute the total cost for each full cycle by evaluating the integral of the loss function from zero to the current cycle length and adding on the audit cost.

d. Compute the expected losses for a fractional cycle, if any, by integrating the loss function between zero and the length of this cycle.

e. Using appropriate discounting factors for each cycle, obtain the total discounted cost as the sum of a finite geometric series and an additive term for the fractional cycle, if any.

f. Divide the total discounted cost by the length of the planning horizon yielding the average discounted cost.

Endwhile

4. From the list of cycle lengths, pick as the optimal cycle the one with the least average discounted cost, breaking ties by choosing the one with the greater length.

5. Stop.

MODEL PERFORMANCE

The algorithm was programmed in WATERLOO BASIC.[15] A data generation subroutine in the program was used to simulate the behavior of the model over random sets of typical input data and an assumed five-year planning horizon. For each unit, the raw AUPS was generated as a random number between zero and nine and the standard audit costs were generated between $3,500 and $35,000, as is typical of these types of costs. The upper bound for the throughput/assets was fixed at $99 million; then, to obtain M, the generated figures were scaled down proportionately so as to lie in the same range as the audit costs. The primary objective of the simulation was to study the behavior of the algorithm, particularly its ability to yield a reasonable distribution of audit schedules.[16]

The loss function exponent β is represented by the raw AUPS scaled by an appropriate factor. The application of a low scaling factor to the raw AUPS leads to a relatively high exponent for the loss function, causing losses to accumulate so rapidly that they more than offset the decrease in audit costs brought about by increasing cycle lengths. Thus, a relatively short cycle yields the minimum of the total cost function; this, in turn, implies that the number of times a unit is audited over a planning horizon will tend to be on the high side. At the other extreme, when a large number is used as the scaling factor, the resulting low exponent for the loss function causes audit costs to dominate the behavior of the total cost function. Both extremes are undesirable since they lead to clustering at opposite ends of the horizontal axis. What is therefore necessary is the exploration of scaling factor magnitudes in a reasonable range in order to determine that subrange or particular value yielding a more or less uniform spread of audit schedules over the planning horizon.

A run size of 200 units[17] was employed, with the AUPS scaling factor incremented in steps of five, from one to fifty. In constructing the distribution of computed schedules under each scenario, the feasible range of schedule values from 0.1 to five years was divided into eight classes, each of size 0.5 years, beginning from one to 1.5 up to 4.6 to five.

In this model we must take into account not only variations in the scaling factor, but also the interest rate. Therefore, in designing the simulation experiment, interest rates of 10, 15, and 20 percent were considered (refer to Figure 7).

The following results emerged:

1. At the lower end, an interest rate of 10 percent causes heavy concentration at the right end of the horizontal axis if the raw AUPS is employed directly in the loss function. An AUPS scaling factor of five changes the shape of the distribution dramatically, and with an AUPS scaling factor of ten, a normal-type shape emerges which is reproduced in Figure 7. The middle frequency is quite high—about 37 percent of the total number of units. In order to balance the workload, units falling in this class can be appropriately redistributed into neighboring classes, especially the one to the left which contains no entries.[18] In respect to scaling factors higher than ten, the behavior of the algorithm is often erratic.

2. The 15 percent interest rate scenario starts in much the same way as the previous one; application of the first two AUPS

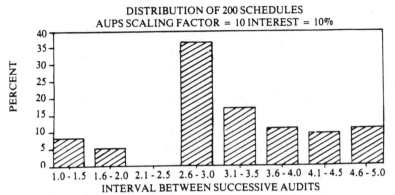

FIGURE 7
Audit Schedule Frequency Distributions
(Discount Rates = 10%, 15%, 20%)

DISTRIBUTION OF 200 SCHEDULES
AUPS SCALING FACTOR = 10 INTEREST = 10%

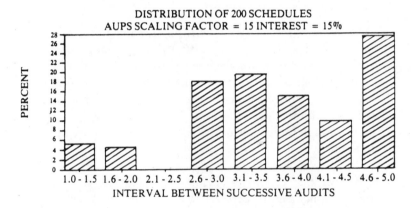

DISTRIBUTION OF 200 SCHEDULES
AUPS SCALING FACTOR = 15 INTEREST = 15%

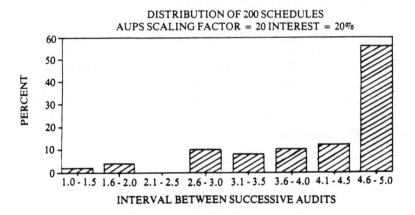

DISTRIBUTION OF 200 SCHEDULES
AUPS SCALING FACTOR = 20 INTEREST = 20%

201

scaling factors of five and ten alters results substantially. Nevertheless, there is a consistent concentration of schedules in the right-most class whose frequency dips initially and then steadily rises. An AUPS scaling factor of 15 causes approximately 27 percent of all schedules—the lowest for this interest rate—to fall in the right-most class (see Figure 7). This configuration, although a good one in present circumstances, may not always appeal to practitioners. The problem can be greatly alleviated if all classes from 2.6–3.0 onwards are shifted to the left by one step. Reclassification of audit schedules in this fashion, and subsequent redistribution if desired, will achieve greater uniformity at the expense of some loss in accuracy, which may not be very significant. For AUPS scaling factors higher than fifteen, the algorithm has a tendency to skew results overwhelmingly to the right, rendering them incapable of use.

3. At an interest rate of 20 percent, more than half the schedules fall in the right-most class over the entire range of AUPS scaling factors examined. Even through redistribution, re-classification, or shifting into adjacent classes, this distortion cannot be removed to any appreciable extent. This implies that for interest rates of around 20 percent or higher, there is an erosion in the power of the algorithm to produce balanced schedules.

It is clear that to obtain reasonable schedules, the user can employ scaling factors between ten and fifteen depending on whether interest rates are closer to 10 or 15 percent, respectively. A good rule of thumb is to start with a one-to-one correspondence between the prevailing interest rate and the AUPS scaling factor. Subsequently, a narrow range of factors around the initial value can be tried. The schedule frequencies so obtained can be redistributed or shifted to the left to achieve better configurations. This flexibility should be of value to practitioners. However, for interest rates close to 20 percent and beyond, use of the algorithm is discouraged.

Conclusions

We have developed and demonstrated what we believe to be an effective, yet simple, approach to the determination of audit

Applications in Auditing

frequencies. The procedure rests on plausible assumptions and is intuitively appealing, performing tradeoffs between audit costs and the losses that accrue in the absence of auditing. Through user-supplied inputs, due recognition is given to the auditor's judgmental process. The model is flexible since it allows the user to experiment with different frequency configurations by changing only a few key parameters such as M, β, r, and C. Of course, the model has some potentially significant limitations which should be recognized.

1. The loss function in our model incorporates several simplifying assumptions (e.g., its shape, rate of increase, and limits) which may not be applicable in practice.

2. The model incorporates several scaling factors (e.g.,for M and β) which are set empirically rather than analytically, and which have a limited range of reasonable operation as outlined above.[19]

3. The model requires an appropriate interest rate. Which rate should be used is an unresolved issue.

4. The model has only been tested by using simulation; thus, its behavior in practice is still unknown, particularly since the range of typical input data is unknown.

5. The model depends upon the auditor's professional judgment about the riskiness of an audit unit. The auditor may not have adequate experience in making such judgments or may not be able to accurately measure or convey appropriate risk scores.

The model output is essentially an audit coverage plan that can be incorporated into an integrated audit planning framework such as the one outlined in the introduction. The next logical step would be to match this coverage with resource availabilities over the planning horizon. Estimates of time requirements, personnel-skill availability, and progress and tenure ratings for audit personnel can be used to balance the workload over the coverage plan, identifying significant shortfalls or excesses in the resources. Once long-range feasibility is assured, detailed task assignments and work schedules can be established accordingly.

203

Footnotes

1. The terms frequency and schedule are closely related. A planning horizon divided into the audit schedule yields the audit frequency and vice versa. The choice of working in either of these units depends on the specific structure and assumptions of the models to follow.

2. The definition of what constitutes an auditable unit powerfully dominates the nature of audit procedures and the nature of benefits to be derived from the audit activity. By avoiding listing an overabundance of small, isolated audit projects, emphasizing instead the integrated aspects of various units, it may be possible to perceive more clearly the significant features of an operational activity and therefore the value of an audit of that activity.

3. This may appear to be a limited view of the internal auditor's role, since auditors can be viewed to perform a more "positive" consultative function in the organization. Any such positive role can be viewed in terms of opportunities for improvement foregone if no audit activity is undertaken, and this opportunity cost serves the same function as the loss in the discussion above.

4. There are those who suggest that it is not the audit that minimizes losses such as the above, but the fear of being audited. This is no doubt true; however, no such fear could be sustained if no audits ever took place. Some auditing is therefore essential, and it is the frequency of this audit activity which is the subject of this paper.

5. Subsidiary issues pertain to the scope of audits, the timing of audit stages, and work assignment to appropriate personnel. In this paper, only the frequency problem is studied.

6. Refer to Barefield (1975, Chapter 3) for a discussion of these factors. Examples of applications may also be found in Gray (1983), Staslee and Breckel (1984), Gresham (1984), and Thompson (1985).

7. Boritz and Jensen (1984) discuss a number of advantages and disadvantages of these methods.

8. One way of validating the ratings might be to have a few senior auditors go through the process independently, then correlate their ratings, identifying areas of strong disagreement. These should be discussed and a consensus reached.

9. The total cost function is traced out for the general case. Hence it is not necessary that its minimum lie at the intersection of the two constituent curves, a situation that always holds for the classical EOQ derivation.

10. This level M may be due to features such as integrity and conscientiousness of personnel and incentives in the system designed to limit the size of possible losses. Whatever the explanation for such a maximum, our model assumes that it exists and can be estimated.

11. Wilson and Ranson (1971) used a similar function in their analysis.

12. This method might, for example, be a more sophisticated version of the Direct Assessment Method (Subjective), requiring segregation of risk factors and units into categories, and then computing, through user-supplied inputs, category-specific weights based on arithmetic/geometric average methods. The relevant category weights could then be brought together and through a process of further averaging, an overall priority score obtained for that unit.

13. Details on the derivation of the following equations are available from the authors.

14. Under this method all terms are transposed to the L.H.S. and equated to zero, the central idea being to start with an interval which the user knows contains the zero of the function. Then, by repeated bisection of this interval, the zero is confined at each iteration to an interval half the size of the preceding one. Repeated application of the method will yield zero of the function to any prespecified degree of accuracy. For a detailed discussion, the reader is advised to refer to any standard text on numerical analysis.

15. The program listing is available from the authors upon request.

16. Of course, to actually validate the schedules requires field tests in specific organizations.

17. A run size of 200 units was chosen after some preliminary experimentation, in order to provide a tradeoff between asymptotic accuracy of audit schedule frequencies and computational time.

18. This is because a value of 2.6 causes the number of complete cycles in the five-period planning horizon to drop to one *for the first time,* leaving a large fractional cycle of size 2.4 years.

19. Rather than fixing AUPS scaling factors through simulation, this study could be extended by establishing a precise relation between the β's and their corresponding AUPS. Key personnel at audit locations can be shown a series of loss functions with differing β's and asked to choose that curve which, in their opinion, most closely matches the potential loss pattern for each audible unit. Next, the β's of the chosen curves can be regressed on the corresponding AUPs (computed in the usual fashion):

$$\beta_I = K_0 + K_1 AUPS_1 + \epsilon_1 \ (I = 1, 2, \ldots n)$$

The least-squares for K_0 and K_1 specify the relation (function) through which a unique β can be obtained for a given AUPS. This refinement could avoid the necessity for estimating AUPS scaling factors using simulation.

References

Barefield, R. M., *The Impact of Audit Frequency on the Quality of Internal Control,* SAR #1, Sarasota, FL: American Accounting Association, 1975.

Boritz, J. E., *Planning for the Internal Audit Function,* Institute of Internal Auditors Research Foundation, 1983.

―――― and R. E. Jensen, "A Hierarchical Assertion-Oriented Approach to Planning Audit Evidence-Gathering Procedures," paper presented at the Symposium on Audit Judgment and Evidence Evaluation, University of Southern California, February 12–13, 1985.

Gray, O. R., "Audit Project Evaluation Methodology," *The Internal Auditor,* June 1983, pp. 31–34.

Gresham, N. K., "Audit Coverage Plan," *The Internal Auditor,* August 1984, pp. 46–48.

Hughes, J. S., "Optimal Internal Audit Timing," *The Accounting Review,* January 1977, pp. 56–68.

Institute of Internal Auditors, *The Standards for the Professional Practice of Internal Auditing,* 1978.

――――, *Survey of Internal Auditing,* 1979.

Jardine, A. K. S., *Maintenance, Replacement, and Reliability,* Pitman Publishing, 1973.

Macchiaverna, P., *Internal Auditing,* The Conference Board, 1978.

Morse, P. M., *Queues, Inventories and Maintenance,* John Wiley & Sons, 1963.

Patton, J. M., J. H. Evans, and B. L. Lewis, *A Framework for Evaluating Internal Audit Risk,* Institute of Internal Auditors, 1982.

Silver E. A. and H. C. Meal, "A Heuristic for Selecting Lot Size

Requirements for the Case of a Deterministic Time-Varying Demand Rate and Discrete Opportunities for Replenishment," *Production and Inventory Management,* Vol. 14, No. 2, 1973, pp. 27–30.

Thompson, G. T., "Comprehensive Audit Planning," *The Internal Auditor,* April 1985, pp. 36–38.

Wagner, H. M., *Principles of Operations Research,* Prentice-Hall, 1975.

Wilson, D. E. and R. D. Ranson, "Internal Audit Scheduling—A Mathematical Model," *The Internal Auditor, July–August 1971, pp. 42–50.*

Internal Control Evaluation: A Computational Model of the Review Process

RAYMAN D. MESERVY,
ANDREW D. BAILEY, JR., and
PAUL E. JOHNSON

Researchers, as well as teachers and practitioners, are interested in the processes that auditors use when making judgments and decisions. While expertise in such fields as medicine, physics, and chess has been studied intensely during the past twenty years (e.g., Klienmutz [1968], Einhorn [1980], Elstein et al. [1978], and Johnson et al. [1982]), comparatively little research has been done in the fields of business and management.

The study and evaluation of internal accounting controls is a problem involving the expertise of well-trained auditors and is a requirement of every audit performed by CPAs. This research examines auditor expertise as it relates to the audit task of evaluating internal accounting controls.

This paper first focuses on expertise and the auditing task of reviewing and evaluating internal controls. The applicability of Decision Support Systems (DSS), Artificial Intelligence (AI), and Expert Systems (ES) to auditing tasks is then discussed. The current research covers the complete process of developing an expert system, but focuses most heavily on the cognitive science issues. The resulting computational model is intended to emulate the expert, i.e., the focus of our work is on understanding the expert's decision processes and not on building a better problem solver. The various methods of assessing the auditor's judgment processes used to build the knowledge base are presented. An expert system shell was used to build a computational model of the resulting process. Validation of the resulting computational model using several approaches is discussed.

Extant Auditing DSS/AI/ES/Applications

There are many views about what should be included as DSSs and their relationship to AI and ES. While no definitive statements of definitions and characteristics for DDS exist, in this paper we use the term Decision Support Systems or DDS in a broad sense to refer to any interactive computer application that helps a decision maker by providing access to large data banks or by implementing a decision model, or both.

Artificial Intelligence (AI) has been defined by Barr and Feigenbaum (1981) as "the part of computer science concerned with designing intelligent computer systems, that is, systems that exhibit the characteristics we associate with intelligence in ...ui ian behavior—understanding language, learning, reasoning, solving problems, and so on."

Expert systems have been defined by Stefik et al. [1982] as "problem-solving programs that solve substantial problems generally conceded as being difficult and requiring expertise. They are called knowledge-based because their performance depends critically on the use of facts and heuristics used by experts." Feigenbaum (1978) says, "We must hypothesize from our experience to date that the problem solving power exhibited in an intelligent agent's performance is primarily a consequence of the specialist's knowledge employed by the agent, and only very secondarily related to the generality and power of the inference method employed. Our agents must be knowledge rich, even if they are methods poor." Thus, expert systems attempt to capture specific knowledge from an acknowledged expert concerning a specific problem domain and to replicate the decision inference process used by this expert. In this paper, expert systems is used in a narrow sense to refer to interactive computer applications that help a decision maker by simulating the specific knowledge and inference processes used by experts in their limited domain of expertise.

208

The development of organized methods of collecting, organizing, and scoring data collected on audits was a long-established practice before the computer. However, the advent of inexpensive computing has opened new horizons. As a result, many of the manual aids previously used by auditors have been or are being converted to computer support systems. These include the systems prepared by the major public accounting firms, as well as private software houses catering to the public and internal auditing communities. Most of these systems concentrate on data collection from client systems, organization, analysis based on descriptive and normative models, statistical sampling methods, and workpaper control. In most cases, they lack the characteristics necessary to be a DSS as defined earlier. The term Decision Aid (DA) might better describe these systems.

In the last several years, auditing firms and academics have become very active in extending the capabilities of Decision Aids by adding menu-driven, interactive components to support the various audit functions. Peat Marwick Main & Co.'s SEACAS, the computerized version of SEADOC (1980), and Arthur Young & Co.'s recently announced ASQ, Auditing Smarter and Quicker, are good examples of this trend. Balachandran and Zoltners (1981) provide an example of possible future directions in this area.

Non-Expert DSS are part of a new wave of technological innovation in the field of auditing. Auditors accept both the technology and the potential of such systems. Within the next several years many such systems will come on line.

In the last few years, numerous projects have been started that attempt to apply expert systems techniques to the development of DSS for auditors. These include the development of TAX-MAN (McCarty, 1977) and TAX ADVISOR (Michaelson, 1982) to provide legal tax advice. TAX ADVISOR is based on the EMYCIN (van Melle et al., 1981) shell. AUDITOR (Dungan and Chandler, 1980) is an expert system for the evaluation of the adequacy of the client's allowance for bad debts. Other systems include those by Braun and Chandler (1982) to aid auditors in Analytic Review, by Hansen and Messier (1982), a model for evaluating EDP Controls, and by Bailey et al. (1985) for internal control evaluation.

There is currently an acceleration of research and development activities for DSS in auditing. The above brief discussion of systems in auditing represents only a small portion of the current

209

interest and activity. Further, this discussion ignores the many studies necessary to the final implementation of such systems. Studies such as that of Biggs (1979) on the going concern judgment process, Mutchler (1984) on the issues of "subject to" opinions, and many others facilitate the future development of DSS for auditors.

Expertise And The Audit Task

Expertise has been defined as "knowledge about a particular domain, understanding of domain problems, and skill about solving some of these problems" (Hayes-Roth et al., 1983). Davis has proposed that the nature of expertise includes the ability to: (1) solve the problem, (2) explain the result, (3) learn, (4) restructure knowledge, (5) break rules, (6) determine relevance, and (7) degrade gracefully (Davis, 1982).

An expert's knowledge consists of both public and private information. Public knowledge includes the facts, theories, and definitions as found in the texts and journals referenced by those studying in the domain. However, experts also possess private information that is not found in any of the public literature. Much of this private knowledge is in the form of rules of thumb which we will refer to as heuristics. Heuristics allow experts to "make educated guesses when necessary, to recognize promising approaches to problems, and to deal effectively with errorful or incomplete data" (Hayes-Roth, 1983). Knowledge engineers, who are concerned with the acquisition and representation of knowledge, concentrate much of their effort on the elucidation and reproduction of such "rules of expertise." Human expertise in problem solving is largely the recognition and use of heuristics. Feigenbaum emphasizes that "experience has taught us that much of this knowledge is private to the expert, not because he is unwilling to share publicly how he performs, but because he is unable. He knows more than he is aware of knowing" (Feigenbaum, 1978).

We consider auditors to be experts in performing certain tasks. The objective of this study was to determine the processes that auditors use in a specific audit task, formalize and implement those processes as a computational model, and then test the model.

Auditing Internal Accounting Controls

The American Institute of Certified Public Accountants (AICPA) (1979) defines internal controls as "the plan of organi-

210

zation and all the coordinate methods and measures adopted within a business to safeguard its assets, check the accuracy and reliability of its accounting data, promote operational efficiency, and encourage adherence to prescribed managerial policies . . . "(Section 320.09) (AICPA, 1972). Mair, Wood, and Davis, in their book *Computer Control and Audit,* make the statement: "Controls act upon things that can go wrong which, in turn, leads to the reduction of exposure" (Mair et al., 1978). Although all public accounting firms evaluate controls and general guidelines have been suggested by several different researchers (Mautz and Winjum, 1981), auditors still have difficulty evaluating the quality of internal control systems.

The general objective in studying accounting internal controls is to satisfy the auditor's second standard of field work: "There is to be a proper study and evaluation of the existing internal control as a basis for reliance thereon and for the determination of the resultant extent of the tests to which auditing procedures are to be restricted" (AICPA, 1972). Thus, the primary purpose is to determine whether the accounting controls are strong enough to be relied upon to produce reliable financial information. If the internal controls are determined to be strong, then the scope of other audit procedures may be more restricted than when the internal controls are determined to be weak. A second objective is to provide the auditor with a basis for constructive suggestions on how to improve the client's internal accounting controls (AICPA, 1972).

Conceptualization Of The Task

The strengths and weaknesses of an internal accounting control system are evaluated by determining control objectives, identifying controls and faults from a description of the system, and then combining the controls and faults into an overall evaluation of the sufficiency with which each control objective has been met. (See Figures 1a and 1b.)

Controls and faults are conceptual objects that can be identified by particular recognizable patterns of data embedded within the statements describing the accounting information system. Controls prevent, correct, or detect system exposures to loss or misrepresentation and may vary in character and extent. Faults act as "red flags" triggering auditor concerns. The identification of a fault does not necessarily indicate a system weakness as there

211

FIGURE 1a
Conceptulization

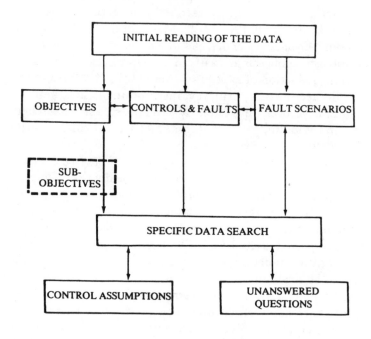

may be offsetting controls, but the identification of a fault generally results in a search for compensating controls.

Auditor associations between specific system designs, and the resulting strength of internal controls, are learned through formal education, case examples, and by performing many similar auditing tasks. These associations permit chains of deductive reasoning to be constructed connecting the structural design of the accounting system and the likely functional strengths and weaknesses of the system. This is typically called prototypic or recognition-based reasoning.

The result of the internal control evaluation task consists of: (1) a suggested list of controls for the compliance testing phase, and (2) a lists of control weaknesses. The list of control weaknesses indicates significant problems discovered during the evaluation process and the resulting exposures that could occur. The

212

FIGURE 1b
Conceptualization Overview

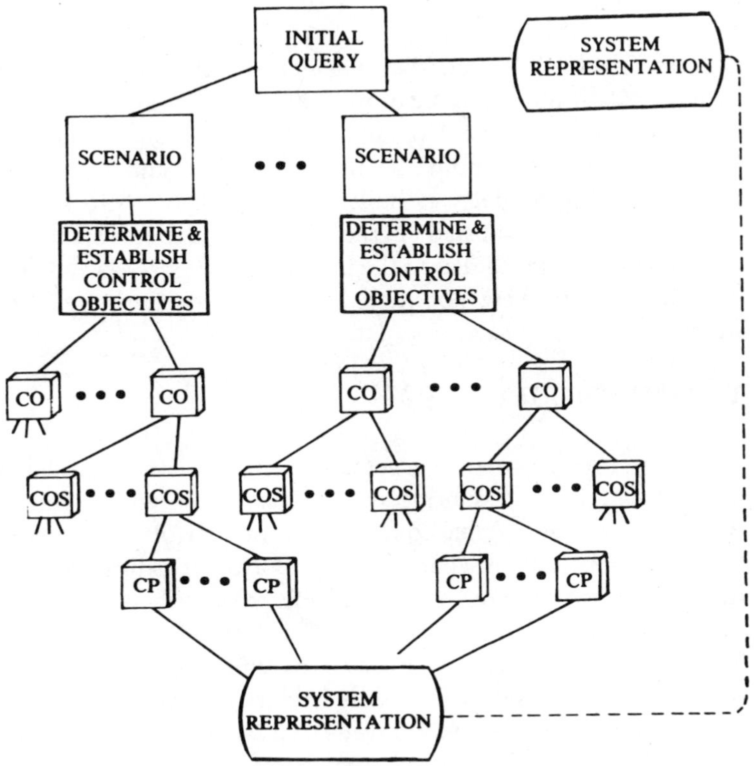

*Not necessarily a tree (overlap)

A Control Objective (CO) is a high-level abstraction of what preventive devices should be used. Control Objectives may be broken down into Control Subgoals (COS). Control Procedures (CP) look for an implementation (a matching pattern) and are the lowest level of control knowledge.

auditor uses this list in establishing subsequent compensating audit steps and for interaction with management. The specific weaknesses identified are combined with the controls to determine sufficiency for each control objective, which in turn results in the auditor expanding some of the substantive tests performed later in the audit.

SUBJECTS

Practicing CPAs in middle management of a large auditing firm served as subjects in the project. Managers in the local office of Peat Marwick Main & Co., an international public accounting firm, participated in both the model building and the cross-validation. The model was built largely with the help of one auditor, who also assisted in the model validation. Six other auditors assisted in validating the model. (See Figures 2a and 2b.) All the subjects were considered expert at the task by their superiors.

TASK DIFFICULTY

There is no unique set of acceptable controls that is considered normative; rather, accounting systems can be configured using a wide variety of acceptable combinations of controls. As a result, the evaluation of internal accounting controls is a difficult task. In addition, experts are generally unable to describe each step in the evaluation process, making it difficult to train new experts. The process is normally taught by providing *ex post* rationalizations of the analysis process and by having novices solve numerous case problems. Behavioral studies clearly indicate that the *ex post* explanations often do not match the process actually followed by the expert (Nesbett and Wilson, 1977).

The evaluation of internal controls has typically relied on such decision support aids as flowcharts and questionnaires concerning the client's accounting systems. The weaknesses inherent in these traditional techniques have been recognized by accountants and accounting firms for some time. The last several years have witnessed the introduction of a number of new approaches intended to regularize the data collection and evaluation process. Previously referenced research suggests a greater likelihood of success on the collection side than on the evaluation side. Nevertheless, public accounting firms hope that these new approaches

FIGURE 2a
Plan of Work

PLAN OF WORK

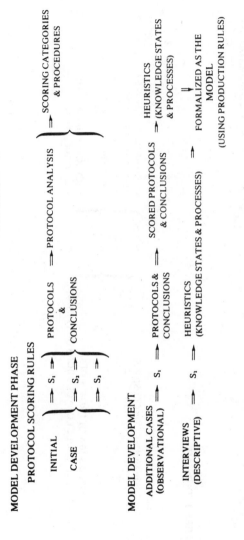

MODEL DEVELOPMENT PHASE
PROTOCOL SCORING RULES

INITIAL ⟹ S₁ ⟹
CASE   ⟹ S₂ ⟹ PROTOCOLS
        ⟹ S₃ ⟹ & CONCLUSIONS ⟹ PROTOCOL ANALYSIS ⟹ SCORING CATEGORIES & PROCEDURES

MODEL DEVELOPMENT

ADDITIONAL CASES ⟹ S₁ ⟹ PROTOCOLS & ⟹ SCORED PROTOCOLS & CONCLUSIONS
(OBSERVATIONAL)   CONCLUSIONS

INTERVIEWS ⟹ S₁ ⟹ HEURISTICS ⟹ HEURISTICS ⟹ FORMALIZED AS THE MODEL
(DESCRIPTIVE)   (KNOWLEDGE STATES & PROCESSES)   (KNOWLEDGE STATES & PROCESSES)   (USING PRODUCTION RULES)

MODEL TUNING PHASE

SEVERAL CASES ⟹
                MODEL ⟹ MODEL TRACE
REFINEMENTS TO ⟹   ⟹ MODEL CONCLUSIONS
KNOWLEDGEBASE*

SEVERAL CASES ⟹ S₁ ⟹ PROTOCOL & CONCLUSIONS ⟹ SCORED PROTOCOL ⟹ SUBJECT & MODEL OUTPUT COMPARISONS RESULTS IN REFINEMENTS TO KNOWLEDGEBASE (SEE ABOVE)

FIGURE 2b
Plan of Work

PLAN OF WORK (CONTINUED)

MODEL VERIFICATION PHASE

GENERAL DATA

THREE CASES:
1 TYPICAL
2 ATYPICAL

MODEL $\Rightarrow$ 3 TRACES
3 SETS OF CONCLUSIONS*

S_1 (PRIMARY)
S_2, S_3, S_6

$\Rightarrow$ 9 PROTOCOLS $\Rightarrow$
$\Rightarrow$ 9 SETS OF CONCLUSIONS*

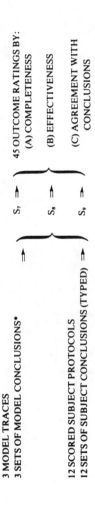

RATER$_1$
RATER$_2$

SCORED PROTOCOLS
(HYPOTHESES CATEGORIES
& REASONING PROCESSES)

$\Rightarrow$ TYPED CONCLUSIONS*

PEER JUDGMENT

3 MODEL TRACES
3 SETS OF MODEL CONCLUSIONS*

12 SCORED SUBJECT PROTOCOLS
12 SETS OF SUBJECT CONCLUSIONS (TYPED) $\Rightarrow$

S_7 $\Uparrow$
S_8 $\Uparrow$
S_9 $\Uparrow$

45 OUTCOME RATINGS BY:
(A) COMPLETENESS

(B) EFFECTIVENESS

(C) AGREEMENT WITH
CONCLUSIONS

*CONCLUSIONS CONSIST OF:
(1) LISTS OF CONTROLS TO BE COMPLIANCE TESTED
(2) LISTS OF CONTROL WEAKNESSES

216

will lead to greater consensus in evaluating internal controls among their field auditors.

THE TASK

Subjects were asked to perform the task of reviewing and evaluating actual audit of workpapers used in audits by Peat Marwick Main & Co. The task was limited to the purchases, payables, and cash distribution transaction cycle as found in manufacturing, wholesale, and retail industries. Specifically, the subjects were asked: (1) to identify control weaknesses or problems, and (2) to make recommendations for specific controls to be compliance tested. The workpapers consisted of SEADOC (Peat Marwick Main & Co., 1980) flowcharts and descriptions of client firms, as prepared by the in-charge auditor. The task was also veridical in that our subjects were managers, who ordinarily do not prepare such documents, but generally do review and evaluate internal controls based on such SEADOC documents prepared by others. Although our study places the manager in a normal and familiar role, the subject would normally be involved in an ongoing relationship with the client. For study purposes, our subjects evaluating internal controls were provided with documentation for clients with an ongoing relationship with the firm but in which no such relationship existed for them personally.

Methodology: Decision Processes

The methods discussed below were employed to help understand the expert auditor's decision processes in analyzing internal controls and to validate that understanding. For this study our focus was on understanding, not on building a better problem solver. The methodology is summarized in two phases, discovery and verification. (See Figures 2a, 2b, and 3 and discussions below.) The notable difference in using these tools to understand the expert process as opposed to a problem solver orientation is the extensive amount of work required in the discovery phase. The discovery phase was composed of two steps, model development and model implementation and tuning. The objective of the discovery phase was the development of a theory of task performance for our expert.

217

FIGURE 3
Research Overview

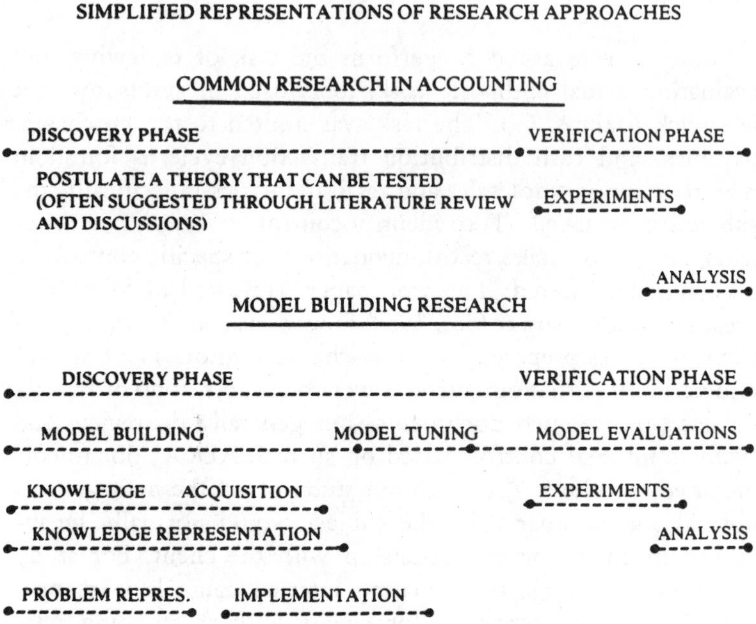

SIMPLIFIED REPRESENTATIONS OF RESEARCH APPROACHES

COMMON RESEARCH IN ACCOUNTING

DISCOVERY PHASE   VERIFICATION PHASE
●- -●- - - - - - - - - - - - - - -●

POSTULATE A THEORY THAT CAN BE TESTED
(OFTEN SUGGESTED THROUGH LITERATURE REVIEW   ●EXPERIMENTS●
AND DISCUSSIONS)

                                       ANALYSIS
MODEL BUILDING RESEARCH   ●- - - - - -●

DISCOVERY PHASE   VERIFICATION PHASE
●- -●

MODEL BUILDING   MODEL TUNING   MODEL EVALUATIONS
●- - - - - - - - - - - - - -●- - - - - - -●- - - - - - - - - - - - - - - - - - -●

KNOWLEDGE   ACQUISITION   EXPERIMENTS
●- - - - - - - - - - - - - - - - - - - -●   ●- - - - - - - - -●
KNOWLEDGE REPRESENTATION   ANALYSIS
●- -●   ●- - - - - -●

PROBLEM REPRES.   IMPLEMENTATION
●- - - - - - - - - - -●   ●- - - - - - - - - - - - -●

(The model must be verified through experimental research similar to any other theory)

The Discovery Phase: Model Development

Preliminary representations of expertise, including key concepts and relationships, were developed from interviews and experimental task data using experts both as collaborators and as subject-informants. These descriptions consisted of problem-solving steps and heuristics that represent auditor judgment in: (a) identifying internal accounting control objectives; (b) identifying controls and faults in the accounting system; and (c) evaluating the system controls, weaknesses, and sufficiency of documentation.

218

Knowledge Acquisition

Research at the University of Minnesota by Johnson (1983b) has isolated general principles of eliciting expert knowledge. This research adapted these approaches and used them to elicit knowledge from our expert auditors. The multi-method approach is summarized in three parts: observational, descriptive, and intuitive methods.

OBSERVATIONAL METHODS FOR KNOWLEDGE ACQUISITION

The observational approach adopted for this study consisted of collecting "thinking-aloud protocols" which were used to identify problem-solving mechanisms being used by experts. These protocols provided information about the organization of the expert's knowledge base, the knowledge it contains, and the control structures used to apply that knowledge. A major difficulty with observational methods is, however, that the very techniques used to determine the reasoning processes may distort those processes (Nisbett and Wilson, 1977; Johnson, 1983a).

Previous experience in cognitive modeling indicates that the decision making behavior of experts cannot be adequately understood by analyzing problem-solving processes alone. Several higher levels of analysis are important to the modeling of expertise. In this study, auditor decision processes were analyzed in terms of: (1) episodes, (2) views or frames of reference, and (3) problem-solving processes. The categories range from the more general decision- and goal-seeking strategy of the subjects, to very specific types of processes which allow the auditor to progress from one state of knowledge about the audit to another.

Macro-analysis of the protocols first identified the higher-order episodes used by the auditor in the decision making process. Episodes involve proposing tentative goals and/or subgoals appropriate for the task, and then doing the analysis necessary to either substantiate or disprove the goals. The macro-goal categories for the task are: (1) Decide on the likely inherent risk category of client and the most appropriate overall audit approach. Such firm categorization is based on understanding the macro-environment within which the firm operates, firm size, growth, industry, and general management characteristics. (2) Decide if there are significant processing controls which can be

219

relied upon and the appropriate compliance tests. (3) Choose which boundary controls for accounts payable to rely upon and the appropriate compliance tests. (4) Choose which controls over disbursements can be relied upon and the appropriate compliance tests. (5) Evaluate the effectiveness of general computer controls and other appropriate firm environment factors. (6) Draw conclusions on overall audit approach, controls to be relied upon, and appropriate audit procedures.

The episodic categories are presented in Figure 4 by dividing and thus standardizing each transcribed auditor protocol into 100 equal units and then classifying each unit in the appropriate category. Figure 4 presents the flow of the protocol from leeft to right. Each asterisk represents a unit of time during the protocol. As can be seen from Figure 4, the episodes are sustained goal-seeking categories. However, these episode goals are somewhat interdependent and must sometimes be suspended until other episodic goals have been reached. Consider the specific processing controls dependent upon the computer as an example. Before conclusions about the specific tests of computer processing controls can be reached, the auditor must first determine the effectiveness of the general computer controls and the extent to which they can be relied upon. Figure 4 allows us to relate how the episodes unfold and their relationship with other activities scored in the protocols.

Auditors also appear to have major frames of reference which allow them to organize and evaluate various aspects of the data cues. The views or frames of reference identified from the auditor protocols were: (1) processing, (2) segregation of duties, (3) electronic data processing (EDP) factors, and (4) the adequacy of the working papers.

The data cues are analyzed by the auditor from each of the above perspectives, then integrated before deciding which controls may be effective, which controls should be compliance tested, what type of compliance tests should be performed, and how large a sample would be sufficient. Our primary subject reported "flipping from one view to another" as he analyzed the data. He also reported significant interactions among these various views of the data. This behavior is evident in his protocols. Figure 4 illustrates, by reading down the Figure for a given time unit that there may be mention of more than one reference frame in any of the protocol units. Also note that the primary frame of reference is processing, which enjoys the most sustained atten-

FIGURE 4*

Graph of Protocol Analysis

```
Subject # 1    Case # C
Total Pages: 16
*************************************************************************************************

                              TASK STAGE (Protocol divided into 100 units)
                0       1       2       3       4       5       6       7       8       9       0  %
EPISODES:       1234567890123456789012345678901234567890123456789012345678901234567890123456789012345678901234567890
General Summary...   1       2       3       4       5       6       7       8       9       0
Processing Overvie******  1       2       3       4       5       **************************  0 42
A/P Addit(Boundry)   ***************************************************  6       7       8       9       0 52
Disbursmnts(Bndry)   1       2       3       4       5       6       7       8       9       0
Conclusions.......   1       2       3       4       5       6       7       8       9   ******  6
                                                                                                100

                0       1       2       3       4       5       6       7       8       9       0  %
VIEWS or FRAMES 1234567890123456789012345678901234567890123456789012345678901234567890123456789012345678901234567890
PROCESSING:
Commitments (PO)..   ********************  *3 *  * * 4       5 *     6       7       8       9       0 23
Recpt.of Goods(RR)   1       2   **********  * 4   5 *     6       7       8       9       0 12
Goods Returned....   1       2       3       4       5       6       7       8       9       0
A/P Additions(INV)  *  ** 1       2   **** ***** 4   ********   ***** *** 7  *  8********* 9  *** * 41
Disbursements(CKS)  *   1       2       3       4   *     *   ******************  9       0 21
Posting to Account** **  1       2       3       4       5       6*      7   *  *8      **      0 9

SEGREGATN.OF DUTIES  1       2       3   ***     5       6       7       8   * 9       0 4
EDP FACTORS.......   1   *   2   *   3       4       5       6*    * 7     8   * ** **   0 9
ADQCY.of WORK.PAPER  1       2       3   4********  5   **** 6       7       8       9       0 11

                0       1       2       3       4       5       6       7       8       9       0  %
COGNITIVE PROCESSES: 1234567890123456789012345678901234567890123456789012345678901234567890123456789012345678901234567890
Read (R)...........*  * *** **** * 2   *** 3   ** *4   ** * *   ******** 7*  ** *8 **  ** *   0 36
Data Search (DS)...   1       2       3       4       5       6       7       8       9       0
Infor.Retrieval(IR)  1       2       3       4       5       6       7       8       9       0
Plan (P)...........   1       2       3       4       5       6       7       8       9       0
Assumption (A).....   1       2       3*      4       5       6       7       8       9       0 1
Conjecture (C).....  **   1       **    *   *   4   *   5   * 6       7       8       9       0 8
Evaluation (E).....  *** * 1   * *2 **   **3 **   *******  *5  *** *6   ***7 ****  * **  ***  *g** 0 40
Question (Q).......   1       2       3       4       5       6       7       8       9       0
Inference (I)......   1       2       3       4       5       6       7       8       9   **** * 5
Generate Altern(GA)  1       2       3       4       5       6       7       8       9       0
Decision Rule (DR).  1       2       3       4       5       6       7       8       9       0
Audit Decision (AD)  1 *     2   *   3   ** 4   5** *  6       7       8       9 *  **    *0 10
                                                                                                100

                0       1       2       3       4       5       6       7       8       9       0  %
WRITTEN RESULTS:  1234567890123456789012345678901234567890123456789012345678901234567890123456789012345678901234567890
Controls to Test...  1                       23      456
Weaknesses & Qstns.          1                                                       2
```

WRITTEN RESPONSES

CONTROLS TO TEST:
1. compliance test: purchasing department's review of authorization for purchases
2. compliance test: comparison of invoice, purchase order, and receiving report
3. compliance test: math check of invoice
4. compliance test: authorization review by controller of check requisition
5. compliance test: accuracy control regarding check requisition
6. compliance test: math control regarding check requisition

WEAKNESSES, PROBLEMS, AND QUESTIONS:
1. why is population of P.O. N/A, management control point if nothing else
2. do not rely on processing controls without special application review

* Figure 4 is an example. A similar figure was prepared for each model and subject protocol on each case.

tion. It should be noted that the working papers themselves are organized primarily from a processing frame of reference.

Decision operators provide the links between individual knowledge states at the micro level. Scoring the protocol for problem-solving processes allows the determination of which operators are used by auditors in their evaluation of internal controls. Figure 4 also provides a list of cognitive operators used during scoring.

Using observational methods, the macro-analysis of the protocol provided the episodes and views around which the model was built. The micro-analysis scoring of the decision processes helped most in the model-building process when scored within the bounds of the specific goals and objectives that direct the search and confirmation processes.

The initial protocol phase of research was followed by a refinement phase in which experts were asked to comment on the episodes and views developed from the protocols and were queried for the appropriate decision rules.

DESCRIPTIVE METHODS FOR KNOWLEDGE ACQUISITION

Descriptive methods of assessing expertise are used to formalize portions of the expert's knowledge by transforming that knowledge into an explicit representation, often in the form of a heuristic or rule. Most existing methods of assessing expertise rely heavily on descriptive methods. The major limitation of the descriptive method is that the more competent an expert becomes, the less able he or she is to describe his or her problem-solving knowledge (Johnson, 1983a). One method of accomplishing this end is through interviews with auditors in which they attempt to characterize their knowledge and skill in the given task situation. The researcher then formulates the response as a production rule. The type of questions asked in this process included the following:

What objectives h do you think of when you see problem data about c?

What evidence (controls or sub-objectives) makes you more certain that objective h is satisfied?

What makes you conclude that objective h cannot be satisfied? (See Moen, 1984.)

222

A second, more direct method is through the creation of a precise "language" in which the expert is asked to describe his or her expertise. The structure of the language is determined by the architecture of the knowledge base. In this case the auditor described his or her lines of reasoning by means of production rules, i.e., If-Then statements.

INTUITIVE METHODS OF KNOWLEDGE ACQUISITION

Intuitive methods for capturing knowledge exist in two forms. In one case, a knowledge researcher interacts with both the auditor and the literature of the field in order to become familiar with its major problem-solving methods, which are then checked against the opinion of other auditors and eventually incorporated into the computer program. A second intuitive method of knowledge involves a researcher who is an expert in the area attempting to describe the basis for his or her own knowledge and skill. Intuition as a means of recovering one's own knowledge is subjective and may not be adequate (Johnson, 1983a). Intuitive methods were used by researchers in the model-building process only when necessary to guide the use of observational and descriptive methods in deriving the production rules.

In addition to the above methods, we referred to textbooks in an attempt to provide a base of reference for the rules (Johnson and Jaenicke, 1980). Although these books did provide a reference point for basic internal control terminology and issues, only those rules elicited directly from the experts were used for model building. This is consistent with our objective of studying auditor decision processes rather than building a new problem solver. In addition, subsequent discussions with the experts indicate that while the textbook rules are generally correct, they do not coincide with the auditor's decision processes.

The products of the knowledge acquisition portion of the research included a representation of auditor expertise in: (a) the identification of specific internal accounting control objectives, (b) the evaluation and review processes, identifying which controls should be further tested for reliance thereon, and (c) the type of processes used in recognizing controls and weaknesses.

223

Knowledge Representation Structures

Production rules were chosen to represent the expert knowledge of an auditor. No claim is made for the universal applicability of such a representation; rather, we rely on the demonstrated utility of rule-based systems in representing problems with characteristics similar to those encountered in analyzing internal controls. Rule-based representations (also referred to as Situation — Action rules or If — Then rules) allow easy modification and explanation, both considered essential for building and then tuning such a computational model. Basically, each rule captures a "chunk" of the domain knowledge, meaningful in and of itself to the domain specialist (Feigenbaum, 1978).

The rules are normally associated with "lines of reasoning" and "episodes" that are comprehensible to the domain expert (Feigenbaum, 1978). Lines of reasoning incorporate the system analysis method and frames of reference employed by the subject. Episodes involve proposing a tentative goal and/or subgoal (hypotheses) and then trying to either substantiate or disprove that goal. Such a generate-and-test frame work has been identified in behavioral studies by Biggs and Mock (1983) and others when studying audit settings. The formulation and maintenance of lines of reasoning and episodes often requires the integration of many different "chunks" of knowledge. It is important that the computational model be able to explain its use of knowledge to the domain expert for both refinement and validation purposes. The computational theory, including the choice of hierarchical structures and the partitioning of the knowledge base into sub-components, is discussed elsewhere (Meservy, 1985).

Model Implementation And Tuning

The preliminary model was implemented as a computational model by using the Galen modeling tool developed at the University of Minnesota (Thompson et al., 1983). Galen's architecture reflects its development in modeling problem-solving processes. Galen's inference engine has the ability to partition the knowledge base, to search for a hierarchical set of goals, to apply forward and backward chaining, and to build and interact with LISP representation of the audit working papers. While demonstrating the generality of Galen, the adaptation of an already proven tool enhanced development productivity. The rules developed above and the Galen inference engine were combined to form the computational model.

THE MODEL

The implemented computational model with its associated rules included approximately 300 If statements. Note that some of the If statements in Galen may represent six or more production rules in other expert systems. The actual implementation of the Galen-based system involved organizing the formalized knowledge into rule teams, along the line of reasoning categories identified from the protocol analysis.

Of the approximately 300 rules in the model, normally only 10 to 25 percent of the rules fire in any given evaluation. These percentages held for the three model traces which were used in the cross-validation test.

MODEL TUNING

After the acquired knowledge was mapped into Galen's representational framework, the system was "tuned." Tuning involved running several prototype internal accounting control information systems descriptions through the evaluation process and, in collaboration with the expert, checking the lines of reasoning and episodes for reasonableness and making adjustments in the rules. Some of the more important aspects of expertise were discovered in this process, i.e., knowing when to discontinue the current line of reasoning or begin another. Aspects of expertise incorporated during the tuning phase included rules about the use of other rules, known as meta rules, which were used by the expert in guiding his or her thinking about each case.

The Verification Phase

It is important in simulation studies that the model not only be built and tuned, but also be tested and verified. Typically, researchers have not been able to formulate single critical experiments which validate such models. Furthermore, because of the small sample size, statistical evaluations of experimental results are generally not available and researchers are constrained to rely

225

on graphical techniques. The approach used in this study included several empirical tests, each of which addressed different types of data and different aspects of the model's behavior.

Verification experiments focused upon comparisons between the control evaluation strategies of the model and the processes employed by human auditors. The framework used to evaluate the model's performance had two major features: (1) tests of the quality of model processes and of cue usage, and (2) tests of sufficiency or adequacy of model outcomes.

Because accounting information systems differ, each represents a new challenge to the model. Therefore, if the model is to be tested, the cases chosen should not represent recombinations of portions of previous cases employed, but totally new cases representing a wide range in risk, reliance, and workpaper documentation. The three cases chosen represent such a range within the confines of the model limitations, discussed earlier. Copies of actual work papers obtained from the firm were used for the three cases.

The computational model was fine-tuned, as previously noted, around the expertise of one individual auditor (the primary subject, S1). The computational model was initially validated against this individual using the three cases, and then it was cross-validated against three additional expert auditors (subjects 4, 5, and 6).

For each case, the primary subject and the other three auditors were asked to read aloud the pertinent data and give "thinking-aloud" protocols while reviewing and evaluating the actual work papers prepared by an in-charge auditor. As part of the task, the subjects were asked to list: (1) recommendations for specific controls to be compliance tested, and (2) weaknesses identified from the system description. At the conclusion of the session, subjects were asked to fill out a participant background questionnaire. The complete problem-solving session for each subject was tape recorded and transcribed. The computational model also received each case and made similar evaluations. In addition to making recommendations for specific controls to be compliance tested and weaknesses, the model provided a trace of all data analyzed and rules fired.

TESTS OF QUALITY OF MODEL PROCESSES AND CUE USAGE

The first type of analysis involves establishing the quality of the evaluation processes employed by the model and the model's response to "critical cues." To establish quality of evaluation processes, the inferences made must not only be "legal," but must be the type of inferences that experts would make. Determining that a sample of model behavior constitutes adequate auditing behavior is not a simple matter. In games, such as chess, it is fairly easy to determine if the model is performing the requisite behavior because the rules used to determine whether a given move is "legal" are well-defined. By contrast, in environments such as internal control evaluation, it is not clear what constitutes a "legal move." Furthermore, as in a game, though all reasoning steps are explainable by logic or rules, some "lines of reasoning" (smaller sets of steps or moves) must be made according to a criterion of quality in order for the task to be done well. In medical diagnosis, for example, typically there is a small set of cues that, if interpreted properly, would lead to a correct diagnosis. Experts may differ in their interpretations of other pieces of information, but they tend to agree more on the interpretation of these critical cues and the use of additional cues to mediate between competing hypotheses (Johnson et al., 1982).

The evaluation framework adopted in the present study requires that the model's rules for performing the evaluation be based on heuristics of expert behavior. The judgment as to whether the model is performing the task is then based on comparisons between the specific acts of model behavior on the task and the behavior of expert auditors. These comparisons focus upon: (1) the identification and use of specific goals and objectives which direct the search and confirmation processes, and (2) the processes linking problem states to one another. The quality of the model's "thinking" process was evaluated by transcribing, scoring, and analyzing each model problem-solving trace against the problem-solving trace of expert auditors as revealed in their verbal protocols. Protocols provide a depth of understanding about judgment and decision making unavailable using other methods. However, as in other methods, the data must be reduced to a structured, objective image of the processes that auditors are using. The analysis is developed by synthesizing the results of two analytical methods: a top-down, global analysis and a bottom-up, problem state/processes analysis (Bouwman, 1978).

The top-down analysis identifies single problem-solving goals from the protocols. Proposed categories are developed through functional analysis of the review task, formalized descriptions of evaluation processes generally, and model fragments found in the auditing literature; an example is the representation or mental picture of the segregation of duties within the purchasing/cash distribution function.

The bottom-up analysis focused on problem-solving states, the basic set of facts, concepts, and hypotheses generated by the subject, and an associated set of reasoning processes (reading, planning, evaluating, searching for information, etc.). Figure 4 contains a list of hypothesized categories for the internal control evaluation and review task. Scoring protocols for reasoning processes permits an understanding of how auditors use past knowledge, generate new knowledge, and the type of processes that link this knowledge together. The analysis provided a "picture" of the path taken by the auditor to perform the task. It differs from the top-down analysis primarily by being more elementary and in finer detail (Malone, 1984).

A third, more general type of analysis, "lines of reasoning" and search strategy, was then determined by analyzing the "protocol graphs" and the sequence of problem-solving goals. Lines of reasoning involve the methods employed by the subjects to solve the task; an example would be the focus on receipt of goods rather than on commitments.

TESTS OF ADEQUACY OF MODEL OUTCOMES

The second type of analysis, for sufficiency or adequacy of model outcomes, was performed to establish that the computational model could identify and evaluate internal accounting controls. The fifteen outcomes from the three cases examined, including the lists described above, were retyped, randomly sorted, and renumbered for each case to hide the original identity and remove inter-case identity. These outcomes were then given along with the cases to three other expert auditors (subjects 7, 8, and 9) to judge. This process is referred to here as a peer review.

The peer review required each subject acting as a reviewer to first read case A and judge the five solutions produced by the model and four subjects. The peer reviewer was then asked to judge each solution for completeness, effectiveness, and agreement with results. The possible range of each evaluation was from one through seven, where one indicated a minimal rating and seven represented *extremely* complete, *extremely* effective or *substantial* agreement with conclusions. After rating all five solutions, the peer reviewer was instructed to divide the solutions

228

into *two* groups based on perceived similarity. Between one and four solutions were allowed in each group. Next, the reviewer was instructed to divide the solutions into *three* groups, again based on similarity. This time between one and three solutions formed a group. At this point the peer evaluation was complete, and the subject proceeded with the next case. These ratings were later analyzed to determine how well the model performed in relation to the person it was modeled after and in relation to the other auditors.

VALIDITY AND CONSISTENCY

After each transcribed protocol and trace was scored, a second scorer or rater, trained in the rules for coding these protocols, again scored portions of the transcribed protocols from the model and for all subjects and cases. The coded protocols from each rater were compared, and the proportion of agreement between the lists developed by each rater for the protocols rated were computed. Cohen's K (Cohen, 1960), an inter-rater reliability coefficient, was employed to adjust for agreement due to chance. Traces generated by the computational model were scored by the same methods used to score subject protocols. The inter-rater reliability analysis, after being adjusted for agreement due to chance, ranged from 65.3 percent to 92.6 percent, with all but three falling in the .7 to .9 range.

Results

This section examines the results of several empirical tests addressing different types of data and aspects of model behavior. The analysis of the experimental data is presented in two parts. The first part, Quality of Model Processes and Cue Usage, examines in detail the scored protocols and model traces, establishing the quality of the evaluation process employed by the model. In the second part, Adequacy of Model Outcomes, peer reviews of the model's and subjects' internal control evaluations are presented and discussed.

Quality of Model Processes and Cue Usage

The quality of evaluation processes used by the model is established by determining that the inferences made by the

229

model are not only all "legal," but of the type experts make. The analytical approach used synthesizes the results of two analytical methods: (1) a top-down, global analysis and (2) a bottom-up, knowledge state/processes analysis. This section analyzes: (1) the hypotheses generated, (2) the processes identified, (3) the cue usage or the order and data attended to, and (4) the lines of reasoning employed. The last two are closely related in this study and will be discussed together.

HYPOTHESIS GENERATION

The major hypotheses generated by the computational model were compared with the major hypotheses generated by expert auditors. The complete set of hypotheses and tentative conclusions employed by auditors in their review is so numerous that in this study we have limited ourselves to the major hypotheses generated. Whereas in medical diagnosis the physician may think of major diseases or disease categories, the auditor thinks in terms of controls, weaknesses, and problems, as well as major objectives.

Questions of interest were:

1. Are the hypotheses generated by the computational model found in the protocols of the primary auditor?

2. Are the hypotheses generated by the computational model found in the protocols of other auditors from the same firm?

Figure 5 is a Hypotheses Graph of the hypotheses generated by the subjects and the model. The graph is organized and presented by case and within each case by model and subject. Only those hypotheses which were employed during the experiment are listed on the left side of the graph. The " + " represents a positive decision, a " − " represents a weakness, problem, or question, and a "?" represents an assumption or basic issue about the hypothesis category. In the context of the auditor review where team decisions are involved, it is often more important that the hypothesis has been effectively dealt with than the " + " or " − " determined. Also, because "?'s" may represent important issues for the auditor that need to be resolved, no great significance should be attached to the distinction afforded by the question mark.

FIGURE 5
Hypotheses Graph

	CASE A					Case B					Case C				
	M	S1	S4	S5	S6	M	S1	S4	S5	S6	M	S1	S4	S5	S6
COMMITMENTS (PO)															
Signature	-												+		
Completeness	+	+	+			-	-	+			-	-			+
Authorization	+	+	+			+	+		+	+	+	+	+		+
Comparisons	+	+			+	+	+		+	+	+	+	+	+	+
RECEIPT OF GOODS															
Blind Copy PO	-														
Signature	-										-				
Completeness			-	+		+	+		+-					+	
Authorization								?+							
Comparisons	+	+		+	+	+	+		+	+-	+	+	+	+	+
Other				+											
A/P ADDITIONS															
Completeness											-			+-	
Authorization			+		+						+	+	+		
Comparisons	+	+		+	+	+	+	+	+	+	+	++	+	+	+
Math Checking				?						+-	++	++		+	+
Other						-	-								
DISBURSEMENTS															
Completeness										?	?				
Authorization						-	?+		-						
Comparisons								+							
Recncl.Bank						+	+				+				
PROCESSING															
Input				+		+	+		+	+	-				
Summarization						+	+	-			-				
Posting						+									
Recncl.Sub-GL						+	+								?
INVENTORY			-												
EDP GENERAL (BNDRY)	+	+		--		+	--			+-	+	-			+-
RELIANCE ON SYSTEM			?-			+	+	+	+	-	-	-	-	-	?
WORKPAPERS									-						
SEGREGATION OF DUTIES											-				
COMMON WITH MODEL		6	2	2	4		12	5	6	8		9	6	6	8
NUMBER OF SUBJECT HYPOTHESES		6	5	5	7		13	8	8	11		9	10	8	9
AGREEMENT WITH MODEL		1	0.4	0.4	0.57		0.92	0.63	0.75	0.73		1	0.6	0.75	0.89
TOTAL COMMON WITH MODEL		27	13	14	20										
TOTAL SUBJECT HYPOTHESES		28	23	21	27										
OVERALL AGREEMENT WITH MODEL		0.96	0.57	0.67	0.74										

It is interesting to note that in the three cases, there is only one hypothesis that was used by the model that was not used by one of the expert auditors, and that use was in the form of a possible weakness: whether a blind copy of the purchase order (PO) had been used in the receiving function. Note also the similarity between the model and the primary subject (S1 from whom the model was developed) as compared to the other subjects involved.

In case A, the model included each of the hypotheses identified by S1. Additionally, the model identified three possible management letter discussion issues not discussed by S1 in case A, but that had been discussed in earlier "tuning" cases. At the bottom of the graph is found the total number of hypotheses the subject and model had in common, the total number of hypotheses the subject included, and the agreement between the two

231

represented by the ratio of common hypotheses to subject hypotheses. Case A represents the lowest overall average agreement between the model and the subjects as a whole, i.e., approximately 60 percent compared to 75.8 percent average agreement for case B and 81 percent average agreement for case C. While not wholly comparable, Ashton (1974) found auditor consensus to be about 70 percent, and Ashton and Brown (1980) found auditor consensus to be 67 percent on average in the internal control-related studies.

In case B, the model and S1 agree on all hypotheses, except that each generated one additional hypothesis. During the three test cases, this was the only instance in which S1 generated any hypothesis that the model did not generate. The model generated seven additional hypotheses (three in case A, one in B, and three in C) not generated by S1, five of which were management issue questions. This fact in conjunction with performance, as discussed earlier in the chapter, may indicate a bootstrapping effect, where the computer model is consistent and never forgets to analyze any possibilities. On the other hand, the model may not yet have some of the meta-rules allowing it to dismiss such questions.

Although case C was unique, there was less variation in the hypotheses generated here than in any other case. S4 was the only auditor that appeared to generate a substantially different set of hypotheses than the model. Note that the hypotheses sets generated by the model for each of the three cases are quite different from each other, at least compared to the similarity of the model and subjects within any given case.

PROBLEM-SOLVING PROCESSES

The reasoning processes allow progression from one knowledge state to another. Figure 4 contains a list of hypothesized processing operators for the internal control evaluation and review task. The list includes operators for information acquisition and retrieval, planning approaches, analyzing the information acquired, and making decisions (taking action). The questions of interest are:

1. Are the reasoning processes produced by the model found in the protocols of the primary auditor?

232

2. Are the reasoning processes produced by the model found in the protocols of other auditors from the same firm?

The most detailed part of the analysis is the fifteen protocol graphs, i.e., one graph is presented for the model and each subject's evaluation of each case. Figure 4 is the Protocol Analysis Graph for Subject 1's evaluation of case C. The graph presents a sequential picture of the goals and cues being attended to, the processes involved, and when the resulting decisions were made.

A vertical line through the Figure 4 graph for any unit of time provides information about what is occurring on several different levels at any instant and allows immediate access to that portion of the protocol. Given any of the auditor's decisions, the graph allows a quick picture of the general processes and the goals and cues that led to that decision. For example, using Figure 4, "Controls to Test," #2 at the bottom of the Figure indicates that S1 decided to compliance-test the comparison of invoices, purchase orders, and receiving reports. By reading across "Written Results" in the Figure for "Controls to Test" over to the number "2," located in the 37th division, we observe that this occurred when S1 was 37 percent of the way through his protocol. Analyzing the 37th column of the graph under "Episodes," S1 had been examining the accounts payable boundary conditions. Further examining column 37 under "Views or Frames: Processing," commitments, receipt of goods, and accounts payable additions (invoices) have all been scored, meaning that all these categories were mentioned at that point in the protocol. Note that invoices had been mentioned frequently between columns 29 and 37 in the graph, whereas commitments and receipt of goods had been mentioned more often in earlier portions of the protocol. Certain lines of reasoning, as discussed later, may also be determined. Finally, under "Cognitive Processes," "Audit Decision" was scored as the process in use. Using the protocol graphs, direct access to that portion of the protocol that produced the second written result for "Controls to Test" is possible by reference to the percent column.

On the right side of Figure 4, the percentage occurrence of each operator is presented. These percentages, averaged for each subject and the model, have been included below as Figure 6. Note that the biggest difference in the model is the high percentage of read operators used. This difference, however, may only

233

FIGURE 6
Reasoning Process Category Analysis
(in percents)

Emphasis of when the model is outside the behavior of the auditors (when the average scored model percentages are outside the boundaries of the average scored protocols of the expert auditors).

	Subj. Avg.	Model	S1	S4	S5	S6	Outside
I. Information Acquisition							
Read	34.9	46.3	34.3	47.3	39.3	18.7	0
Data Search	1.2	0.0	1.0	1.3	0.3	2.3	-.3
Information Retrieval	0.8	0.0	0.3	0.0	2.0	1.0	0
Total	37.0	46.3	35.7	48.7	41.7	22.0	
II. Plan							
Plan	2.1	0.0	0.7	0.3	4.3	3.0	-.3
Total	2.1	0.0	0.7	0.3	4.3	3.0	
III. Analytical							
Assumption	2.9	0.0	0.7	0.7	6.0	4.0	-.7
Conjecture	6.8	5.7	8.0	2.0	6.7	10.3	0
Evaluation	33.0	32.7	41.0	27.7	26.3	37.0	0
Question	1.9	0.3	0.0	5.0	1.7	0.7	0
Inference	1.0	2.0	1.7	0.7	0.7	0.7	.3
Total	45.3	40.7	51.3	36.0	41.3	52.7	
IV. Action							
Generate Alternative	0.0	0.0	0.0	0.0	0.0	0.0	0
Decision Rule	0.0	0.0	0.0	0.0	0.0	0.0	0
Audit Decision	15.6	13.0	12.3	15.0	12.7	22.3	0
Total	15.6	13.0	12.3	15.0	12.7	22.3	
Final Total	100.0	100.0	100.0	100.0	100.0	100.0	

be the result of the scoring rules used on the trace and/or the way the model reads in the data, displaying it on the trace.

At the right of Figure 6 is a column labeled "outside." Whenever the model is outside the range of percentages found in the four expert protocol averages, the difference is marked in this column. Note that the model was outside the given range four times, but never by more than one percent. In addition, in those instances when the model was outside the given range, it was not more than one percent different from the primary subject (S1).

In general, the operators scored for in the model are quite consistent with the operators found in the expert protocols. Note the relatively high percentages of the read, evaluation, and audit decision operators scored. The next highest operators are the conjecture and assumption operators. Auditors evaluating internal accounting controls make numerous tentative evaluations or judgments, dealing with uncertainty by raising questions, building conjectures, posing assumptions, and proposing numerous tentative evaluations. The use of discrete assumed outcomes rather than probabilistic assessments of uncertainty is consistent with the findings of Biggs et al. (1985) and with Doyle's (1983) "reasoning by assumption." No probabilistic remark, such as "I'm 75 percent positive that invoices are adequately accounted for," was found in any of the protocols.

No explicit decision rule was ever mentioned by the experts while completing the internal accounting control evaluation. This result is consistent with the protocols from subjects S1, S2, and S3.

In summary, although some differences were found in the degree to which operators were used and/or graphed, the operators employed in the model were found in the primary subject's and the other experts' protocols.

CUE USAGE AND LINES OF REASONING

The cues and problem-solving goals attended to are examined at two different levels, episodes and views or frames of reference. As defined earlier, episodes are sustained goal-seeking categories. However, episodes are somewhat interdependent and must sometimes be suspended until other decisions have been reached. Figure 4 allows us to relate how the episodes unfold and their relationship with other problem-solving activities.

In addition to episodes, auditors appear to use major frames of reference through which they view data. Such frames of reference allow them to organize and evaluate various aspects of specific data cues. The views through which client data are evaluated are also contained in the upper portion of the graphs. The representations for these views indicate more fragmented goal-seeking activities than those for episodes. Auditors may engage in several of these views simultaneously, and/or switch back and forth very quickly between them.

The following analysis examines the percentages of these activities for each case. The percentages for case A are presented in Figures 7 and 8.

Note that in case A, the percentage of time spent in each category by the model was within the range used by the four expert subjects. This indicates that a normal percentage of the protocol was spent in the major goal-seeking efforts and use of relevant cues. As most auditors would expect, the major amount of effort by all subjects was in regard to the accounts payable boundary condition.

Examination of the views or frames of reference within the above episodes revealed that the model spent an abnormal per-

FIGURE 7
Episodic Goal Percentage — Case A
(in percents)

	CASE A						
	M	S1	S4	S5	S6	Avg.	Outside
General Summary	5	18	14	0	12	9.8	0
Processing Overview	9	6	6	9	19	9.8	0
A/P Additions (Boundary)	81	68	68	85	69	74.2	0
Disbursements (Boundary)	0	0	0	0	0	0	0
Conclusions	5	8	12	6	0	6.2	0
Totals	100	100	100	100	100	100	

FIGURE 8
View or Frames of Reference Percentage - Case A
(in percents)

	CASE A						
	M	S1	S4	S5	S6	Avg.	Outside
Processing							
Commitments	44	10	14	32	22	19.5	12
Receipt of Goods	26	20	29	33	56	34.5	0
Goods Returned	0	0	0	0	0	0	0
A/P Additions	16	16	29	34	31	27.5	0
Disbursements	1	3	0	0	6	2.3	0
Posting to Accounts	6	1	0	0	10	2.8	0
Segregation of Duties	16	9	12	4	5	7.5	4
EDP Factors	15	24	15	20	47	26.5	0
Adequacy of Working Papers	0	0	0	1	0	.3	0

cent of time with purchase commitments compared to S1 and the other experts. This may indicate too careful an analysis by the model, requiring too many rules, or it may indicate the commitment rules were improperly organized in the knowledge base.

The model also spent more time on segregation-of-duty issues in case A than any of the experts. Part of this difference may be that the auditors didn't specifically verbalize segregation issues. There appears to be considerable variance among the auditors, as well, in the commitment and segregation-of-duty categories.

For case B, the model spent more time on the accounts payable boundary conditions and less time on the processing controls than any of the expert auditors. Related to the boundary conditions, substantially more time was again spent examining commitments. Although similar conditions are noted in case C, a major difference is the time experts spent examining commitments.

With few exceptions, upon examining the relative percentages and the protocol graphs, it can be seen that the model is performing the task in a manner similar to auditors, and in the same order.

LINES OF REASONING

The order of patterns of problem-solving activities is of particular interest in determining the nature of both human and model reasoning. These ordered patterns of data-search and problem-solving goals may be expressed in terms of the concept of "lines of reasoning." Lines of reasoning are represented by the methods subjects employ to solve the task. The two questions of interest were:

1. Are the lines of reasoning produced by the model found in the primary subject's protocols?

2. Are the lines of reasoning produced by the model found in the additional subjects' protocols?

The most prominent sequence of reasoning steps is found in the episodic graphs. The general pattern among all of the auditors on case A was to: (1) examine the general information, (2) take a brief look at the processing overview information, and (3) then spend the majority of the time examining the accounts payable boundary conditions. The model and two of the subjects (including S1) briefly rechecked the information on the processing overview flowchart before concluding.

Regarding the episodic reasoning in case B, the model, S1, and S6 first examined general and processing controls, respectively, then spent more time on the a/p boundary controls; used less time on disbursement boundary controls; and then returned to use the majority of time on the processing controls. Of the other two auditors, S4 examined all the information sequentially without returning, whereas S5 seemed to go back and forth several times.

While examining case C, the model, S1, and S6 used the same basic episodic strategy (Figure 4). S4 also employed the same strategy examining C as B, while S5 used a very different

237

FIGURE 9
Episodic Goal Percentage - Case B
(in percents)

	CASE B M	S1	S4	S5	S6	Avg.	Outside
General Summary	2	3	2	4	18	5.8	0
Processing Overview	34	61	41	48	48	46.4	-7
A/P Additions (Boundary)	43	24	20	20	23	26.0	19
Disbursements (Boundary)	18	12	18	13	9	14.0	0
Conclusions	3	0	19	15	2	7.8	0
Totals	100	100	100	100	100	100	

FIGURE 10
View or Frames of Reference Percentage - Case B
(in percents)

Processing	CASE B M	S1	S4	S5	S6	Avg.	Outside
Commitments	25	13	12	14	9	12.0	10
Receipt of Goods	17	10	12	16	16	13.5	1
Goods Returned	0	0	0	0	0	0	0
A/P Additions	20	14	34	41	24	28.3	0
Disbursements	24	31	25	22	29	26.8	0
Posting to Accounts	20	30	18	11	19	19.5	0
Segregation of Duties	11	7	3	2	18	7.5	0
EDP Factors	15	10	7	10	27	13.5	0
Adequacy of Working Papers	0	2	0	0	1	.8	0

approach (examining the boundary controls first without even looking at the processing controls.) The peers rated S5's solution set the lowest on case C. The model, S1 and S6 (whose solutions were ranked the highest by the peer experts on all three cases) used the same basic episodic approaches.

An intermediate level of analysis, views or frames of reference, was also analyzed. Each of the views could likewise be thought of as a "line of reasoning," along with the manner in which they interact.

An examination of the processing category in case A revealed that the model showed a definite sequential pattern between (first) commitments, (second) receipt of goods, and then (third)

FIGURE 11
Episodic Goal Percentage - Case C
(in percents)

	CASE C						
	M	S1	S4	S5	S6	Avg.	Outside
General Summary	2	0	0	4	0	1.2	0
Processing Overview	34	42	59	71	52	51.6	-8
A/P Additions (Boundary)	63	52	35	25	48	44.6	11
Disbursements (Boundary)	0	0	0	0	0	0	0
Conclusions	1	6	6	0	0	2.6	0
Totals	100	100	100	100	100	100	

FIGURE 12
View or Frames of Reference Percentage - Case C
(in percents)

	CASE C						
Processing	M	S1	S4	S5	S6	Avg.	Outside
Commitments	29	23	16	17	30	21.5	0
Receipt of Goods	22	12	4	12	23	12.8	0
Goods Returned	0	0	0	0	0	0	0
A/P Additions	40	41	50	30	29	37.5	0
Disbursements	6	21	13	3	3	10.0	0
Posting to Accounts	17	9	5	16	16	11.5	1
Segregation of Duties	9	4	20	3	2	7.3	0
EDP Factors	11	9	11	10	49	19.5	0
Adequacy of Working Papers	4	11	0	0	0	2.8	0

a/p additions, referring back to the other categories evaluated as needed. The primary subject, S1, also showed the same definite pattern. In contrast, S6 had a definite reasoning pattern of focusing on the receipt of goods, and then brought in commitments and additions as appropriate. The pattern for S4 was almost opposite that of the model and S1, while S5 produced a mixed approach more similar to S6.

For case B, the sequential evaluation of commitments, receipt of goods, and a/p additions were all evident when processing the a/p boundary conditions. Subjects 5 and 6 again had a definite focus on the receivables, and only included other information as appropriate. This is referred to as a mixed approach. The approach for S1 in case B appeared to be more mixed.

Examining case C revealed that the model and S1 (Figure 4) again show the stepped approach, with S4 stepped, but just the opposite. Subjects 5 and 6 appear to again have a more mixed approach.

239

Although auditors may examine the accounts payable process-ing stream before examining the disbursements processing stream, or first examine inputs to the processing system before examining summarization and posting types of controls, those patterns were not prominent in the limited protocols gathered. Other scoring methods may also be found that would highlight various levels and lines of reasoning not evident from existing scoring methods.

On the global level of analysis, each expert appeared to care-fully and systematically examine all available cues. Although there was some directed search among the documents, it ap-peared to be minimal.

Adequacy of Model Outcomes

The peer evaluations were next analyzed to determine if there were substantial differences between the model and the primary subject (the modeler), or the other expert auditors. Good simula-tion models solve tasks in the same manner as experts, par-ticularly similar to the expert modeled. The two questions of interest were:

1. Are there substantial differences between the outcomes of the primary auditor and the model as judged by experts?

2. Are there substantial differences between the outcomes of the model and the three auditors as judged by experts?

The three cases were analyzed by case and by subject in a blind review. Here we present only the combined results. The follow-ing figure presents ordinal relationships for the various solu-tions, as determined from the ratings of S7, S8, and S9. Ties are scored for the higher category.

For each of the three categories, completeness, effectiveness, and agreement with results, the model obtained five first-place ratings, three second-place ratings, and either a third-place or a fourth-place rating. The model had the most first-place ratings for completeness and effectiveness, and tied for the largest number of first-place ratings for agreement with results. How-ever, out of the fifteen first-place ratings, eight were ties for first

240

FIGURE 13
Place Rankings by Category
as Determined by Peer Reviewers

Completeness	1st	2nd	3rd	4th	5th
Model	5	3	1		
S1	3	2	4		
S4	1		2	3	3
S5		1	1	4	3
S6	4	3	1	1	

Effectiveness	1st	2nd	3rd	4th	5th
Model	5	3		1	
S1	4	3	2		
S4	1	1	2	2	3
S5		3	2	2	2
S6	4	2	1	2	

Agreement	1st	2nd	3rd	4th	5th
Model	5	3		1	
S1	4	2	3		
S4	1	1	2	1	4
S5		2	1	2	4
S6	5	2	1	1	

Totals	1st	2nd	3rd	4th	5th
Model	15	9	1	2	
S1	11	7	9		
S4	3	2	6	6	10
S5		6	4	8	9
S6	13	7	3	4	

place. Six of the thirteen first-place ratings for S6 were also ties. Six of the eleven first-place ratings for S1 were without ties. Examining the results for relatively poor performance, the outputs for the model, S1, and S6 were never judged the worst solutions.

Another type of analysis involves weighting and combining the ordinal rankings. Each first place was assigned five points, each second place received four points, each third place received three points, etc., and the results were added. The total for the model was 118, the total for both S1 and S6 was 110, and the points for S4 and S5 were 63 and 61, respectively. Caution must be used in interpreting these ordinal results. The peer reviewers were also asked to separate each case's solution into two groups and then into three groups. The results for how often the model was placed in the same group with each of the auditors are indicated in Figures 14 and 15.

Analyzing the above two tables over all cases and all subjects, the model appears to be the most like the modeler (S1). It is interesting to note that for both the two and three groupings, the

241

FIGURE 14
Combined Comparison of
Groupings - Two Groups

	Model	S1	S4	S5
S1	8			
S4	3	4		
S5	1	2	5	
S6	6	5	4	4

FIGURE 15
Combined Comparison of
Groupings - Three Groups

	Model	S1	S4	S5
S1	8			
S4	2	2		
S5	1	2	1	

model has been placed in the same group with each subject at least once. Figures 13, 14, and 15 support the conclusions that: (1) there is no substantial difference between the outcomes of the primary auditor and the model as judged by experts, and (2) there is no substantial difference between the outcomes of the model and the three auditors as judged by experts. The model appears to be adequately performing the task of reviewing and evaluating internal accounting controls.

In conclusion, the model appears to simulate the processes of expert auditors, particularly the auditor after whom it was modeled. As indicated earlier in this section, a network of tests is necessary to validate a simulation model. Such a network of tests has been employed, but further validation is always appropriate.

Conclusion and Extensions

In the process of building and testing the computational model, a theory was formulated of the kind that Allen Newell and Herbert Simon call "dynamic" (Newell and Simon, 1972). Dynamic theories represent the initial state of psychological systems, such as human memory, in the form of symbol structures and the procedures for manipulating these structures (i.e., mental operations). Typical dynamic theories are formalized as computer algorithms, allowing the theory to be tested, which in turn allows future states of the system to be predicted (Johnson,

1983). The dynamic theory encompassed in the simulation model presented here allowed the model to be tested. Furthermore, the theory can now be manipulated or perturbed, allowing new predictions to be examined.

Point predictions occur when exact predictions of how a given task will be done under variations in the knowledge base and alternative task conditions can be hypothesized (Johnson, 1983). Suggestions for future research include systematically manipulating the model, creating and examining new hypotheses, and constructing specific task materials from which differential lines of reasoning, assumptions, and "garden paths" resulting in suboptimal solutions can be predicted. Such predictions can be worked out either by analysis of expert thinking or by examining the behavior of the simulation model (Johnson and Hassebrock, 1982).

Another extension to the present model is to join a powerful internal control model and query language, TICOM (Bailey et al., 1985) under the control of an expert system decision model. Such a union would allow the resulting system to query the user for appropriate modeling information to represent the client's system as a TICOM model. Then, based on the questions of interest, decision rules could be employed to query the model, combining results for appropriate recommendations. The resulting system would allow both individual companies and auditors to make effective and efficient evaluations of internal accounting controls.[1]

Footnotes

1. Researchers interested in pursuing any of these issues should: (1) see Bailey et al. (1985) for information concerning software and manuals related to TICOM, (2) obtain a copy of Meservy (1985) from the Michigan Microfilm Library, as it contains the complete code for the model discussed in this paper, and (3) contact the Artificial Intelligence Research Center at The University of Minnesota to obtain information on the use of the Galen program.

References

American Institute of Certified Public Accountants (AICPA), *Statement on Auditing Standards,* November 1972, AU Section 320.

Ashton, R. H., "An Experimental Study of Internal Control Judgments," *Journal of Accounting Research,* Spring 1974, pp. 143–157.

——— and P. R. Brown, "Descriptive Modeling of Auditors' Internal Control Judgments: Replication and Extension," *Journal of Accounting Research,* Spring 1980, pp. 269–277.

Barr, A. and E. A. Feigenbaum, *The Handbook of Artificial Intelligence, Volume I,* Heuris TechPress, 1981.

Bailey, A. D., Jr., G. L. Duke, J. Gerlach, C. Ko, R. D. Meservy, and A. B. Whinston, "TICOM and the Analysis of Internal Controls," *The Accounting Review,* April 1985, pp. 186–201.

————, ————, P. E. Johnson, R. D. Meservy, and W. Thompson, "Auditing, Artificial Intelligence, and Expert Systems," in *Decision Support Systems: Theory and Application,* North-Holland, Forthcoming.

Balachandran, B. V. and A. A. Zolters, "An Interactive Audit-Staff Scheduling Decision Support System," *The Accounting Review,* October 1981, pp. 801–812.

Biggs, S. F, "An Empirical Investigation of the Information Processes Underlying Four Models of Choice Behavior," in *Behavioral Research in Accounting II,* (ed.), by T. Burns, The Ohio State University, 1979, pp. 35–81.

————, W. F Messier, Jr., and J. V. Hansen, "A Study of the Predecisional Behavior of Computer Audit Specialists in Advanced EDP Environments," University of Florida ARC working paper No. 84-1, 1985.

———— and T. J. Mock, "An Investigation of Auditor Decision Processes in the Evaluation of Internal Controls and Audit Scope Decisions," *Journal of Accounting Research,* Spring 1983, pp. 234–255.

Bouwman, M. J., "Financial Diagnosis: A Cognitive Model of the Processes Involved," unpublished Ph.D. dissertation, Carnegie-Mellon University, 1978.

Braun, H. M. and J. S. Chandler, "Development of an Expert System to Assist Auditors in the Investigation of Analytical Review Fluctuations," research proposal, University of Illinois, 1982.

Cohen, J., "A Coefficient of Agreement of Nominal Scales," *Educational and Psychological Measurement,* Vol. 26, 1960, pp. 37–46.

Davis, R., "Expert Systems: Where Are We? And Where Do We Go From Here?" *The AI Magazine,* Spring 1982, pp. 3–22.

Doyle, J., "Some Theories of Reasoned Assumptions: An Essay in Rational Psychology," working paper CS-813-125, Computer Science Department, Carnegie-Mellon University, May 1983.

Dungan, C. and J. Chandler, "Development of Knowledge-Based Expert Systems to Model Auditors' Decision Processes," unpublished paper University of Illinois, 1980.

Einhorn, H. J., "Learning From Experience and Suboptimal Rules in Decision Making," in T. S. Wallsten (ed.), *Cognitive Processes in Choice and Decision Behavior,* Lawrence Erlbaum Associates, 1980, pp. 1–20.

Elstein, A. S., A. S. Shulman, and S. M. Sprafka, *Medical Problem Solving: An Analysis of Clinical Reasoning,* Harvard University Press, 1978.

Ericsson, K. A., and H. A. Simon, *Protocol Analysis: Verbal Reports as Data,* MIT Press, 1984.

Feigenbaum, E. A. "The Art of Artificial Intelligence—Themes and Case Studies of Knowledge Engineering," Fifth International Joint

Conference on Artificial Intelligence, Cambridge, MA, 1977, pp. 1014–1029.

Hansen, J. V. and W. F. Messier, "Expert Systems for Decision Support in EDP Auditing," *International Journal of Computer and Information Sciences*, October 1982, pp. 357–379.

Hayes-Roth, F, D. A. Waterman, and D. B. Lenat, (eds.), *Building Expert Systems*, Addison-Wesley, 1983.

Johnson, K. P., and H. R. Jaenicke, *Evaluating Internal Control*, John Wiley & Sons, 1980.

Johnson, P. E., "The Expert Mind: A New Challenge for the Information Scientist," *Beyond Productivity: Information System Development for Organizational Effectiveness*, Th.M.A. Bemelmans (ed.), North-Holland, Elsevier Science Publishers, 1984, pp. 367–386.

———, "What Kind of Expert Should A System Be?", *The Journal of Medicine and Philosophy*, 1983, pp. 77–97.

———, F. Hassebrock, A. S. Duran, and J. Mollar, "Multimethod Study of Clinical Judgment," *Organizational Behavior and Human Performance*, Vol. 30, 1982, pp. 201–230.

Kleinmuntz, B., "The Process of Clinical Information by Man and Machine," in B. Kleinmuntz (ed.), *Formal Representations of Human Judgment*, New York: John Wiley & Sons, 1968, pp. 149–186.

Loebbecke, J. K., "Auditing Research State of the Art: Auditing Approaches, Methods, Programs, and Procedures," Presented at Peat Marwick Main & Co. Audit Research Conference, May 1981.

Mair, W. C., D. R. Wood, and K. W. Davis, *Computer Control & Audit*, The Institute of Internal Auditors, Touche Ross & Co., 1978.

Mautz, R. and J. Winjum, "Criteria for Management Control Systems," Financial Executive Research Institute, 1981.

McCarty, "Reflections on TAXMAN: An Experiment in Artificial Intelligence and Legal Reasoning," *Harvard Law Review*, March 1977, pp. 837–893.

Malone, N. P., "A Strategy for Knowledge-Based Decision Support: Decision Making Expertise in Corporate Acquisitions," unpublished Ph.D. dissertation proposal, University of Minnesota, 1984.

Meservy, R. D., "Auditing Internal Controls: A Computational Model of the Review Process," Ph.D. dissertation, University of Minnesota, 1985.

Michaelsen, R. H., "An Expert System for Federal Tax Planning," working paper, University of Nebraska, 1982.

Moen, James B., "Algorithms and Data Structures in Galen," working paper, University of Minnesota, 1984.

Mutchler, J. F, "Auditors' Perceptions of the Going Concern Opinion Decision," *Auditing: A Journal of Practice and Theory*, Spring 1984, pp. 17–30.

Nisbett, R. E. and T. D. Wilson, "Telling More Than We Can Know: Verbal Reports on Mental Processes," *Psychological Review*, May 1977, pp. 231–259.

Newell, A. and H. A. Simon, *Human Problem Solving*, Prentice-Hall, 1972.

Peat Marwick Main & Co., *Research Opportunities in Auditing*, 1984.

———, *Systems Evaluation Approach: Documentation of Controls (SEA-DOC)*, 1980.

Stefik, M., J. Aikins, R. Balzer, J. Benoit, L. Birnbaum, F Hayes-Roth, and E. Sacerdoti, *The Organization of Expert Systems: A Prescriptive Tutorial*, Xerox Palo Alto Research Centers, 1982.

Thompson, W. B., P. E. Johnson, and J. B. Moen, "Recognition-Based Diagnostic Reasoning," *IJCAI Proceedings*, 1983, pp. 236–238.

van Melle, W., E. H. Shortliffe, and B. G. Buchanan, "EMYCIN; A Domain-Independent System that Aids in Constructing Knowledge-Based Consultation Programs," *Pergamon-Infotech State of the Art Report on Machine Intelligence*, Vol. 9, No. 3, 1981, pp. 249–263.

Knowledge-Based Expert Computer Systems In Auditing

JESSE F. DILLARD and
JANE F. MUTCHLER

1. Introduction

Artificial intelligence (AI) is the area of computer science concerned with designing systems that exhibit the characteristics associated with intelligent human behavior. Expert systems are a means of applying AI techniques within specific, complex domains such as auditing. The knowledge identification required to design an expert system as well as the system itself provide a means for identifying and explaining how human experts store, access, and process information. From an applied standpoint, the system can perform as an intermediary between human experts and/or authoritative pronouncements which provide the basis for its structure and knowledge and users who utilize the system as a decision guide or task consultant.

Research related to expert auditing systems contributes directly to, and is viewed as extensions of, two current areas of interest. The first attempts to understand and explain auditor decision processes. (See Libby, 1981 for a review.) The second attempts to automate audit tasks, increase effectiveness and efficiency, and increases decision consistency across auditors. The widespread application of statistical sampling is indicative of these efforts. Several of the Big Eight public accounting firms are currently moving toward implementing expert systems within the audit environment (Elliott, 1984).

Audit researchers are currently applying expert systems tech-

247

nology in several areas including analytical review (Braun, 1986), auditor opinion formulation (Dillard et al., 1983a), EDP auditing (Hansen and Messier, 1982), and internal control (Dungan, 1983). The purpose of this paper is to generally provide guidance for expert system research and development in auditing and more specifically to report on the development of a prototype system. The illustrative example used is the decision processes related to formulating audit opinion decisions. Methodological issues are addressed, practical issues related to the complex domain of auditing are discussed and theoretical issues associated with expert system design are evaluated.

The next section discusses the stages in expert system development. The third section describes the methodology used to develop a prototype system for the going concern opinion decision using professional standards.[1] The fourth section proposes criteria that should be considered when designing and evaluating knowledge-based expert systems in auditing. The final section presents a summary and conclusions.

2. Stages of System Development

Expert systems development can be viewed as a three stage sequential process with each stage reflecting a different level of expertise or system sophistication.[2]

1. Decision support stage

2. Intermediate expert support stage

3. Expert system stage.

The first stage focuses on task specification and the system architecture. The result is a knowledge-based decision support system. This stage is carried out by identifying the task and human experts within the area and representing the knowledge in such a way that it can be understood and encoded into a computer system. The primary decision hierarchy, decision points and linkages are identified. This results in a detailed description of the task and the domain knowledge needed in carrying out the task. The resulting design provides, at one level, a detailed description of the decision process. Requisite databases (e.g., industry statistics) are identified. The requisite analytic capabilities needed to carry out the task and the point at which

248

they are utilized are identified. A first approximation of the decisions that must be made, their sequence and their relationship to prior and/or future decisions is obtained. The task description is encoded into a computer system. The system provides a means for testing the proposed structure in online, interactive sessions with human experts. The intelligence in a first stage system is the decision structure, its sequence, hierarchy, and component linkages, which provide the framework for building a sophisticated knowledge-based expert system.

From an applications perspective, the first stage system confronts the user with the decisions that must be made but requires that the user actually carry out the logical processes. The decisions are broken down into their lowest components so that the decision maker is presented the many intermediate decisions that are combined in order to arrive at the final decision required. Again, this is intelligence only in the sense that the intermediate decisions are presented to the decision maker in a sequence representing the hierarchical decision structure. The decision results are also formatted, aggregated, and presented to the decision maker where called for at different points in the sequence.

The intermediate expert support stage begins with the stage one decision support system. The second stage validates and extends the structure developed in the first stage by comparing it with expert behavior and evaluating its assessment of historical cases. In effect, the first stage results, represented in the prototype decision support system, can be viewed as a set of hypotheses to be empirically tested using multiple evaluation methods such as protocol analysis, linear modeling, and sensitivity analysis.[3] This process provides a detailed, systematic investigation of expert decision processes which result in a more sophisticated system as well as more detailed and accurate models of expert behavior than are currently available.

From a developmental perspective as the structure is refined, it also can be made more "intelligent" because the decision processes are better understood. In the second stage the intermediate decisions will begin to be "compiled." That is, all the steps will not have to be carried out by the user. The system will have the capability of inferring some of the needed intermediate results. Prior research (Hayes-Roth et al., 1983) indicates that this requires the implementation and encoding of decision heuristics[4] as well as the availability of requisite databases.[5]

The third stage in developing expert systems involves the construction of a system which contains extensive reasoning, learning, and language capabilities and which can be applied to more general and expanded decision making tasks and situations. No AI system currently meets all these objectives in any domain.[6] The remainder of this paper will focus on the design of an expert system through stage one using the going concern audit opinion as the audit task of interest.

3. Expert System Development for the Going Concern Opinion Decision

3.1. PROBLEM SELECTION

Given the current level of technological development, one of the most critical components in successful expert system construction is selecting an appropriate decision task. The task should be fairly precisely definable and somewhat limited in scope. For our purposes, this requires that the task of interest be a subtask, or a specialty task, within the overall audit opinion process.

A general question arises as to whether the going concern opinion decision is an appropriate task domain for expert systems applications. Two major criteria appear to be met. First, it is an environment where expert judgment is required before the task can be carried out. There appear to be no tractable algorithmic solutions due to the environmental complexity of the task domain. Second, there is an identifiable set of recognized experts and codified knowledge relating to the decision task.

The decision appears to be a diagnostic type of decision where a judgment is made at a given point in time reflecting the expert's understanding of the conditions at that time. There are a set of predetermined conditions which reflect past experience and professional consensus. The current conditions, as they are understood, are evaluated within this context to arrive at a decision.[7] Expert judgment is a primary component in the process. From this perspective, the going concern opinion decision seems somewhat analogous to medical diagnosis, an area where extensive expert systems work has been undertaken.[8]

250

Figure 1: An Overview of the Auditor's Opinion Process (Felix and Kinney, 1982)

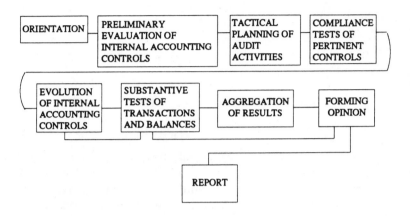

The model presented in Figure 1 represents the auditor's opinion formulation process (Felix and Kinney, 1982). Each stage can require many and varied judgment tasks not to mention significant interactions among the cells. However, some sequencing of tasks is present. For example, generally compliance tests are undertaken prior to substantive tests, and audit opinion formulation is undertaken after the audit results are known. Theoretically the decision as to the type of opinion rendered by the auditor is made after the completion of the audit process. Thus, the opinion decision can be defined such that the audit results are parameters whose values are known.

The opinion alternatives faced by the auditor are summarized in Figure 2.

Generally speaking there are different sets of decision criteria associated with each opinion category. Thus each can be viewed separately in terms of system design. That is, if the assumption that the opinion decision can be viewed such that the results of the audit process are known parameters, a separate and distinct expert system can be constructed for each opinion category. Thus each could be the focus of an expert computer system. This paper focuses on the unusual uncertainties categories in general and specifically on the going concern opinion.[9]

The going concern opinion is a fairly well defined task within

	Not Material	Material	Very Material
GAAP	Clean	Except For	Adverse
Unusual Uncertainty	Clean	Subject To	Disclaimer
Scope	Clean	Except For	Disclaimer

FIGURE 2
Auditor Opinion Options

the audit opinion domain. Focusing on the going concern opinion decision restricts the system to a more manageable level of complexity. Yet such a system would provide an integral part to a more complete expert system of the audit opinion process.

The next section presents an analysis of the task domain. The results are a set of decision processes specified in such a way that they can be encoded into an expert system.

3.2. TASK DOMAIN

The subject-to opinion is the general domain of interest. If an uncertainty arises which has the potential to materially affect the financial statement results, the auditor decides if a qualified opinion is needed. The circumstances giving rise to uncertainties can range from relatively simple litigation loss contingencies to relatively complex cases of entity failure.

From an information processing perspective, the major diagnostic task of the auditor is to construct a benchmark or model for evaluation, given the parameters of the entity being evaluated. Once reasonable standards are determined, an evaluation of the entity in relation to the standards is undertaken. Based on preliminary evaluations of auditor behavior and prior experience in other complex domains and accounting problem solving, the auditor's decision process appears to follow a hierarchical branching structure originating around a series of diagnostic questions. However, it does not appear that this structure is called until there is reason to believe that an unqualified opinion is not appropriate. This is suggested by the following statement in Statement on Auditing Standards No. 34 (SAS No. 34).

252

In an examination of financial statements in accordance with generally accepted auditing standards, the auditor does not search for evidential matter relating to the entity's continued existence because, in the absence of information to the contrary, an entity's continuation is usually assumed in financial accounting. Nevertheless, the auditor remains aware that auditing procedures applied primarily for other purposes may bring to his attention information contrary to that assumption. (para. 3)

Once there is reason to believe that the opinion may have to be qualified, evidence (AICPA, 1981; Mutchler, 1984) suggests that the auditor assesses the following dimensions, among others, of the entity:

1. Management ability and plans

2. Cash flow potential

3. Performance in relation to industry

4. Performance in relation to prior years

5. Mitigating factors.

Specific diagnostic questions focusing on these dimensions are addressed by the auditor and should be included in the system's hierarchical branching structure.

The following example questions relate to the assessment of cash flow potential.

- Has management prepared a cash flow forecast?
- Is the cash flow forecast reasonable and verifiable?
- Can bankers verify lines of credit?
- What is the degree of certainty associated with future sources of cash flow?

There are many related questions included in a hierarchical branching structure used by an auditor for the going concern

253

opinion decision. For example, SAS 34 directly addresses auditor decision making in the presence of going concern uncertainties. In doing so, it describes "contrary information" that may cast doubt on the ability of an entity to continue in existence, and further points out "mitigating factors" which may discount the significance of any problem. An analysis of each of these dimensions provides inputs for the final audit opinion. The following discussion presents a detailed task analysis of the going concern audit opinion decision as specified by SAS 34 and provides illustrations as to how the results are encoded to construct the prototype stage one system.[10]

3.3. PROTOTYPE STAGE ONE SYSTEM

The following discussion illustrates the development of a stage one prototype system based on the decision processes implied in SAS 34. First, the proposed system architecture is presented. Second, the decision hierarchy is specified. Next, the decision hierarchy is applied to develop a prototype stage one system by specifying the decision nodes in terms of the decisions that must be made at that point. This process is illustrated using decision frames[11] from the resulting stage one prototype system.

Based on research in accounting related areas[12] the general architecture presented in Figure 3 is proposed. The task support system is a network of frames each representing a decision-action state which is related to making the decision of interest. The guidance system is a network of frames which provide suggestions, rules and methods for making the decisions required in the task support system. The guidance system would parallel the task support system. The task action system provides a package of support programs for data access, statistical analysis, etc. The external interface system provides for the automatic production of requisite documentation, audit trails, etc. The task support structure is the heart of the system. The structure is encoded in an information organization program that represents, organizes, and links the decision frames or episodes. That is, one frame represents each decision identified. This frame is linked to all other relevant frames as well as the needed databases and prior decision results.

Software used in this project to construct the stage one prototype is ZOG developed by Newell, Robertson, McCracken,

Figure 3: Architecture

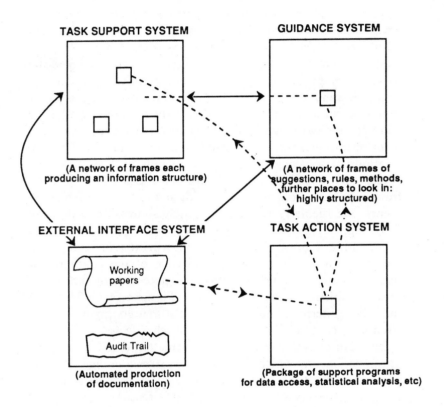

TASK SUPPORT SYSTEM

(A network of frames each
producing an information structure)

GUIDANCE SYSTEM

(A network of frames of
suggestions, rules, methods,
further places to look in:
highly structured)

EXTERNAL INTERFACE SYSTEM

Working
papers

Audit Trail

(Automated production
of documentation)

TASK ACTION SYSTEM

(Package of support programs
for data access, statistical analysis, etc)

and Ramakrishna (Robertson et al., 1977; Robertson et al., 1979). The system has been applied in several different situations (Chandrasekaran et al., 1983b; Fox and Palay, 1980; Mantei and McCracken, 1979; Ramakrishna, 1981). This system provides only the structure, editing and manipulating facilities. All the task specific content knowledge must be constructed within the framework.

3.3.1. The Decision Hierarchy

The decision hierarchy based on SAS 34 provides the initial outline (or basic structure) for the stage one prototype system and provides a first approximation of the task representation. This analysis, as does SAS 34, begins at the point which the auditor has cause to suspect that a going concern opinion may have to be issued. The auditor begins by evaluating contrary information. The decision sequence is presented in Figure 4. First, the auditor determines if the contrary information relates to solvency problems. SAS 34 identifies two classifications: negative trends and other indications. In evaluating negative trends the auditor determines whether there are recurring operating losses, working capital deficiencies, negative cash flows from operations, and/or adverse key financial ratios. Other indications of solvency problems are defaults on loan or similar agreements, arrearages in dividends, denial of usual trade credit from suppliers, noncompliance with statutory capital requirements, and the necessity of seeking new sources or methods of financing.

The auditor must also evaluate information that may raise questions about the continued existence of the entity in the future. These are indications that the potential for future solvency problems exists. As shown in Figure 5, SAS 34 breaks these into internal matters and external matters giving specific circumstances to be considered under each.

The auditor evaluates contrary information in the light of any mitigating factors which are present. As shown in Figure 6, SAS 34 categorizes mitigating factors into those that relate to solvency problems and those that relate to potential solvency problems.

3.3.2. Decision Frames

Each cell in Figures 4, 5, and 6 represents a decision, or a set of decisions, made by an auditor in arriving at the going concern opinion determination and represents the first, rather abstract, level of decision making. The decisions can be represented by a series of frames. Two types of analysis are implied. The first relates to establishing a factor's existence. The second evaluates the factor's potential impact on the entity. The relevance of the second type of analysis is dependent upon the first level determinations. For example, if recurring operating losses are not

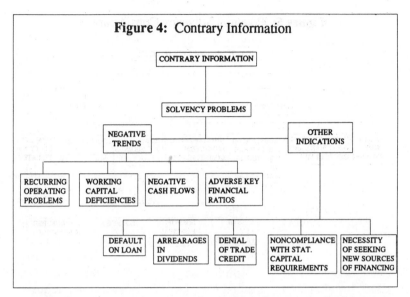

Figure 4: Contrary Information

present there is no reason to evaluate them in terms of mitigating factors.

The following discussion describes the stage one prototype system based on SAS 34. The system is comprised of approximately 190 frames. The illustrative issue addressed is working capital deficiencies. As shown in Figure 4, once the entity has been identified as a problem firm, contrary information relative to solvency problems is evaluated. The following frame specifies the alternatives to be considered.

Frame PMM2:

Two classifications of solvency problems should be considered.

Negative Trends (PMM3)

Other Indications (IO1)

Assuming the decision maker selects negative trends, the following frame appears indicating that four negative trend categories are to be considered.

Figure 5: Potential Solvency Considerations

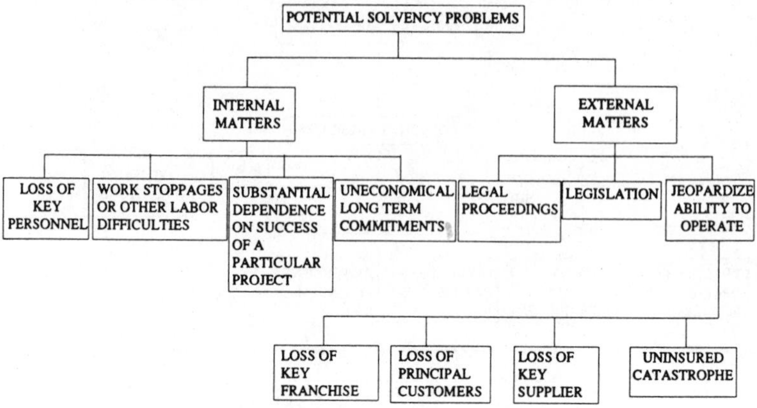

Frame PMM3:

The following is a list of negative trends that should be consid-⟩ ered when evaluating solvency problems.

Recurring Operating Losses (OI1)

Working Capital Deficiencies (WC1)

Negative Cash Flows from Operations (NC1)

Adverse Financial Ratios (AF1)

These represent states to be considered. The balance of this example assumes that "Working Capital Deficiencies" is chosen. The next frame represents attributes along which this state is evaluated.

Frame WC1:   (next: WC12)

The evaluation of the impact of working capital deficiencies on the solvency condition of the entity necessitates consideration of the following:

Deterioration rate (WC2)

258

Figure 6: Mitigating Factors

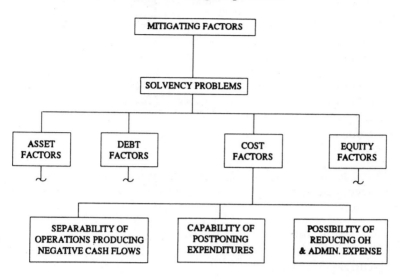

Permanence of Influence (WC6)

Susceptibility to Internal Influences (WC10)

Pervasiveness Within the Entity (WC11)

Each of these components is evaluated. For example, deterioration rate is evaluated as to whether it is rapid or gradual. Then, given that the rate is rapid/gradual, the system user is confronted with the question, what is the impact on the entity's solvency position? It should be noted that this stage one system structures the task and presents the decisions to be made. There is no inference capability within the system. After the attributes of a state are evaluated, the state impact on the solvency position is determined. As illustrated in the following frame, the decisions, or evaluations, relative to attributes and the effect of the attributes on the states are preliminary to a decision of the state impact on solvency position. In a stage two system, given the attribute evaluations, a state evaluation could be made by the system thus relieving the decision maker of the activity.

259

Frame WC12:   (next: WC1)

The following is a summary of your responses to questions evaluating the impact of working capital deficiencies on the solvency position of the entity.

Deterioration rate   *rapid   significant (4)*
Permanence of influence *permanent   Moderate (3)*
Susceptibility of internal
  influences   *susceptible (3)*
Pervasiveness   *very pervasive (5)*

What is the impact of the working capital deficiencies on the solvency position of the entity using the five point scale provided below?

Very significant—5   (WC13)
Significant—4   (WC13)
Neutral—3   (WC13)
Insignificant—2   (WC1)
Very insignificant—1   (WC1)

Next, mitigating factors relating to working capital deficiencies are considered. For example, does management have plans for overcoming working capital deficiencies? The frame presented below illustrates the factors to be considered in evaluating management's plans for overcoming working capital deficiencies.

Frame WC14:

Evaluate the following factors that are a part of management's plan for overcoming the working capital deficiencies.

Asset Factors   (WC15)

Debt Factors   (WC33)

Cost Factors   (WC45)

Equity Factors (WC58)

The factors are evaluated in terms of proposed management actions directed toward overcoming working capital deficiencies. The following frame sequence illustrates the decision sequence incorporated into the system relating to cost factors.

260

Frame WC45:   Cost Factors   (next: WC14)

Which of the following actions are part of management's plan for overcoming working capital deficiencies?

Separating operations producing negative cash flows (WC46)

Postponing expenses (WC48)

Reducing expenses (WC53)

Our hypothetical decision maker notes that management is planning to postpone maintenance expenses and is guided through the frame sequence.

Frame WC48:   Postponing Expenses   (next: WC45)

Which of the following expenses are to be postponed?

Maintenance expense (WC49)

Research and Development (WC51)

Frame WC49: Maintenance Expense

Is it feasible to postpone maintenance expense as specified in management's plan?

Yes (WC50)

No (WC48)

Don't know

Frame WC50:   (next: WC48)

What is the effect on working capital of postponing maintenance expense?

Very significant—5
Significant—4
Neutral—3
Insignificant—2
Very insignificant—1

After the initial evaluations are made, a summary is presented and the overall impact of management's plans relating to cost factors on working capital deficiencies is evaluated. After each factor is evaluated, the overall impact of management's plans relating to working capital deficiencies is determined. Next, the effect of working capital deficiencies, in light of management's plans for reducing them, on the entity's solvency position is determined. The primary and intermediate decision sequences are evaluated and combined to determine if substantial doubt remains about the entity's ability to continue in existence. If so, the following guidance is provided by SAS 34.

> In such a case he [or she] should consider the recoverability and classification of recorded asset amounts and the amounts and classification of liabilities in light of that doubt. (para. 11)

The auditor combines all prior judgments with the recoverability assessment in arriving at the final opinion decision.

The preceding discussion outlines the decision process implied by SAS 34 in making going concern audit opinion decisions. The decisions have been identified and specified in such a way as to be encoded into a stage one decision support system. As stated previously, it represents a first order approximation of the decision process required in making the going concern opinion determination. From a research perspective it provides a detailed structure for building a more intelligent system through further specification and inclusion of reasoning capabilities. From a practical perspective, the stage one system provides decision support by guiding the user through the decision sequence.

3.4. STAGE TWO PROTOTYPE DEVELOPMENT

Stage two evaluates the proposed structure by comparing it with actual expert behavior. Several benefits accrue. First, from a pragmatic perspective, the comparisons provide indications as to where the auditor deviates from the procedures specified by the authoritative pronouncements. Second, the comparisons are a means of verifying the first stage system. If both are similar, there is at least some support for the system's validity. Third, expert behavior adds specificity to the stage one system.

262

Two procedures can be used to acquire the needed expert knowledge:

1. in-depth interviews and

2. verbal protocols.

In-depth interviews are carried out by directing questions to an expert concerning the hypothesized decision processes. For example, SAS 34 provides no guidance as to how one determines the deterioration rate on the entity's solvency position caused by working capital deficiencies. The interview can be used to better understand how the decision is made and identify the cues used by the expert.

Protocol analysis is another way of acquiring expert knowledge. Two alternative approaches might be useful. First is to have the expert think aloud during an interactive session as he or she goes through the stage one prototype. Second, experts can be presented with cases and asked to think aloud as they evaluate the case.[13] As more knowledge is gained, expert decision processes can be articulated more precisely. More realistic cases can be constructed from the interview results and historical data such as working papers. Verbal protocols can be collected from experts as they make audit opinion decisions. Protocol analysis is explained by Newell and Simon (1972), its strengths and weaknesses are discussed by Ericsson and Simon (1980), and it has been applied in accounting research (Bhaskar and Dillard, 1979; Dillard et al., 1982; Biggs and Mock, 1983; Hansen et al., 1981).

4. Design Criteria

Criteria are needed for designing and evaluating expert systems. The following set of criteria set forth by Bobrow (1975) in a discussion of representation is proposed. They are not "how to" criteria,[14] but represent general guidelines for expert system research. While it may not be feasible to empirically test each criterion in detail, they represent fundamental issues critical to expert systems research from the standpoint of scientific legitimacy as well as long term real world applications.[15]

- How do objects and relationships in the world correspond to the units and relations encoded in the system?

263

- In what ways do the operations in the system correspond to actions in the world?
- How can system knowledge be used in mapping the world state?
- How can information be added to the system without further external input?
- How are units linked to provide access to appropriate knowledge?
- How are two structures compared for equality and similarity?
- What knowledge does a system have to have about its own structure and operation?

The first three criteria relate to how well the system corresponds to the "real world." The last four relate to the system's awareness of itself, and its ability to "learn." The first requires expertise in the domain of interest; the related issues are legitimate audit research issues. The second set requires AI expertise and represents fundamental AI issues that are yet to be resolved.[16] It should be noted that by employing the suggested criteria, the researcher is forced to be concerned not only with the decision outcome but also the process used to arrive at the outcome. It appears that predictive accuracy is the primary criterion currently being used in evaluating auditing research. This leads to the question of what is the research's objective. Is it to explain human behavior or to predict an outcome or result of human behavior? And which of these is appropriate and under what circumstances?[17] From a short run application perspective, predictive accuracy is the appropriate criterion. Prediction of bankruptcy is a good example. Linear models using a limited number of cues have been shown to be very good predictors of bankruptcy. Two observations can be made from the expert systems perspective. First, there is little about the human expert's decision processes that can be learned from this approach. Second, if the task can be carried out by an algorithm then there is no need to build an expert system to do it. From a longer run research perspective, understanding decision processes is important not only for building good expert systems but also for gaining meaningful insights into auditors' decision making behavior.

264

5. Summary and Conclusions

The purpose of the preceding discussion has been to describe expert system development both in general and specifically as applied to the auditor's opinion decision. Two points need emphasis. The first is the importance of understanding the problem being investigated, and the second is the extensive time commitment required to build expert systems (Hayes-Roth, et al., 1983). Three stages in system development are identified. The results of the first stage is a knowledge-based decision support system which represents a detailed outline of the expert behavior of interest, in this case the audit opinion decision. The system provides a means for testing the proposed framework in online, interactive sessions with human experts. The intelligence in this first stage system is the decision structure, its sequence hierarchy and component linkages. These provide the basic components for building the more sophisticated knowledge-based expert systems of stages two and three. A methodology for developing an expert system for the going concern opinion has been presented as well as evaluation criteria and issues which should be addressed when carrying out expert system research.

There is a need for more basic research into the behavior of expert decision makers. The central determinant of effective use of knowledge is how it is organized. Issues of representation should come after the organizational structure of knowledge that is needed for problem solving has been clarified. The methodology presented above provides a means for achieving this objective.

As more audit related expert systems are built, system developers should become more mindful of system interfacing. The audit task can be viewed as a series of intermediate decisions which are made by different people. These people could be viewed as specialists in their areas and would be consulted in forming the audit opinion similar to the consultation of medical specialists during a diagnostic evaluation of a patient. Thought needs to be given as to how these specialists should interact with one another and how they should interface with the "opinion" expert.

One of the major benefits of research on expert systems is that it forces the researcher to examine important task domains in detail. The process not only contributes to the researcher's

265

knowledge base but also can lead to a self-examination process by the auditing firm. This evaluation process can lead to overall improved decision making, the potential for decreasing inconsistencies in the opinion decision across auditors and in ultimately decreasing audit risk.

Footnotes

1. For purposes of this report, the term "going concern opinion" refers to either a qualification or a disclaimer issued for going concern uncertainties.

2. It might be noted that at one level, expert system development does not differ a great deal from the development of more traditional types of computer systems. That is, problem identification, problem specification, algorithm identification and specification, and translation into machine-readable code are required. The major difference is the nature of the problem or task or interest. Expert systems projects address fairly ill-defined tasks for which no algorithmic solution is known (or if known is not feasible). Expert systems employ symbolic representation and inference, heuristic search and domain specific problem-solving strategies as integral components of the computer system. These are not incorporated in traditional systems.

3. This is an "expert consensus" validation approach. Thus, it is preferable that a set of experts other than those who might have participated in the first stage are used.

4. Decision heuristics are identified throughout the three stages with increased specificity required as one attempts to increase the system's inferencing capabilities.

5. System interfaces with requisite databases and other decision support facilities can present a major impediment in constructing AI systems (Chandrasekaran et al., 1983a).

6. The most sophisticated systems are currently in the area of medical diagnosis (See Hayes-Roth et al., 1983 for a review) but they fall short of possessing these requirements.

7. The "correct" answer becomes evident only with the passage of time. However, the decision must be made prior to that time. The appropriateness of the decision is not necessarily determined by whether it is "correct" but whether it is the same conclusion that an expert faced with the same facts would reach.

8. There are some rather important differences between the two areas. The most fundamental one appears to be associated with the standards, or benchmarks, used for comparisons. The medical diagnostic domain appears to have fairly well established models and precisely measurable cues. The problem is that there are many possible outcomes (diseases) to consider. In the auditing domain, the appropriate benchmarks are not as precisely established or as accurately measured. To a greater extent, the auditor must first construct a normative model of each entity and then compare the model with the entity's current condition as he or she understands them at the time. The major focus is constructing the normative model of the entity, not making and evaluating the comparisons. This does not appear to be the case in medical diagnosis. Further, the auditor generally faces a smaller set of possible outcomes. These differences do not diminish the applicability of expert systems in the audit opinion domain. They do however suggest that medical expert systems might require modification before they are applied within an auditing context.

9. The subject-to opinion issued for going concern uncertainties is no longer a valid option in Canada. However, the considerations relating to the going

concern opinion decision are relevant in assessing failure to disclose a potential going concern problem which would constitute a GAAP departure.

10. This procedure will represent a complete stage one system only if SAS 34 represents a complete description of the decision process; however, authoritative pronouncements provide an appropriate basis from which to begin developing the decision support system.

11. The term frame is not used in a theoretical sense as does Minsky (1975) but in a technical sense referring to the representation of a decision and to presentation on the terminal screen.

12. A prototype system for military procurement price analysis has been constructed using this system. (See Dillard et al., 1983b and Ramakrishna et al., 1983).

13. These knowledge acquisition procedures can also be used to acquire knowledge for building the stage one prototype system.

14. Several other sets of more procedural criteria have been proposed by several authors. The reader is referred to (Hayes-Roth et al., 1983).

15. The proposed criteria are based on the assumption that the most promising strategy for expert system development currently is to attempt to reflect expert problem-solving behavior.

16. This is not to suggest that audit research should not address these issues, only that fundamental theoretical development will also be required. AI researchers are probably better equipped in these areas.

17. See Waller and Jiambalvo (1984) for an interesting discussion of the related issues.

References

American Institute of CPAs, *The Auditor's Considerations When a Question Arises About An Entity's Continued Existence, SAS No. 34,* New York: AICPA, 1981.

Bhaskar, R. and J. F. Dillard, "Human Cognition in Accounting: A Preliminary Analysis," T. J. Burns (ed.), *Behavioral Experiments In Accounting II.,* The Ohio State University, 1979.

Biggs, S. F. and T. J. Mock, "An Investigation of Auditor Decision Processes in the Evaluation of Internal Control and Audit Scope Decisions," *Journal of Accounting Research,* Spring 1983, pp. 234–255.

Bobrow, D. G., "Dimensions in Representation," D. G. Bobrow and A. Collins (eds.), *Representation and Understanding,* Academic Press, 1975.

Braun, H. M., "An Application of Expert Systems to Study the Decision Process Used by Analytical Review Information for Audit Decisions," Ph.D. dissertation, University of Illinois, 1986.

Chandrasekaran, B., J. F. Dillard, and K. Ramakrishna, *The Design of an Expert System for Contract Price Analysis,* Technical Report I and II, Department of Computer and Information Science, The Ohio State University, April 1983.

———, *The Design of an Expert System For Contract Price Analysis,* Phase III Technical Report. Department of Computer Science and Information Science, The Ohio State University, September 1983.

Dillard, J. F., R. Bhaskar, and R. G. Stephens, "Using First-Order Cognitive Analysis to Understand Problem Solving Behavior: An

Example From Accounting," *Instructional Science,* Vol. 11, 1982, pp. 71–92.

———, and ———, "Expert Systems for Audit Opinion Decisions," The Ohio State University, 1983.

———, J. F. Mutchler, and K. Ramakrishna, "Knowledge-Based Expert Systems for Price Analysis: A Feasibility Study," *Federal Acquisition Research Symposium,* Williamsburg, VA: U. S. Air Force, December 1983.

Dungan, C. A., *A Model of an Audit Judgment in the Form of An Expert System,* Ph.D. dissertation, University of Illinois, 1983.

Elliott, R. K., Comment on "Auditing Research in Accounting Doctoral Programs," T. J. Burns (ed.), *Doctoral Programs in Accounting,* The Ohio State University, 1984.

Ericsson, K. A. and H. A. Simon, "Verbal Reports as Data," *Psychological Review,* Vol. 87(3), May 1980.

Felix, W. L. and W. R. Kinney, "Research in the Auditor's Opinion Formulation Process: State of the Art," *Accounting Review,* April 1982, pp. 245–271.

Fox, M. S. and A. J. Palay, "Machine-Assisted Browsing for the Naive User," J. L. Divilbiss (ed.), *Public Access to Library Automation,* University of Illinois, 1980.

Hansen, J. V. and W. F. Messier, "Expert Systems for Decision Support in EDP Auditing." *International Journal of Computer and Information Sciences,* 1982, pp. 357–379.

———, ———, and S. F. Biggs, "Software Development for Implementation Testing of Artificial Intelligence Methods in EDP Auditing," research proposal, University of Florida, 1981.

Hayes-Roth, F., D. A. Waterman, and D. B. Lenat, "An Overview of Expert Systems," F. Hayes-Roth, D. A. Waterman, and D. B. Lenat (eds.), *Building Expert Systems,* Addison-Wesley, 1983.

Libby, R., *Accounting and Human Information Processing,* Prentice Hall, 1981.

Mantei, M. and D. L. McCracken, "Issue Analysis With ZOG, a Highly Interactive Man-Machine Interface," *First International Symposium On Policy Analysis and Information Systems,* Duke University, June 1979.

Minsky, M., "A Framework for Representing Knowledge," P. Winston (ed.), *The Psychology of Computer Vision,* McGraw-Hill, 1975.

Mutchler, J. F., "Auditors' Perceptions of the Going Concern Opinion Decision," *Auditing: A Journal of Practice and Theory,* Spring 1984, pp. 17–30.

Newell, A., and H. A. Simon, *Human Problem Solving,* Prentice-Hall, 1972.

Ramakrishna, K., *Schematization As An Aid To Organizing ZOG Information Nets,* Ph.D. dissertation, Computer Science Department, Carnegie-Mellon University, August 1981.

———, J. F. Dillard, T. G. Harrison, and B. Chandrasekaran, "An Intelligent Manual For Price Analysis," *Federal Acquisition Research Symposium.* Williamsburg, Virginia: U. S. Air Force, December 1983.

Robertson, G., A. Newell, and K. Ramakrishna, *ZOG: A Man-Machine*

Communication Philosophy, Technical Representative Computer Science Department, Carnegie-Mellon University, August 1977.
————, and D. McCracken, *The ZOG Approach To Man-Machine Communication* Technical Representative Computer Science Department, Carnegie-Mellon University, October 1979.
Waller, W. and J. Jiambalvo, "The Use of Normative Models in Human Information Processing Research in Accounting," *Journal of Accounting Literature,* Vol. 3., 1984, pp. 201–226.

Scheduling the Monitoring of EDP Controls in Online Systems

JAMES V. HANSEN and
WILLIAM F. MESSIER, JR.

1. Introduction

Corporate management establishes systems of internal control to aid in effectively meeting corporate goals. In designing sound systems of internal control, management is concerned with providing reliable data, safeguarding assets and records, promoting operational efficiency, and encouraging adherence to corporate policy.[2] Another concern that has recently entered the picture is the Foreign Corrupt Practices Act of 1977 (FCPA), which requires management to maintain "proper record keeping systems." Unfortunately, this law provides few operational definitions to guide managerial compliance. Mautz, et al.,[2] found that management's typical reaction to the compliance aspect of the FCPA was in the form of increased systems documentation, and that this had done little to alleviate concern about the adequacy of controls in an environment characterized by dependence on computers for accurate financial reporting and operational efficiency.

The latter problem is of considerable importance because of the pervasiveness of computer-based systems in all types of organizations, and the fact that today's EDP systems are undergoing major design changes. The primary reasons for these

271

design changes are that: (1) many users feel that their current batch systems are not sufficiently responsive, (2) an increasing number of users are trained in at least one programming language and desire to have hands on control over processing, and (3) the relative costs of equipment and software to support online operations are making online systems more attractive. These developments create something of a dilemma for EDP auditors,[1] since methods for the control and audit of online computer systems are still undergoing development.[2]

In general, online means that the user is interfacing with the computer system under direct control of the central-processing unit. However, to the EDP auditor it may also mean that: (1) data files are readily accessible; (2) programs are memory resident; (3) local/remote terminals are connected via dedicated/dial communications; (4) the user is performing inquiry response, record update, and online data entry and/or report generation; (5) the system should provide for restart and recovery; (6) the system should insure privacy and security of exit/entrance passwords, programs, files, resource allocation, and maintenance controls; (7) the system should control double updates, lack of update, and file recovery; (8) the system should control the network and insure data validity, routing, and security; (9) the system should provide complete audit trails. Applications not only include real-time programs involving inquiry, update, and dispatching, but also remote batch transactions and remote job entry (RJE). While remote batch transactions and RJE are subject to loss of transaction data during transmission, real-time applications are subject to human data-entry errors, loss of control over access, and hardware or software failure during application processing. Moreover, there is the danger of parts of the transaction trail being unaccounted for.

In online systems the *processing* controls mimic to some degree the standard controls found in a batch processing system. However, in an online system there is necessarily an emphasis on *programmed* controls because of concurrent processing and increased accessibility of files and programs. The bulk of online programmed controls reside in the supervisory program, implying substantially more effort in the development of test data than with a batch system. For example, batch testing will never need to test the effectiveness of message handling or control of intelligent terminals. The EDP auditor is generally examining complex software which can make control failures difficult to immediately detect. As technology advances, overall control of EDP processing will require (1) continued upgrading of controls, and (2) methods and schedules for monitoring their effectiveness. While considerable research effort[3] has addressed the design and reliability of internal control systems, little attention has been devoted to the *monitoring* issue; yet, the American Institute of Certified Public Accountants' Special Advisory Committee on Internal Accounting Control[2] has emphasized that one of management's responsibilities is to "monitor compliance" of their internal control system.

The implementation of new controls requires close monitoring to determine if those controls function as desired. Existing techniques also require attention to determine how well they operate in the online environment where a failure could easily go undetected for a costly length of time. Because of the heavy reliance on programmed controls, costs of control dysfunction[4] could be critical. In this paper we are concerned with the effective scheduling of monitoring of EDP controls so that such failures do not become disasters and the costs of checking are balanced against the costs of dysfunction. We view the computer, itself, as a proper tool in this monitoring process.

2. A GENERAL MODEL

Thorough testing of compliance in online systems can be achieved through: (1) development of embedded modules which allow the introduction of test transaction into the system at random intervals, (2) tagging of transactions to trace live data through the system (at each processing step the interaction of the tagged data with other data can be captured and logged—or displayed on output devices), (3) extending application programs to detect transactions which meet certain predetermined requirements, and (4) maintaining an audit log of specific events, such as attempts to override a password, unauthorized access to a data file. To study these cases, we elaborate on the analysis of Keller.[6] A general formalization of the monitoring process can be specified as follows:

Let the cost per inspection of status be k_0 and we assume that the longer the period between a failure and its detection, the greater the loss from the failure. Of course, the more frequently the system is monitored, the lower will be the loss of undetected failure $C(T)$ and the higher will be the total cost of monitoring.

273

An optimal inspection schedule minimizes the expected sum of these two costs (loss from control failure and monitoring costs).

Suppose that monitoring is so frequent that it can be described by a smooth density function $n(t)$ denoting the number of inspections per unit time. This is particularly relevant in the context of using embedded audit modules which can, theoretically, monitor at any time. It follows that $1/n(t)$ is the time between inspections and $\frac{1}{2}n(t)$ is the expected time interval between dysfunction and the check that detects it. How is this so? Consider for simplicity a uniform probability density function. If $n(t)$ is, say, sixty inspections per hour, then $1/(n(t)) = \frac{1}{60}$ is the average delay between one inspection and the next. Thus, if inspections are performed every $\frac{1}{60}$ seconds, the expected time lapse from failure to detection is $1/(2n(t)) = \frac{1}{120}$ seconds.

Suppose that the first dysfunction occurs at time t. The expected loss will be $C(\frac{1}{2}n(t))$ and the cost of testing will be $k_0 \int_o^t n(s)\,ds$. Let $F(t)$ be the probability of dysfunction between time 0 and time t, so that $F^1(t)$ is its probability density function. F is a nondecreasing function with $F(0) = 0$ and $F(t_1) = 1$, and the system will evidence dysfunction by t_1. The expected cost, E, up to detection for the first dysfunction is

$$E = \int_0^t \left[k_0 \int_0^t n(s)\,ds + C(1/2n(t)) \right] F'(t)\,dt \tag{1}$$

This is the cost if dysfunction occurs at time t, multiplied by the probability density of dysfunction at time t, integrated over all possible dysfunction times. We desire to produce an investigating function $n(t)$ that minimizes E.

We can make (1) more tractable if we let $x(t) = \int_o^t n(s)\,ds$, whereby $x^1(t) = n(t)$ and (1) becomes

$$E_{min} = \int_0^t |k_0 x(t) + C(1/2x'(t))| F'(t)\,dt \tag{2}$$

subject to $x(0) = 0$, and $x(t_1)$ free. The resulting Euler equation is

$$k_0 F'(t) = -d|C'(1/2x'(t) F'(t)/2x(t)'^2|/dt \tag{3}$$

In order to proceed we utilize the transversality condition (see the Appendix), and if x_1 is free, then $F^1_x = 0$ at t_1 becomes

$$-C'F/2x'(t)^2 = 0 \text{ at } t_1 \tag{4}$$

Separating variables and integrating produces

$$k_0 F(t) = -C'F'(t)/2x(t)'^2 + c \qquad (5)$$

Letting $\gamma = c/k_o$, we can rewrite (5) as

$$C'(1/2n(t))/n^2(t) = 2k_0|\gamma - F(t)|/F'(t) \qquad (6)$$

Therefore

$$-C'F'(t)\, 2n^2(t) = k_0|\gamma - F(t)| \qquad (7)$$

so that (4) leads to

$$k_0|\gamma - F(t_1)| = 0 \qquad (8)$$

Since $F(t_1) = 1$, from (8) we have

$$\gamma = 1 \qquad (9)$$

Substituting (9) in (6) yields

$$C'(1/2n(t))/n^2(t) = 2k_0|1 - F(t)|\, F'(t) \qquad (10)$$

which implies the optimal monitoring schedule $n(t)$. The larger the conditional probability of density of failure $F^1(t)/(1-F(t))$ at time t, given survival to time t, the smaller the cost of checking, the larger the loss from undetected failure; hence the more frequent the monitoring.

One of the most troublesome problems facing the auditor of online systems is how to obtain assurance that proper controls are operating correctly. Methods such as the integrated test facility[5] (ITF) hold potential for online systems since they allow the entry of test transactions into the system concurrent with normal transactions. Concurrency is necessary since problems and inconsistencies must be identified quickly so that preventive auditing can be exercised. ITF techniques provide evidential information about the controls and logic of the system. They have been found to be particularly useful when used with program tracing methods. Procedures which aid in determining the presence of unauthorized program instructions, incorrect program paths, or unused program segments are termed program tracing. This is generally a straightforward procedure, since most support software includes a capability whereby the auditor can easily activate a trace routine and receive a complete listing of the sequence of procedures that were executed during the program run. ITFs can be implemented at any time, without the necessity of organizational personnel knowing when such monitoring is occurring.

These techniques tend to evaluate the type of processing controls where failure may result in relatively constant losses over the short term. For example, the failure to validate transactions will likely result in a typical number of errors per run, the cost of which may be relatively constant. Suppose we process 200 transactions per run with an average of three erroneous identifiers (e.g., not on the master file, not coded as a new record, etc.) This could result in, say, a one day delay in billing customers, with a corresponding "constant" cost to the firm.

In this case we proceed as follows. Denoting constant proportionality by

$$C(t) = k_1 \qquad (11)$$

then $C^1(t) = k_1$ and Eq. (6) yields

$$n(t) = \left| \frac{k_1 F'(t)}{2k_0 |\gamma - F(t)|} \right|^{1/2} \qquad (12)$$

and (1) becomes

$$E = \left| \frac{k_0 k_1}{2} \right|^{1/2} \int_0^\infty \left| F' \int_0^t \left(\frac{F'}{\gamma - F} \right)^{1/2} ds + (\gamma - F)^{1/2} (f')^{1/2} \right| dt \qquad (13)$$

Integrating, we derive

$$E = \left| \frac{k_0 k_1}{2} \right|^{1/2} \int_0^\infty \left| (F')^{1/2} \frac{1 - F + \gamma - F}{(\gamma - F)^{1/2}} \right| dt \qquad (14)$$

For any value of F, the integrand in (14) is minimized when $\gamma = 1$. Therefore, (14) yields

$$E = (2k_0 k_1) \int_0^\infty (F')^{1/2} (1 - F)^{1/2} dt \qquad (15)$$

With $\gamma = 1$, (11) produces the result

$$n(t) = \left| \frac{k_1 F'(t)}{2k_0 |1 - F(t)|} \right|^{1/2} \qquad (16)$$

From (14), we see that the value $y = 1$ makes the expected monitoring cost equal to the expected value of $C(T)$. Therefore the expected number of tests is $E/2k_0$.

3. Embedded Audit Modules

Embedded audit modules have evolved from the need to monitor and report unusual transactions. Such systems have become more prevalent with the development of improved software for supervisory transactions. Embedded modules are typically designed to monitor all transaction activity and to notify the auditor of any activities having special audit significance, such as unauthorized attempts to access the system or dollar amounts in excess of certain limits. Typically, the module will write all relevant information concerning such transactions on a file called the audit log. The auditor then periodically requests a print-out of the audit log and inspects the transactions recorded there. It is the schedule for monitoring the log which is of interest in this section.

We note that *tagging* can also be used as a method of pursuing the same audit objective. With tagging, selected records are identified by a special code. As application programs process these records, audit modules capture all data concerning the tagged records and record it in an audit file. In this situation the auditor must again determine when and how often to inspect this file.

Intelligent terminals which are programmable and loadable only by the host computer are a lesser hazard to the security of a system than a locally programmable and loadable mini-computer used as an intelligent terminal. The use of locally programmable intelligent terminals can introduce the prospect of other exposures. The exposures are based on the possibility that the terminal may be used to access the information requested by other users connected through the same intelligent terminal. That is, a user loads the terminal with a program which appears normal and legitimate but which also monitors all of the activities occurring at the terminal. This program intercepts all data requested and generated by each user. It can also intercept passwords as users sign on. The hazards from a penetration of this sort are obvious. Security requires some method whereby the host processor can determine that all attached intelligent

277

terminals perform those functions which are authorized and intended and that they do nothing else.

The design of a data security system must include appropriate preventive measures to protect against this threat. To avoid the surreptitious introduction of monitoring type programs into an intelligent terminal, the host system must be able to check the program status of the terminal. Random interrupts of the processing at the terminal must be permitted to allow its contents to be examined without warning. This, again can be accomplished with an embedded module.

The primary objective of embedded modules is to detect exception or unusual conditions. Frequently the underlying probability distribution of unusual occurrences, such as an unauthorized attempt to access, is not known. We address this issue as follows. For the constant loss case, E, is given by (15). Maximizing this with respect to F results in the Euler equation

$$d[(F')^{-1/2}(1-F)^{1/2}]/dt + (F')^{1/2}(1-F)^{-1/2} = 0 \qquad (17)$$

which produces

$$(1-F)F'' = (F')^2 \qquad (18)$$

Since t does not appear in (17), it has the solution

$$F' = c/2(1-F) \qquad (19)$$

where c is an integration constant. This leads to

$$F^2 - 2F = -ct + c_0 \qquad (20)$$

Since $F(0) = 0$, $c_0 = 0$ and (19) becomes

$$F(t) = 1 - (1-ct)^{1/2} \qquad (21)$$

Since $F(c^{-1}) = 1$ and F is nondecreasing

$$F(t) = 1 \qquad \text{for} \quad t > c^{-1}$$

From (16) and (21) we have

$$n(t) = 1/2 \left[\frac{k_1 c}{k_0} \right]^{1/2} (1-ct) - 1/2, \qquad 0 \leqslant t \leqslant c-1 \qquad (22)$$

278

From (15) we derive

$$\max_{F} \min_{n} E(n, F) = (k_1 k_0/c)^{1/2} \qquad (23)$$

From (23) the expected loss is seen to be a decreasing function of c. Thus we impose the conditions $F(t) = 1$ for $t \geq t_0$ and the maximum of E is obtained when $c^{-1} = t_0$. We conclude that the optimum monitoring schedule is given by (22) with $c = t_0^{-1}$.

4. Software Monitors

A software monitor is a program inserted into the code of a system to collect performance measurement data. There are two types of software monitors: events-drive and sampling. The model we propose is not necessary for the former, since it executes a measurement when prompted by some type of internal event.

The second type is more appropriate to the model. It is exemplified by the auditor who wishes to evaluate the efficiency with which an interactive program executes various decision models that users call selectively to aid their decision making process. The auditor wants to focus on those that are used most frequently and consume the most time.

Sampling software monitors collect performance data when a signal is received from some timing device. The timing device may generate signals randomly or after constant intervals. When a signal occurs, the software monitor accesses system tables to obtain resource consumption data. Sampling software monitors cause less system interference than event-driven software monitors because they are invoked less often. The principal decision to be made when using a sampling software monitor is how frequently events should be inspected. In such instances, historical data or error types and rates may allow the development of a density for particular types of control failure. When such data are available, we should use it in our model for scheduling inspections.

We can apply results from the initial model development to illustrate this model. The exponential distribution is frequently the appropriate model where the outcome is the duration of time until some occurrence and where there is no aging effect. In particular,

$$F(t) = 1 - e^{-\lambda t} \tag{24}$$

and from (16) the density of monitoring activity is

$$n(t) = \left[\frac{k_1 F'(t)}{2k_0(1 - F(t))}\right]^{1/2} = \left[\frac{k_1 e^{-\lambda t}}{2k_0 e^{-\lambda t}}\right]^{1/2} = \left[\frac{\lambda k_1}{2k_0}\right]^{1/2} \tag{25}$$

Therefore, from (15), the expected cost is

$$E = (2k_0 k_1)^{1/2} \int_0^\infty (F')^{1/2}(1 - F)^{1/2}\, dt$$

$$= (2k_0 k_1) \int_0^\infty (\lambda e^{-\lambda t})^{1/2}(e^{-\lambda t})^{1/2}\, dt \tag{26}$$

$$= \left[\frac{2k_0 k_1}{\lambda}\right]^{1/2}$$

And, the desired number of inspections is

$$\frac{E}{2k_0} = \left[\frac{2k_0 k_1}{\lambda 4k_0 2}\right]^{1/2} + \left[\frac{k_1}{2\lambda k_0}\right]^{1/2} \tag{27}$$

5. Conclusion

Effective monitoring of controls is necessary to insure the protection of data against unauthorized disclosure, modification, restriction, or destruction. Increased recognition that accounting data in a computer system must be protected was a development brought on by the three factors which caused a significant increase in the vulnerability of computer systems.

First, many more individuals now have access to many more computer systems. The increased application of the computer to daily business practice makes the computer installation an integral part of many organizations. Shared resources and jointly used data have become the normal mode of computer operation. Also, direct interaction with the computer, once the prerogative of the programmer or operator, has become a commonplace activity for the most casual of computer users.

Second, many more individuals are being trained in computer science. Thus the detailed knowledge of how to manipulate computer systems is more pervasive instead of being confined to small isolated groups.

Third, because the amount of data which may be stored in a

computer system is very large, the value of this stored information can be sufficiently large in many instances to make its theft worthwhile.

Confronted with the growing complexity of computer technology and a complex array of economic and regulatory constraints, the EDP auditor will be forced to utilize more sophisticated and comprehensive methods of control. An important issue is the schedule for monitoring controls in online systems. Reliability theory has formed the traditional framework for scheduling control monitoring. Its methods become very complicated, however, when a large number of tests are involved.[4] This situation, which is characteristic of the EDP audit environment, is better handled by the methods outlined in this paper.

Appendix

Suppose only the initial value is given with all other values to be chosen optimally, i.e.,

$$\text{Maximize} \int_{t_0}^{t_1} (F(t), x(t), x'(t))\, dt \qquad \text{(A1)}$$

subject to

$$x(t_0) = x_0 \qquad x_0, t_0, t, \text{ given} \qquad x(t_1)\, \text{free}$$

Let $x(t)$ be optimal and $x(t) + g(t)$ be continuous on $[t_0, t_1]$ satisfying the initial conditions. That is $g(t_0) = g(t_1)$ is free.

For the family of admissable functions $x(t) + ag(t)$, with $x(t)$ and $g(t)$ fixed, the value of (A1) depends on a, that is

$$g(a) = \int_{t_0}^{t_1} F(t, x(t) + ag(t), x'(t) + ag'(t))\, dt \qquad \text{(A2)}$$

which achieves its maximum at $a = 0$ since x is optimal. Then we have

$$g'(0) = \int_{t_0}^{t_1} |F_x(t, x, x')\, g + F_{x'}(t, x, x')\, g'|\, dt = 0 \qquad \text{(A3)}$$

Integrating the second term by parts, with $F'_x = u$ and $g'\, dt = dv$, yields

$$(F_{x'}, g)_{t=t_1}| - \int_{t_0}^{t_1} (g\, dF'_x/dt)\, dt \qquad \text{(A4)}$$

since $g(t_0) = 0$. Now substituting into (A3) produces

$$\int_{t_0}^{t_1} g(F_x - dF'_x/dt)\, dt + (F_x, g)_{t=t_1}| = 0 \qquad (A5)$$

Now (A4) must be zero for all differentiable functions satisfying $g(t_1) = 0$. Thus, the optimal function x must satisfy the Euler equation

$$F_x(t, x, x') = dF'_x(t, x, x')/dt \qquad (A6)$$

Since x satisfies (A4), condition (A5) infers the requirement

$$F'_x(t_1, x(t_1), x'(t_1))\, g(t_1) = 0$$

for any candidate $g(t_1)$. Recalling that $g(t_1)$ is unrestricted, the implication is that $F'_x = 0$ at t_1 if x_1 is free. This is termed the transversality condition.

Footnotes

1. We use EDP auditor here to include both internal auditors or external auditors (CPAs).
2. See Hansen and Messier[3] for a discussion of the difficulties currently facing EDP auditors.
3. See, for example, Cushing,[3] Hamlen,[4] Stratton,[8] and Yu and Neter.[9]
4. Dysfunction is used to represent control failure or the occurrence of un-desired processing.
5. An integrated test facility is the establishment of a "dummy" entity through which data can be processed; for example, a fictitious store, dealer, department, customer, employee, subsidiary, account, or any other basis of accumulating accounting information. After the entity is established, the author can process transactions using the client's actual application systems. See AICPA.[1]

References

American Institute of Certified Public Accountants, *Computer-Assisted Audit Techniques,* AICPA, New York, 1979.

American Institute of Certified Public Accountants, *Report of the Special Advisory Committee on Internal Accounting Control,* AICPA, New York, 1979.

Cushing, B. "A Mathematical Approach to the Analysis and Design of Internal Control Systems," *The Accounting Review,* Vol. 4, No. 1, 1974, pp. 24–41.

Hamlen, S. S. "A Chance-Constrained Mixed Integer Programming

Model for Internal Control Design," *The Accounting Review,* Vol. 55, No. 4, 1980, pp. 578–593.

Hansen, J. V. and W. F Messier, Jr., "Expert Systems for Decision Support in EDP Auditing," *Int. J, Comp. Inform. Sci.,* Vol. 11, No. 5, 1982, pp. 357–379.

Keller, J. B., "Optimum Checking Schedules for Systems Subject to Random Failure," *Management Science,* Vol. 4, No. 3, 1974, pp. 256–260.

Mautz, R., W. Kell, M. Maher, A. Merton, R. E. Reilly, D. E. Severance, and B. White, *Internal Control in U.S. Corporations: The State of the Art,* Financial Executives Research Foundation, New York, 1980.

Stratton, W. O., "Accounting Systems: The Reliability Approach to Internal Control Evaluation," *Decision Sciences,* Vol. 12, No. 1, 1981, pp. 51–67.

Yu S. and J. Neter, "A Stochastic Model of the Internal Control System," *J. Accounting Research,* Vol. 11, No. 2, 1973, pp. 273–295.

Part IV

APPLICATIONS IN ACCOUNTING

O'Leary and Munakata present an accounting-based prototype expert system to design aggregated financial statements for accounting information systems for use by decision makers. The authors set the background for AI and ES in accounting by discussing aggregation functions in accounting information systems (AIS). A series of conceptual implementation issues are also discussed, including accounting language processing, vocabulary representation, and accounting tuples.

O'Leary and Lin describe the conceptual foundations for the development of an expert system for cash flow analysis. The proposed system, denominated CFA, uses two accounting-based models: ratio analysis and the statement of changes in cash flow. It takes financial information as input and as output to provide diagnostics and rationale.

Steinbart and Gal examine the role of expert systems in accounting research. Their conceptual examination posits a theoretical background that examines issues such as the nature of problem-solving behavior, symbolic information processing, and to the building of prototypes. The paper concludes with the use of expert systems as research tools.

An Accounting Prototype Expert System

DANIEL E. O'LEARY, and TOSHINORI MUNAKATA

Introduction

For the past decade or so, extensive work has occurred in knowledge-based expert systems. More recently, accounting researchers have focused on developing knowledge-based expert systems for accounting problems. This paper discusses a system for use in developing aggregated financial statements in the design of an accounting information system. AGGREGATE develops *aggregated* financial statements to be used in accounting information systems (AISs). For example, AGGREGATE would use as input Table I and produce Table II as output. AGGREGATE is designed to simulate the approach of a human accountant designing financial statements for an AIS by using heuristics and other rules of thumb in the computer program in order to accomplish that task.

AGGREGATE was developed using the computer language PROLOG. AGGREGATE uses a frame-based knowledge representation with an inference engine that is a combination of forward chaining and backward chaining designed to solve the specific problem.

Artificial Intelligence and Expert Systems

Artificial Intelligence (AI) is that part of computer science aimed at developing computer programs that perform tasks

287

TABLE I
An Input Example—Financial Statement Before Aggregation
BOSTON EDISON COMPANY—DECEMBER 1963

	Dollars	Transactions
Cash	$ 4,048,773	167,354
Special-Deposits	1,166	87
Working-Funds	242,495	608,959
Notes Receivable	53,004	911
Customers' Accounts Receivable	17,448,883	17,392,927
Other Accounts Receivable	479,353	74,945
Fuel Stock	1,218,478	75
Plant Materials, Supplies, and Merchandise	7,176,643	8,056
Prepaid Insurance	369,210	894
Other Prepaid Items	10,028	742
Rents Receivable	40,607	962
Miscellaneous Current and Accrued Assets	61,032	1,480
Net Electric Plant In-Service	327,802,559	109
Electric Plant Construction-In-Progress	21,609,430	723
Net Steam Plant In-Service	10,520,537	15
Steam Plant Construction-In-Progress	179,584	76
Net Nonutility Property	2,167,063	201
Other Investments	1,758,042	1,358
Unamortized-Discount Series-D Bonds	41,501	80
Refunding-Costs Series-G Bonds	341,875	120
Temporary-Facilities	18,249	1,040
Deferred-Debits Federal-Income Tax	990,800	89
Deferred-Debits Miscellaneous	321,644	1,655
Nonutility Property Additions	82,193	842
Deferred-Debits Sewer-Use Tax	12,037	895

This example is constructed by the authors for illustration purposes from information given in Lev (11). For example, the order of the items is rearranged and the number of transactions is added.

requiring intelligence and which, for the moment, humans are more capable of doing (Barr and Feigenbaum, 1982; Rich, 1983). Expert Systems (ESs) are a branch of AI. ESs are computer programs that can perform a task in a specific task domain as well as a human expert can perform the same task (Barr and Feigenbaum, 1982; Davis and Lenat, 1982; Hayes-Roth et al., 1983).

ACCOUNTING EXPERT SYSTEMS

There are a number of accounting expert systems (AESs) that have been developed for commercial use. Peat Marwick Main &

TABLE II
Final Output of the System—An Aggregated Internal Accounting Statement for Table 1 Input.

Category No.	Original No.	Title	Dollars	Transactions
1	1	Cash	$ 4,048,773	167,354
1	2,3	Special-Deposits and Working-Funds	243,661	609,046
1	4,5	Prepaid Insurance and Other Prepaid Items	379,238	1,636
1	6,7,8,9	Receivables	18,021,847	17,469,745
1	10,11	Fuel Stock and Plant Materials, Supplies, and Merchandise	8,395,121	8,131
1	12	Miscellaneous Current and Accrued Assets	61,032	1,480
2	13,14	Other Investments and Temporary-Facilities	1,776,291	2,398
2	15	Net Electric Plant In-Service	327,802,559	109
2	16	Electric Plant Construction-In-Progress	21,609,430	723
2	17,18	Net Steam Plant In-Service and Steam Plant Construction-In-Progress	10,700,121	91
2	19,20	Net Nonutility Property and Nonutility Property Additions	2,249,256	1,043
3	21,22	Unamortized Discount Series-D Bonds and Refunding-Cost Series-G Bonds	383,376	200
3	23,25	Deferred-Debits Federal Income Tax and Deferred-Debits Sewer-Use Tax	1,002,837	984
3	24	Deferred-Debits Miscellaneous	321,644	1,655

289

Co. is currently testing an AES to analyze bank loans (Willingham and Wright, 1984). Coopers & Lybrand has implemented a system for tax accrual planning (Shpilberg and Graham 1986a and 1986b). Other AESs include prototype systems, such as the AES developed in this paper, e.g., TAXADVISOR (Michaelsen, 1984), AUDITOR (Dungan and Chandler 1985), EDP AUDITOR (Hansen and Messier, 1982 and 1986), and ICES (Grudnitski, 1986).

TAXADVISOR, an AES designed for use in estate planning, was developed using EMYCIN. AUDITOR, designed for auditing the allowance for bad debts account, was developed using AL/X. EDP AUDITOR, an AES designed for use in auditing EDP systems, was developed using AL/X. ICES, designed to facilitate the elicitation of knowledge from an auditor about the internal control environment, was developed using EMYCIN.

AES prototypes provide a useful tool in accounting research and in accounting practice. Accounting research uses AES prototypes to determine the feasibility of developing an AES in a specific area, to understand the judgments and heuristics used in a specific decision and as an aid in understanding a specific judgmental area: if you can't program a decision-making process, it is likely that it is not understood. Accounting practice can use AES to supplement or replace decision makers.

Aggregation of Accounts in AIS

Aggregation of accounts in internal financial accounting reports is a practical problem faced by the accounting information systems designers, even though managers theoretically can use their firm's accounting database to ascertain the information required to meet their needs. However, for a variety of reasons financial reports are prepared for managers, thus eliminating the need for them to analyze the database directly. These reasons include the need to:

(1) develop accounting information systems that provide decision makers with the information necessary to make good decisions

(2) design information systems that are cost-beneficial

(3) develop responsibility-based accounting information systems and

(4) meet security requirements.

First, sometimes it is thought that the decision maker should be provided with all available information. However, in Ackoff's classic paper (1967), it was noted this can lead to an over-abundance of irrelevant information. The level of aggregation can affect the quality of the decisions made by a manager (White, 1983). This suggests that there is some "appropriate" level of aggregation that is somewhere between "all the available information" and "too much" aggregation.

Second, information systems should be cost-beneficial. The negative impact of information availability of aggregation should be offset by other factors. Although aggregation can decrease the quality of decisions, it is not necessarily cost-beneficial to present decision makers with a highly unaggregated set of accounts. This occurs for two primary reasons. First, the decision-making time increases as the amount of aggregation decreases (White, 1983). Too much time spent on one decision can lead to a sacrifice in the quality of another decision. The use of aggregation provides a trade-off between the amount of time spent on each of a portfolio of decisions. Second, the cost of maintaining an unaggregated system is larger than the cost of a more aggregated system. For example, a larger number of accounts means more coding errors on the entry of information into the system and larger resource requirements for maintenance of the system.

Accounting information systems usually are responsibility-accounting systems. Such an accounting system assigns responsibility to a manager for organizational performance and provides the manager with a series of accounting reports that summarizes the relevant information necessary to manage. For example, the president of a company is not responsible directly for the dollars spent on paper clips, so a financial statement for the president would not directly include that account. However, the president may be responsible for the total supplies expenditures for the firm via a profit figure. Consequently, all the individual accounts that go into supplies would be aggregated for the president's report.

An accounting system also has a number of accounts that have security and other considerations. These accounts must be aggregated to ensure that the contents are not discovered by the general population of the firm. For example, accounts that relate

291

to firm strategies or executive salaries are not of concern to all firm members. These accounts must be aggregated to camouflage underlying critical information.

THEORETIC CONSTRUCTS AND EMPIRICAL FINDINGS

There has been limited theoretical and empirical work in the aggregation problem in AIS. Lev (1969) used entropy or "information theory" to analyze the aggregation problem in AIS. He maximized the information content in the reports provided to management. Information theory was used to measure the information content. However, that approach has been criticized for a number of reasons (e.g., Feltham, 1972 and Ronen and Falk, 1973).

ACTUAL APPROACHES TO AGGREGATION IN AIS

Since there is no generally accepted framework for the aggregation of financial statement information, designers of AIS generally use multiple sources of knowledge to develop aggregated financial statements:

1. Theoretical/Empirical Findings

2. Design Heuristics

3. User Requirements

4. Materiality Requirements

The limited theoretical and empirical work on aggregation in internal financial statements has suggested some judgmental heuristics. For example, Lev's (1969) entropy-based analysis suggested aggregating accounts whose dollar balances are a small percentage of the total dollar balance of the set of accounts.

Design heuristics derive from the apprenticeship nature of the development of AIS that occurs in accounting firms and from the subsequent design of AIS. One of the authors has previously worked in developing AISs and some of his experience has been built into AGGREGATE.

User requirements help define the level of aggregation of accounts on financial statements. For example, as noted above, the president does not need to know supply expenditures, yet he or she may find that executive salaries is a critical account.

Materiality requirements suggest that the dollar balance in the accounts affects the aggregation of accounts. For example, a materiality level typically of 5% of a given standard quantity is used by accountants.

IMPLEMENTATION OF THE AGGREGATION OF FINANCIAL STATEMENTS

AGGREGATE uses three basic steps to develop aggregated financial statements:

1. Determining the accounts that should be aggregated

2. Identifying the sets of accounts that can be aggregated with each other and

3. Choosing between alternative sets of potential account aggregations.

Determining the accounts that should be aggregated involves identifying those accounts that for some reason (e.g., lack of importance or for security reasons) should be aggregated with other accounts. Identifying the accounts that can be aggregated is the process of determining which accounts are somewhat similar so that it makes "sense" to aggregate those sets of accounts. Choosing between alternative sets of potential aggregations is the process of meeting the constraints that have been identified while providing decision makers with the necessary decision-making information.

Determining The Accounts That Should Be Aggregated

To provide management with a financial statement that allows it to focus on important decision-making variables, the financial reports they receive should reflect the "important" accounts. Those unimportant accounts can be aggregated with other accounts to develop an aggregated financial statement. The development of AGGREGATE lead to the recognition of three sources of information on which to base the decision to aggregate or not aggregate an account:

1. Activity Level

2. User Requirements

3. Security Requirements

ACTIVITY LEVEL

Activity levels of an account provides a measure of the importance of the account to a decision maker. Human accountants routinely use two measures to determine the activity level of an account: the dollar amount of the account and the number of transactions of the account.

AGGREGATE also uses these same measures of activity levels. If both of these measures are below a certain level, then AGGREGATE indicates that those accounts should be aggregated. AGGREGATE uses heuristic-based percentages of the total dollar volume and the total number of transactions. In addition, the totals are based on the category totals of the type of assets—for example, current assets. AGGREGATE uses materiality percentages of the category totals.

USER REQUIREMENTS

Human accountants also determine unique user requirements. This is particularly important in cases where accounts are determined to be insignificant (as above), but the user regards them as important. Typically, each firm has a set of expenses that it may consider important but other firms may not. Alternatively, an account may show as important in the above analysis but it may not be important to the particular manager. AGGREGATE can be extended to accommodate these requirements.

SECURITY REQUIREMENTS

A third approach used by accountants is to determine if there are any potential security leaks in the disclosure of particular accounts. For example, executive salary expenditures may be an appropriate account for just a select set of personnel—possibly only the president. Since AGGREGATE is only a prototype, this is not yet a major concern.

294

Identifying Sets Of Accounts That Can Be Aggregated

Next, the human accountant must determine which accounts make "sense" to aggregate with the accounts that have been determined to require aggregation. For example, in Table I, the human accountant would likely decide that it makes "sense" to aggregate the first three items, "Cash," "Special-Deposits," and "Working-Funds," while the accountant would decide that it may not make "sense" to aggregate "Cash" and "Net Electric Plant In-Service." What knowledge does the accountant use to make such a decision?

ACCOUNTING LANGUAGE PROCESSING

The accountant has a vocabulary of accounting words that describe the accounts. These accounting words have implicit characteristics associated with them. Two primary characteristics are time frame and liquidity. For example, "Cash" is a short-term and highly liquid asset, whereas, "Net Electric Plant In-Service," is a long-term asset with very little liquidity. Because those characteristics are different it may not make "sense" to aggregate those particular assets.

Concepts of a "vocabulary of accounting words" and "characteristics" suggest *natural language processing* used in AI (e.g., Reitman, 1984). We could employ some of the techniques developed for natural language processing. An alternative, however, is to develop an approach that meets the specific needs of our problem domain.

ACCOUNTING VOCABULARY REPRESENTATION IN AGGREGATE

Accounting vocabulary representation in AGGREGATE is implemented as follows. First, given an account title, the "importance level" (called the *hierarchical level*) of each word is determined. Level 1 is treated as the most important and Level 8, the least important—for example, "Net (Level 6), Electric (Level 4), Plant (Level 1), and In-Service (Level 2)." Such hierarchical levels are assigned to the words so the significance of the words in determining the characteristics of the account title are not equal. That is, in each title there is a "key word" and less important words. To determine the characteristics of an account title, the key word must be found.

AGGREGATE uses the hierarchical levels found in a table referred to as "Hierarchical Levels of Accounting Words" (see Table III). This table, in the form of a list, is given to AGGRE-GATE as a priori knowledge.

Not every word in the table has a unique level. For example, the word "Plant" in "Net Electric Plant In-Service" is a key word, i.e., Level 1. However, the "Plant" in "Plant Materials, Supplies, and Merchandise" is not a key word, but instead is a Level 5 word. The latter is identified by the fact that there is another Level 1 word in the title.

This table is not the only table that could be constructed to represent accounting language. Because this table was designed to meet the needs of this application, it reflects the asset side of the balance sheet, general accounting knowledge, and selected industry knowledge required for this application.

Levels were designed to group conceptually similar account-ing words that the system would encounter. Level 1 includes the set of key words that AGGREGATE recognizes. Level 2 sum-marizes the state of plant assets. Level 3 defines the descriptors associated with receivables. Level 4 reflects the industry-specific descriptors. Level 5 includes the set of descriptors that are not key words, but are the same as key words (e.g., Plant Asset as opposed to Plant Supplies). Level 6 summarizes the descriptors deriving from the depreciation or amortization of assets. Level 7 includes the miscellaneous asset descriptors. Levels 5, 6, and 7 words generally are not required to derive the "meaning" of the particular accounting descriptor.

Given that AGGREGATE has found the Level 1 word in a given title, it uses that Level 1 word to determine the charac-teristics associated with the title. The characteristics provide the "meaning." The characteristics are based on the two dimensions of time frame and liquidity. These dimensions are typically used by accountants to develop financial statements. Generally, the time frame determines the category in which the asset is in-cluded (e.g., current or long-term). In addition, the liquidity determines the order of appearance within a category. Table IV shows the set of characteristics for time frame and Table V shows the characteristics for liquidity. Table VI shows the assets in Table I sorted according to those categories.

296

Table III. Hierarchy Levels of Accounting (Level 1 is the highest)

Level 1

plant,* property, investments, equipment, cash, special-deposits, working-funds, receivables, stock, supplies, merchandise, materials, prepaid, current, accrued, unamortized discount refunding-cost, temporary-facilities, deferred-debits, inventory

Level 2

In-service, in-progress

Level 3

notes, accounts, rent, bonds

Level 4

Electric, steam, fuel, nonutility, construction customers, insurance, series-D, series-G, tax

Level 5

plant* (if there are no other components that are Level 1)

Level 6

net

Level 7

other, items, additions, miscellaneous, assets

Level 8

(all other words that do not appear in Levels 1 through 7)

*Note: "plant" is in Levels 1 and 5.

Table IV. Vocabulary set of accounting words for time frame

A1. Current (short term)
   cash, special-deposits, working-funds, receivable, stock, supplies, merchandise, materials, prepaid, current, accrued, inventory

A2. Long term
   investments, plant, property, equipment, temporary-facilities

A3. Deferrals
   unamortized-discount, deferred-debits, refunding costs

Table V. Vocabulary set of accounting words for liquidity

B1. cash, special-deposits, working funds
B2. investments
B3. prepaid
B4. receivable
B5. merchandise, inventory
B6. supplies, stock, materials
B7. current, accrued
B8. temporary-facilities
B9. equipment
B10. plant
B11. property
B12. deferred-debits, refunding-costs, unamortized discount

TABLE VI

The input items are classified into three categories and rearranged based on their characteristics; their category and serial numbers are also assigned.

Category (A No.)	B No.	Serial No.	Title	Dollars	Transaction
1	1	1	Cash	$ 4,048,773	167,354
1	1	2	Special-Deposits	1,166	87
1	1	3	Working-Funds	242,495	608,959
1	3	4	Prepaid Insurance	369,210	894
1	3	5	Other Prepaid Items	10,028	742
1	4	6	Notes Receivable	53,004	911
1	4	7	Customers' Accounts Receivable	17,448,883	17,392,927
1	4	8	Other Accounts Receivable	479,353	74,945
1	4	9	Rents Receivable	40,607	962
1	6	10	Fuel Stock	1,218,478	75
1	6	11	Plant Materials, Supplies, and Merchandise	7,176,643	8,056
1	7	12	Miscellaneous Current and Accrued Assets	61,032	1,480
2	2	13	Other Investments	1,758,042	1,358
2	8	14	Temporary-Facilities	18,249	1,040
2	10	15	Net Electrical Plant In-Service	327,802,559	109
2	10	16	Electric Plant Construction-In-Progress	21,609,430	723
2	10	17	Net Steam Plant In-Service	10,520,537	15
2	10	18	Steam Plant Construction-In-Progress	179,584	76
2	11	19	Net Nonutility Property	2,167,063	201
2	11	20	Nonutility Property Additions	82,193	842
3	12	21	Unamortized Discount Series-D Bonds	41,501	80
3	12	22	Refunding-Cost Series-G Bonds	341,875	120
3	12	23	Deferred-Debits Federal Income Tax	990,800	89
3	12	24	Deferred-Debits Miscellaneous	321,644	1,655
3	12	25	Deferred-Debits Sewer-Use Tax	12,037	895

TABLE VII
Selected Asset Characteristics

A) Time Frame:

1. Current assets (short)
2. long-term investments
3. deferrals

B) Liquidity: (see Table V)

C) Depreciation:

1. nondepreciated (land, cash)
2. amortize (patent royalties)
3. depreciated (buildings, machines)

D) Use:

1. in operations
2. not used in operations
3. in progress (being built)

E) Cost:

1. historical
2. tied to market value
3. valuation method

F) Commodity:

1. yes (gold)
2. no

(cash)

G) Physical Existence:

1. yes (land, building, cash)
2. no (deferral)

H) Source:
(n/r / a/r)
(not receivable,
acct. receivable)

1. customers
2. affiliated companies
3. other

I) Asset Type:

1. ordinary asset
2. contra asset
3. deferral
4. claims

TABLE VIII
The Accounts to Be Aggregated

Category No.	Serial No.	Title	Dollars	Transactions
1	2	Special-Deposits	$ 1,166	87
1	4	Prepaid Insurance	369,210	894
1	5	Other Prepaid Assets	10,028	742
1	6	Notes Receivable	53,004	911
1	8	Other Accounts Receivable	479,353	74,945
1	9	Rents Receivable	40,607	962
1	10	Fuel Stock	1,218,478	75
1	12	Miscellaneous Current and Accrued Assets	61,032	1,480
2	13	Other Investments	1,758,042	1,358
2	14	Temporary-Facilities	18,249	1,040
2	18	Steam Plant Construction-In-Progress	179,584	76
2	19	Net Nonutility Property	2,167,063	201
2	20	Nonutility Property Additions	82,193	842
3	21	Unamortized Discount Series-D Bonds	41,501	80
3	25	Deferred-Debits Sewer-Use Tax	12,037	895

TABLE IX
The Set of Potential Tuples for Aggregation

The elements in the tuples are Serial Numbers in Table VII.

(1, 2, 3)	(1, 2)	(1, 3)	(2, 3)
(4, 5)	(6, 7, 8, 9)	(7, 8)	(10, 11)
(15, 16, 17, 18)	(15, 16) (15, 17)	(16, 18)	(17, 18)
(19, 20)	(21, 22, 23, 24, 25)	(21, 22)	(23, 25)

TABLE X
A Priority Queue Showing the Order of Procedures for the Tuples

* indicates an item to be aggregated.

Tuple	Aggregation Density	Cardinality	Distance
(12*)	1.00	1	0
(4*, 5*)	1.00	2	359,182
(13*, 14*)	1.00	2	1,739,793
19*, 20*)	1.00	2	2,084,870
(6*, 7, 8*, 9*)	0.75	4	17,408,276
(2*, 3)	0.50	2	241,329
(21*, 22)	0.50	2	300,374
(23, 25*)	0.50	2	978,763
(1, 2*)	0.50	2	4,047,607
(10*, 11)	0.50	2	5,958,165
(17, 18*)	0.50	2	10,340,953
(7, 8*)	0.50	2	16,969,530
(16, 18*)	0.50	2	21,429,846
(21*, 22, 23, 24, 25*)	0.40	5	978,763
(1, 2*, 3)	0.33	3	4,047,607
(15, 16, 17, 18*)	0.25	4	327,622,975

DEVELOPMENT OF POTENTIAL AGGREGATION TUPLES

To develop the potential aggregation sets (tuples), the human accountant would use the accounts that require aggregation and look for other accounts that makes sense to aggregate with them. First, accounts with the same A (Table IV) and B (Table V) numbers are grouped together as "original tuples." For example, in Table VIII, assets 15, 16, 17, and 18 constitute an original tuple since they have the same A number 2 and B number 10. These tuples represent one type of potential aggregation of accounts: the set of accounts that have the same time frame and liquidity.

Second, another type of potential aggregation is derived from the original tuples by considering their subsets. If a subset contains at least one Level 2, 3, or 4 word in common, then the subset is a potential aggregate; otherwise, it is not considered for aggregation. For example, the subset (15, 16) is a potential aggregation tuple since both accounts 15 and 16 contain a com-

302

mon Level 4 word "Electric." Subset (15, 16, 17) is not a potential aggregate since there is no common Level 2, 3, or 4 word for all the accounts. Table IX shows the set of potential aggregation tuples for the example.

This second process derives its rationale from using additional information in the development of a potential aggregation tuples—it allows the grouping of more closely related sets of assets. In addition, this process is frequently used in the development of aggregated financial statements.

Choosing Between Alternative Aggregations

Given the set of potential aggregation tuples, the AIS system designer must choose between the available alternative aggregations. AGGREGATE uses two heuristic rules to guide the search: (1) minimize the number of accounts that are aggregated, subject to the constraint of aggregating the appropriate accounts (based on the entropy approach of Lev (1969)), that is, choose those sets for aggregation that include more rather than fewer accounts that require aggregation as measured by the aggregation density; and (2) group together similar sized accounts, that is, those with a similar cardinality. This rule is based on practical experience and an analysis of the entropy approach. AGGREGATE uses a heuristic based on these two rules. The results of this approach on the example are summarized in Table X.

Summary

This paper describes an accounting-based prototype expert system that is designed to take as input a set of accounts and characteristics of those accounts (e.g., dollar balances) and develop aggregated financial statements that meet the needs of decision makers. Such statements are provided to decision makers because it is not necessarily cost-beneficial to provide the decision maker with all the information in planning and control systems that make use of responsibility-accounting systems. It is also necessary to meet certain security requirements.

The system first identifies those accounts that need aggregation. Then the system determines which accounts it makes "sense" to aggregate. Finally, the system chooses which aggregations meet certain criteria.

References

Ackoff, R. L., "Management Misinformation Systems," *Management Science,* Vol. 14, No. 4, 1967, pp. 147–156.

Barr, A. and E. A. Feigenbaum, *The Handbook of Artificial Intelligence,* Vol. 2, W. Kaufman, 1982.

Davis, R. and D. B. Lenat, *Knowledge-Based Systems in Artificial Intelligence,* McGraw-Hill, 1982.

Dillard, J. and J. Mutchler, "Knowledge-Based Expert Computer Systems for Audit Opinion Decisions," unpublished paper presented at the University of Southern California, Symposium on Expert Systems, February, 1986.

Duda, R. O., J. Gaschnig, and H. Peter, "Model Design in the PROSPECTOR Consultant System for Mineral Exploration," in D. Michie (ed.) *Expert Systems in the Microelectronic Age,* Edinburgh University Press, 1979.

Dungan, C. W. and J. Chandler, "Auditor: A Micro-computer-based Expert System to Support Auditors in the Field," *Expert Systems,* October 1985.

Feigenbaum, E. A. and J. Feldman, *Computers and Thought,* McGraw-Hill, 1963.

Feltham, G. A., *Information Evaluation,* American Accounting Association, 1972.

Grudnitski, G., "A Prototype of an Internal Control Expert System for the Sales/Accounts Receivable Application," unpublished paper presented at the University of Southern California, Symposium on Expert Systems, February 1986.

Hansen, J. V. and W. F Messier, "Expert Systems for Decision Support in EDP Auditing," *International Journal of Computer and Information Sciences,* Vol. 11, No. 5, 1982, pp. 357–379.

———, and ———, "A Preliminary Investigation of EDP-XPERT," *Auditing: A Journal of Practice and Theory,* Vol. 6, No. 1, Fall 1986, pp. 109–123.

Hayes-Roth, F, D. A. Waterman, and D. B. Denat, (eds.), *Building Expert Systems,* Addison-Wesley, 1983.

Lev, B., *Accounting and Information Theory,* American Accounting Association, 1969.

Michaelson, R. H., "An Expert System for Federal Tax Planning," *Expert Systems,* Vol. 1, No. 2, 1984, pp. 149–167.

Reitman, W., (ed.), *Artificial Intelligence Applications for Business Proceedings of the NYU Symposium,* May 1983, Ablex, Norwood, N.J., 1984.

Rich, E., *Artificial Intelligence,* McGraw-Hill, 1983.

Ronen, J. and G. Falk, "Accounting Aggregation and the Entropy Measure: An Empirical Approach," *Journal of Accounting Research,* Vol. —, No. —, October 1973, pp. 696–717.

Shortliffe, E. H., *Computer-Based Medical Consultations: MYCIN,* American Elsevier Publishing Co. Inc., 1976.

Shpilberg, D. and L. E. Graham, "Developing ExperTAX: An Expert System for Corporate Tax Accrual and Planning," unpublished paper presented at the University of Southern California, Symposium on Expert Systems, February 1986.

Shpilberg, D., and L. Graham, "Developing ExperTAX: An Expert System for Corporate Tax Accrual and Planning," *Auditing: A Journal of Practice and Theory,* Vol. 6, No. 1, Fall 1986, pp. 75–94.

White, C. E., "Aggregation in Internal Accounting Reports and Decision Making: A Field Experiment Approach," presented at the American Association of Accountants' national meeting in New Orleans, 1983.

Willingham, J. and W. Wright, "Development of a Knowledge-based System for Auditing the Collectibility of a Commercial Loan," paper presented at the TIMS/ORSA meeting in Boston, April 1984.

An Expert System For Cash Flow Analysis

DANIEL E. O'LEARY, and
W. THOMAS LIN,

One of the most important problems facing management is the management of its cash. Cash flow analysis is a critical part of cash management, concerning itself with budgeting cash flows and diagnosing the causes of positive and negative changes in cash flows. Cash flow analysis is also used to diagnose potential problems and to plan solutions to managing the firm's cash flows.

The purpose of this paper is to discuss a prototype expert system for cash flow analysis. The system, CFA, (CASH FLOW ANALYZER), uses rules based on ratio analysis and a budgetary statement of changes in cash flow in order to budget cash flow, diagnose the source of cash flow problems and to make recommendations.

Recent Developments in Expert Systems

Artificial intelligence can be defined as the study of how to make computers exhibit the characteristics associated with intelligence in human behavior. It includes the simulation of human activities such as robotics, natural language, vision systems, and expert systems.

Expert systems perform tasks normally done by knowledgeable human experts. They are developed by programming the computer to make decisions using the processes and knowledge of the expert.

Expert systems usually have five major components: a knowledge acquisition subsystem, a knowledge base, an inference engine, an explanation module, and the language interface (Lin, 1986). The knowledge acquisition module requires the accumulation, transfer, and transformation of expertise from the expert to the system. Interactive computer systems use interviewing to obtain this knowledge.

The knowledge base provides the set of knowledge that the system uses to process the data. Typically, this is the domain specific knowledge that the expert would use to solve the problem. Knowledge can be represented a number of ways. One of the most frequently used methods is the rule-based approach. Rule-based knowledge representation generally takes the form of "if . . . (condition) then . . . (consequence/goal)." The rules may or may not include a numerical level of confidence or probability of occurrence.

The inference engine provides the basis for using the knowledge base to process the database. In a rule-based system, the inference engine normally uses either a forward or backward chaining approach. Forward chaining reasons toward a goal. Backward chaining reasons backward from the goal to determine if or how the goal can be accomplished.

The explanation module can explain why the system reached a particular decision or why the system is requesting a particular piece of information. The language interface provides English-like query language or graphics for the user to interact with the expert system.

Applications of Expert Systems in Management Accounting

There have been a number of different prototype expert systems built to solve accounting problems. Recent surveys are given by Akers et al. (1986), Lin (1986), and O'Leary (1986 and 1987).

Other than this paper, there has been at least one other application of expert systems to management accounting problems. Palladium has developed an expert system for use by corporate management in capital budgeting problems (Reitman, 1985). Other possible applications of expert systems in management accounting include transfer pricing, variance analysis, performance analysis, and corporate planning and budgeting.

In addition, the cash management problem is a fertile area for the application of expert systems technology to two other management accounting tools: linear programming and forecasting. O'Leary (1986) discussed using expert systems in linear programming to help formulate the program and analyze the output by taking advantage of the structure of the problem and the meaning in the variables. Such an approach could be used in cash management. Similarly, an expert system could be used to formulate and interpret the results of forecasts used in cash management. Such a system would take advantage of the domain of cash management to provide meaning to the variables.

Cash Management Models

There have been a number of analytic models developed for the cash management problem. One of the first models proposed for cash management was the EOQ inventory model (e.g., Beehler, 1983). This lead to the application of other inventory models for cash management problems (e.g., Neave, 1969).

Forecasting techniques of varying complexity have been used to estimate cash inflows and outflows. Some of the approaches used included regression analysis and time series.

Unconstrained decision rules based on probability theory also have been developed (e.g., Bierman and McAdams, 1962). Linear programming (Orgler, 1972) and goal programming (O'Leary and O'Leary, 1982) have also been proposed for the cash management problem in order to meet the constraints of cash flow problems.

Unfortunately, analytic models often are not used because users do not understand them or because the assumptions of the model do not fit the situation (Fabozzi, 1976). For these reasons, an expert system designed to interface with the user, using general models that the user understands, e.g., accounting models, may prove to be more useful than some of the analytic models.

An expert system for cash management can be useful to both large and small businesses. Large businesses that have experts specializing in cash management can benefit from an expert system for a number of reasons. First, an expert system would bring to bear a consistent set of knowledge in cash management problems. This could ensure that top management's goals and objectives are considered cash management problems. Second, the system could be used to make recommendations on the routine decisions, while the expert concentrates on the more unusual problems. Small businesses that may not have the expertise of larger businesses can use the expert system as a source of expertise.

CFA—Cash Flow Analyzer: An Expert System

CFA is a preliminary prototype expert system designed to aid the user in cash flow management. Such an exploratory prototype model is a first step in understanding the development of expert systems for the cash management problem. CFA is a system designed to help the user diagnose cash flow problems, budget cash flows, and plan solutions. The general structure of CFA is given in Exhibit 1.

CFA uses two accounting-based models: ratio analysis and the statement of changes in cash flow. Ratio analysis has been used in at least two previous expert systems. Bouwman (1983) used accounting ratio analysis as the basis of an expert system to diagnose difficulties of firms. Biggs and Selfridge (1986) used accounting ratio analysis as an aid in the development of the "Going Concern" judgment that faces the auditor.

Financial statement analysis provides a number of alternative ratios that can be used in the analysis (e.g., Bernstein, 1978). Ratios can be used to provide insight into the liquidity of the current asset group and the availability of cash. Ratios also can be used to access the cause of cash problems. These ratios can provide information on the source of cash problems and lead to prescriptive recommendations.

The ratios can be compared to benchmarks. If a ratio does not fall within a prespecified range of the benchmarks, then the system can prescribe actions to mitigate the situation. In addition, the trend of ratios can be analyzed to determine if the apparent state of the system is changing and if it is changing, then in what direction the change is occurring. Finally, the ratios can be compared to other ratios to determine the relative strength of the ratio. For example, in cash management, accounts payable turnover is likely to be related to accounts receivable turnover. Thus, relative changes in one ratio can suggest actions in the other.

Both the standards on which the benchmarks are based and the extent and direction of the movement of the ratios should be

310

GENERAL MODEL OVERVIEW

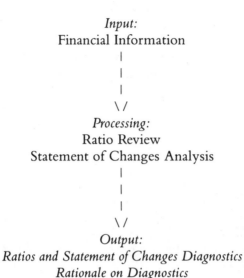

Input:
Financial Information

|
|
|
\ /

Processing:
Ratio Review
Statement of Changes Analysis

|
|
|
\ /

Output:
Ratios and Statement of Changes Diagnostics
Rationale on Diagnostics

EXHIBIT 1.

developed with the particular firm and industry in mind. In addition, the actions that the ratios suggest should also be developed in concert with the needs of the particular firm. The ratios used in CFA are summarized in Exhibit 2.

The statement of changes in cash flow provides another accounting model that has not been used in the development of previous expert systems, but has been used by accountants to analyze cash flow. The format of this statement can be modified for decision-making purposes. For example, the changes can be grouped by changes in assets, liabilities, stockholders' equity, cash inflows, and discretionary and nondiscretionary cash outflows. Placing the assets in these categories allows the system to make recommendations based on the information that describes that category of outflows. As with the ratios, the actions and the parameters on which the parameters are based are a function of the firm's policies and unique needs. Accordingly, CFA would have to be adapted to the unique situation.

CFA is a rule-based expert system developed using the expert system shell EXSYS. As noted above, there are three types of

LIQUIDITY-BASED RATIOS

Proportion of Cash in Current Assets
(Cash + Cash Equivalents)/Current Assets

Cash Available to Pay Current Obligations
(Cash + Cash Equivalents)/Current Liabilities

Current Ratio

Current Assets/Current Liabilities

Quick Ratio
(Current Assets-Inventory-Prepaid Expenses)/(Current Liabilities)

Accounts Receivable Turnover Ratio
Net Sales on Credit/Average Accounts Receivable

Inventory Turnover Ratio
Cost of Goods Sold/Average Inventory

Accounts Payable Turnover Ratio
Purchases/Accounts Payable

EXHIBIT 2.

rules that use ratio information: comparison of a ratio to a standard, comparison of a ratio to a previous value of the ratio, and comparison of ratios to each other.

A sample rule of the first type would be:

If ((Cash + Cash Equivalents)/Current Assets) is less than cash in current assets-standard, then examine the possibilities to increase cash.

A sample rule of the third type would be:

If accounts payable turnover is less than accounts receivable turnover

Then stretch accounts payables.

The rules that use the statement of changes in cash flow are of a similar nature. For example, the following is a sample rule that compares a quantity to a standard.

If net operating cash flows are less than the net operating cash flow standard

Then make arrangements to borrow.

Summary

This paper discussed an expert system for cash flow analysis based on traditional accounting models of cash flow. The scope of expert systems in cash management can range from the current system to systems that include and explain the output from analytic tools such as linear programming or forecasting tools.

This system and other such cash management systems can aid cash flow analysis in a number of ways. First, they can lead to a consistent analysis of the input data, minimizing the inconsistencies of human information processing. Second, they can analyze the information at the "initial screening level" and let the expert spend his or her time analyzing the more difficult aspects of the problem. Third, such systems allow the transfer of cash management expertise to those firms that do not have such expertise.

References

Akers, M. D., G. L. Porter, E. J. Blocher, and W. G. Mister, "Expert Systems for Management Accountants," *Management Accounting,* March 1986.

Beehler, P. J., *Contemporary Cash Management,* John Wiley & Sons, 1983.

Bernstein, *Financial Statement Analysis,* Irwin, 1978.

Bierman, H. and A. K. McAdams, *Management Decisions for Cash and Marketable Securities,* Graduate School of Business and Public Administration, Cornell University, 1962.

Biggs, S. and M. Selfridge, "GC-X: A Prototype Expert System for the Auditor's Going Concern Judgment," paper presented at the University of Southern California Symposium on Expert Systems, February 1986.

Bouwman, M., "Human Diagnostic Reasoning by Computer: An Illustration From Financial Analysis," *Management Science,* Vol. 29, No. 6, June 1983.

Fabozzi, F. F. and J. Valente, "Mathematical Programming in American Companies: A Sample Survey," *Interfaces,* Vol. 7, 1976, pp. 93–98.

Lin, W. T., "Expert Systems and Management Accounting Research,"

Management Accounting News and Views, Vol. 4, No. 1, Spring 1986, pp. 11–13.

Neave, E. H., "The Stochastic Cash Balance Problem with Fixed Costs for Increases and Decreases," *Management Science,* Vol. 16, 1969.

O'Leary, D., "Expert Systems in Mathematical Programming," in *Military Artificial Intelligence Applications,* Operations Research Society of America Monograph, forthcoming.

———, "The Use of Artificial Intelligence in Accounting," in *Expert Systems for Business,* B. G. Silverman, (ed.), Addison-Wesley, 1987.

——— and J. O'Leary, "A Goal Programming Approach to a Hospital Cash Management Problem," in Proceedings of the Fifteenth Annual Hawaii International Conference on System Sciences, 1982.

Orgler, Y. E., *Cash Management,* Wadsworth, 1972.

Reitman, W., "Application of Artificial Intelligence Technology to Management in the '80s," unpublished paper presented at the Forum on Artificial Intelligence in Management, Richmond, VA, May 1986.

The Role of Expert Systems in Accounting Research

PAUL J. STEINBART and
GRAHAM GAL

The nature of expert systems and their role in accounting research have recently become topics of discussion (Messier and Hansen, 1983; White, Luzi, and Craig, 1983; Luzi and White, 1984). Expert systems are computer programs which use knowledge about a task domain to solve complex problems, and reach answers that are similar to those of a human expert. Accounting researchers have built expert systems to perform such tasks as planning for individual estate taxes (Michaelsen, 1982), determining the collectibility of delinquent accounts receivable (Dungan, 1983; Dungan and Chandler, 1983), setting the preliminary materiality level to be used in planning an audit (Steinbart, 1984), and evaluating the quality of internal controls in the revenue cycle (Gal, 1985). Work is also currently underway to build expert systems for performing analytical reviews (Braun and Chandler, 1982), analyzing EDP controls in advanced computer systems (Hansen and Messier, 1983), and issuing a going concern opinion (Dillard, Mutchler, and Ramakrishna, 1983).

One way to view expert systems is as sophisticated decision aids. Indeed, this point of view is apparent in much of the actual accounting research on expert systems (Braun and Chandler, 1982; Dungan, 1983; Dungan and Chandler, 1983; Hansen and

Messier, 1983; Michaelsen, 1982) and also in several discussions of the role of expert systems in accounting research (Messier and Hansen, 1983; White, Luzi, and Craig, 1983). However, the construction of an expert system also involves detailed descriptive research of current decision-making behavior in order to uncover the knowledge to make accurate decisions. Consequently, the construction of an expert system can be seen as a method for structuring descriptive empirical research on decision making. Indeed, researchers in artificial intelligence cite this as one of the characteristics differentiating work on expert systems from traditional computer programming:

> The aim here [in building an expert system] is thus not simply to build a program that exhibits a certain specified behavior, but to use the program construction process itself as a way of explicating knowledge in the field, and to use the program text as a medium of expression of many forms of knowledge about the task and its solution (Davis and Lenat, 1982, p. 471).

Recent work in accounting on expert systems reflects this alternative view (Dillard, Mutchler, and Ramakrishna, 1983; Gal, 1985; Luzi and White, 1984; Steinbart, 1984).

We believe that this latter view better reflects the potential role of expert systems in accounting research on human decision making. The ultimate goal of that research is to find ways to improve the quality of the decisions that are made. This goal requires first an understanding of how decisions are currently being made (Ashton, 1982; Libby, 1981). Building and organizing the knowledge base of an expert system is one method for conducting the necessary descriptive research of current decision-making practices. Moreover, building an expert system is a better method for conducting descriptive research than the traditional research methods used in accounting research on decision making. Those traditional methods (e.g., the Lens model [Brunswik, 1955a, 1955b]) concentrate on measuring the magnitude of the relationships between various information inputs and the resulting decision. Although this methodology provides evidence about what information is important to a decision, it does not explain why that information is important or how it is used. In short, traditional methods ignore the judgment process, focusing instead on the decision outcome:

The decision analyst is misdirected by the importance of the moment when the decision maker identifies a selection. We are seduced by language and common sense into believing that the choice is the decision. Yet . . . the choice is the end product of the decision, the moment when we see the pigeon in the magician's hand. The decision is the process of arriving at a choice, the process by which the pigeon got into the magician's hand (Carroll, 1980, p. 69).

In contrast, building an expert system focuses attention on the judgment process. The expert system must be explicitly programmed concerning what information it should gather and how it should use that information to make a decision. The result is a better understanding of how that decision is made.

The remainder of this paper is organized as follows. We begin by discussing the theoretical background for building expert systems. Next we describe the research method. Then we review several accounting studies to illustrate the benefits of using this methodology. We conclude by evaluating the implications of building expert systems as a structured method for descriptive accounting research on decision making.

Theoretical Background

Research on expert systems is related to studies of problem-solving behavior in the fields of cognitive psychology and artificial intelligence. Research in cognitive psychology has developed a theory about the nature of problem solving. Work in artificial intelligence has extended that theory and has also proposed methods for implementing and testing that theory.

THE NATURE OF PROBLEM-SOLVING BEHAVIOR

Newell and Simon's (1972) research provided many of the essential elements of the currently accepted theory about the nature of problem-solving behavior. That theory is summarized as follows.

Decision makers are seen as being symbolic information processors. They possess a store of knowledge about various task domains and a store of solution methods applicable to different types of problems. Sophisticated cognitive activities (e.g., problem solving, decision making, etc.) can be described as a search through those memory stores for knowledge appropriate to the task at hand. That search is guided by informal rules of thumb (heuristics) which represent the effects of experience. Moreover, it is also influenced by the decision maker's subjective interpretation of the requirements of the task (not by the "objective" task description). Finally, decision making is a conditional process and is sequential in nature. The choice of what information to acquire next and the evaluation of that information is influenced both by the information previously acquired and its interpretation. We now discuss some of these ideas in more detail.

Symbolic information processing

Symbolic information processing consists of the manipulation of nonnumerical concepts to make inferences. Many researchers in cognitive psychology and artificial intelligence believe that the decision maker's knowledge is represented by symbols and that reasoning consists of manipulating those symbols. Some even argue that the ability to manipulate symbols is a prerequisite of intelligence (Newell, 1980). In their Turing Award lecture, Newell and Simon (1976) argue that the concept of a physical system that is able to use and manipulate symbols, and its accompanying hypothesis that humans and computers use similar symbols, is the most fundamental contribution to the joint work of artificial intelligence and cognitive psychology.

Symbols are more than mere abstract tokens that stand for some concept; they actually contain the semantic meaning of the concept and provide the means for accessing that meaning. For example, attached to the symbol "Cash" would be a property list of factual and experiential knowledge about cash (e.g., that it is a current asset, it is easy to misappropriate, etc.). All of these facts about cash are available to the decision maker whenever the symbol is processed; it is the task context that determines which properties are relevant in the given situation.

Symbols are important because they can be used to represent goals. Both Newell (1982) and Pylyshyn (1981) discuss the description of behavior in terms of goals, beliefs, and intentions. They point out that most behavior is purposive and goal-directed. Moreover, goals account for two fundamental characteristics of problem-solving behavior: (1) its interruptibility, and (2) its temporal correlations (Newell 1980). Problem-solving activity can be interrupted and later resumed without having to

318

start over from the beginning. In addition, the fact that problem solving often entails a series of decisions that relate to a common goal produces temporal correlations in cognitive behavior.

Heuristic Search

Heuristic search is believed to be the principal mechanism underlying intelligent problem-solving behavior in both humans and computers (Simon, 1980). To say that search is heuristic means that it is guided by knowledge about the particular task under consideration and that knowledge about the problem area is used to quickly focus on the crux of the problem. In contrast, blind search strategies exhaustively list and examine every possible action that can be taken until a goal or solution is found. Consider, for example, the task of solving cryptarithmetic problems. These problems are of the form BEST + MADE = MASER (from Raphael [1976]). The goal is to assign a unique digit to each letter so that the equation is arithmetically correct. A blind search would examine each potential combination of assignments of digits to letters. Although such a strategy is guaranteed to produce an answer, it could involve considering up to 1,814,000 possible assignments. In contrast, a heuristic search would utilize basic knowledge about arithmetic to reduce the size of the search space. For example, the letter M must equal 1 because that is the largest equation that can be generated by adding two single digit numbers together. Using this one item of domain-specific knowledge reduces the size of the search space by a factor of 10. (Incidentally, the answer to the problem is: $M = 1$, $A = 0$, $B = 9$, $D = 8$, $S = 6$, $T = 7$, $R = 2$, $E = 5$.)

There are two reasons why heuristic search is necessary for intelligent problem solving. The first relates to efficiency constraints (such as time or cognitive complexity) which may preclude its use as demonstrated by the above example. Therefore a human problem solver must select methods that overcome these limitations. If a problem solver has some knowledge about the way in which problems in the task area might be solved, then the selection of heuristics will produce efficient solutions. The problems faced by auditors in evaluating the information contained in the financial statements is an example of problem solving within a set of constraints. An auditor could decide to do a 100 percent audit. This would provide a very high level of assurance but it would be very costly. In reality an auditor (or team of auditors) use various heuristics to decide on the information that should be examined and the relation of this set of information to the items that were not examined.

The second reason, which is perhaps more important for accounting decisions, is that for many problems there isn't a well-defined algorithm that is guaranteed to produce a solution. Often there may not even be a clearly defined criterion to evaluate the final decision (consider, for example, making materiality judgments). Such problems are called ill-structured or ill-defined problems. In most of these cases the decision maker can break the problem down into important subproblems that need to be solved, but does not have any set method or order for solving those subproblems. Instead, the decision maker relies upon prior experience and the particular facts known about the current case to guide behavior.

Simon (1980) has argued that the principal mechanism of intelligence is the ability to deal with problem-solving environments through the use of heuristic search. Simon discusses learning and heuristics in terms of adaptation. Learning, he argues, is a semi-permanent adaptation to the environment in which certain types of knowledge about the environment were obtained. Heuristics then are the short-term adaptations to particular situations.

There have been a number of studies in accounting that examined auditors and their reliance on heuristics (Kinney and Ueckert, 1982; Joyce and Biddle, 1981a and 1981b). These studies have concluded that in certain situations auditors use heuristics (anchoring and adjustment in these studies) and therefore respond inappropriately to the experimental situations. Einhorn (1980) has suggested that the heuristic problem solving that is observed in a particular situation is the result of the application of meta-heuristics to generate rules to meet the observed structure of the problem. If the use of heuristics is a response to a particular situation, then it is important to investigate these heuristics in relation to the task content that is facing the decision maker.

Importance of task content

Task content plays an important role in decision making because it influences the decision maker's subjective interpretation of what is required. There are numerous examples of this in the pyschology literature. Einhorn and Hogarth (1982, 1984) found that changing the composition of the set of alternatives to a given hypothesis in a manner that did not alter the objective probability of that hypothesis nevertheless did change the subjective probability attached to that hypothesis. Adelman (1981) reported that realistic task content facilitated subjects' ability to learn from outcome feedback. Similarly, both Cox and Griggs (1982) and Hoch and Tschirgi (1983) found that subjects' ability to reason with syllogisms improved markedly when the syllogisms included realistic causal relationships with which subjects were familiar. Kahneman and Tversky (1979) and Tversky and Kahneman (1981) found that changing the wording of gambles changed the perceived content of a task and produced reversals in preference. Finally, Newell and Simon (1972) and Hayes and Simon (1977) both found that differences in content between problems with identical formal structural properties also affect performance quality.

In particular task situations in which a person does not have the necessary experience this research suggests that the problem solver will identify an inappropriate structure and the heuristics generated to solve the problem will either be inefficient or inappropriate. On the other hand there is evidence that a person with the necessary experience in a particular problem domain will generate heuristics that will be appropriate or efficient. Card, Moran, and Newell (1983) connected experience with control knowledge in their study. They noted that with low levels of experience a person performing the experimental task "wandered" in search of a particular goal. As experience increased, the person became more efficient at controlling the search for that goal. The ability of experience to make problem solving more efficient was also identified by Klix (1979) in a study that contrasted mathematically-gifted people with normal adults. When these individuals were presented with difficult math problems, the gifted group "revealed in the first trial a higher efficiency in their strategy (p. 3)." That is, they were able to gain information on the problem structure in a more intensive fashion than the control group. A similar observation was made by Chi, Feltovich, and Glaser (1981) in their study of the way in which experts and novices solved physics problems.

The resulting conditional nature of decision making means that traditional mathematical approaches to modeling decision behavior (e.g., regression) are inappropriate for a number of reasons. First, they assume that all information is evaluated simultaneously (Gibbons, 1982). Second, they do not take into

321

account the situations that cause certain heuristics to be generated. Finally, the traditional statistics-based analyses of decision making have been criticized on the grounds that they do not explain the decision process.

> The problem, of course, is that statistical methods are not good models of the actual reasoning process, nor were they designed to be. . . . (they are) for the most part, "shallow," one-step techniques which capture little of the ongoing process actually used by expert problem solvers in the domain (Davis, Buchanan, and Shortliffe, 1977, p. 39).

> . . . the output of a quantitative mechanism, be it numerical, statistical, analog, or physical (nonsymbolic), is too structureless and uninformative to permit further analysis. Number-like magnitudes can form the basis of decisions for immediate action . . . but each is a "dead end" so far as further understanding and planning is concerned, for each is an evaluation and not a summary. A number cannot reflect the considerations that formed it (Minsky 1975, p. 275).

In place of traditional mathematical and statistical models of decision making, the use of production systems has been proposed as a tool to model the decision maker's process. Production systems have been proposed because of the ability of these systems to model particular aspects of the problem-solving behavior. One of the more important features of these models is that they use and manipulate symbols in the process of making decisions. The symbols that are selected in the construction of a production system are similar to those used by a person that deals with similar problems. An additional feature of production systems concerns the way in which the rules that are used in problem solving are formulated. In production systems the rules that govern the action of the system are formulated so as to capture not only the particular actions that a person uses to solve a problem, but also the situations that resulted in the selected action. Thus the importance of content on the selection of heuristics becomes an explicit part of the model.

> A final advantage of PSs (production systems) is their *ability to represent the role of the environment in governing the (subject's) behavior* in a way that a more conventional process model cannot. *For a PS presents the set of possible actions that the subject can take together with*

the basis on which he decides between them, whereas a flow chart or algorithm states only the outcome of that decision (Young, 1978, p. 397, emphasis added.)

The production system architecture has formed the basis of many expert systems (particularly rule-based ones); we discuss the nature of that architecture next.

PRODUCTION SYSTEMS

A production system is a model of contingent behavior consisting of three parts: (1) a knowledge base, (2) an executive control or "inference engine," and (3) one or more working memories (Feigenbaum, 1979; Hayes-Roth, Waterman, and Lenat, 1978; Newell, 1973, 1980).

The knowledge base consists of two general types of knowledge: procedural and declarative. Declarative knowledge pertains to certain symbols which will be used by the procedural component of the knowledge base. The procedural knowledge represents the decision maker's knowledge of how problems in the domain might be solved. They are represented in the form of IF-THEN statements called production rules. The following is an example of such a rule found in the expert system AUDITPLANNER (Steinbart, 1984):

IF: 1) the client is a public entity, and
       2) there is no significant concern about the client's liquidity or solvency

THEN: assume that the principal external user's of the client's financial statements are primarily interested in the results of current operations.

In this example two symbols are being used to solve for a certain subgoal in the process of determining a preliminary value for materiality. The symbol "client" is being examined for two of its properties: its ownership structure (public entity) and its financial health (solvent). In the conclusion portion of this production the property "interested in" for the symbol "principal users" has been assigned the value "results of current operation." It should be evident that the symbols used are similar to those that might be used by a person that makes decisions in this domain. This production also represents a heuristic that a par-

323

ticular auditor may use to determine what users of the financial statements will be interested in.

If a rule is selected and the premise(s) of a rule are satisfied by the facts known about the case the rule is executed ("fired") and the conclusion is added to the current knowledge about the case. The order in which the rules are examined is governed by the control strategy used by the inference engine. The two most common control strategies are backward chaining (goal driven) and forward chaining (data driven).

In a backward chaining strategy the conclusions of the rules in the knowledge base are examined to determine which ones, if fired, would accomplish the goal under consideration. The premises to those rules are then examined to see whether they are satisfied by the facts already obtained for the current case. If they are, the rule is fired and the system solves the task. If the status of the premises can not be determined, then ascertaining the status of those premises becomes established as a new set of subgoals to pursue. The remaining rules in the knowledge base are then examined to find those whose firing would satisfy the new subgoal. The process continues either until a rule is found whose premises are known to be true or false or until the system cannot locate rules which pertain to the current subgoal. In the former case, firing that rule sets off a chain of reasoning that makes some conclusion about the current task (establish an appropriate materiality level), while the latter case requires the system to ask for additional information about the case.

A forward chaining strategy, in contrast, begins by examining the premises of all rules. Those rules whose premises are satisfied are fired, and the resulting inferences change the set of facts and inferences describing the situation. Consequently, the premises of other rules may now be satisfied and they too are fired. The process continues until a rule is fired which concludes about the goal.

Neither strategy is inherently superior to the other; indeed, both have been the basis of successful expert systems outside of accounting. The basis for choosing between them lies in the characteristics of the task. Nilsson (1979), in contrasting these two approaches, identifies backward reasoning (goal driven) as more appropriate in situations that have few goals and many pieces of data. Nilsson also calls the backward chaining approach a form of planning in that a chain of actions is constructed which will cause the pieces of data that are examined to affect the particular goal under consideration. The use, in contrast, of a forward chaining (data driven) strategy would be more appropriate to situations in which the data to be used are restricted as compared to the possible goals. In an auditing context it would appear that the goal-driven approach would be more appropriate as auditors gather and review data that pertain to the goal.

The working memories serve as scratch pads. The facts known about the task situation are stored here, as are any inferences that have been made. The preceding overview was necessarily brief; for more details on the production system architecture, the reader is referred to Steinbart (1984). We now turn to the psychological status of the production system architecture and also review alternative organizations that have been suggested.

THE PRODUCTION SYSTEM ARCHITECTURE AS A THEORY OF COGNITIVE BEHAVIOR

Newell and Simon (1972) have suggested that the human mind is organized along the lines of a production system:

> We confess to a strong premonition that the actual organization of human programs closely resembles the production system organization. . . . We cannot yet prove the correctness of this judgment, and we suspect that the ultimate verification may depend on this organization's proving relatively satisfactory in many different small ways, no one of them decisive (pp. 803–804).

The production system architecture has certainly proved to be relatively satisfactory in modeling a wide variety of cognitive behavior. Cognitive psychologists have used it to model learning (Anderson, 1982, 1983; Young, 1978; Young and O'Shea, 1981) and speech understanding (Newell, 1979). Researchers in artificial intelligence have used this architecture to build expert systems to perform such tasks as medical diagnosis (Shortliffe, 1976) and the molecular analysis of chemical compounds (Buchanan, Sutherland, and Feigenbaum, 1969, 1970).

The flexibility in the types of tasks that can be modeled using the production system architecture is one indication of the power and generality of the notion. Another is the fact that it can be used to model behavior at several levels of abstraction:

325

Firstly, with the least commitment in the architecture, is what one might call the *language level*. Here, PSs are used because of their suitability as a language for expressing certain kinds of computations. The *content* of the PS may express a psychological theory, but the notation is chosen on grounds of its computational convenience. . . . Secondly, one can find a number of studies which operate at what one might call the rule level. At this level there is a commitment to the psychological reality of rules, i.e., to the idea that the cognitive "program" is structured as a PS, and also perhaps to some aspects of the conflict resolution. But this commitment does not necessarily extend to the details of the architecture adopted. . . . Lastly, there is the *immediate processor level*, at which the PS architecture is itself intended as a theory of the structure of human cognitive processes. The allowable actions on the righthand side of the rules, for example, are taken to be the "elementary information processes" of the cognitive system (Young, 1979, p. 43).

Pylyshyn (1973) makes a distinction between competence and performance theories of cognitive behavior. Competence theories attempt to explain the underlying structures and processes which generate the cognitive behavior, while performance theories examine how this knowledge is used in problem solving. Cognitive psychologists have tended to work more at the immediate processor level as a tool in the development of competence theories of cognitive behavior; at that level, the role of the inference engine has been likened to that played by attention (Ueckert, 1980). The knowledge base and working memories have been compared to long-term and short-term memory, respectively (Newell, 1970, 1979). The work of Anderson (1983) is a good example of a production system which was developed as a theory at the immediate processor level. Researchers in artificial intelligence, on the other hand, have tended to operate at either the language or rule levels and are interested in generating theories of performance in a particular area.

There is no "correct" level of abstraction; it all depends upon the nature and purpose of the research using the production system architecture. We argue, however, that for studies of decision-making behavior in applied fields such as accounting, it is best to work at the language and rule levels. The focus is then on understanding the logic underlying task performance (e.g., how do auditors set the materiality level to use in planning an audit?, how do auditors evaluate internal control quality?), rather than on the mechanics by which knowledge is recalled and manipulated. Work at these levels involves using the production system architecture to build performance models of expert problem solvers which use knowledge gathered from these experts to generate the process.

ALTERNATIVES TO THE PRODUCTION SYSTEM ARCHITECTURE

There exists some controversy about whether the production system architecture is adequate for representing all the knowledge needed in expert systems. Aikins (1983), for example, argues that representations of prototypical situations are critical to performance and that such information can best be represented by means of knowledge structures called frames.

Minsky (1975) describes frames as data structures which organized several kinds of information about stereotypical situations. Some of the information pertains to the use of the frame, while some provide default values for important domain variables. This notion of frames was similar to the idea of schemas as the means for organizing topical knowledge (Bartlett, 1932; Schank and Abelson, 1977).

The status of schemas has itself been a topic of controversy. Abelson (1981) reviewed a number of studies which tended to support the existence of schemas as static knowledge structures. Anderson (1982, 1983), on the other hand, has developed a comprehensive theory of learning and skill acquisition based on the production system architecture. He also points out that a production system can simulate the operation of a schema system (1983, p. 38). Clancey (1983) similarly argues that frames can be implemented dynamically in expert systems by means of what he calls "meta-rules" whose premises describe general event scenarios. Moreover, Schank (1980) himself no longer sees complete schemas as static structures, but rather as a set of structures that reside at various levels with the script for a particular event being dynamically created in response to task demands.

SUMMARY

The production system architecture has successfully served as the basis for building expert systems in a variety of task domains. Although alternative architectures have been proposed (schemas), production systems can simulate them. The question about which architecture correctly reflects the human cognitive organization, although interesting, does not affect the use of rule-based expert systems for descriptive accounting research on decision-making behavior. The reason is that such research uses the production system architecture primarily as a means to express the contents of expertise underlying the performance aspects of professional judgment, and does not purport to be a model at the immediate processor level described earlier. The next section discusses the procedure for building an expert system.

Building an Expert System

The construction of an expert system is an iterative process. The researcher first builds a prototype version of the system, then lets the subject use the system to make judgments for actual cases, notes the changes suggested by the subject, modifies the knowledge base accordingly, and then lets the subject use the modified version. This cycle continues until the subject is satisfied that the system is performing correctly, at which time other subjects may be asked to use and evaluate the system. If the evaluation is favorable, the researcher can then analyze the contents of the knowledge base to learn more about how a particular judgment is made.

BUILDING THE PROTOTYPE

There are a number of software tools (e.g., EMYCIN, EX-PERT, AL/X, etc.) available to simplify the construction of an expert system. These tools provide a shell for the expert system, which contains the bookkeeping functions needed to organize and maintain the knowledge base and the inference engine that controls the way in which the knowledge base will be applied to the particular task. Consequently, the researcher is freed from having to program the system and can concentrate on acquiring, structuring, and analyzing the knowledge base used to make the decision.

Each software tool has features that are useful for different types of decision tasks; therefore, the choice of which tool to use should follow a formal analysis of the task to be studied. Stefik et al. (1983) discuss the different generic activities performed by decision makers and describe the features that are needed in expert systems designed to make those judgments. For example, EMYCIN (Van Melle et al., 1981) is the shell of an expert system called MYCIN (Shortliffe, 1976) which was designed to diagnose infectious blood diseases. EMYCIN is, therefore, an appropriate tool for diagnostic tasks. Stefik et al. point out that a major part of diagnosis involves interpreting data, much of which may be incomplete or erroneous. Thus, EMYCIN should also be useful for audit judgments relying upon interpretation.

Once a software tool has been selected, it is necessary to build the initial knowledge base. Several alternative methods exist for acquiring the requisite knowledge. One method is to encode textbook knowledge, such as a firm's written guidelines in their audit manuals. This approach has been used to build the initial prototypes of expert systems designed to make medical diagnoses (van Melle et al,. 1981) and has also been used in accounting by Michaelsen (1982). Textbook knowledge can also be supplemented by structured interviews; this was the approach used by Dungan (1983), Steinbart (1984), and Gal (1985). Another approach involves collecting verbal protocols of subjects making the decision of interest, the approach adopted by both Hansen and Messier (1983) and Dillard, Mutchler, and Ramakrishna (1983).

The approaches are all similar in that the person constructing the system uses the knowledge obtained from the experts or from the textbooks as a basis for formulating the rules that will be used by the system. An alternative approach uses an inductive approach to the formulation of the rules in the knowledge base. The inductive acquisition of the knowledge base requires the researcher to provide the system with a number of examples which consist of different parameter values and the conclusion that was reached for a particular goal. The system induces a rule based on the information in the examples when a sufficient number of examples have been provided. Michie (1982) has suggested that this method of developing a knowledge base is appropriate in cases in which the experts are better able to construct examples of their decision process.

The choice of which method to use should be dictated by the nature of the task being studied (for some decisions there may be no written guidance) and by the time constraints on the research (clearly, a protocol analysis will significantly increase the time involved in building the prototype system). No method is inherently superior because all are used only to build the initial knowledge base. Once the expert begins using the system to make real decisions any flaws or inconsistencies will become apparent and suggested revisions will be offered.

The final decision that needs to be made when building the prototype is the choice of subject(s) to provide the expertise. This is not an easy decision, for several reasons. First, there is a significant time commitment required of the subject. For example, the construction of AUDITPLANNER, an expert system designed to make planning stage materiality judgments, involved five half-day sessions with an audit partner. Second, there is the problem of determining expertise. The CPA examination serves to establish a minimum level of competency, but no tests exist to establish expertise. Because expertise is linked to experience, most studies have looked to audit managers or partners. However, empirical evidence of a lack of consensus among auditors in making many audit judgments raises the problem of which auditor is the "expert." This last point may not be quite as serious as it appears at first glance though, because there may be no unique answer to many judgments. For example, materiality judgments may reflect personal attitudes toward risk, for which no normative answer is appropriate. Consequently, it may be important to build many different expert systems to make the same judgement as a means of developing a taxonomy of judgment models. Simon (1980) notes that taxonomic research played an important role in advancing knowledge in the biological sciences, and argues that it will probably play a similar role in studies of judgment and should, therefore, be encouraged.

EVALUATING THE EXPERT SYSTEM

The majority of the time involved in building an expert system is spent in revising the system in response to the subject's recommendations. At some point, however, this iterative refinement process must stop so that the system can be analyzed. This raises the issue of how to evaluate an expert system.

Einhorn (1974) discusses some necessary conditions that might be applied to the evaluation of expertise in a particular area. He argues that in areas with a well established criterion it might be possible to evaluate global judgments based on this criterion, although he also raises some questions about problems with this approach. There is an additional problem in task domains that do not have a criterion to evaluate the final judgment. This would seem to include most judgments in accounting and auditing. In problem domains that do not have a criterion Einhorn suggests that the presence of convergent validity or agreement among experts might be appropriate. He points out, however, that this issue is also not so simple:

> The concept of agreement can itself be thought of in two ways: (a) agreement "in fact" and (b) agreement "in principle." The former refers to actual agreement of evaluation, whereas the latter refers to agreement with respect to weighting and combining policy, that is, how the global evaluation is to be formed once the inputs are specified. . . . Therefore, agreement in fact will be a function of weighting and combining similarity and similarity in coding cues. On the other hand, it should not be assumed that agreement in principle is easy to achieve. This is due to the fact that learning in a probabilistic environment may be quite difficult. This implies that there is great room for individual differences . . . (p. 563).

The lack of any clearcut measure of human expertise in many judgments makes the evaluation of an expert system problematic. If we cannot tell who is an expert, how can we determine whether an expert system is indeed "expert?" Nevertheless, an expert system must be evaluated, and Gaschnig et al. (1983) discuss appropriate means for doing so.

The first point that they make is that the method of evaluation necessarily must depend upon the purpose of the research. Expert systems developed as research tools for structuring descriptive research should be evaluated in terms of the correctness of their general line of reasoning; that is, do they approach the judgment in a proper way and take into account important nuances? The focus is on ascertaining whether the system is getting the right answers *for the right reasons.* In contrast, the evaluation of an expert system intended for use as a decision aid must additionally focus on the answers produced by the system.

These different motivations require different methods of testing. If the focus is solely on performance, blind evaluation of the system may be necessary to control for prejudices either for or against having computers make the particular judgment in question. MYCIN was evaluated by having a panel of experts make a set of diagnoses along with MYCIN; the answers were then recoded to disguise their source and the panel then evaluated each answer (Yu et al., 1979a, 1979b). On the other hand, if the focus is on evaluating the reasoning process itself, then a different method of evaluation should be used:

> The expert system needs to be exercised within a wide-ranging series to test situations aimed at discovering ways to make the system fail. The experts engaged in evaluating system performance must have full access to all aspects of behavior, so that they can push and probe, looking for weaknesses and deficiencies. This would seem to rule out blinded, comparative studies as an appropriate framework for expert system evaluation, at least in the early stages in the development life cycle (Gaschnig et al., 1983), p. 252).

Moreover, it is not necessary to carry the development of an expert system to the point where it can be commercially released for use as a decison aid in order to use the system as a tool in descriptive research:

> Once a system begins generating performance, it becomes an important part of the laboratory apparatus available to the knowledge engineer and cognitive analyst to gain fresh insights into the domain of expertise for which the system was built. The true goal of evaluation should not be to show how well a system does what it was designed to do but, rather, to gain a greater appreciation of the process, structure, and limits of expertise. This system can later be parlayed into new levels of expert performance in successive system developments (Gaschnig et al., 1983, p. 252).

Note again the emphasis on understanding, as opposed to merely programming the system to perform some task, similar to the statement by Davis and Lenat at the beginning of this chapter. Further, just as the development of human expertise is an ongoing process, so too the development of an expert system should not be viewed as a one-time effort.

Expert Systems as Research Tools

Lack of realism has been a major complaint voiced by participants in laboratory studies of accounting decision making. The following comment is typical:

All participants claimed that they needed more information because of the many factors which merit consideration in materiality decisions. Typically, questions were asked concerning the firm's balance sheet, environment (industry and economic conditions), history, management, accounting policies, previous materiality decisions, etc. (Moriarity and Barron, 1979, p. 106)

The construction of an expert system avoids this lack of realism because, as previously mentioned, subjects can use the system to make judgments in real situations. Consequently, building an expert system increases the external validity of descriptive research on decision making.

Another advantage of building an expert system is that it helps to clarify how a particular judgment is made. Traditional research methods merely measure the magnitude of the impact of an information input on a decision, without explaining how that item is used. The rules in the knowledge base of an expert system, on the other hand, explicitly indicate the way in which an item of information affects a decision.

For example, the authoritative literature mentions that in making a materiality judgment the auditor should take into consideration both the nature of the entity and the needs of the users of the client's financial statements (AICPA, 1983). The following rules in AUDITPLANNER (Steinbart, 1984) illustrate exactly how these factors enter into the judgment process:

IF: 1) the client is a public entity, and
         2) there is not any significant concern about the liquidity or solvency of the client

THEN: assume that the principal external users of the client's financial statements are primarily interested in the results of operations.

IF: 1) the principal external users of the client's financial statements are primarily interested in the results of operations, and
         2) income from continuing operations is above the break-even level,

THEN: the materiality judgment should be based on the amount of income from continuing operations.

333

Other rules lead to the conclusion that the users of the financial statements of privately-held companies are most interested in measures of financial position and, therefore, that materiality should be based on either current assets or stockholder's equity.

There are also some examples of the way in which certain data that are generally considered important actually affects the judgment about the quality of an internal control system. For instance, there is the general notion that for any given control weakness there are also compensating controls which can overcome these problems (Arens and Loebbecke, 1980). The following rules from the INTERNAL-CONTROL-ANALYZER (Gal, 1985) illustrate particular instances in which the auditor has identified certain compensating controls and reached conclusions about certain subgoals in the overall evaluation process:

IF: 1) The accounts receivable cash receipt functions are adequately separated, OR
       2) The accounts receivable cash receipt functions are adequately supervised

THEN: there are not any problems with incompatible functions for accounts receivable cash receipts

IF: 1) Sales orders are not specifically authorized, and
       2) There is an approved customer list that is used by the employee taking sales orders,

THEN: the controls for authorization of sales orders is effective.

There are other rules in the knowledge base which identify situations that would cause the auditor to look for an incompatible separation of duties, such as companies with small accounting departments. There are also rules that demonstrated the relationship between certain subgoals and the overall evaluation of internal controls such as the importance of controls over cash receipts in relation to the controls over sales orders.

Conclusion

Traditional methods for analyzing judgment behavior such as regression fail to explain the process by which those judgments are made. Consequently, accounting researchers have begun to turn to alternative research methods which focus more directly on the judgment process. One such method is the construction of expert systems, as explained in this paper; another is the analysis of verbal protocols (Biggs and Mock, 1983; Larcker and Lessig, 1983).

The two methods share much in common: they both allow the study of decision making in realistic environments and they both produce explanations of how and why certain factors affect the judgment process. Moreover, the two methods can be used in conjunction, as we pointed out in our discussion of building the prototype version of an expert system.

We feel, however, that there are significant advantages to building an expert system as opposed to conducting a protocol analysis. First, because of the time involved in both performing and analyzing verbal protocols, typically only a small number of decisions can be studied. In contrast, the process of refining an expert system entails the use of the system to make judgments in as wide a variety of situations as possible.

A second advantage of expert systems over verbal protocols is in completeness of analysis. Verbal protocols provide only a partial trace of the reasoning process (Ericsson and Simon, 1981). Moreover, there is an increasing body of evidence that the degree of verbalization is inversely related to the level of expertise possessed by the subject (Card, Moran, and Newell, 1983; Anderson, 1982, 1983). The implication is that richer protocols can be obtained by studying auditors with less experience; the question is, do we want to study those subjects' behaviors? This problem does not exist when building an expert system because subjects are not asked to verbalize their actions. They are asked, however, to use a system to make judgments. If they disagree with the system's conclusions, they use the debugging features to track down the cause of the error and then supply a rule for correcting that problem. Thus, the expert system probes for specific rules for specific situations.

Perhaps the major advantage of the expert systems methodology over verbal protocol analysis is that the former provides a means for testing the completeness of the analysis. The expert system either makes an appropriate judgment, or it does not. No such method for testing the sufficiency of analysis exists for verbal protocols.

We believe that expert systems will play an increasingly important role in future decision-making research in accounting. The construction of such systems will add rigor to descriptive field studies of current decision behavior. In addition the analysis of the resulting knowledge base should provide insights into the nature of the decision process used by the expert. Those insights, in turn, may then be used to design better laboratory experiments which more accurately measure the importance of different information items. Thus, the expert systems methodology should become another tool in the multi-method approach to the study of human decision-making behavior.

References

Abelson, R. P., "Psychological Status of the Script Concept," *American Psychologist,* July 1981, pp. 715–729.

Adelman, L., "The Influence of Formal, Substantive, and Contextual Task Properties on the Relative Effectiveness of Different Forms of Feedback in Multiple-Cue Probability Learning Tasks," *Organizational Behavior and Human Performance,* Vol. 27, 1981, pp. 423–442.

Aikins, J., "Prototypical Knowledge for Expert Systems," *Artificial Intelligence,* February 1983, pp. 163–210.

American Institute of Certified Public Accountants, *Statement on Auditing Standards No. 47: Audit Risk and Materiality in Conducting an Audit,* AICPA, 1983.

Anderson, J. R., "Acquisition of Cognitive Skill," *Psychological Review,* Vol. 89, No. 4, 1982, pp. 369–406.

————, *The Architecture of Cognition,* Harvard University Press, 1983.

Arens, A. A. and J. K. Loebbecke, *Auditing: An Integrated Approach,* Prentice-Hall, 1980.

Ashton, R. H., *Studies in Accounting Research #17: Human Information Processing in Accounting,* American Accounting Association, 1982.

Bartlett, F C., *Remembering: An Experimental and Social Study,* Cambridge University Press, 1932.

Biggs, S. F and T. J. Mock, "An Investigation of Auditor Decision Processes in the Evaluation of Internal Controls and Audit Scope Decisions," *Journal of Accounting Research,* Spring 1983, pp. 234–255.

Braun, H. M. and J. S. Chandler, "Development of an Expert System to Assist Auditors in the Investigation of Analytical Review Fluctuations," research proposal, University of Illinois, 1982.

Brunswick, E., "Representative Design and Probabilistic Theory in a Functional Psychology," *Psychological Review,* May 1955a, pp. 193–217.

————, "In Defense of Probabilistic Functionalism: A Reply," *Psychological Review,* May 1955b, pp. 236–242.

Buchanan, B. G., G. L. Sutherland, and E. A. Feigenbaum, "Heuristic DENDRAL: A Program for Generating Explanatory Hypotheses in Organic Chemistry," in B. Meltzer and D. Michie (eds.) *Machine Intelligence,* Vol. 4 Edinburgh University Press, 1969, pp. 209–254.

————, "Rediscovering Some Problems of Artificial Intelligence in the

336

Context of Organic Chemistry," in B. Meltzer and D. Michie (eds.) *Machine Intelligence*, Vol. 5, Edinburgh University Press, 1970, pp. 253–280.

Card, S. K., T. P. Moran, and A. Newell, *The Psychology of Human-Computer Interaction*, Lawrence Erlbaum Associates, 1983.

Carroll, J. S., "Analyzing Decision Behavior: The Magician's Audience," in T. S. Wallsten (ed.), *Cognitive Processes in Choice and Decision Behavior*, Lawrence Erlbaum Associates, 1980, pp. 69–75.

Chi, M. T. H., P. J. Feltovich, and R. Glaser, "Categorization and Representation of Physics Problems by Experts and Novices," *Cognitive Science*, April–June 1981, pp. 121–152.

Clancey, W. J., "The Advantages of Abstract Control Knowledge in Expert System Design," *AAAI-83: Proceedings of the National Conference on Artificial Intelligence*, pp. 74–78.

Cox, J. R. and R. A. Griggs, "The Effects of Experience on Performance in Wason's Selection Task," *Memory and Cognition*, September, 1982, pp. 496–502.

Davis, R., B. Buchanan, and E. Shortliffe, "Production Rules as a Representation for a Knowledge-Based Consultation Program," *Artificial Intelligence*, February 1977, pp. 15–45.

—— and D. Lenat, *Knowledge-Based Systems in Artificial Intelligence*, McGraw-Hill, 1982.

Dillard, J. F., J. F. Mutchler, and K. Ramakrishna, "Knowledge-Based Expert Computer Systems For Audit Opinion Decisions," working paper, The Ohio State University, 1983.

Dungan, C. W., "A Model of an Audit Judgment in the Form of an Expert System," unpublished dissertation, University of Illinois, 1983.

—— and J. S. Chandler, "Analysis of Audit Judgment Through an Expert System," working paper #982, University of Illinois, 1983.

Einhorn, H. J., "Expert Judgment: Some Necessary Conditions and an Example," *Journal of Applied Psychology*, October 1974, pp. 562–571.

——, "Learning from Experience and Suboptimal Rules in Decision Making," in T. S. Wallsten (ed.), *Cognitive Processes in Choice and Decision Behavior*, Lawrence Erlbaum Associates, 1980, pp. 1–19.

—— and R. M. Hogarth, "A Theory of Diagnostic Inference: I. Imagination and the Psychophysics of Evidence," working paper, University of Chicago, 1982.

——, "A Theory of Diagnostic Inference: Judging Causality," working paper, University of Chicago, 1984.

Ericsson, K. A. and H. A. Simon, "Verbal Reports as Data," *Psychological Review*, May 1980, pp. 215–251.

Feigenbaum, E. A., "Themes and Case Studies of Knowledge Engineering," in D. Michie (ed.), *Expert Systems in the Microelectronic Age*, Edinburgh University Press, 1979, pp. 3–25.

Gal, G., "Using Auditor Knowledge to Formulate Data Model Constraints: Expert Systems for Internal Control Evaluation," dissertation proposal, Michigan State University, 1984.

Gaschnig, J., P. Klahr, H. Pople, E. Shortliffe, and A. Terry, "Evaluation of Expert Systems: Issues and Case Studies," in F. Hayes-Roth,

D. A. Waterman, and D. B. Lenat (eds.), *Building Expert Systems,* Addison-Wesley, 1983, pp. 241–280.

Gibbons, M., "Regression and Other Statistical Implications for Research on Judgment Using Intercorrelated Data Sources," *Journal of Accounting Research,* Spring 1982, pp. 121–138.

Hansen, J. V. and W. F. Messier, Jr., "A Knowledge-Based Expert System for Auditing Advanced Computer Systems," ARC working paper 83-5, Brigham Young University, 1983.

Hayes, J. R. and H. A. Simon, "Psychological Differences among Problem Isomorphs," in N. Castellan, Jr., D. B. Pisoni, and G. R. Potts (eds.), *Cognitive Theory:* Vol. 2 Lasrence Erlbaum Associates, 1977, pp. 21–41.

Hayes-Roth, F., D. A. Waterman, and D. B. Lenat, "Principles of Pattern-Directed Inference Systems," in D. A. Waterman and F. Hayes-Roth (eds.), *Pattern-Directed Inference Systems,* Academic Press, 1978, pp. 577–601.

Hoch, S. J. and J. E. Tschirgi, "Cue Redundancy and Extra-Logical Inferences in a Deductive Reasoning Task," *Memory and Cognition,* March 1983, pp. 200–209.

Joyce, E. J. and G. C. Biddle, "Anchoring and Adjustment in Probabilistic Inference in Auditing," *Journal of Accounting Research,* Spring 1981a.

————, "Are Auditors' Judgments Sufficiently Regressive?" *Journal of Accounting Research,* Autumn 1981b.

Kahneman, D. and A. Tversky, "Prospect Theory: An Analysis of Decision under Risk," *Econometrica,* March, 1979, pp. 263–291.

Kinney, W. and W. Ueckert, "Mitigating the Consequences of Anchoring in Auditor Judgments," *The Accounting Review,* January 1982, pp. 55–69.

Klix, F, "On the Interrelationships between Natural and Artificial Intelligence Research," in F Klix (ed.), *Human and Artificial Intelligence,* North-Holland, 1979, pp. 1–9.

Larcker, D. F and V. P. Lessig, "An Examination of the Linear and Retrospective Process Tracing Approaches to Judgment Modeling," *The Accounting Review,* January 1983, pp. 58–77.

Libby, R., *Accounting and Human Information Processing: Theory and Applications,* Prentice-Hall, 1981.

Luzi, A. D. and C. E. White, Jr., "The Audit Concerns Model: An Extension of Auditing Theory Through Expert Systems Methodology," AMIS working paper 84-4, Pennsylvania State University, March 1984.

Messier, W. F Jr. and J. V. Hansen, "Expert Systems in Accounting and Auditing: A Framework and Review," ARC working paper 83-4, University of Florida, August 1983.

Michaelsen, R. H., "A Knowledge-Based System for Individual Income and Transfer Tax Planning," unpublished Ph.D. dissertation, University of Illinois, 1982.

Michie, D., "Experiments on the Mechanization of Game Learning," *The Computer Journal,* January 1982.

Minsky, M., "A Framework for Representing Knowledge," in P. H.

Winsten (ed.), *The Psychology of Computer Vision*, McGraw-Hill, 1975, pp. 211–277.

Moriarity, S. and F. H. Barron, "A Judgment-Based Definition of Materiality," *Supplement to the Journal of Accounting Research*, 1979, pp. 114–135.

Newell, A., "Remarks on the Relationship Between Artificial Intelligence and Cognitive Psychology," in R. B. Banerji and M. D. Mesarovic (eds.), *Theoretical Approaches to Nonnumerical Problem Solving: Proceedings of the IV Systems Symposium at Case Western Reserve University*, Springer-Verlag, 1970, pp. 363–400.

————, "Production Systems: Models of Control Structures," in W. G. Chase (ed.), *Visual Information Processing*, Academic Press, 1973, pp. 263–526.

————, "Harpy, Production Systems, and Human Cognition," in R. A. Cole (ed.), *Perception and Production of Fluent Speech*, Lawrence Erlbaum Associates, 1979, pp. 289–380.

————, "Physical Symbol Systems," *Cognitive Science*, April–June 1980, pp. 135–183.

————, "The Knowledge Level," *Artificial Intelligence*, January 1982, pp. 87–127.

———— and H. A. Simon, *Human Problem Solving*, Prentice-Hall, 1972.

————, "Computer Science as Empirical Inquiry: Symbols and Search," *Communications of the ACM*, March 1976, pp. 113–126.

Nilsson, N. J., "Some Examples of Artificial Intelligence Mechanisms for Goal Seeking, Planning, and Reasoning," in F. Klix (ed.), *Human and Artificial Intelligence*, North-Holland, 1979, pp. 11–36.

Pylyshyn, Z. W., "The Role of Competence Theories in Cognitive Psychology," *Journal of Psycholinguistic Research*, 1973, pp. 21–50.

————, "Psychological Explanations and Knowledge-Dependent Processes," *Cognition*, Vol. 10, 1981, pp. 267–274.

Raphael, B., *The Thinking Computer: Mind Inside Matter*, W. H. Freeman, 1976.

Schank, R. C., "Language and Memory," *Cognitive Science*, Vol. 4, 1980, pp. 243–284.

———— and R. Abelson, *Scripts, Plans, Goals, and Understanding*, Lawrence Erlbaum Associates, 1977.

Shortliffe, E. H., *Computer-Based Medical Consultation: MYCIN*, American Elsevier Publishing Co. Inc., 1976.

Simon, H. A., "Cognitive Science: The Newest Science of the Artificial," *Cognitive Science*, Vol. 4, 1980, pp. 3–46.

Steinbart, P. J., "The Construction of an Expert System to Make Materiality Judgments," unpublished dissertation, Michigan State University, 1984.

Stefik, M., J. Aikins, R. Balzer, J. Benoit, L. Birnbaum, F. Hayes-Roth, and E. Sacerdoti, "Basic Concepts for Building Expert Systems," in F. Hayes-Roth, D. A. Waterman, and D. B. Lenat (eds.), *Building Expert Systems*, Addison–Wesley, 1983, pp. 59–86.

Tversky, A. and D. Kahneman, "The Framing of Decisions and the Psychology of Choice," *Science*, January 13, 1981, pp. 453–458.

Uecker, H., "Cognitive Production Systems: Toward a Comprehensive

Theory on Mental Functioning," in F. Klix and J. Hoffman (eds.), *Cognition and Memory*, North-Holland, 1980, pp. 33–39.

van Melle, W., A. C. Scott, J. S. Bennett, and M. Peairs, *The EMYCIN Manual*, Stanford, 1981.

White, C. E. Jr., A. D. Luzi, and D. L. Craig, "Knowledge-Based Expert Systems for Auditing Professionals," AMIS working paper 83-10, Pennsylvania State University, August 1983.

Young, R. M., "Strategies and the Structure of a Cognitive Skill," in G. Underwood (ed.), *Strategies of Information Processing*, Academic Press, 1978, pp. 357–401.

————, "Production Systems for Modeling Human Cognition," in D. Michie (ed.), *Expert Systems in the Microelectronic Age*, Edinburgh University Press, 1979, pp. 35–45.

———— and T. O'Shea, "Errors in Children's Subtraction," *Cognitive Science*, April–June 1981, pp. 153–177.

Yu, V. L., B. G. Buchanan, E. H. Shortliffe, S. M. Wraith, R. Davis, A. C. Scott, and S. N. Cohen, "Evaluating the Performance of a Computer-Based Consultant, *Computer Programs in Biomedicine*, Vol. 9, 1979a, pp. 95–102.

————, L. M. Fagan, S. M. Wraith, W. J. Clancey, A. C. Scott, J. F. Hanigan, R. L. Blum, B. G. Buchanan, and S. N. Cohen, "Antimicrobial Selection by a Computer: A Blinded Evaluation by Infectious Disease Experts," *Journal of the American Medical Association*, Vol. 242, 1979b, pp. 1279–1282.

Part V

APPLICATIONS IN PRACTICE

Part V focus on the applications of expert systems in practice at some of the "Big Eight" accounting firms and the Turban & Mock article on the meaning of expert systems to the executive. Shpilberg and Graham describe the "ExperTAX" system used for corporate tax accrual and planning, a system where, more than twenty experts have devoted over 1000 hours to the system's development. The system was developed using a shell developed by the authors using the LISP language. A separate knowledge base maintenance system is used to update tax knowledge.

Kelly, Ribar, and Willingham analyze the essence of an expert system for the auditor's loan loss evaluation. They explain why AI technology offers significant benefits for the audit researcher. They also describe the CFILE (credit file) system prototype in detail, including the results of a comparison of auditor and model judgments.

Smith & Temple developed the "Mortgage Loan Analyzer" (MLA) as a tool for underwriters to evaluate residential loan applications. The system first gathers data, prompts the underwriter to review specific aspects of the loan application process, applies other information and guidelines to the situation, and finishes by generating a loan evaluation report. MLA is a practical solution to a business problem.

Developing ExperTAX^{sm}: An Expert System for Corporate Tax Accrual and Planning

DAVID SHPILBERG and LYNFORD E. GRAHAM

Recently, articles about the use of expert systems in account-ing and auditing have begun to appear in the audit literature (Longair, 1983; Stoner, 1985), and special audit research con-ferences focusing on the issue (USC, 1984 and 1986) have been scheduled. These trends are indicative of the growing degree of interest by researchers in the technology of these systems.

Expert systems is a branch of the discipline termed "artificial intelligence," or AI. An expert system may be defined as a system that

- handles real-world, complex problems requiring an ex-pert's interpretation, and

- solves these problems using a computer model of expert human reasoning, reaching the same conclusions the ex-pert would reach if faced with a comparable problem (Weiss and Kulikowski, 1984, p. 1).

As additional artificial intelligence software tools for developing expert systems become available at reasonable cost, and the power, speed, and portability of micro-computers increase, more and more audit and professional service tasks become likely candidates for assistance from expert systems. The potential gains in competitive advantage and productivity embodied in the use of this new technology, the ever-increasing complexity and volume of tax, regulatory, and professional accounting and auditing standards, and the increasing sophistication of business environments combine to create a situation in which such systems will be most welcome. Various possible applications to the audit environment have been cited in the literature (Elliott and Kielich, 1985; Dungan and Chandler, 1985).

This paper presents a case study on the development of an expert system in an audit and tax environment. The study points out issues identified in the development process that are of interest to those researchers currently experimenting with expert systems. In addition, the case study may alert researchers to issues and areas of research related to expert systems where their efforts can lead to an advance in knowledge.

This paper describes the key issues surrounding the development of a knowledge-based expert system called ExperTAX. It provides guidance and advice, through issue identification, to auditors and tax specialists in preparing the tax accrual for financial statement purposes. It also identifies relevant issues for tax planning, tax compliance, and tax service purposes.

The Problem

Tax accrual, the process of identifying tax-book differences and explaining differences between statutory and effective tax rates, is an audit task requiring specialized training and considerble time. In connection with tax services provided to most audit clients, the client's tax strategy, timely filing issues, and planning opportunities are also identified during the course of the audit.

Many accounting firms have developed questionnaires, forms, or checklists that facilitate the gathering of information necessary to conduct the tax accrual and tax planning functions. These questionnaires are usually completed by staff accountants in the field and may be brought back to the office or left in the field for analysis. At the client's location, an audit manager conducts the accrual analysis, and a tax manager, either in the office or at the client's location, reviews the analysis and identifies tax planning issues and opportunities. If these issues or opportunities are significant, the case is referred to more experienced personnel for further analysis and/or interaction with the client.

The process, as described, is quite efficient. Knowledge is leveraged to the field by the use of specialized questionnaires. Information is gathered by staff accountants and utilized by audit and tax managers not only to conduct the tax accrual computation, but also to corroborate their tax accounting practices and identify tax planning opportunities. Senior experts are brought in on a timely basis when they are clearly needed.

The problem is that practical realities limit the efficiency of the process. Tax accrual questionnaires are perceived by audit personnel to be long, complicated documents. On the other hand, tax professionals are concerned that such questionnaires attempt to simplify and standardize rather complex situations. Audit staff assigned to the task are concerned primarily with the tax accrual computation, and may not be aware of the detailed tax planning implications of some of the information collected. Other questions clearly address tax issues that are beyond their audit expertise and, while perhaps important to the tax function, may not be directly relevant to the task at hand.

The analysis by both the audit and tax managers of all the required information is a complex task. While the tax accrual computation requires some time, identifying tax planning issues and opportunities is a much more demanding task. Reviewing the issues may necessitate several rounds of on-site information gathering to complete the questionnaires and answer follow-up questions. In the process of this review, the tax and audit reviewers must focus their expert attention on both simple and complex issues. The physical timing of this task creates considerable stress on tax planning efficiency.

The Solution

A tax accrual support system should actively guide the staff accountant through the information gathering process, efficiently directing the individual to the relevant issues and pointing out the specific importance of the information requested. This will motivate the accountant to obtain the data and educate him or her on the potential ramifications of the information requested. Such a system would improve the staff accountant's productivity as well as the quality of the information gathered; it would also accelerate the accountant's training process.

Once the issue of efficient collection of relevant information has been dealt with, processing the information on a timely basis, in adequate depth, and by the appropriate experts becomes the knowledge "bottleneck." Better information does not by itself alleviate the problems associated with the audit and tax managers' reviews. If anything, it increases their need for larger blocks of time near year-end to adequately examine all the known facts and to identify the relevant issues.

Thus, to meaningfully improve the process, the support system should go beyond the efficient collection of information. It should be capable of analyzing and synthesizing the information to identify relevant issues to be brought to the attention of the audit and tax managers. If the support system routinely uncovered and described most of the basic tax accrual and planning issues, so that the attention of the experts could be directed to the higher-level issues, the process would be more efficient. This would effectively eliminate the expert-resource-intensive task of routine information analysis, except for cases in which critical issues require the attention of highly specialized personnel.

In summary, a support system that would significantly enhance the current tax accrual and planning process should include the following features:

1. The ability to efficiently guide, motivate, and educate a staff accountant in the process of collecting information.

2. The ability to quickly and thoroughly analyze the information collected and identify the relevant issues.

To address those requirements, Coopers & Lybrand has developed ExperTAX, a knowledge-based expert system supporting the corporate tax accrual and planning process. ExperTAX functions as an "intelligent" questionnaire, guiding the user through the information gathering process. It asks only those questions that are relevant to the client situation, is capable of sifting through issues that require clarification, and requests additional information when needed. It is also capable of explaining why a question is being asked and why the response is relevant. In addition to its ability to gather information and identify tax accrual and planning issues, it keeps track of any relevant questions still unanswered and documents all the questions asked, answers given, and user-generated "marginal notes."

ExperTAX's knowledge base consists of over 1,000 frames, rules, and facts derived from knowledge engineering sessions conducted with over twenty senior tax and audit experts at Coopers & Lybrand. ExperTAX has been developed in common LISP and runs on IBM-PC XT, AT, or IBM-compatible personal computers. The following sections describe ExperTAX in greater detail.

Knowledge Engineering: Designing the Product's Environment

Knowledge engineering is defined in this paper as the process of designing the expert system to:

1. facilitate its use

2. maximize its ability to leverage expert knowledge

3. facilitate the knowledge acquisition process

4. optimize system efficiency and

5. produce a cost-efficient solution.

A process of meta knowledge acquisition should precede the gathering of specific facts and rules. The process encompasses understanding the expert system's tasks, exploring product delivery, environments, identifying the experts, defining the structure of the knowledge base, distilling its technical requirements, and selecting the software and hardware for implementation and delivery.

UNDERSTANDING THE EXPERT SYSTEM'S TASKS

The current operating environment for the tax accrual process and related functions is summarized in Table 1. As can be seen from Table 1, the process consists of a number of phases and involves professionals of differing backgrounds. To aid in the conduct of the process, several supporting instruments are used

347

TABLE 1
Current Tax Accrual Process

Task	Person(s) Responsible	Site	Support Instruments	Duration (Hrs.)	Cumulative Elapsed Time (Days)	Output	Level of Expertise	Type of Expertise
Audit Strategy/Planning								
1. Prepare Tax Strategy Summary	In-charge accountant (ICA) or audit manager	Client/Office	Prior-year info (summary, questionnaire, tax returns), preliminary financials, client discussion	1	2	Completed Tax Strategy Summary	Medium	Audit and tax
2. Review Tax Strategy Summary and identify alternate tax strategies	Audit and tax managers and partners	Office	Completed Tax Strategy Summary	2	10	Memoranda, possible client discussions	High	Audit and tax
Preliminary Fieldwork								
3. Complete TAX questionnaire	ICA	Client	Prior-year info, preliminary financials, client discussion			TAX questionnaire responses, notes, schedules	Medium	Audit and tax
4. Review data for tax accrual issues	Audit manager	Office	Prior-year info, completed TAX			Memoranda	High	Audit
5. Review data for tax planning/compliance issues and develop alternative tax strategies	Audit manager, tax manager, and audit and tax partners	Office	Prior-year info, completed TAX			Memoranda, client discussions	High	Tax
Year-End Fieldwork								
6. Gather tax accrual data, compute accrual, and update questionnaire	ICA	Client	Memoranda, financial statement data, updated TAX			Financial statement numbers, tax return schedules	Medium	Audit
7. Perform a final review of tax accrual and TAX	Audit manager Tax manager	Client Client/	Tax accrual workpapers, updated TAX			Memoranda	High	Audit and tax
8. Make a final identification of issues and alternative strategies	Engagement managers and partners	Office Office	Updated TAX questionnaire			Reports to clients, memoranda	Very high	Audit and tax

348

and interim reports are produced. All these factors and their interactions have to be considered if an effective expert system is to be developed.

The expert system would help improve the tax accrual process if it could reduce the time devoted to specific tasks, reduce the time elapsed from start to finish, maintain the quality of the output, and reduce the time demands and pressures on high-level expertise.

To improve data gathering, the expert system would have to animate the questionnaire functions, asking only relevant questions and explaining the reasons for the required information in the context of the client's situation. The process would allow more specialized questions to be asked, would improve the average quality of the initial responses, and would tend to eliminate the need for additional data-gathering sessions. In terms of input and output requirements, the expert system should allow the user to enter the required information in response to the questions, using a multiple-choice format supported by user-desired or required notes, explanations, and schedules.

The most time-consuming tasks for managers are those associated with the analysis of the completed questionnaires. Over the course of the engagement, identifying and studying tax accrual and tax planning issues may take several days of expert time over several weeks of elapsed time. Since all the information used for these tasks could be captured in the completed questionnaires, the expert system should be able to conduct those tasks more efficiently, utilizing a knowledge base extracted from the experience and know-how of tax accrual and tax planning experts.

EXPLORING PRODUCT DELIVERY ENVIRONMENTS

By their nature, expert systems are serious consumers of computer power. They function more efficiently using specialized hardware (e.g., LISP machines) or fairly large dedicated general-purpose computers. Specialized hardware offers the added advantage of providing user-friendly software environments that are particularly productive in the context of quick prototyping of expert system functions. Several commercially available software environments contribute to making these programming environments even more productive.

When dealing with the issue of a delivery environment for the product, one has to come to grips with the operational restrictions that the environment might impose. For the tax accrual function, the data-gathering task takes place at the client's location and is generally carried out by a senior (in-charge) staff accountant. Only an expert system that can be resident in an easily obtained on-site computer will be feasible for this task. Hundreds of IBM-compatible computers are currently utilized by staff at client sites. If those computers could be used to support the expert system, chances for its successful implementation would be noticeably enhanced.

IDENTIFYING THE EXPERTS

Typically, very few experts are used while developing an expert system. This occurs for a number of reasons, usually due to the fact that experts are a scarce resource, and in many domains, one expert is all that is needed. In the area of U.S. taxation, there are many areas of expertise. At Coopers & Lybrand this expertise is distributed throughout the firm. ExperTAX used many experts during the construction of its knowledge base, and the knowledge base now represents their collected knowledge.

The task of identifying the professionals whose expertise should be tapped in constructing the knowledge base of the system is significant. There are people who are "experts" in the execution of the process; that is, they know what materials should be gathered, the order in which information should be collected, and the most efficient order in which to answer the various questions. There are other experts who know what questions to ask and why, and what follow-up questions may be required to identify a relevant issue. There is yet another group of experts who are particularly good at summarizing the results and presenting the information for analysis. Finally, there are experts who can construct viable alternative strategies, given the information presented to them. All of those experts have a role in the tax accrual and planning process. Thus, for the expert system to satisfactorily perform its support tasks in the data gathering, analysis, and planning modes, it will have to incorporate expertise from several sources.

Although most tax managers could do a good job of performing the various tax accrual and planning tasks, they would probably not be as effective in each of the specific areas of the process as some specialized experts would be. Thus, it is conceivable that by bringing together the right experts for the right tasks, the resulting expert system could provide a consistent quality of response in a more efficient manner than would result from the experts acting alone. It is through the integration of the experts' collective specialized knowledge that the tax accrual expert system comes alive.

DEFINING THE STRUCTURE OF THE KNOWLEDGE BASE

The most difficult task associated with the knowledge engineering function is to determine an adequate structure for the knowledge base. This task requires the most abstract level of knowledge acquisition, since neither the experts nor the knowledge engineer initially has a frame of reference on which to base their discussions.

In early exchanges with the experts, they described their tasks in holistic terms (i.e., "focus on the main issues," "analyze all the relevant data," "base our analysis on experience," "react to the particular characteristics of the client"). They described the process in terms that criticized the shortcomings of questionnaires and emphasized the value of unstructured, yet careful, analysis. However, the evidence clearly suggests that most analysis is based on the information gathered through the existing questionnaires and, on some occasions, through additional requests for specific data.

To bring structure to the process and to facilitate our understanding of the dynamics of the process, a simulation experiment was conducted. An experienced auditor provided a real case for which the tax accrual process had recently been completed. He provided all the basic work-paper and tax return information that had been used to process the case. Two other experienced auditors, one in audit and one in tax, were asked to identify the specific information required to conduct a complete tax accrual process for the client in question.

A conference room with a long table in the middle was divided by a curtain. All the case information was gathered and deposited on the left side of the table, including the forms and questionnaires deemed relevant. A staff accountant with no previous practice experience in the tax accrual process was selected at random and asked to sit at the left side of the table. Two

351

experienced audit and tax people were given blank questionnaires and forms and were asked to sit at the right side of the table, separated by the curtain from the staff accountant and the case data.

The staff accountant was informed that it was his responsibility to conduct a successful tax accrual process for the client. He was told that he currently had all the necessary information in front of him, and most importantly, a panel of experts behind the curtain. The experts were told that it was their responsibility to guide the staff accountant toward the successful completion of the tax accrual process. They were instructed to actively guide him with verbal advice and to answer questions when asked. They were unable to go to the other side of the curtain to explain; only oral communication was allowed.

The process was videotaped with two cameras and observed by the knowledge engineering team. Several variations of the process were conducted for a total of twelve hours over three days. At the end of the experiment, the knowledge engineering team had a clear picture of the basic structure of the knowledge base and the minimum requirements for the user screen interface. A first prototype of the expert system could then be built.

DISTILLING TECHNICAL REQUIREMENTS

A careful analysis of the expert system simulation exercise was the basis for distilling the technical requirements of the system.

1. The process should be driven by a "smart" questionnaire. The expert system has to continuously probe for information, deciding which questions to ask and in what order. In addition, it has to have the ability to explain why a question is being asked and reveal some of the implications associated with the answers. This was found to be particularly important in motivating and guiding the user to gather the relevant data.

2. The data-gathering process should be conducted first. The analysis of the data gathered should be executed only on demand, after part or all of the data have been gathered. The system also needs to produce written reports detailing the information gathered and documenting the accrual process and planning issues raised.

352

3. The knowledge base needs to be organized in frames. The frames are to be classified by the context of the knowledge (e.g., inventory, receivables) and by the type of knowledge they represent (i.e., questions, issues, facts). The knowledge base has to be easy to maintain, since the tax field is in constant flux and the audit and tax planning process may be revised.

4. The user interface needs to be highly interactive. Staff auditors will spend considerable time communicating with the system and will be highly sensitive to the system's responses. The screen display should be simple and self-explanatory, yet allow the user to control the process at all times, permitting the insertion of free-flow text whenever the user considers it necessary to make a note. The "why" explanations should be easily invoked but only at the user's request, since most auditors do not need to refer to this information for every question. The process sequence should be easily controllable by the user, allowing questions to be skipped for later completion.

5. The size of the knowledge base will be substantial, containing over 1000 frames, rules, or facts. The search structure, however, will tend to be wide and shallow, usually allowing fast conversion on a forward chaining mode. The wide and shallow format follows from such considerations as the system's broad coverage of numerous subject areas and the relatively few questions required in each area to identify an issue. The process is to be controlled by a fact-finding forward chain. Backward chaining will not be a frequently invoked function. It will be required only when changes in previously introduced facts become necessary. The number of text lists to be stored and randomly accessed for display as "why" messages or for the construction of issue reports will be substantial, and they will be components of the frames. However, the length of individual message units tends to be brief, rarely exceeding ten lines of text.

6. The findings reported above were used to build the first ExperTAX prototype. It was used interactively during the knowledge acquisition sessions that followed. While the expert system continued to evolve throughout this process, it required only minor modifications to the user interface, inference engine, and knowledge base structure.

SELECTING SOFTWARE AND HARDWARE

The analysis of the product delivery environment strongly suggested an IBM-compatible computer as the recommended hardware for delivery of the ExperTAX system. Based on that requirement, commercially available expert system programming environments for the IBM-PC were carefully evaluated.

Several products, such as Expert-EASE, Exsys, and M.1, ranging in price from $150 to $15,000, were identified and studied. First-cut prototypes were developed on those considered most promising. Several proved easy to use and versatile enough to accommodate some version of the desired prototype. However, they all failed to satisfy the technical specifications deemed essential for ExperTAX. In many cases screen design was not flexible enough to support the level of dialogue interaction required, response time was judged to be unbearably slow, or the facility to explain the system's slow, or the facility to explain the system's reasoning was too rudimentary. In some, the size of the knowledge base was severely restricted or the quality of displayed and printed output was unacceptable.

It was decided that the system would have to be custom designed using a suitable programming language. Common LISP was selected because it is relatively mature and versatile and is rapidly becoming the standard LISP dialect for Artificial Intelligence work in the United States (Winston and Horn, 1984). From among the Common LISP implementation vehicles available for the IBM-PC, Gold Hill Computers' Golden Common LISP (1985) was selected for the project. It is a reasonable subset of Common LISP and its code operates very efficiently in the IBM-PC environment.

IBM PC-ATs were used during the prototyping phase, but the product was designed to run on an IBM PC-XT or compatible unit with 640 kilobytes of memory. The disk storage requirement for the knowledge base is under ten megabytes. To enhance the quality of the user interface, a high-resolution color monitor is supported as optional equipment. A laser printer is the preferred output vehicle for printed reports.

ExperTAX Components

ExperTAX is a rule-based expert system program especially designed to accommodate the requirements of the tax accrual

354

and planning process as conducted at Coopers & Lybrand. While it was designed for a single purpose, the ExperTAX shell has proved to be a flexible programming environment for other kinds of questionnaire-driven expert systems.

ExperTAX consists of four main components:

1. The inference engine is responsible for controlling the logic search through the knowledge base, firing the appropriate rules, tracking the inference process, and communicating with the user through the user interface.

2. The knowledge base is responsible for harboring all the frames, rules, and facts that constitute the expertise of the system, and for making them available upon request to the inference engine and the user interface.

3. The user interface is responsible for the control of the screens and keyboard used by the system to communicate with the user, as well as the generation of all the printed reports. Its operation is controlled by the user. The information it displays comes directly from the knowledge base, and the information it takes in is used by the inference engine to direct its search processes and to enrich the output documentation.

4. The knowledge base maintenance system is responsible for supporting the modification of frames, rules, and facts in the knowledge base. It is independent of the other three modules and is designed to facilitate the maintenance of the knowledge base by the designated organizational group.

INFERENCE ENGINE

The ExperTAX inference engine is a forward chaining, rule-based system. It incorporates a frame manager, a facts database, and a rule interpreter. Two types of frames are recognized by the frame manager, those associated with questions to be asked (question frames) and those associated with valid issues (issues frames). The frames can also be grouped in sections to be executed one at a time in any prescribed order. Within a section, the frame manager controls the execution of frames. The inferencing from question frames and issue frames takes place at different times.

The actual inferencing process is controlled by the rule interpreter, which uses the facts deposited in the facts database by the user interface. The rule interpreter focuses on the rules contained in the frames activated by the frame manager. It compares the left-hand side of the rule (the If part of an If-Then rule) with known facts in the database. When a match is found, the rule is executed. The execution of a rule, also known as rule firing, consists of implementing the instructions contained in the right-hand side of the rule fired (the Then part). This can result in one of several actions: the set of known facts in the facts database may be modified, an information string may be sent to the user interface as output, the execution control may be transferred to the user interface, or a fact or documentation string may be requested from the user interface. The rule interpreter will continue to search the same section of frames in the knowledge base until it fires a rule that transfers control to the user interface.

The ExperTAX inference engine keeps track of the inference chain created by the successive firings of rules, allowing for the display of specific reasoning associated with conclusions. The inference engine permits interruption and resumption of the inference process at any stage, and backtracking of the process for alternative fact evaluation.

KNOWLEDGE BASE

The ExperTAX knowledge base stores information as "frames." Some information relates to how and when to use the frame, some to what should happen next, and some to what to display or print. A frame can include several rules. There are two types of frames in the ExperTAX knowledge base: question frames and issue frames. They differ in the number and type of attributes (also called slots), procedures, and facts associated with them.

The question frames include the following attributes: Questions, Preconditions (rules), Possible Answers (rules), Marginal Note Instructions, and Why Messages. The attributes include attached procedures that can evaluate facts and fire rules, display information, request additional facts, and transfer control to other frames. Figure 1 presents a typical question frame.

FIGURE 1
Coopers & Lybrand
Question Frame
ExperTAX Knowledge Base
Documentation—Question QA17

November 13, 1985

What is client's bad-debt write-off method for TAX purposes?
S—Specific charge-off
R—Reserve method

Summary: Bad debt write-off method

Precondition: (QZI IS A): Accrual or Cash
Basis IS Accrual

Possible Answers:
S—Specific charge-off
(Clarifying explanation required.)
R—Reserve method
Follow-up Questions:
QA19—Bad-debt reserve method
QA20—Difference between BOOK and TAX reserve
QA21—Bad-debt recoveries to reserve

WHY Message:

In a typical environment, the Reserve method over time will result in larger tax deductions than the Specific charge-off method.

The issue frames are simpler than the question frames. They include only a Rule attribute and a Display attribute. The attached procedures evaluate facts, and fire and issue displays. Figure 2 presents a typical issue frame.

357

FIGURE 2
Coopers & Lybrand
Issue Frame
ExperTAX Knowledge Base
Documentation—General Rules
Issue P4

November 12, 1985

The IRS has indicated that it will not allow the taxpayer who is using the Completed Contract method of accounting to also elect LIFO. See proposed long-term contract regulations which are contrary to Peninsula Steel Products and Equipment Co. v. Comm., 78 TC 1029 (1982).
Rule:
(QA2 IS C): LT Contract TAX method IS Completed Contract AND
(QB14 IS L): Method of accounting for inventory IS LIFO
OR
(QB14 IS B): Method of accounting for inventory IS Both LIFO and FIFO
Issue on PLAN List

The frames are further classified by sections, which are groups of frames that share an execution sequence. The number of frames in a section and number of sections in the knowledge base are restricted only by the storage limitation of the hardware and software environment.

USER INTERFACE

The user interface of ExperTAX controls the screen display used for communicating with the user and the printer commands necessary for formatting and issuing reports. The screen layout consists of three active horizontal windows. The top window displays information identifying the section being analyzed. The middle window displays long and short forms of the questions being asked, the precondition that fired the current rule, and the valid answers. The lower window is used to present clarification messages (why messages), when requested, and to type in "marginal note" information when requested by the system or the user. Figure 3 presents a sample screen display.

FIGURE 3
Screen Display

Coopers & Lybrand
Tax Accrual and Planning
Expert System Inventory
(Section B)

Any Inventory: Yes

Does the client include any of the following items in inventory for TAX purposes?

Real Estate

Materials and supplies not held for sale (e.g., office supplies)

Deferred cost under the Completed Contract method

Consigned goods to which the client does not have title

Summary: Non-inventory items

QB3   Answer one of:(YN)—

The items mentioned above may be treated as inventory items for BOOK purposes, but may not be treated as such for TAX purposes. (Ref. Atlantic Coast Realty v. Comm., Rev. Rul. 59-329, Reg. 1.471-1.)

F1-Note F2-Skip F3-Why F5-Back

The user interface is operated through a system of nested menus that allows the user substantial control of the inference process. At virtually any point in the process, the user can return to a menu that allows for an orderly interruption of the process or for the resumption of the process at a different session or frame.

The printed reports generated by the user interface include lists of all issues identified by ExperTAX, audit trails of all

359

questions asked and answers received, notes taken during the sessions, and specialized forms issued when additional documentation is required. Figure 4 presents a sample of an issues report.

FIGURE 4
Coopers & Lybrand
Issues Report
ExperTAX Planning Issues
and Ideas
February 7, 1986

The following planning ideas and issues should be reviewed to determine their applicability to the client. Some may be inappropriate because of immateriality. Others may represent issues which should be examined closely.

- The IRS has indicated that it will not allow the taxpayer who is using the Completed Contract method of accounting to also elect LIFO. See proposed long-term contract regulations which are contrary to Peninsula Steel Products and Equipment Co. v. Comm., 78 TC 1029 (1982).

- Since the client is not determining market value based on bid price, it may not be complying with Reg. Sect. 1.471-4. Under ordinary circumstances, market value means the current bid price prevailing at the current inventory date. If no open market exists, a taxpayer may use such evidence of fair market value as may be available.

- LIFO inventory may not be valued for tax purposes using the lower-of-cost-or-market method!! The IRS may terminate the taxpayer's LIFO election if LIFO inventory is valued at lower-of-cost-or-market. See Rev. Proc. 79-23. In limited situations, a taxpayer may be able to change to the Cost method and preclude the IRS from terminating its LIFO election. See Rev. Proc. 84-74. Market write-downs are required to be included in income under the provisions of Sec. 472(d) when LIFO is elected.★★

- Items such as real estate, office supplies, consigned goods and deferred costs under the Completed Contract method should not be included as inventory items for TAX purposes and therefore the LIFO inventory method or lower-of-cost-or-market method may not be used for these items. Client should consider changing to the proper method for treating these items. Ref. Atlantic Coast Realty

360

Co. v. Comm., Rev. Rule 59-329 and Reg. Sect. 1.471-1.★★

• Direct material, direct labor and indirect (overhead) costs must be included in inventory costs!! This will require a change to accounting method which requires prior IRS approval. If request for change is NOT filed, a penalty may be imposed. A voluntary change may not be filed once a taxpayer has been contacted in any manner by the IRS. The spread period for such a change may not exceed three years. See Rev. Proc. 84-74.

• It is normally appropriate to look at the general economic conditions, risk of industry, and financial condition of specific customers as judgmental factors in establishing an appropriate level of reserves for bad debts. If the client now wishes to consider these factors in establishing reserve levels, it may constitute a change in accounting . . .

KNOWLEDGE BASE MAINTENANCE SYSTEM

The ExperTAX knowledge base maintenance system is an independent software system designed to update, modify, and expand the knowledge base. The system includes a frame editor, logic evaluator, and rule interaction display.

The frame editor permits the user to state the different components of a frame in simple English. It edits the information entered for consistency and completeness and helps the user correct omissions or inconsistencies.

The logic evaluator checks for possible conflicts in logic between the rules in the frame being edited and the rules contained in currently valid frames. If an inconsistency is discovered, the evaluator suggests editorial action that would resolve the situation. For example, the system will diagnose the case where a question frame with a structure control rule would transfer to an undefined question, or where a question can not be asked because of an improper precondition. It will also diagnose the case where an issue frame contains a rule whose antecedent cannot be true (such as "the answer to Q1 is A AND the answer to Q1 is B," and other more complex cases).

The rule interaction display allows the user to dynamically observe all the frames affected by changes in the frame being edited. This permits the user to better visualize the changes in operating procedure that could be implicit in modifications of a frame with several complex rules or follow-up routines.

Knowledge Acquisition: Building the Knowledge Base

Knowledge acquisition is defined in this paper as the interactive process of "training" the expert system to the point at which it is capable of delivering a level of performance considered satisfactory for the task to be performed. It is the phase of the project during which detailed gathering of rules and facts takes place. It is a process of careful selection of experts, of exhaustive interactive sessions for knowledge capture, of fine-tuning enhancements to the system shell, and of careful validation of the knowledge base logic, structure, and information.

SELECTING THE EXPERTS

A careful observation of the current tax accrual and planning process reveals several sources of expertise:

1. The audit and tax specialists who design and maintain the support tools (e.g., questionnaires) used in the field.

2. The engagement auditors who gather data for the process.

3. The managers and partners who review the data and issue recommendations.

4. The tax auditors and consultants who specialize in various complex areas of the tax planning process and are regularly used as expert resources by managers and partners on engagements.

As described earlier, the initial attempt to infer a structure for the knowledge base utilized a simulation experiment. The experts that participated in those sessions came from the four sources mentioned above. This allowed the knowledge engineering team to gain an understanding of the experts' likely role in the detailed knowledge acquisition process.

From those sessions, it was concluded that the existing questionnaires were a good frame of reference for the tax accrual process. They had been carefully designed and incorporated considerable expertise. While they were not as comprehensive as some experts would have liked and were rigid in their format and a bit cumbersome to administer, they constituted a good

362

frame of reference for the tax accrual process and were being used regularly throughout Coopers & Lybrand. Thus, it was decided that the first source of expertise to be used for the ExperTAX knowledge base would be the existing tax accrual and planning support tools, such as the questionnaire and the audit and tax specialists currently responsible for its maintenance and support.

The expert system simulation sessions also brought home the fact that the knowledge base had several clearly defined subsets or sections dealing with different areas of specialization (e.g., inventory, accounts receivable). Detailed problems related to these areas are routinely supported by different professionals acting as consultants on specific engagements. A variety of specific areas of expertise were identified as being specialized enough to require separate treatment. Since it is always easier to work with narrowly defined knowledge bases, it was decided to address each of those areas one at a time, but only after conducting some general sessions to identify possible interactions between areas.

To implement the process described above, the second source of expertise utilized was the one provided by the generalists. Audit and tax managers and partners who regularly conduct tax accrual and planning processes were consulted on the validity of the basic expertise structure of the questionnaire. These practitioners helped to validate the control process and user interaction features of the system and to identify some areas of cross-correlation between knowledge frames.

The largest pool of experts utilized were specialist tax consultants, who currently serve as expert resources supporting the practice managers and partners. These experts proved to be highly receptive to the structured question framework for knowledge acquisition, since it seems to closely resemble the process they often follow in acquiring information and giving advice over the telephone. By the end of the process, more than twenty experts had devoted over 1000 hours to the project and had helped transform the prototype questionnaire-based knowledge base into an extensive pool of knowledge capable of efficiently supporting in-depth analyses in many areas of expertise.

The final group of experts asked to participate in the knowledge acquisition process were the staff auditors who currently gather data in the field. Together with the tax and audit managers, they participated in the field validation of successive versions of ExperTAX, comparing and reporting on its performance *vis a vis* reports they had prepared for clients.

INTERACTIVE KNOWLEDGE ACQUISITION

Interactive knowledge acquisition is the process of incorporating expert knowledge into an existing expert system at the same time as the knowledge is transmitted by the human expert to the knowledge engineer. The expert system is being "trained" on-site by the expert, with the help of the knowledge engineer, who acts as an information broker. The knowledge engineer ensures that the new knowledge is in phrases that are compatible with the structure of the expert system, elicits explanations and clarifications from the expert, questions the order of or need for the information supplied by the expert, and runs the expert system continuously to let the expert observe the effects of the newly acquired knowledge.

All ExperTAX knowledge acquisition sessions (except for the simulation sessions described earlier) were conducted "live" with the computer. After some initial sessions were completed, a functional prototype of ExperTAX was built. This prototype was then used in all the following working sessions with experts.

The ideal knowledge acquisition session involves one knowledge engineer, a computer with the latest version of the expert system, and one or two experts. The dynamics of these sessions are such that the experts very quickly begin to structure their responses to closely resemble the favored syntax and logic of the expert system structure. The experts become further motivated by observing their suggestions and comments being immediately introduced into the knowledge base. They see how the expert system is "learning" and how the system's advice begins to closely resemble their own. They can also observe when certain rules or facts put into the system affect the behavior of the system in undesirable ways (e.g., when such rules lead to "blind alleys" or attempt to "train" the system beyond the desired level of expertise). Thus, they can correct the mistake immediately, suggesting alternative approaches to address the point.

The net result is a highly efficient knowledge acquisition process in which the quality of the information exchange between the knowledge engineer and the experts is greatly enhanced by the instant feedback provided by the evolving expert system.

ENHANCING THE EXPERTAX SHELL

While the final version of ExperTAX closely resembles the original prototype developed, it nevertheless incorporates a few significant changes deemed relevant by the experts as a result of the interactive knowledge acquisition sessions. The friendly and productive programming environment provided by the Exper-TAX shell in particular, and LISP in general, made it feasible to expediently modify ExperTAX to accommodate new perceived user needs as the knowledge acquisition process progressed.

When it became obvious that a new feature should be incorporated (e.g., the ability to go back to a previous question, add "why" messages of extended length, or create special forms of schedules to be printed when required), it was added to the system by the knowledge engineering team immediately after the session. The additions were usually available for review at the next scheduled session. The opportunity to observe emerging patterns of use by the experts testing the system permitted the search patterns and knowledge storage and retrieval rules to be designed to minimize system response times, without changing the hardware requirements.

This process of incremental software development yielded a final product closely tailored to the needs of the audit and tax professionals. Only the original prototype was based on a formal software system design. The final product was the result of incremental enhancements of the prototype, which were made possible by the interactive knowledge acquisition sessions and the highly productive programming environment provided by the ExperTAX shell and LISP.

KNOWLEDGE BASE VALIDATION

The exhaustive validation of an expert system's knowledge base is a difficult task. Logic tests should be run to ensure the consistency of the knowledge base, and the system should be tested against the experts in an extensive array of situations. One way, possibly the best way, to validate a pool of knowledge is for professionals that were not involved in the development process to conduct an independent validation of its performance. There are two potential problems with this approach. First, different professionals might have different approaches to arriving at a specific conclusion. Second, the sheer number of possible combinations of responses that the system is capable of producing makes it difficult to test the system exhaustively.

Our approach to the problem was to select a group of practice partners and managers in different offices and ask them to test the system for a representative set of their clients. A knowledge engineer supervised the process and ensured that all relevant comments made during the sessions were noted. The practice partners and managers familiarized themselves with ExperTAX by running random exercises and evaluating the system's responses. Once they were satisfied with the overall performance, they processed several client cases whose tax accrual and planning process had recently been completed, and compared the system's responses with their personal evaluations of the cases. Some issues were raised as to the clarity of the wording of specific questions, explanations, or recommendations. These issues were brought back to the experts who contributed those areas to the knowledge base and appropriate modifications of the knowledge base were made.

While the knowledge base validation was by no means exhaustive, it did suggest a procedure to be followed for the ongoing monitoring of the system's performance. For example, it is clear that practitioners in the field will continually face situations that might not be directly addressed by the system. In some cases, it will be desirable to enhance the knowledge base to handle the situation. This decision will be evaluated by the group within the organization responsible for maintaining the knowledge base. The knowledge maintenance group will be able to conduct a continuous validation of the knowledge base and an ongoing evaluation of its performance, as well as respond to changes in the environment that dictate modifications to its frames, rules, or facts.

ExperTAX at Work: A Sample Session

The first thing ExperTAX does is to present a menu that allows the user to make a selection from a series of options. While there are several possible choices nested in various menus, they basically deal with the choice between starting to work with a new client or continuing a job for a recurring client. To illustrate, assume we are starting with a new client, Artificial Company, a highly successful manufacturer of smart computers. ExperTAX would start by asking some questions from the

366

preliminary section of its knowledge base. It would quickly discover that Artificial accounts for its transactions on an accrual basis, is a privately held company, and is interested in tax minimization strategies. That general information would help Exper-TAX structure its search procedures and access frame sections so as to minimize unnecessary paths, and then load into memory those subsets of the knowledge base that contain rules more likely to be fired.

If we join an ExperTAX session where inventory issues related to the write-down of obsolete goods are being aired, the middle window on the ExperTAX screen displays the following question:

How does the client value these obsolete goods?

C—Cost

S—Selling price less direct cost of disposition

Summary: Net realizable value method

The user always has the option of answering the question, asking why the question is being asked, or skipping it altogether. He elects to answer C. The middle window of ExperTAX changes its display to the following:

Net realizable value method: Cost

Do the obsolete goods include any excess inventory items which are sold under an agreement which allows the client to repurchase the items at a predetermined price?

Summary: Thor Power Sham Transaction

At this point, the user elects to press the "Why" key. The lower window displays the following statement (the middle screen is still displaying the question):

The IRS has held that a sale of items under an agreement to repurchase at a predetermined price is not a sale and thus the excess inventory must be continued to be valued at cost.

Having read the explanation, the user answers the question and continues in a similar manner until ExperTAX finishes with the section and returns to the selection menu.

Once the user has finished the inventory section, he or she might elect to continue with another section, to look at the issues raised so far, or to print those issues and the accompanying documentation. If he or she elects to look at the issues raised, they would appear in the middle window, one at a time, together with the specific answers that triggered them. For example:

LIFO inventory may not be valued for tax purposes using the lower-of-cost-or-market method!! The IRS may terminate the taxpayer's LIFO election if LIFO inventory is valued at lower-of-cost-or-market. See Rev. Proc. 79-23. In limited situations, a taxpayer may be able to change to the Cost method and preclude the IRS from terminating its LIFO election. See Rev. Proc. 84-74. Market write-downs are required to be included in income under the provisions of Sec. 472(d) when LIFO is elected.★★

Reasoning:

Method of accounting for inventory:
LIFO
Inventory valuing: Lower of cost or market

★★—These issues require a change in accounting method for which approval must be requested within 180 days of the beginning of the tax year.

Once the user has answered all relevant sections, a complete printed report can be generated. The report would list all issues raised, segmented by type (e.g., accrual, planning). It would also list all questions asked and responses received during the session

368

and all notes taken by the user, whether voluntarily or because of prompts by the system to further explain an answer.

The ExperTAX report would then be used by the audit and tax managers or partners in charge of the engagement to prepare the final tax accrual and issue their tax planning recommendations to the client. Figure 4 shows part of the Planning Issues section of a typical ExperTAX report.

Issues and Suggestions For Further Research

A number of observations came to mind during the development of ExperTAX that may be of interest to researchers in identifying areas for further scholarly research or to those interested in experimenting with the technology. Some of those issues are discussed further below.

IDENTIFYING THE EXPERTS

An important element in the development of an expert system is the identification of experts. It is illogical to attempt to develop an expert system if recognized expertise does not exist. The identification of experts in the practice environment is a complicated task, perhaps because so many support mechanisms are used by practitioners for certain tasks (questionnaires, informal and formal consultations, texts, etc.). Together these support mechanisms contribute to the high quality of professional output. However, this may tend to make it difficult to identify a knowledge "czar" whose estimates, processes, or knowledge are clearly superior to what the system and mix of staff, support tools, and consulting skills produce in the rendering of normal client service. Clearly, the delivery of consistent, high-quality service is a primary objective for the practice of public accounting.

The more narrowly technical expertise is defined, the easier it may be to define an expert to begin the knowledge acquisition process. For example, a "LIFO" expert may be easier to identify than an "inventory" expert. But problems may arise if the LIFO expert is unfamiliar with the process being supported by the system. The expert may have little or no knowledge of the tax accrual or planning process and may be more attuned to the special project environment than the audit environment. Thus,

369

identifying the right "expert" may be a critical and difficult task in applying this technology to some types of problems.

KNOWLEDGE BASE MANAGEMENT

To justify the development of the initial system, knowledge base management and maintenance must be evaluated and considered feasible. From a distant vantage point, the development of an expert system may appear similar to the development process of any other software product. However, the parallels become blurred when one considers the specialized expertise necessary to evaluate or design system shells in a commercial environment, the interactive growth of the system (rather than the detailed design and programming stages), the more complicated issues of quality assurance, and the technical expertise needed to supervise system growth and updating.

Groups such as the national organizations of the functional specializations (e.g., audit and tax), EDP development groups, and decision support groups may all interact in the development process and are candidates for the continuing management and oversight of such systems. It remains an open but important question as to how the maintenance of such systems should be handled. The new technological environment provides an opportunity to reconsider the issue in light of organizational factors and efficiency.

SYSTEM DISTRIBUTION AND SECURITY

The existence of a competitive environment introduces significant issues into the expert system development process that are not encountered in more traditional software development environments. The handling of those issues may be influenced by whether the system will be sold commercially or will be resident only within the domain of the developer. One such issue that may be raised is whether the client will know (or care) that expert systems technology was applied during the engagement. This issue will affect the distribution process and publicity surrounding product releases.

Security is a heightened concern in expert systems. Such systems are no longer akin to computer software templates with only the capacity to manipulate numbers, but may also contain the accumulated knowledge of a firm. Communicating and distributing the product, protecting the software, and at the same time providing an environment that does not constrain authorized users in its application is a practical problem. While the value of such a system may diminish over time if not continuously updated and maintained, the implications of the system's misappropriation or unauthorized use or transfer are more significant than with many other software products. Accordingly, organizational and hardware and/or software controls assume increased importance in the design and distribution of such systems.

OTHER ISSUES

Some issues, such as the organization and mechanism by which projects are identified, assigned priority, managed, and maintained, are very important to developers of support systems but may yield limited independent research opportunities. Other issues that may have research potential flow from some of the aforementioned topics—for example:

1. The need to better understand what is meant by "expertise."

2. More tools and techniques to evaluate and simulate real-world environments.

3. Continued research into methods of extracting and capturing expertise.

The purpose of this paper has been to describe an application of AI technology (expert systems) to a real-world environment. It has attempted to go beyond a simple recitation of hardware and software options and capabilities, since that would hardly constitute a contribution to the research literature. We hope that the case presented will assist researchers in understanding more of the issues and areas that may be conducive to future research.

Conclusions

The ability to apply expert systems technology to develop audit practice aids is being made more economical and feasible by the increasing power and availability of micro-computers and expert systems tools that operate in that changing micro-computer environment. Since these trends for micro-computers and expert systems tools are likely to continue, increasing numbers and types of solutions to problems that could not be produced or delivered today cost-effectively will become possible in the future.

Once researchers have obtained a sufficient understanding of the mechanics of the technology, attention must be directed to identifying areas for future worthwhile scholarly research. The expert systems area needs this identification to remain a topic of useful research interest.

References

Dungan, C. W. and J. S. Chandler, "AUDITOR: A Microcomputer-Based Expert System to Support Auditors in the Field," *Expert Systems*, October 1985, pp. 210–221.

Elliott, R. K. and J. A. Kielich, "Expert Systems in Auditing," *Journal of Accountancy*, September 1985, pp. 130–131.

Gold Hill Computers, *Golden Common LISP*, Gold Hill Computers, 1985.

Longair, R., "What 'Expert Systems' Will Mean for Auditors," *Chartered Accountant in Australia*, November 1983, pp. 27–29.

Stoner, G., " 'Expert Systems': Jargon or Challenge?", *Accountancy* February 1985, pp. 142–145.

USC, *Symposium on Expert Systems and Audit Judgment*, University of Southern California, 1986.

———, *Symposium on Expert Systems and Audit Judgment Research*, University of Southern California, 1984.

Weiss, S. M. and C. A. Kulikowski, *A Practical Guide to Designing Expert Systems*, Rowman and Allenhead, 1984.

Winsten, P. H. and B. K. P. Horn, *LISP Second Edition*, Addison-Wesley, 1984.

Interim Report on the Development of an Expert System for the Auditor's Loan Loss Evaluation

KIRK P. KELLY, GARY R. RIBAR, and
JOHN J. WILLINGHAM

Introduction

The Audit Research Group at Peat Marwick Main &Co. has been interested in Artificial Intelligence and Expert Systems for a number of years. Under the auspices of the Research Opportunities in Auditing program, we have funded a number of academic research projects on the application of AI to the audit task. With the growing interest in the field and the advances in technology, it was decided to undertake a project oriented toward the development of an application model. The initial thrust was to build a prototype model for testing and evaluation with the implicit intent that the model would eventually be developed into a useful audit tool for field work. This paper reports on the project in terms of the rationale for the project, the current status of the project, and the future directions for this project.

Rationale for Expert Systems

The rapid advances in computer technology and ensuing applications requires that those engaged in the accounting and

373

auditing profession be involved in exploring new application opportunities. Artificial intelligence and expert systems are clearly in the forefront of these technologies; however the conventional wisdom of expert system developers suggests that considered applications ought to be limited to environments that exhibit certain characteristics. For example, it is suggested that there should be clearly definable experts in the problem task, that there should be appropriate measures of correct vs. incorrect judgments, and problems should be small yet have a high payoff.

The auditing environment has some unique characteristics that tend to make it a less likely candidate for successful deployment of expert systems. For example, many areas of auditing do not have a feedback mechanism that allows for determination of correct vs. incorrect decisions. Auditing is more process-oriented than results-oriented, wherein the quality of work is judged not by results, but by traces of process to be found in the work papers. Moreover, auditors learn acceptance of processes that may diverge significantly from their own as long as they "appear reasonable." A side effect of this is that we do not have a set of clearly defined "experts" whose technical skills find "material errors" in an audit with a significantly higher frequency than other auditors.

While these factors may mitigate against using expert systems, we do not believe that they are fatal. The issue surrounding the feedback and correctness of judgments in the audit environment is, we believe, a knowledge representation issue that will clarify itself through the knowledge engineering tasks. We also believe that there is expertise, albeit spread out, and that the professed need for a singular expert is a knowledge engineering problem that can and will be addressed pragmatically as the art of knowledge engineering advances.

We believe that AI technology offers the following significant benefits:

1) *Support of Field Work:* We believe that there are any number of applications for the AI technology that when harnessed, can be used as tools in the support of auditing field work, thereby freeing the auditor from many of the more mundane tasks and making the work of the auditor significantly more interesting. At the same time, the technology can lead to a greater consistency in the quality of field work, and hopefully reduce the time requirements for the field work.

2) *Diffusion of knowledge:* The complexity of modern audit-

ing as dictated by the complexity of modern business, leads to areas of audit specialization. Expertise relates to certain industries, such as banking or oil and gas, and across industries as in EDP auditing. Even within industries, there are pockets of expertise, e.g., in the banking industry there are those who are expert in auditing community banks, moderate size banks, and the extremely large banks. Additionally, many banks themselves perform in specialized industries, e.g., agricultural banks, oil and gas, etc. The data or information available in these varying circumstances require varying types of expertise. It is very difficult if not impossible for one auditor to be expert in all these areas. By capturing the expertise in specialized areas, however, we can provide knowledge where the expert is not available.

3) *Uniformity of documentation:* Through the proper design of an expert system, the required documentation to support a given judgment can be automatically provided as the output of the judgment exercise and included in the working papers of the audit. This not only provides uniformity of documentation, but also frees the auditor from another time-consuming and costly chore.

4) *Staff Training Aids:* Training is an extremely costly investment in a large public accounting firm. Technological advances are providing the potential vehicles for both increasing the effectiveness of training while concurrently reducing the huge costs involved.

5) *Research:* We should not forget the role of research in the design of expert systems. Designing expert systems is research-oriented, in that problems chosen are seldom well enough understood to be solved algorithmically. The knowledge engineering process can and should lead us to a greater understanding of the problem, thereby advancing our knowledge.

Based on the above reasoning, a decision was made to embark on the development of an expert system that would at once provide insights into the development process, provide knowledge about resource requirements, and produce a useful audit tool.

Selecting a Project

Since the project to be developed had multiple objectives, it was agreed that the project should be of a very limited scope and

375

nature, yet have the potential for a very high payoff. Additionally, since we were not overly committed to the expert system technology, we wanted to attempt the development at a minimal investment. The decision was therefore made to develop the model in a micro-computer environment using commercially available development shells.

Hoping for the potentially high payoff, we wanted to focus on a problem that was meaningful to our firm's audit practice and yet might be successful given the constraints we were imposing. Since bank audits are a large part of our audit practice, it was decided to focus on a problem in that area. We found that there was significant support from bank audit partners in the form of enthusiasm and willingness to invest expert bank auditors' time and cooperation. This was considered important, since we knew the development work would require a considerable amount of time and effort from bank experts at no small cost.

The next issue was to settle on a specific problem. We were guided by two considerations: 1) the problem had to be small enough to accomplish within a reasonable time, and 2) it had to be sufficiently important within the context of a bank audit. An area of bank audits that filled both of these requirements was the loan loss evaluation, the process of estimating the dollar amount of the reserve for the bank's portfolio of loans. This problem is basically a classification problem, which is a type of problem that has been successfully attacked by rule-based systems before. (Most commercially available developments tools for micro-computers are rule-based.)

Project Description

Since we did not have an in-house AI capability for the development of such a system, we contracted the project to an outside consultant. The consultant's project proposal suggested the following stages of development:

1) Review of current literature

2) Development of a preliminary model of the loan loss evaluation process

3) Implement the preliminary model as a computer program

4) Extended knowledge acquisition to include the process of expert loan evaluation

5) Combine knowledge into a final task expertise model and complete prototype expert system.

The proposal intitially indicated the above stages would require nine months to complete, employing one full-time consultant with the availability of audit experts in the loan loss evaluation task. To date we are somewhere in the fourth stage. What follows is a description of our model and how the system works.

Description of Model

For ease of reference, we have named the model CFILE, for *credit file* analysis. The current working model is based on the conceptual model shown in Figure 1. The model is modularized and illustrates the various factors going into the reserve judgment. The first column of factors to the left of the reserve conclusions are "level one subgoals" and the second column is composed of "level two subgoals" which go into the level one goals. For example, the conclusion on the current financial condition of the borrower is based on conclusions concerning the borrower's short term liquidity, financial risk, and business risk. These judgments are reached internally by the model with the exception of the industry profitability and volatility, which temporarily are user inputs.

The consideration underlying the control structure of CFILE is efficiency. Efficiency is often considered one of the hallmarks of the expert. Like an expert, the model is designed to arrive at a conclusion as soon as possible with the minimum amount of information.

A session with CFILE begins with screens explaining the purpose of CFILE and what it will do. Immediately following this the user is asked some basic information about the loan including its size, when it is due, and what kind of collateral and/or guarantees exist relating to the loan.

What CFILE asks next depends on the answers to the initial questions. If, for example, it is indicated that there are bank deposits pledged as collateral, CFILE will be ask a series of questions about those bank deposits. These include questions about access and financial strength, which are the two level two subgoals relating to collateral. CFILE will want to know whether or not the bank has the legal right to dispose of the collateral in the event of a default. It might also be asked if those bank deposits were pledged as security for another loan. If the model concludes that there is adequate access to those deposits and their strength is sufficient to cover the loan, the analysis would stop with a no-reserve decision.

If the bank deposits were not sufficient, the model would start dealing with the three level one subgoals that are needed to perform an analysis on an unsecured loan; current financial condition, overall loan history, and expected net cash flow. The model would ask the usual questions about hard data such as the current ratio of the borrower and would also ask about soft information, such as whether or not the borrower is planning any major projects that are going to be financed through the use of current assets. Again how many of these subgoals would be pursued and to what extent would depend on the situation. For example, if the loan were due in the next twelve months and the borrower had a very strong current financial condition, no reserve would be necessary and the system would conclude without asking any questions about loan history or expected cash flow.

The system has some other interesting features. In general the questions are asked in an abbreviated form. This is useful for the experienced user who will be familiar with the system. For example, the question about major projects alluded to above would appear as illustrated in Figure 2. However, help screens are available throughout to provide more details and guidance. The help screen for the same question as shown previously appears in Figure 3.

Another feature of the system is the ability to do a limited sensitivity analysis. It is possible for the user to see how sensitive the conclusion is to a particular question. For example, one might be interested in determining the impact of the loan officer's opinion of the borrower's liquidity (see Figure 4), given an otherwise constant set of input judgments.

Figures 5 and 6 illustrate the conclusion reports provided by the model. Both conclusions came from identical information except for the response to the question noted in Figure 4. One can see that in this case, the answer to the question had a fairly substantial impact. There is a difference in the evaluation of current financial condition which leads to different conclusions. In one case, we find an evaluation of the current financial condition of the borrower as weak and a conclusion of a 25 to 34%

reserve before considering collateral. In the other we find a moderate evaluation leading to a no-reserve conclusion.

This facility is useful to both user and developer. It gives the user who is uncertain about the appropriate response the ability to see the impact of alternatives without repeating a lot of data entry. It gives the developer a tool for testing the reasonableness of the rules in the system.

Perhaps the most important feature in this system is the user's ability to find out why a question is being asked. Through a function key one can look at the rule that has caused a specific question to be asked, and in turn ask about that rule. Figure 7 illustrates the screen that would appear asking about the loan officer's view of the borrower's liquidity. In this way it is always possible for the user to understand the line of reasoning that the system is using. This not only allows the user to understand the basis for the conclusion the system reached but facilitates review and avoids the blanket acceptance or rejection that is common with algorithmic systems. The model becomes a transparent box which is essential to the audit review process and it places the user in a position to be able to make constructive criticisms, which may aid in further system developemnt.

Limitations of Current Model

The current model has limited capabilities that have resulted from design decisions intended to keep the project manageable. CFILE applies only to loans that are due on demand or within one year and are either unsecured or secured by bank deposits or marketable securities. The model requires two years of audited financial information or three years of unaudited financial information on the borrower and is limited in its ability to perform and integrate cash flow analysis into its decision process. The model is further limited by its inability to deal with situations involving bankruptcy and liquidation analysis.

These limitations resulted from design decisions made early in the project and compose a major portion of the work yet to be performed. Again, our intent was to build a working prototype model that we hoped would be easily expanded to cover situations through the addition of modules to the knowledge base. It is envisioned that the prototype will then be of assistance in the future for knowledge engineering work.

With the prototype model working it was decided that we should test the system against the modeled "expert" to determine how well we captured the experts' decision model. A field test of CFILE was carried out in late February and early March of 1986.

Field Test of CFILE

For a number of reasons dealing with logistics, time constraints, and purpose, the field test was not set up as an experimental design, but rather as a pilot test to determine if we were on the right path with our model. It provided us the opportunity to deal with actual loan files in bank audit environments and to compare how different auditors performed the tasks in process as well as judgment.

The testing was carried out at four of our client banks. Two of the banks are large regional banks and the other two are smaller community banks. A total of sixteen cases were chosen either from client's listings of unsecured loans or with the assistance of the local audit team. First priority was given to loans which had a reserve allocated to them either by the audit team or by the bank's internal loan review department.

Each case was reviewed by each of three subjects, two at the partner level and one at the senior accountant level. The partners chosen were both from our bank audit practice. One of the partners was the "expert" employed in the development of the model. The other partner had only a cursory understanding of the model. The senior accountant had neither bank audit experience nor knowledge of the model to be tested. Our intent here was to see how much the model might assist the novice in the field and whether the senior accountant level is the appropriate level for performing this task during an actual audit.

Cases were reviewed first without the use of the model and then with the use of the model by each of the three people. Unfortunately, one of our partner subjects, the "expert," was unable to participate at the first bank setting due to illness and therefore only evaluated ten of the sixteen cases.

The results of the test are summarized in Figure 8. By way of explanation, CFILE uses nine reserve classifications: no reserve, 1 to 10%, 11 to 15%, 16 to 24%, 25 to 34%, 35 to 44%, 45 to 59%, 60 to 74%, and 75 to 100%. All analyses of the data were made using these ranges. If the reserve suggested by the subject fell into the same range or on the border, the comparison was marked OK. If the reserves fell in different ranges, the number of ranges by which they were different was noted. Starred entries indicate that one party suggested a reserve and the others did not. In addition the cases were analyzed for a comparison of the reserve vs. no reserve decision.

Comparisons were made between individual judgments, both with and without the use of the model. This allowed us to consider how closely the unaided partner's judgments agreed on the same loan and how closely the non-expert judgment agreed with the partners. Additional comparisons were made between the partners' judgments without the model in order to determine if the system was moving the non-expert judgment closer to the partner judgment. The loans were also analyzed according to whether no reserve or some reserve was required without respect to the reserve amount in order to test how the model did on the reserve vs. no reserve decision.

SUMMARY OF RESULTS

The following table summarizes the results of the individual's judgments compared to the model's judgments when the model is used by that individual.

	All Cases		Res vs. No Res		Reserve Cases	
	Agree	Disagree	Agree	Disagree	Agree	Disagree
Expert partner	90%	10%	90%	10%	100%	0%
Second partner	69%	31%	81%	19%	33%	67%
Senior	62%	38%	88%	12%	20%	80%

In terms of the test's first objective, i.e., determining whether the system is consistent with the judgments of the designated expert, the results are very positive. On ten loans, the model's judgment is consistent with the expert partner's judgment nine times. Reserve vs. no reserve decisions were consistent in 90% or nine out of ten loans. In three cases where the expert and the model both suggested a reserve, the reserve amounts are in agreement. On the one disagreement, the model suggested a reserve of 11%–15% while the partner suggested no reserve. We feel that these results are very positive and we intend to expand the scope of the model to produce a significant audit tool.

The second partner's percentages do not look quite so good in terms of agreement with the model. The second partner evaluated sixteen loans. The model agreed eleven times while disagreeing on five of those loans. These results become much more positive, however, when viewed in relation to other data. First of all, the percentages improve when looking at the agreement between a reserve vs. no reserve judgment. Here the model disagreed on only three loans. If we then scrutinize the degree of disagreements we note the model was never more than two classifications away from the second partner.

In attempting to explain the disagreement we note that the two partners' judgments, independent of the model, agree in nine of ten or 90% of the cases, (with only one classification separating them on the one disagreement). Since the use of the model is the only variable, and we know that the model is constant when given the same inputs, we hypothesize that the problem is not in the model itself, but in the user/model interface. We explain this as follows. The expert partner, who was instrumental in the design of the model, fully understands the questions and the impact of the responses on the model since he essentially wrote the questions. The other users of the system only had the cryptic wording of the questions and the help screens to indicate what the questions were intended to ask. To support this, we looked at the model's consistency of performance across users. We have forty-two runs of the model which consisted of running ten cases three times, once by each subject and six cases two times by the subjects which we designate as partner-2 and senior. This provides us with thirty-six two-way comparisons. Of these thirty-six, twenty runs involving ten of the sixteen cases had complete three way agreement. All of these agreed on zero reserve. In the additional sixteen comparisons, involving only six of the cases, the consistency of the model was significantly different, agreeing with itself only five times or 31% of the time when a reserve is indicated.

Based on this it appears that the model performs well on the easy cases that require no reserve, but struggles when the case becomes more difficult and where more user judgment comes into play. While one reason for the degradation may be the user interface, we also suspect that the depth of the knowledge base may be inappropriate, thereby requiring too much user judgment in interpreting what the model is asking for. If the model were sufficiently robust to deal with facts rather than user judgments about, for example, the strength of the current ratio, we would expect that a good deal of the inconsistency would disappear. Yet another cause may be the attempt to be too specific about the amount of the reserve. In attempting to specify the ranges, it is possible that we have overrefined, attempting to be more specific than the experts themselves. While this may be a cause, we tend to discount it somewhat since there was no definable pattern to the disagreements between the model and the user. The model was not consistently higher or lower nor off by one or two classifications. The differences appeared to be more random, leading us to believe that the shallowness of the model's knowledge coupled with the user/model interface are the major problems.

We could apply the same analysis to the figures associated with the senior subject performing the task; however, in this case, we are not primarily interested in whether the model agreed with the senior. Since one of the objectives of the model is to improve the inexperienced decision maker's ability to emulate the partner decison, the more important data deal with how the senior's judgment independent of the model compared to the partners' judgment independent of the model, and then, how the model altered the senior's judgment in relation to the partners.

The data indicated that the senior's unaided judgments agreed with the partners' unaided judgments in only 69% of the cases. This, of course, is expected based on experience and knowledge of the senior. Ideally, when using the model, the senior's judgments should be closer to the partners' decisions. The data show that the model did alter the senior's decision in four of the cases; however the model moved toward the partners' decision on only two loans and moved further away from the partners' decisions on the other two loans. While these results are inconclusive, we again hypothesize that the interface or communication problem cited above is the major culprit. In any event, negative conclusions should not be drawn on the basis of this test. Further testing with improved user interface will provide more insight in this matter.

SUMMARY OF FIELD TEST RESULTS

Based on the results obtained from the field test we conclude that the model performs very well within the stated limitations of the design and when used by the expert who was involved in the design of the model. We must also conclude that the model performs less well in the hands of others.

This problem can be thought of as an interface or communication problem that may be very simple to rectify, or may require a considerable amount of effort. The solution lies in determining how to structure the questions in such a manner that, given a specific loan, user responses to the model's questions will be consistent. Some of this may be accomplished through restructuring the existing questions and some may be accomplished through training users in the use of the model. A third and more time-consuming solution is to enhance the model's knowledge base to a depth that allows the model to work from more basic information.

Additional Insights From Field Testing

Through observation and recording verbalized protocols of certain cases we were able to gather additional knowledge that a) lends more support to our hypotheses above and b) provides a focus for the immediate development work that is required. Since the analysis of the protocols is not yet complete, we will informally discuss these in the following paragraphs.

We are pleasantly surprised by finding that our bank partner's unaided judgments agreed in nine out of ten loans and disagreed by only one reserve classification on the tenth. We are fortunate that this one case is included in the six cases for which we have protocols, and these protocols provide a plausible explanation for the partners' disagreement.

The second partner made reference in the protocol to having just recently read an article in a leading business journal concerning the borrower's history of problems, actions taken, and forecast for their survival. (In a later discussion we found he had read the article on the airplane en route to the lending bank's city). The expert partner made no such reference to any additional outside information. The article provided an optimistic outlook for the company's ability to turn its problems around and survive in its market. While both partners recommended a rather high reserve (75% and 50%), the second partner was lower, perhaps indicating the impact of the article on the amount of his reserve judgment. This would indicate the need for the model to account for more soft data in greater detail than currently available. This is further supported in other parts of the various transcripts.

While we have not yet completed our analysis of the protocols, they appear to provide clear evidence that there is a significant weighting differential based on two primary characteristics of data; the recency of the data in relation to the date of evaluation, and the independence of the source of the information. While this is not terribly surprising, it is surprising in that the degree of change in the weighting appears to be significant. While we have not yet drawn any conclusion, it appears at this point that the model will have to account for these information characteristics.

Another fact that is becoming increasingly evident is the need for the model to deal with cash flow. It was originally thought that cash flow projections would not be a significant factor until we expanded the scope of the model to longer time horizons. Our protocols clearly indicate otherwise. In fact, as soon as a loan is considered to be a candidate for a reserve, the cash flow model comes into play. Furthermore, as the loans become increasingly suspect, there is a point when the partners change to a liquidation model, attempting to determine how much the bank may salvage from a liquidation and/or bankruptcy proceeding. These are important considerations even within our limited scope model.

Conclusions

We are basically pleased with the results of our field test not only because they indicate the model provides results consistent with the expert, but also because we believe that the model will provide significant assistance to the senior in the field. While we are aware that in the longer term the model's knowledge base must be expanded depthwise, we also believe that many of the user/model communication problems can be rectified through a restructuring of questions and help screens, as well as training of the intended users.

Our intention is to pursue the development of this model in three directions: a) to improve the interface to the point we can release the model to the bank practice personnel for more extensive field tests, b) to improve the model's current scope by increasing the depth of its knowledge and provide the ability to deal with the cash flow and liquidation requirements, and c) to begin expanding the scope of the model to handle other types of security and time horizons.

FIGURE 1

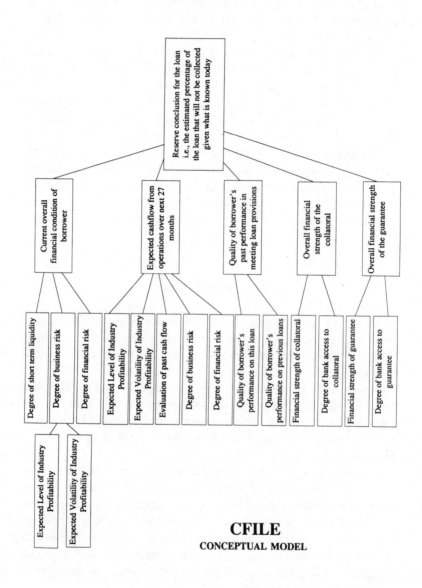

CFILE
CONCEPTUAL MODEL

FIGURE 2

PMM CFILE Preliminary Version 2.02 November 25, 1985

Select what describes

current assets used for new commitments

no

yes
2 UNKNOWN   3 REPORT   4 EXPAND   5 MENU   6 HELP

FIGURE 3

PMM CFILE

Based on your judgment, is there a significant chance the borrower will use a substantial amount (i.e., at least 25 percent) of current cash, accounts receivable, and marketable securities or incur a significant amount of new short term liabilities for commitments to finance a major new project?

A major new project could be an acquisition, stock repurchase or an expanded advertising campaign, or plant expansion program. A yes response would also be appropriate here if the borrower is involved in a continuing problem situation (e.g., a legal dispute) such that it is possible (FASB #5) that a new significant liability will emerge for the borrower.

enter no   if any new commitments will not use significant current assets or generate significant new current liabilities.

enter yes if new commitments will use significant current assets or generate significant new current liabilities.

---

2 RESTART   5 GO BACK   6 HELP   7 EXIT

FIGURE 4

PMM CFILE

Based on your judgment, if a set of financial statements were to be generated as of today, do the comments provided by the loan officer suggest to you that the loan officer, based on his/her knowledge of the borrower's current financial condition, believes the borrower is in a strong, moderate, or weak short term liquidity condition?

enter
   strong   if the loan officer believes the short term liquidity condition of the borrower is strong

   moderate   if the loan officer believes the short term liquidity condition of the borrower is moderate

   weak   if the loan officer believes the short term liquidity condition of the borrower is weak

---

2 RESTART   5 GO BACK   6 HELP   7 EXIT

FIGURE 5

PMM CFILE CONCLUSIONS

Client Name: ABC BankCorp
Audit Period: 12–31–85

Borrower: XYZ Company

Analysis prepared by Joe Auditor on 12–1–85

Extent of available information is adequate.
Based on the available information, the following factors are indicated:

Industry prospects: expected profitability = moderate.
                     expected profit volatility = high.

Intermediate conclusions (scaled from very weak to very strong):
   Current financial condition is weak.
   Future cash flow potential is weak.
   Borrower's past loan performance is moderate.

The amount of the loan is $150,000.

The loan is covered by bank deposits having an accessible value of $100,000. Of this, $90,000 is considered available to cover the loan.

No guarantee is available for this loan.

A reserve of 25 to 34% of the loan would appear appropriate, if it were unsecured. After considering the collateral available, no reserve would appear to be required.

I agree with the conclusion suggested by the system and the underlying reasoning.

_____, Preparer.

FIGURE 6

PMM CFILE CONCLUSIONS

Client Name: ABC BankCorp
Audit Period: 12–31–85

Borrower: XYZ Company

Analysis prepared by Joe Auditor on 12–1–85

Extent of available information is adequate.
Based on the available information, the following factors are indicated:

Industry prospects: expected profitability = moderate.
                    expected profit volatility = high.

Intermediate conclusions (scaled from very weak to very strong):
    Current financial condition is moderate.
    Future cash flow potential is weak.
    Borrower's past loan performance is moderate.

The amount of the loan is $150,000.

The loan is covered by bank deposits having an accessible value of $100,000. Of this, $90,000 is considered available to cover the loan.

No guarantee is available for this loan.

No reserve appears to be required.

I agree with the conclusion suggested by the system and the underlying reasoning.

_____, Preparer.

FIGURE 7

PMM CFILE Preliminary version 2.02 5 November, 1985
The highlighted fields indicate the antecedent
and conclusion being pursued.
The rule currently being pursued is:

RULE 3850
IF
PMM quick ratio is (are) weak
AND current ratio is (are) moderate
AND current ratio trend is (are) decreasing
AND loan officer liquidity judgment is (are) strong
THEN
stliquid is (are) very strong CF 0
AND stliquid is (are) strong CF 0
AND stliquid is (are) moderate CF 100
AND stliquid is (are) weak CF0
AND stliquid is (are) very weak CF0

2 ALL RULE   3 OR CLASS   4 FORWARD   5 GO BACK
6 HELP   7 EXIT

Figure 8
CFILE TEST RESULTS

Loan	PMM or Bank Eval	Expert Partner w/o CFILE	Expert Partner w/ CFILE	Expert Partner Difference	Second Partner w/o CFILE	Second Partner w/ CFILE	Second Partner Difference	Senior w/o CFILE	Senior w/ CFILE	Senior Difference	Partner Divergence	Average Ptr Judgement (AP) w/o CFILE	AP vs Snr w/o CFILE	AP vs Snr w/ CFILE
D2	n/a	n/a	n/a	n/a	0	0	OK	0	0	OK	n/a	0	0 OK	OK
D3	0	n/a	n/a	n/a	0	0	OK	0	0	OK	n/a	0	0 OK	OK
D8	n/a	n/a	n/a	n/a	0	0	OK	0	0	OK	n/a	0	0 OK	OK
D10	0	n/a	n/a	n/a	0	0	OK	10	0	OK	n/a	0	0 -1	-2
D11	0	n/a	n/a	n/a	0	13	*2	18	20	OK	n/a	0	0 -2	
D13	0	n/a	n/a	n/a	10	0	*1	20	0	*2	n/a	10	10	1
P1	2	0	13	*2	0	13	*2	25	52	2	OK	0	0 -3	-4
P3		0	0	OK	0	0	OK	0	0	OK	OK	0	0 OK	OK
P4	68	67	67	OK	75	67	OK	60	40	1	1	71	71 OK	
P6	52	75	87.5	OK	50	87.5	OK	60	13	4	OK	62.5	62.5 OK	5
M-P1	n/a	0	0	OK	0	0	OK	0	0	OK	OK	0	0 OK	OK
M-P2	n/a	0	0	OK	0	0	OK	0	0	OK	OK	0	0 OK	OK
M-P4	n/a	0	0	OK	0	0	OK	0	0	OK	OK	0	0 OK	OK
M-D5	n/a	0	0	OK	0	0	OK	0	0	OK	OK	0	0 OK	OK
M-D6	n/a	87.5	87.5	OK	90	52	2	70	87.5	1	OK	88.75	88.75	1
M-D7	n/a	0	0	OK	0	0	OK	0	0	OK	OK	0	0 OK	OK

Note: Evaluations are given in percentages of the outstanding loan balance.
Differences are in number of CFILE categories.
Starred differences also indicate a disagreement about the reserve vs. no reserve decision.

SUMMARY STATISTICS	Expert Partner w/ & w/o CFILE		Second Partner w/ & w/o CFILE		Senior w/ & w/o CFILE		Agreement between Partners		Average Partner Judgment vs. Senior w/o CFILE		Average Partner Judgment vs. Senior w/ CFILE	
ALL CASES												
AGREEMENTS	9	90%	11	69%	10	63%	9	90%	11	69%	11	69%
DISAGREEMENTS	1	10%	5	31%	6	38%	1	10%	5	31%	5	31%
AVE. CATEGORIES DISAGREEMENT	1		1.8		1.8		1		1.6		2.6	
RESERVE VS NO RESERVE DECISIONS												
AGREEMENTS	9	90%	13	81%	14	88%	10	100%	13	81%	13	81%
DISAGREEMENTS	1	10%	3	19%	2	13%	0	0%	3	19%	3	19%
CASES WITH RESERVES												
AGREEMENTS	3	100%	1	33%	1	20%	2	67%	2	50%	1	33%
DISAGREEMENTS	0	0%	2	67%	4	80%	1	33%	2	50%	2	67%
AVE. CATEGORIES DISAGREEMENT	0		2		2		1		1		3	

393

Expert Systems: What They Mean To The Executive

EFRAIM TURBAN and
THEODORE J. MOCK

"The real existence, the real promise of Artificial Intelligence, is that all those fairy tales that we have heard about, talking lamp posts and such, are not just fairy tales. Soon they will all start coming true."

Allen Newell
Founding President of the American Association of Artificial Intelligence

"Artificial Intelligence is here!" announced a 1984 cover story in *Business Week.* Indeed, the era of "artificial" intelligence and "expert" systems may be upon management, as is evidenced by the flow of reports about successful applications of Artificial Intelligence (AI) in publications such as *Computerworld* and *Datamation.* Some call it the greatest technological advance since the control of fire by man. It is clearly the newest buzzword in managerial circles. The American Association for Artificial Intelligence reports that close to 5000 people attended its most recent annual meeting. Governments and companies are pouring millions of dollars into Artificial Intelligence research, and stiff international competition is developing between Japan, England, and the United States in AI research.

Is AI a reality? Not yet, according to a lead story in a 1984 issue of *Fortune* and according to a new book titled *The AI Business.* Caught between the unprecedented optimism on the one hand, and the cautious pessimism on the other, is the corporate executive. Should he join the bandwagon now, so he won't miss a great opportunity? Should she wait to see if AI is just another fad? Or should he take an intermediate course of action? And what is this all about, anyway?

To help executives think more clearly about AI, we've assembled a number of questions that are frequently asked by executives about that portion of AI called Expert Systems. Because we believe that Expert Systems (ES) could have a major effect on corporations in the near future, we offer answers that are based on information collected from several users of ES, including General Electric, Litton, IBM, Digital Equipment, Xerox, Hughes Aircraft, TRW, Fairchild Industries, and Texas Instruments.

Question No. 1: *What are Expert Systems?*

Answer: Expert Systems are decision-making or problem-solving computer programs based on research in Artificial Intelligence. These systems have reached a level of performance comparable to that of a human expert in certain complex (usually narrow) problem areas.

The notion of an Expert System is so fluid that the definition is changing as quickly as the field itself. *"It's a moving target,"* according to Xerox Corporation, which is developing an ES to aid in the design of copying and publishing equipment. Perhaps the best advice regarding the definition of ES is given by Litton Corporation: *"Do not try to define ES; try to find out how to make it work."*

The difficulty in defining ES has already resulted in several computer products that are labeled ES, but are probably not. To be classified as an ES, a computerized system should properly exhibit certain characteristics and capabilities (which brings us to our next question!).

Question No. 2: *What are the major characteristics and capabilities of Expert Systems?*

Answer:

- Reasoning capabilities.
- Use of bodies of knowledge (expertise) in the form of facts and procedures to solve complex, unstructured problems in a specific problem area.

396

- Use of informal, judgmental knowledge to conduct effective search for "good-enough" (heuristic) solutions.
- Effective and efficient problem-solving expertise.
- Built-in explanations so that the manager can understand the assumptions, the line of reasoning, and the process leading to a solution generated by the computer.
- Capabilities in several phases of the decision-making process as well as in different decision-making approaches.
- End-user oriented, flexible, and non-threatening; its dialogue is conducted in everyday English.

In summary, an ES replaces human intelligence with machine intelligence for certain tasks, although *critical* tasks still must be done by human minds.

Question No. 3: *What are the major advantages of ES?*

Answer:

- Preserving, replicating, and disseminating crucial expertise that could otherwise be in danger of extinction, or in short supply, or is inequitably distributed through the corporation.
- Saving money (since human expertise is usually very expensive).
- Better quality. Some ES prove to do a better job than humans (that is, they make fewer mistakes, they are more consistent, and their advice is easily documentable).
- Handling complexities. ES can handle unstructured and complex problems that no other *computerized* system can.
- Compatibility with many managers' decision styles (since ES programs are based on judgment).
- Use as training vehicles both for nonexperts and for improving the expertise of experts.
- Freeing experts from simple and routine advice and activities, and enabling them to concentrate on more creative tasks such as research and development.
- Improving customer service levels due to the timeliness of service. (You do not have to wait for the human expert to arrive.

Question No. 4: *Can you give specific examples of successful ES applications in business?*

Answer: The following are representative examples:

☐ *Expert Configurator (XCON).* This program is used to make custom designs of Digital Equipment Corporation's computer systems (VAX-11). Using a set of more than 2500 rules, XCON examines a customer's specifications, determining whether all the necessary components are included. It then draws a set of diagrams to show the proper relationships among the components. Prior to the use of this ES, errors by human checkers had been costing $10–20 million per year; after, most of the errors were eliminated.

☐ *Computer-Aided Trouble-Shooting System (CATS-1).* CATS-1 is one of the first ES designed for routine operation on the shop floor and the first to run on a micro-computer for industrial use (at General Electric). This system included, in 1983, over 500 rules to cover about 50% of the problems that locomotive repair shops encounter. (1500 rules were expected by 1985, covering over 80% of the problems.)

☐ *Automated Cable Expertise (ACE).* This ES was developed by Bell Labs to monitor the repair of phone cables. By zipping through regular maintenance reports, the system is able to pinpoint spots for repairs and preventive maintenance.

☐ *Database Access and Analysis.* The U.S. Treasury developed an ES that automatically reads and analyzes large databases for patterns and trends so that critical situations requiring human action could be identified. A similar ES was developed by the International Monetary Fund, where the database is on a mainframe but the analysts use their personal computers for accessing the data and conducting analyses.

☐ *Maintenance of Complex Equipment.* Sophisticated electronic systems pose considerable maintenance problems. An example of an ES that handles such problems is ARBY, which was developed at General Dynamics Corporation to diagnose malfunctions. Another example is DART, used at IBM to diagnose "sick" computers.

398

☐ *Tax Advisor (TAD).* This system is not only able to fill out IRS tax forms, but also advises the user on issues such as what income must be reported, and what expenses are deductible. The Tax Advisor could become a forerunner of a home ES, since its future price is estimated to be less than $10,000 (down from the current $60,000). TAD could also be used on a time-sharing basis, since one uses it very infrequently (see Question 9). Presently, H&R Block is negotiating with the manufacturer about installing TAD in its local offices.

☐ *Auditing (AUDITOR).* This ES can assist auditors in assessing a company's allowance for bad debts. The knowledge was captured from expert auditors who listed the factors that are important in examining the allowances, their relative importance, and their interrelationships.

☐ *Intelligent Factories.* Westinghouse, together with scientists from Carnegie-Mellon University, developed an ES that ensures that all the machines in a factory are working at a high level of efficiency. The system, called the *intelligent factory,* can monitor the scheduling of machine tasks to minimize downtime. In addition, the system is able to design work to flow through a plant as quickly as possible. The system monitors breakdowns and presents the manager with the best alternative method of production until repairs can be made.

☐ *Corporate Planning.* Arthur D. Little, Inc., is developing an ES for the strategic management of technology in a company. This system, labeled CORP, is designed to aid in technology planning, resource allocation, and analysis of the impact of new technologies on a business. The system can be used to analyze complex sets of relationships between products and technology.

Question No. 5: *What types of problems can I solve with an ES?*

Answer: In theory, an ES could replace any expert, in any area of specialty. However, applications such as those listed in the answer to Question No. 4 can be classified into the following generic categories:

- Diagnosing faults and problems.
- Repairing deficiencies discovered in the diagnosis.
- Monitoring and controlling (comparing performance to plan, signaling exceptions).
- Analyzing data and determining causal relationships.
- Predicting and forecasting.
- Interpreting information.
- Planning and scheduling.
- Instructing and training.
- Designing (software, production process).
- Improving managerial actions (managing projects and factories).

Question No. 6: *What Expert Systems are now in the developmental stage?*

Answer: It is very difficult to document what is being done since most companies expect their systems to give them a competitive advantage and therefore consider R&D information confidential. But here are our best guesses:

Finance and Banking
- Stock portfolio management.
- Designing information systems for retail banks.
- Asset-liability management.
- Loan approvals and auditing.

Operations (production)
- Fault diagnosis in networks and machines equipment.
- Preparing complex bids (in the construction industry).

Accounting and Auditing
- Estate planning and tax advisement.
- Executing and analyzing internal auditing.
- Charging back costs to users in a computer time-sharing system.
- Auditing advanced EDP systems.

Marketing and Sales

• Packaging insurance products.

General Management

• Advice on application of management by objectives.

• Selection and use of forecasting techniques.

• Analysis of failing companies.

• Scheduling business trips and business meetings.

Computers and Information Systems

• Data center evaluation.

• Selecting and maintaining hardware and software.

• Designing chips and integrated circuits.

• Information resource management and retrieval.

Human Resources

• Matching personnel to jobs.

• Arranging compensation packages.

Question No. 7: *How much does it cost and how much can I save?*

Answer: To build a complex ES may take fifteen to twenty man-years of work at a cost of several million dollars. However, using certain ES tools (such as generators) can reduce the cost and the construction time significantly.

An Expert Systems generator is software used to build an ES. Together with special hardware, generators cost in the range of $50,000 to $250,000. To this basic cost, one should add the cost of knowledge acquisition, training, support services, and the like. ES generators for micro-computers are selling for as little as $95, but they are limited in their capabilities. Time-sharing and leasing options are available from several vendors. A general purpose ES (such as the Management Edge) that performs *limited* organizational diagnosis sells for only $295. There are very few general purpose ES on the market at the present time, but their use for the home may mushroom soon.

The savings one may realize from using ES will vary. A typical consultation with an ES for hard-rock mineral exploration costs $10, versus a charge of $1,000 by a human consultant. As with

401

any new technology, savings are difficult to estimate, since they must include developmental costs and intangible benefits. Digital Equipment reports annual savings of $15 million from ES.

Most users report that they get *"a reasonable return on their investment,"* but they emphasize that the efficient solving of complex problems is more important than the dollars and cents saved.

Question No. 8: *Can I use ES on my existing computer?*

Answer: Most large scale ES require special computers (such as a LISP machine). However, there is a clear trend for producing standard software which will fit all sizes of computers.

Question No. 9: *Can I time-share ES?*

Answer: At the present time, there are very few ES available on a time-sharing basis. But we know of at least the following two systems that are currently in place:

☐ *Questware* (available from Dynaquest Corporation) helps business people to select hardware and software. To use the system, a business person calls an 800 number and completes a thirty-minute telephone interview. From the response to the question, *"What kind of business are you in?"* the computer develops additional questions which it then asks the client. The client gets a printed report outlining suggested types of hardware and software, price ranges, and training and support requirements. The cost of the advice is only $189. The system is being expanded to include problem-solving and diagnostic sessions regarding computer systems.

☐ *The Intelligent Machine Model (TIMM).* While Questware is a general purpose ES, TIMM represents a time-sharing approach to ES construction. Available from General Research Corporation, TIMM is an ES generator.

Question No. 10: *What are the major limitations of ES?*

Answer: The following limitations have been reported by users of ES:

- Expertise is hard to extract from humans (because experts have difficulty in explaining how they make decisions).
- The approach of each expert to situation assessment may be different.
- ES decisions are very uninspired as compared with those of a creative natural intelligence.
- It is difficult, even for a super-expert, to abstract good situation assessments when he or she is under time pressure.
- The knowledge acquisition usually requires a Knowledge Engineer.

Question No. 11: *And what about future ES?*

Answer: Some of the limitations discussed in the previous question may be eliminated by development of smarter systems.

One of the ways to look at future ES is to examine the plans for the so-called Fifth Generation Computer project in Japan. The project is developing a faster, denser circuitry to create a new class of superintelligent computers. These applications systems will handle many forms of input: voice, handwritten characters, video images, and printed text. These computers will be able to learn from experience, associate, draw inferences, and make decisions. They will be the engine of the future information society, small, robust, and inexpensive. They will appear as a utility, as commonplace and easy to use as the telephone.

There is no doubt that the Fifth Generation Computer and similar research efforts will eliminate some of the ES limitations; others may never be removed. The machine, no matter how smart it is, will be inferior in some areas to the human mind. (For an explanation of the inherent limitations of AI, see Charles Van Doren's "The Future of Knowledge Systems" *NM* Vol. 2, No. 1.)

Question No. 12: *What are some of the major questions to which I'll need answers if I decide to start using ES?*

Answer: Depending on the situation, you are most likely to encounter the following questions:

- Where should ES be applied?

- What vendor(s), software, and/or hardware should be used?

- Should you buy, lease, or time-share the computer technology?

- What can be expected from an ES and when?

- How are AI experts recruited?

- How are the experts you want to use as a source of knowledge to be identified, and how can their knowledge be acquired?

- What changes in the structure of your organization will occur (for example, in the distribution of power)?

- How is an AI consultant selected?

What are the answers to these problems? It depends; answers are situational, and many of these problems cannot be solved (at least for the moment) by a machine. For the time being, you will have to rely on human expertise.

Question No. 13: *So what should I do?*

Answer: A progressive company can no longer ignore projections like a recent one by Arthur D. Little, Inc., which estimated that the AI field could be $11 billion in the 1990s. All the same, it is clear that the risk of investing money in AI is very high. Hence, a reasonable approach is the one adopted by Litton Industries, where a team of top executives recommended making a commitment to ES, but to be cautious. In other words, you should undertake ES slowly and carefully. The time-sharing availability should be carefully explored before any purchase is made. On the other hand, buying an ES generator for a micro can be a modest way to start. The availability of ES generators provides a unique opportunity to participate in the AI business with little cost and risk. The least that you can do is join the American Association of Artificial Intelligence (AAAI) and attend their annual meetings.

AI capabilities provide an opportunity to do business differently, but adopting and applying the technology requires managerial innovation, since the technology is tentative and developing rapidly; therefore, it sometimes fails. They also may have a significant impact on organizational structure, on power allocations, on the number of positions—in short, on people. Therefore, the use of ES technology must be planned explicitly. But when used with insight, it pays.

The Mortgage Loan Analyzer— An Expert System for Underwriting Residential Mortgage Loans

DRAKE W. SMITH and DAVID J. TEMPLE

One of the most important steps in lending money to a potential homeowner is underwriting the loan application package. Underwriters analyze data about the borrowers and the property and decide if the loan represents an acceptable risk. Their role is to ensure that all secondary mortgage market, government, and lending institution requirements are met. The burden of these requirements has increased as the role of the secondary market, competition for customers, and concern over the quality of loan portfolios have escalated in the past decade. This article discusses the development of the Mortgage Loan Analyzer (MLA) expert system. MLA assists underwriters by managing the detailed requirements and general rules of thumb, allowing the underwriter to concentrate on making subjective decisions and evaluating risk. Arthur Andersen & Co. developed

MLA in Seattle and anticipates several installations will result from a national marketing effort begun on 1 June 1987.

The first section of this article presents an overview of MLA. The second section describes how underwriting was identified as a potential information systems application and why expert systems technology was selected. Section three describes the people involved in creating MLA and how their qualifications and personal characteristics made the development possible. The fourth section outlines the development process and critical success factors, and the final section examines the requirements for successful implementation and describes the reactions of underwriters and management to MLA.

I. The Mortgage Loan Analyzer (MLA)

Arthur Andersen & Co. developed MLA as a tool for underwriters. The system helps underwriters make approval decisions on residential mortgage loans. It analyzes each loan for potential risks and evaluates the loan's adherence to underwriting guidelines and policies. MLA uses expert systems technology to improve the quality of both the lending decision and the supporting documentation.

MLA helps reduce risk by assisting the underwriter in evaluating hundreds of factors from numerous documents. The underwriting process is both difficult and risky because of the large amount of information in a loan file. MLA handles much of the detail, freeing the underwriter to handle more analytical and judgmental tasks. Thus, MLA improves the consistency of decisions by evaluating all loans using the same criteria. It also records the underwriter's reasons for accepting or denying a loan and provides an expert system-generated report documenting the supporting analysis. Another advantage of MLA is it allows lending institutions to use underwriting expertise to its fullest potential. Experienced underwriters are a scarce and costly resource. During periods of high volume, mortgage companies historically have increased underwriting staffs by hiring experience away from competitors. Many underwriters experience stress from the details and pressures of the profession. These factors culminate in high turnover rates and shortages of experienced personnel.

MLA's processing is broken into four steps (Exhibit I). First, data from the loan application, credit report, verification of

EXHIBIT I.

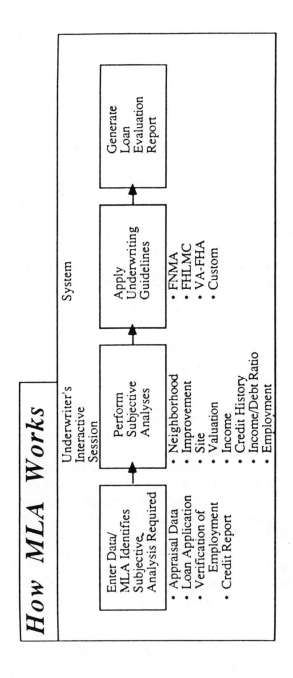

How MLA Works

System

Underwriter's Interactive Session

Enter Data/ MLA Identifies Subjective Analysis Required
- Appraisal Data
- Loan Application
- Verification of Employment
- Credit Report

Perform Subjective Analyses
- Neighborhood
- Improvement
- Site
- Valuation
- Income
- Credit History
- Income/Debt Ratio
- Employment

Apply Underwriting Guidelines
- FNMA
- FHLMC
- VA-FHA
- Custom

Generate Loan Evaluation Report

employment, and property appraisal is downloaded to MLA from the institution's automated loan origination system or entered manually by a clerk. The underwriter is then prompted to review specific aspects of the loan package, such as the borrower's future employment prospects or knowledge of the property's neighborhood. Next, secondary market, government, and lender guidelines are applied to the subjective information and raw data.

The Loan Evaluation Report is then generated. It lists MLA's inferences on the positive and negative aspects of the loan and conditions that must be satisfied before approval. The underwriter's rationale for accepting or rejecting the loan is included. This formatted report replaces the notes typically written by the underwriter and becomes part of the permanent loan file (Exhibit II).

Note that the system does not make the approval decision. Extreme circumstances may compensate for some of the advantages and disadvantages listed on the report. Therefore, ultimate responsibility for the lending decision rests with the underwriter.

II. Applying Expert Systems Technology to a Business Problem

In mortgage lending institutions throughout the country, underwriters have stacks of loan files on their desks. At the same time, potential homeowners spend a month or more waiting to find out if their loans have been approved. Underwriting is a key bottleneck and the main business problem in residential mortgage lending. This bottleneck is caused by three factors. First, underwriting expertise is expensive and has an inelastic supply in the short run. Second, each loan takes thirty to ninety minutes to review. Third, large fluctuations in loan volume cause unstable work loads. Reducing any of these factors would produce a significant payback.

Expert systems technology was selected as the tool to solve this business problem. The appropriateness of this selection is evident when the underwriting task is subjected to Waterman's (1986, Chapter 11) guidelines. These guidelines determine whether or not the development of an expert system is possible, justifiable, and appropriate.

EXHIBIT II.

Loan Evaluation Results
Loan Number 151977

Borrowers: #1–John Smith
#2–Sue Smith

Property Address: 12345 9th Ave., Kent, WA 98032

Messages: Exceeds FNMA Total Obligations-to-Income ratio guidelines.

1. Standard Calculations:
    a. Loan to Value: 85.0%
       It is advisable to reduce the loan amount for the following reasons:
       Borrower(s) credit history shows problems.
    b. Income Ratios:
       Housing Expenses to Income: 26.3%
       Total Obligations to Income: 37.3% (Exceeds FNMA guidelines)

2. Credit Analysis:
    Borrower #1—
    Borrower has good employment and income stability but borrower has a history of slow payments.
    Borrower #2—
    Borrower has good employment and income stability but credit history shows actions taken against borrower for non-payment of obligations.

3. Income and Expense Analysis:

Monthly Income	$ 3303
Housing Expenses/Month	$ 868
Liabilities/Month	$ 365
Total Liquid Assets	$ 8389
Total Debt (non-REO)	$ 6209

4. Neighborhood Analysis: Good
    Favorable Factors:
       Comments are favorable. Neighborhood is predominantly owner-occupied and property is priced at or near the predominant price for the neighborhood.
    Unfavorable Factors: Neighborhood is mixed use.

411

5. Site Analysis: Good
   Favorable Factors:
   Comments are favorable and site has a good view.
   Unfavorable Factors:
   Utilities are not all publicly provided.

6. Improvements Analysis: Good
   Favorable Factors:
   Improvements have energy efficient items. Other comments are favorable, and property's effective age is lower than its actual age.
   Unfavorable Factors:
   Combined effective age and remaining economic life shows an unusually long life for improvements.

   7. Valuation Analysis: Fair
   Favorable Factors:
   None
   Unfavorable Factors:
   Property has a large amount of physical deterioration.
   Comparable #1—
   Net adjustments exceed 15% of sales price.
   Comparable #2—
   Appraiser has not adjusted for sales concessions.
   Comparable #3—
   Price/living area out of line with Subject. Square footage not similar to Subject, and property is located too far from subject.

LOAN CONDITIONS

1. Mortgage insurance is required by FNMA.
2. A satisfactory certification or inspection report is required for the private water supply.

1. Is expert system development possible? Expert systems can be developed when all of the following are true (pp. 128–129):

- The task does not require common sense
- The task requires only cognitive skills
- Experts can articulate their methods
- Experts agree on solutions
- Genuine experts exist
- The task is not too difficult
- The task is not poorly understood

By limiting the scope of the system, it was possible to develop MLA using expert systems technology. According to the list of requirements above, completely automating the underwriting function would not be possible using this approach. The subjective aspects of the underwriting task—those that require applying common sense, evaluating risk or using judgment—clearly can not be automated. However, much of the task is performed using rules of thumb that can be articulated by experts and are standard in the industry. For example, several above-average appraisal ratings for a neighborhood indicate the subject property is in an especially good neighborhood. In addition, although underwriting is subjective to some extent, experts exist and can agree on a basic set of rules comprising sound underwriting practice. Because most of the secondary market and government requirements are already documented, the task, although complex, is well understood and not prohibitively difficult. It is also important to note that the volatility of these requirements makes developing and maintaining an underwriting system in a third or fourth generation language prohibitively expensive.

2. Is expert system development justifiable? Expert systems technology can be justified by any of the five criteria below (pp. 130–131):

- The task solution has a high payoff
- Human expertise is being lost
- Human expertise is scarce

413

• Expertise is needed in many locations
• Expertise is needed in a hostile environment

The residential mortgage loan underwriting process can be justified using three of these criteria: scarce expertise, a high payoff, and multiple locations. The first characterizes human expertise as a limited resource. Although there is currently no critical shortage, experienced underwriters are a valuable resource. If underwriter productivity can be increased and expertise duplicated with an expert system, then the effort and expense required for development is justified. The fourth item above refers to expertise being needed in many locations. Many institutions would like to decentralize underwriting geographically so underwriters are more in touch with local market conditions. However, this is often outweighed by the need for centralized control and uniform underwriting practices. By using MLA, an organization gains control over how this function is performed.

3. Is expert system development appropriate? An expert system is appropriate when the nature, complexity, and scope of the task satisfy the following requirements (pp. 131–133):

Nature	• The task requires symbol manipulation
	• The task requires heuristic reasoning
Complexity	• The task is not too easy
Scope	• The task has practical value
	• The task is of manageable size

Since much of the information on a loan application is symbolic and the process of balancing advantages and disadvantages is heuristic, the nature of the underwriting task fits well in this framework. Given the voluminous requirements established by the Federal National Mortgage Association, the Federal Home Loan Mortgage Corporation, the Veteran's Administration, the Federal Housing Administration, and other secondary market investors, the underwriting task meets the criteria above for complexity. In regard to scope, there is great practical value to improved lending practices for banks and their customers. Finally, analyzing a loan package is a large task. However, because it can be broken down into different modules for employment, income, credit history, valuation analysis, etc., the expertise already has a logical structure. This structure makes its large size manageable. Therefore, an expert system solution to this problem is possible, justifiable, and appropriate.

III. The People Involved

The domain expert and knowledge engineer involved in the project were critical to the success of MLA's development. The domain expert had the background, experience, and credentials to qualify as a true mortgage loan underwriting expert. She had a broad perspective of the domain due to her extensive experience in banking and mortgage lending. Prior to underwriting, she was employed both as a bank branch manager and a legal secretary, and was a veteran of eighteen home purchases. This background allowed her to view underwriting, a process which is typically isolated from the customers, as an integral part of the mortgage industry.

After holding these positions, she worked at her current savings and loan company as an underwriter for five years. When promoted to Assistant Vice President, Senior Underwriter, the additional responsibility further broadened her perspective of the underwriting task and validates her credentials as a domain expert. This company, an Arthur Andersen & Co. client, is one of the larger loan originators in Washington state. It has an extremely low mortgage delinquency rate and a very high rate of loan acceptance by FNMA.

In addition, the expert was interested in using systems technology, specifically, and learning about computers in general. As an example of her commitment to applying systems technology, she initiated the use of word processing in her department. She also attempted to generate enthusiasm for the MLA project at all levels within the organization. This not only created interest among management, but also helped the underwriters gain confidence in the system by knowing that an expert they respected had a direct role in developing MLA. Finally, the domain expert understood the systems development process, allowing her to communicate effectively with the knowledge engineer.

The MLA knowledge engineer, a senior analyst with Arthur Andersen & Co., worked as both a functional and technical analyst in previous information systems projects. Although she did not have extensive mortgage lending experience, her commitment to learning the underwriting task and the banking industry by consulting secondary sources (e.g., Hess, 1986), and her close contact with the domain expert, allowed her to quickly understand the mortgage lending environment. The combination of the knowledge engineer's commitment and the motivation and availability of the domain expert were key factors in the successful development of the Mortgage Loan Analyzer.

IV. System Development

After determining that expert systems technology was appropriate for this application, the next step was to determine the implementation hardware and software. In order to implement MLA in mortgage lending institutions nationwide, the system had to run on their conventional data processing equipment: micro-computers, mini-computers, or mainframes. The expert system shell, AION Corporation's Application Development System (ADS), was chosen for a number of reasons. First, ADS ran on IBM-AT compatibles and System 370 architecture mainframes. It was a rule-based system and thus followed the structure of the expertise the system would model. Underwriting also required a backward chaining knowledge base. As issues are identified in the loan file, further research produces evidence that supports or refutes the issue. For example, if the loan-to-value ratio is greater than 90%, the underwriter would look for adequate reserves in savings to cover at least three payments. The shell was also strong procedurally, which allowed the knowledge engineer to organize and control program execution. In addition, it had good message and report-generating capabilities, a straightforward screen editor, and features that could be customized as needed by Arthur Andersen & Co.'s clients.

As mentioned earlier, most of the system's high level design was dictated by the existing structure of underwriting requirements. This design was fine-tuned through interviews with the domain expert. The knowledge engineer determined whether or not the structure of the regulations and policies paralleled the procedures used by the underwriters. After verifying the structure of the knowledge with the domain expert, the knowledge engineer began the detailed construction of the system. Since the

416

Mortgage Loan Analyzer
System Design

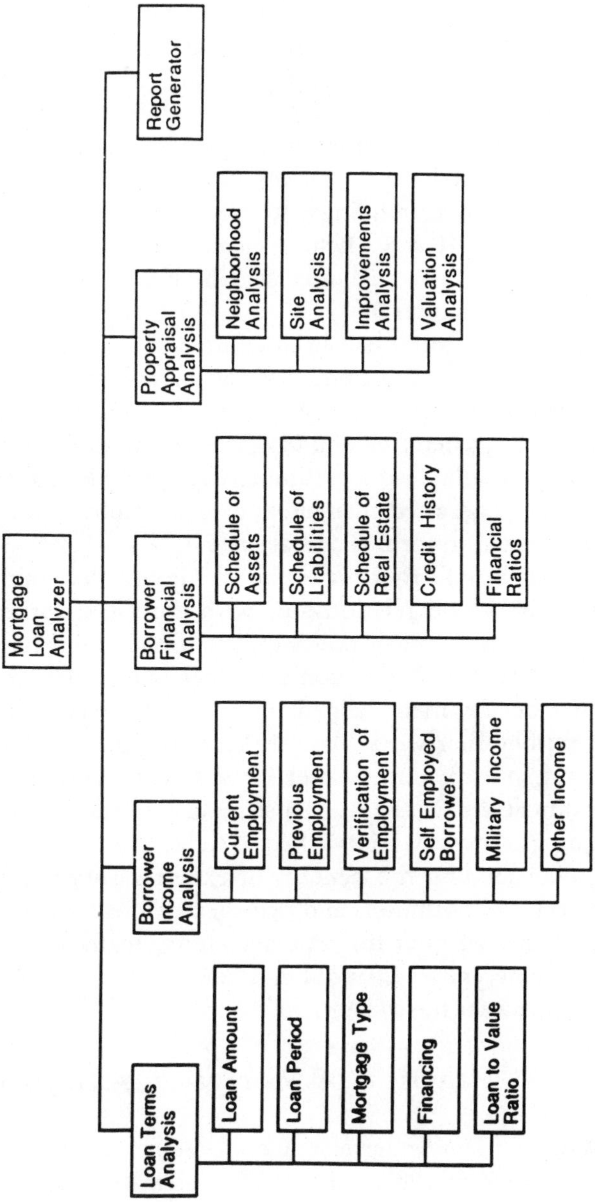

EXHIBIT III.

underwriting task had been broken down into five manageable modules, each module became a subsystem (Exhibit III).

These subsystems were built after reviewing case examples with the domain expert. The knowledge engineer asked questions to obtain a clear understanding of each task. As each module was completed, the knowledge engineer ran the case examples again, using the expert system's modules. The domain expert suggested improvements and clarified the knowledge engineer's misunderstandings. Iteratively developing the modules based on actual cases helped ensure that the knowledge base would model the actual underwriting process (Klahr and Waterman, 1986, Chapter 9).

After all modules had been completed, the validation test of the system was conducted by all the underwriters. Discrepancies between their manual analysis of the file and the results generated by the system were noted. The test included 100 loan files. Even though this was a preliminary test, reactions were positive. The users' suggested changes were reviewed by a committee and implemented to form the final system.

Several key factors made the six-month development effort successful. Good relationships with the users during development helped establish user support. The knowledge engineer's close contact with the domain expert and other underwriters during development helped the users understand the system's role within their work place. MLA was designed as an assistant or tool, not an underwriter replacement. This working relationship also gave the users a sense of ownership and an understanding of how MLA worked.

Understanding the benefits of expert systems technology is important to both users and management for a successful implementation. Without that understanding, managers will not devote the necessary financial and personnel resources, and users will not accept the system.

V. Reaction of Mortgage Institutions

When Arthur Andersen & Co. began marketing MLA nationwide in June of 1987, it became apparent that the first obstacle was differentiating between MLA and systems that perform other lending functions, such as point scoring or loan origination and tracking systems. Point scoring systems assign numerical values to various factors in the loan file and produce a rating

418

for the loan. MLA analyzes the complex interrelationships between those factors and applies both numeric and symbolic data to underwriting guidelines. Origination and tracking systems prepare documents and report on the status of loans within a bank's "pipeline." MLA performs neither of these functions. Therefore, the first challenge was to generate awareness of MLA as a new type of application employing new technology. An important part of generating this awareness was providing a rudimentary description of the technology. Upper management and chief underwriters in mortgage lending have responded enthusiastically to both the concept and design of MLA.

The most interesting result of marketing MLA has been how institutions identify new uses for the system. Many institutions are interested in using MLA to pre-qualify loans. Pre-qualification serves three purposes. First, it helps ensure that only completed, quality loans go to underwriting. Second, it instills an "underwriting attitude" in the employees taking loan applications. Third, the most appropriate loan products can be quickly selected to fit a customer's situation. Another application of MLA is using the loan evaluation report to demonstrate the quality of each loan to secondary market investors. Investors could use MLA to screen incoming loans. MLA can also be used as a training tool to help new underwriters analyze previously underwritten loans to get a feel for the process. Finally, MLA could be used by auditors to judge the quality of prior lending decisions to satisfy secondary market loan compliance standards.

VI. Conclusion

The rapid development and initial success of the Mortgage Loan Analyzer demonstrates that expert systems technology can help automate functions where it was previously not feasible. However, successful development depends upon several factors. Some of these are unique to expert systems, but most are required when developing and implementing any new system. The critical success factors include management commitment, project team commitment, and a strong development methodology. Although close user contact is essential in any development project, it is especially important when developing an expert system because it models complex human expertise. A final key success factor is that users and management must have a basic understanding of expert systems and the benefits this tech-

419

nology can provide. This is essential for gaining support for the system during development and implementation.

MLA is a practical solution to a real business problem. By institutionalizing and disseminating underwriting expertise, MLA helps improve the quality of the underwriting decision, relieve the bottleneck in the loan pipeline, and improve customer service.

References

Hess, J. L., (ed.), *Residential Mortgage Lending,* Chicago IL: The Institute of Financial Education, 1986.

Klahr, P., and D. A. Waterman (ed.), *Expert Systems Techniques, Tools, and Applications,* Addison-Wesley, 1986.

Waterman, D. A., *A Guide to Expert Systems,* Addison-Wesley, 1986.

About the Contributors and the Editor

ARTIFICIAL INTELLIGENCE, COGNITIVE SCIENCE,
AND COMPUTATIONAL MODELING IN AUDITING
RESEARCH

Andrew D. Bailey, Jr. is Arthur Young Professor of Accounting at The Ohio State University.

Karl Hackenbrack is a graduate student at The Ohio State University.

Prabuddha De is Associate Professor of Accounting and Management Information Systems at The Ohio State University.

Jesse Dillard is Associate Professor of Accounting and Management Information Systems at The Ohio State University in Columbus.

ON THE FUTURE OF KNOWLEDGE-BASED
ACCOUNTING SYSTEMS

William E. McCarthy is a Professor of Accounting at Michigan State University.

EXPERT SYSTEMS AND MANAGEMENT
ACCOUNTING RESEARCH

Thomas W. Lin is a Professor of Accounting at the University of Southern California.

DECISION SUPPORT AND EXPERT SYSTEMS IN
AUDITING: A REVIEW AND RESEARCH
DIRECTIONS

Mohammad J. Abdolmohammadi is an Associate Professor at Boston University.

421

A COMPUTATIONAL VIEW OF FINANCIAL ACCOUNTING STANDARDS

Jagdish S. Gangolly is an Associate Professor at the State University of New York at Albany.

EXPERT SYSTEMS IN AUDITING: THE STATE OF THE ART

William F. Messier, Jr. is an Associate Professor at the University of Florida.

James V. Hansen is a Professor at Brigham Young University.

THE USE OF RULE-BASED EXPERT SYSTEMS TO INVESTIGATE THE EFFECTS OF EXPERIENCE ON AUDIT JUDGMENTS

Graham Gal is an Assistant Professor at the University of Massachusetts at Amherst.

Paul J. Steinbart is an Associated Professor at Memphis State University.

SCHEDULING INTERNAL AUDIT ACTIVITIES

J. Efraim Boritz is an Associate Professor at the University of Waterloo.

D. S. Broca is a Lecturer in Management at the University of Lethbridge.

INTERNAL CONTROL EVALUATION: A COMPUTATIONAL MODEL OF THE REVIEW PROCESS

Rayman D. Meservy is an Assistant Professor of Accounting and Information Systems, Carnegie-Mellon University.

Andrew D. Bailey Jr. is an Arthur Young Professor of Accounting and Management Information Systems at The Ohio State University.

Paul E. Johnson is a Professor of Management Science at the University of Minnesota.

422

KNOWLEDGE BASED EXPERT COMPUTER SYSTEMS IN AUDITING

Jesse F. Dillard is an Associate Professor of Accounting at The Ohio State University.

Jane F. Mutchler is an Assistant Professor of Accounting at The Ohio State University.

AN ACCOUNTING PROTOTYPE EXPERT SYSTEM

Daniel E. O'Leary is an Assistant Professor at the University of Southern California.

Toshinori Munakata, is an Professor at Cleveland State University.

EXPERT SYSTEM FOR CASH FLOW ANALYSIS

Daniel E. O'Leary is an Assistant Professor at the University of Southern California.

Thomas W. Lin is a Professor of Accounting at the University of Southern California.

THE ROLE OF EXPERT SYSTEMS IN ACCOUNTING RESEARCH

Graham Gal is an Assistant Professor at the University of Massachusetts at Amherst.

Paul J. Steinbart is an Associated Professor at Memphis State University.

DEVELOPING EXPERTAX: AN EXPERT SYSTEM FOR CORPORATE TAX ACCRUAL AND PLANNING
David Shpilberg is managing partner of the Decision Support Group of Coopers & Lybrand.
Lynford E. Graham is a partner in the National Auditing Directorate of Coopers & Lybrand, New York, N.Y.

INTERIM REPORT ON THE DEVELOPMENT OF AN EXPERT SYSTEM FOR THE AUDITOR'S LOAN LOSS EVALUATION
Kirk P. Kelly is an Assistant Professor of Systems at Rice University in Houston.

Gary S. Ribar is a Manager at Peat Marwick Main & Co.
John J. Willingham is a Partner at Peat Marwick Main & Co.

EXPERT SYSTEMS: WHAT THEY MEAN TO THE
EXECUTIVE
Efraim Turban is Professor of Systems Science at the
University of Southern California
Theodore J. Mock is the Arthur Andersen Alumni Professor
of Accounting at the University of Southern California.

THE MORTGAGE LOAN ANALYZER
Drake W. Smith, Arthur Andersen & Co., Seattle
David J. Temple, Arthur Andersen & Co., Seattle

The Editor

*Miklos A. Vasarhelyi is a member of the technical staff at A. T. T.
Bell Laboratories and adjunct professor of accounting at Columbia
University. He was Associate Professor of accounting and director the
Center of Accounting Research at Columbia University until 1987.*